Praise for *The Screenwriter's Bible*

A "bible" for those of all persuasions. Whether you are a rank beginner who needs instruction, or an old pro who needs reminding, you could not do better than Dave Trottier's book. A brilliant effort by a first-class, dedicated teacher." —William Kelley, Academy Award–Winning Writer, *Witness*

"Love your book—very practical. I've kept it near my desk since high school and I still go back to it." —Travis Beacham, Screenwriter, *Pacific Rim, Clash of the Titans, Dog Days of Summer*

"An invaluable resource—a treasure chest of useful information—not only for new writers but also for seasoned veterans." —Professor Richard Walter, UCLA Screenwriting Faculty Chairman

"Whenever I am writing, I have The Screenwriter's Bible *close at hand for reference."* —Ellen Sandler, Emmy-Nominated Co-Executive Producer, *Everybody Loves Raymond*

"Good, common sense. Sets up practical guidelines without encroaching on the writer's creativity. Easy to follow—feels like a workbook that will be used and not just read. The author is encouraging, but reminds the writer of the realities of the business." —Candace Monteiro, Partner, Monteiro Rose Dravis Agency

"Contains chapter and verse on all aspects of screenwriting, and addresses every key and fundamental principle from how far to indent dialogue to how to speak to the agent's assistant." —*Script* Magazine

"Offers all the essential information in one neat, script-sized volume. . . . New screenwriters will find The Screenwriter's Bible *invaluable; experienced screenwriters will find it an excellent addition to their reference shelf."* —Hollywood Scriptwriter

"If you have the gift, this book will show you how to use it." —Victoria Wisdom, Producer-Manager and Former Literary Agent at ICM and Becsey Wisdom Kalajian

"An excellent resource book and overall guide that can be of tremendous assistance to answering the many questions that screenwriters have." —Linda Seger, Author, *Making a Good Script Great*

"Delivers more in 400 pages than can be found in several screenwriting books. A true gem that measures up to its title." —*Writer's Connection*

The Bible Provides Clear Answers to Crucial Questions:

- How do I get discovered in today's difficult, crowded marketplace?
- How do I sell my script if I don't have an agent? How do I find an agent?
- How do I get in the game now, even if I don't live in L.A.?
- How do I summon my muse and spark my creative energy?
- What is the Character/Action Grid, and what makes it so fast and effective in evaluating and revising my work?
- What common formatting mistakes turn off agents and readers?
- What are the tricks to effective scene construction and transition?
- What is the single most important key to writing great dialogue? And what are the seven deadly dialogue sins?
- How do I write a query letter or one-sheet that will get my script read?
- How do I build a winning, compelling pitch? What are the unwritten rules?
- What "breakthrough" strategies can jump-start my screenwriting career?
- What is meant by the "heart of the story," and how do I get mine beating?
- How do I break into television, the New Media, and other lesser-known markets?
- What are the 10 keys to creating captivating characters?
- What basic plot paradigms do virtually all stories utilize?
- How do I find the "high concept" in my own script so that I can sell it?
- Where can I find a clear writing process that will motivate me to finish my script?
- How can I add dimension, depth, and emotion to virtually any story?
- How do I bring my characters to life and fascinate readers?
- What are the 10 tools every writer needs (and few have) before approaching the market?
- Where do contests fit in my strategic marketing plan?
- Where can a new writer get free feedback?
- How does Hollywood really work?
- How is a spec script different from a shooting script, and how do I write it?
- What writing opportunities are often overlooked by screenwriters?

It's all in *The Bible*.

Here's what the sixth edition contains:

- The spec-formatting guide recommended by agents, readers, and producers.
- A sensible plan to jump-start your writing career and get in the game now.
- More on character development and dialogue writing that will help make your characters compelling and clear.
- The latest in proper screenplay format. This section has been completely updated and expanded by "Dr. Format" himself, with additional examples of virtually every conceivable formatting situation. Shows correct format plus how to apply it.
- Timely new advice on creating and delivering pitches, and writing one-sheets.
- An updated marketing section that includes ways to get "discovered" in today's crowded marketplace.
- More than 50 pages of sample scenes written in proper format, and a complete analysis of each.
- Plenty of worksheets with detailed instructions that will guide you in creating a laser-sharp strategic marketing plan.
- More tips, techniques, and pointers on writing a successful screenplay.
- Specific up-to-date marketing advice. There are more effective ways to get read and get assignments than sending query letters to agents—find out what these are.
- Includes over a half-dozen writing and revising exercises with suggested revisions to help you excel in your writing craft.
- Two sample treatments, a Hollywood coverage, and a sample release form.
- Hundreds of examples and illustrations that you can apply right now to your own writing or script marketing project.
- An extensive, easy-to-use index.

Completely up-to-date and completely reliable

EVERYTHING YOU NEED UNDER ONE COVER

The Screenwriter's Bible—your authoritative source

THE SCREENWRITER'S bible

THE SCREENWRITER'S BIBLE

A COMPLETE GUIDE TO WRITING, FORMATTING, AND SELLING YOUR SCRIPT

6TH EDITION EXPANDED & UPDATED

BY DAVID TROTTIER

SILMAN-JAMES PRESS
Los Angeles

Ethan Chodos, Excerpt from *Two Dogs and a Fish*, © Ethan Chodos
Natalia Garcia, Excerpt from *Personalities*, © Natalia Garcia
Chris Philpott, Excerpt from *Undecided*, © Chris Philpott
George Mullen, Excerpt from *Target Mona Lisa*, © George Mullen
Chris Wilson, Excerpt from *Just My Luck*, © Chris Wilson
Deana Costner, Excerpt from *Kissin' Cousins*, © Deana Costner
Ryan Tremblay, Excerpt from *Vicious Cycle*, © Ryan Tremblay
Lori Liddy and Sue Holzinger, Excerpt from *Getting What We Want*, © Lori Liddy and Sue Holzinger
Denise Ann Wood, Excerpt from *Quality of Life*, © Denise Ann Wood
Barbara Reitz, Excerpts from *The Blue Lobster*, © Barbara Reitz
David S. Freeman, *The 'It' Girl*, © David S. Freeman
Excerpts from *Dr. Format* column, reprinted courtesy of *Script* magazine, © David R. Trottier
Conversation with Taylor Russo ("A Dynamite Experience") used with permission
Martin Carbonella, Excerpt from *Knife in My Heart*, © Martin Carbonella
Debi Tuccio, Excerpt from *Oh What a Night*, © Debi Tuccio. Reprinted courtesy of *Script* magazine
Leslie Paonessa, coverage of *The Secret of Question Mark Cave*, © Leslie Paonessa, All Rights Reserved
Daniel Stuenzi, Excerpt from *The Helpers*, © Daniel Stuenzi
Jose Barranca, *A Cuban Cigar* query letter, © Jose Barranca
Kerry Cox, *Bed of Lies* query letter, © 1993 The Hollywood Scriptwriter, All Rights Reserved
Joni Sensel, Excerpts from "More Queries From Hell" and *The Wizard of Oz* query letter, © 1993 *Northwest Screenwriter*, All Rights Reserved. Reprinted courtesy Joni Sensel and *Northwest Screenwriter*.
Jeff Warshaw, *The Silk Maze* query letter, © Jeff Warshaw

10 9 8 7 6 5 4 3 2 1

Library of Congress Cataloging-in-Publication Data

Trottier, David.
The screenwriter's bible : a complete guide to writing, formatting, and selling your script / by David Trottier. -- 6th Edition.
pages cm
Includes index.
ISBN 978-1-935247-10-4 (alk. paper)
1. Motion picture authorship. 2. Television authorship. I. Title.
PN1996.T76 2014
808.2'3--dc23

2013049186

Cover design by Heidi Frieder

Silman-James Press
www.silmanjamespress.com

Contents

BOOK IV: Writing and Revising Your Breakthrough Script: A Script Consultant's View

BOOK V: How to Sell Your Script: A Marketing Plan

Introduction to the sixth edition of *The Bible*

Twenty years ago, in response to student and client requests, I created the first edition of *The Screenwriter's Bible.* Where has the time gone? Since then, I have coached aspiring writers around the world. And throughout this period, I have come to understand that there are core principles and techniques that help screenwriters get off to a fast start. The result is the sixth edition of my work, which I believe to be the best edition of the bunch, and clearly the timeliest.

In fact, this 20th Anniversary Edition is dedicated to you, the developing screenwriter or pro, and to the students and clients who have inspired me with their dedication and creative vision. You have made this edition possible.

In this volume, I help you begin the screenwriting and script selling journey and guide you along the way. Not that you won't need help and encouragement from others—you will—but every aspect of screenwriting is covered in this work. That's why I call it *The Screenwriter's Bible.*

There are five guidebooks in *The Bible.* Each book is self-contained and can be read independently of the others. In addition, each can be used as a handy reference. You will find yourself turning to *The Bible* again and again. Most writers, regardless of experience, will benefit from a thorough reading of all five books. Here's a helpful insight into each book or section:

- *Book I: How to Write a Screenplay* is based on my award-winning audio series and national seminar. My hope is that you'll find it a concise and clear presentation of screenwriting essentials. Use it as a primer or as a refresher when you're stuck. Books I and II can be used concurrently as you write your script. In fact, Book I will occasionally refer you to Book II (actually a *work*book) at appropriate junctures.

- *Book II: 7 Steps to a Stunning Script* is a workbook that takes you step by step through the writing process. The first step deals with creativity, "summoning your muse," and overcoming blocks. The other six steps include the pre-writing, writing, and revision phases.
- *Book III: Proper Formatting Technique* not only provides the crucial formatting standards by which your script will be judged, but teaches something of screenwriting itself. Even if you have a complete knowledge of formatting, reading this book will improve your writing style. This formatting guide has become the *de facto* industry spec screenplay formatting standard.
- *Book IV: Writing and Revising Your Breakthrough Script* is an annotated guide to spec writing. Since samples of spec scripts are so rare, this section will prove valuable to you because you must write a spec script to break into the business. Try your hand at revising the poorly written sample scenes and then compare your versions with mine. Also review the first nine pages of an actual spec script with my line-by-line analysis.
- *Book V: How to Sell Your Script* presents a detailed marketing plan with useful worksheets that takes the mystery out of selling to Hollywood and to the many other screenwriting markets. The plan is comprehensive as well as specific. With it, you'll be able to target your market with effective sales strategies.

(Note: *The Screenwriter's Bible* is sold with the understanding that neither the publisher nor the author is engaged in rendering legal advice. If legal assistance is required, the services of an entertainment attorney or other competent professional should be sought.)

I invite you to share with me your reactions to *The Bible*, and I hope it becomes a help and a guide to your personal writing success. I wish you the best.

Keep writing,

Dave Trottier
dave@keepwriting.com

HOW TO WRITE A SCREENPLAY

BOOK I

A Primer

How stories work

THE NEXT GREAT SCREENWRITER

You may have heard that breaking into the movie business is tough. It is.

However, if you write a script that features a character that has a clear and specific goal or desire, and there is strong opposition to that goal, leading to a crisis and an emotionally satisfying ending, your script will automatically find itself in the upper 10%. Few developing screenwriters have mastered even the *basics* of screenwriting.

If your script also presents a well-crafted story built on an original concept or premise and featuring a fascinating character with which people can become emotionally involved, there are agents and producers awaiting the advent of the next great screenwriter.

You can be that next great screenwriter if you work hard, learn your craft, and develop discipline. You'll need to apply the fine art of pleasant persistence. And there are going to be disappointments. But you can do it! Now stop for just a moment and say that to yourself.

All successful screenwriters begin in the same way. All write one or more feature-length scripts of about 100 pages or so. Even if you want to write for television, your best means of entering the industry is via a feature script that you can use as a sample or a pilot.

Book I is designed to help you write that one spec script that's going to get you noticed. What is a spec script? It's the script you're writing now on the speculation that someone will buy it later. Unless you are being paid in advance to write, you are writing a spec. Book II gives you specific direction in the writing process. Book III is your industry standard formatting and style guide, while Book IV will provide additional help in applying formatting and spec writing principles to the nitty-gritty of the actual writing. Book V helps you sell your script and/or find work.

THE STRENGTH OF THE SCREENPLAY FORM

A screenplay differs from a stage play or novel in a number of ways.

A novel may describe a character's thoughts and feelings page after page. It's a great medium for expressing internal conflict. A stage play is almost exclusively verbal; soap operas and sitcoms fit into this category. A movie is primarily visual. Yes, it will contain dialogue—it may even deal with internal things—but it is primarily a visual medium that requires visual writing. I have seldom read a "first screenplay" that did not have too much dialogue and too little action. You may have that same common tendency to tell rather than show.

Picture a **stage play** in which a babysitter cuts paper dolls with her scissors. The children are upstairs playing. From the other side of the room, a robber enters. He approaches her with a knife. Just in time, she turns and stabs him with the scissors. Not particularly suspenseful. In an actual stage play, these people would probably talk to each other for 10 minutes before the physical confrontation, because the conflict in a stage play generally comes out in dialogue. That's the strength of the stage play form.

A **novel** may focus on the thoughts and feelings of each character. That's the strength of the novel form—inner conflict. Perhaps the babysitter contemplates suicide, and this is the robber's first job. Neither is sure he/she can go through with it. These inner conflicts manifest themselves through inner dialogue.

However, a **screenplay** will focus on the visual and emotional aspects of the scene. The scissors penetrate one of the paper dolls. The doorknob slowly turns. The babysitter doesn't notice. Outside, the dog barks, but the kids upstairs are so noisy that the babysitter doesn't hear the dog. A figure slides in through the shadows. His knife fills the screen. He moves toward her. The dog barks louder. The intruder inches closer. But she is completely absorbed in cutting paper dolls. He looms over her. His knife goes up. The dog barks louder still. She suddenly becomes aware, turns, and impales the man with the scissors. He falls. His legs twitch and finally become still. She drops the scissors and screams.

The focus here is on the action—the drama—because movies are primarily visual. Yes, there are notable exceptions, but you are wise to use the strength of the medium for which you have chosen to write. Inner conflict is great, dialogue is important to bring out interpersonal conflict, but make your screenplay visually powerful. *Showing* through action usually works better than *telling* with dialogue. Even in character-driven "dialogue" scripts, add visual touches.

For example, the Gran Torino automobile in *Gran Torino* can be seen as a symbol of Walt's traditional American male values as he sees them. The house in *Up* is a symbol of Carl's wife Ellie and his memories of her. Likewise, Ellie's *My Adventure Book* becomes a symbol of the theme. Her book inspires Carl to have a new adventure. Always look for opportunities to make the abstract visual and the internal external. I will mention the importance of visual writing and creating cinematic moments throughout *The Screenwriter's Bible*.

THE IMPORTANCE OF BEING STRUCTURED

Your screenplay must be well structured because you want your story to survive once the director and other collaborators take your work of art and make it their own—you want the story to endure. This is one reason William Goldman emphasized in his book *Adventures in the Screen Trade* that "screenplays are structure."

Art—whether it's a painting, a flower arrangement, a rock ballad, or your story—is a union of form and content. Accordingly, the *content* of your story requires a dramatic structure or *form* to give it shape. Structure is the skeleton on which you hang the meat of your story. And without that skeletal framework, your story content falls flat like a blob of jelly, incapable of forward movement.

Most beginning writers just begin writing without much thought of story structure— where are their stories going and how will they end? Soon, writer's block sets in. One of your first writing steps will be to construct a skeleton, a structural model of some kind.

Aaron Sorkin, in writing *The Social Network*, spent a lot of time figuring out how to "frame" his character-driven screenplay about the founder of Facebook. He finally settled on the deposition hearing as a way of giving the story content shape or structure.

Aristotle was right

Aristotle wrote in his *Poetics* that drama (and that includes comedy, since comedy is drama in disguise) has a beginning, a middle, and an end. You've heard this before. Traditionally, the beginning comprises about 25% of the story, the middle is approximately 50%, and the end is about 25%. These are the basic proportions of the three-act structure. If you like to think in terms of four acts, then Act 1 is the beginning, Acts 2 and 3 are the middle, and Act 4 is the end. A seven-act structure still has a beginning, middle, and end. Shakespeare's five-act plays have a beginning, middle, and end, as does the five-act *Four Weddings and a Funeral*.

Because a screenplay is about 90–110 pages (120 pages at the most), the beginning is usually the first 15 to 25 pages. The middle is the next 50 pages or so, and the end is the last 10–25 pages. Obviously, the exact length can vary, but the middle will always be the largest section.

Setup, complications, and resolution

All great screenplays have a beginning, a middle, and an end. In the beginning, you set up your story; that is, you grab the reader's attention, introduce your thesis, and establish the situation for conflict. During the middle, you complicate matters and develop the conflict, which should build to some kind of crisis. In the end, you conclude the story and resolve the conflict. The end is the payoff for the reader, for the audience, and for you. Put your hero in the proverbial tree, throw rocks at her, and then get her out. Boy meets girl, boy loses girl and tries to get her back again, boy gets girl. Beginning, middle, and end.

What about *DOA*? It opens with the ending . . . or does it? Granted, it opens with the end of the central character's life, but not with the end of the story. What is this story really about? It is not about the central character's death, it's about who killed him. The dramatic premise is this: Can he find his killer before he dies? The story ends when he finds his killer. This is just a creative way of using the basic model.

In *Back to the Future*, the beginning takes place in 1985, the middle in 1955, and the end in 1985 again. A very simple overall framework.

THE TWO KEY TURNING POINTS

Twists and turns

How do you get from the beginning to the middle and from the middle to the end? *Turning points*. They are also called *transition points*, *action points*, *plot points*, and *character crossroads*. Turning points are the twists and turns. They are the important events that complicate or even reverse the action, such as cliffhangers, revelations, and crises. Structure organizes these events into a story.

Your story may have dozens of turning points, but the two that facilitate the transitions from act to act are key to your story's success. The first big turning point ends Act 1 (the beginning) and moves the reader (and the audience) to Act 2 (the middle). It could be called the *Big Event* because it is usually a "big event" that dramatically affects the central character's life.

The second major turning point moves the reader into Act 3 (the end) and the final showdown. This is the *Crisis*. Of all the crises in your story, this is the one that forces the central character to take the final action, or series of actions, that will resolve the story. Let's look at some examples.

How big an event?

In the film *Monsters University*, Mike is a "scare major" at the university. Ever since he was six, he has dreamed about attending college and working at Monsters, Inc. Dean Abigail Hardscrabble warns students that if they flunk the final, they'll be dropped from the scare program. So Mike studies hard while a fellow student, Sulley, relies on his natural gifts to get by. One night, Sulley steals a rival college's mascot, a pig, which escapes. Mike captures the pig, but Sulley takes the credit and is admitted to a top fraternity. The resulting rivalry between the two students causes Hardscrabble to fail them both and drop them from the program.

Is this not a big event that changes Mike's life? How can he possibly find a way to get Hardscrabble to readmit him to the program? And what will he do with the anger he feels towards Sulley, who has destroyed his childhood dream?

As you can see, this plot point clearly sets up everything that follows, both in terms of the action and the relationship. Please note that, in this case, the Big Event does not involve bombs or a car chase. The Big Event is "big" in terms of its meaning to the central character.

Steven Spielberg said that, in the best movies, someone "loses control [of his/her life] and then somehow has to regain it" (from *The Films of Steven Spielberg* by Douglas Brode). The Big Event causes that loss of control. In *Cast Away*, that moment comes when Chuck Noland is cast away. In *Ghost*, the Big Event is the murder of Sam Wheat (played by Patrick Swayze). In this case, he literally loses his life, and that's a pretty big event.

Natalie's new plan could ground Ryan (George Clooney) in *Up in the Air*. Andy Dufresne (Tim Robbins) in *The Shawshank Redemption* is incarcerated. In *The Incredibles*, Bob Parr is lured to a remote island for a top-secret assignment. Gil (Owen Wilson) is transported to 1920s Paris in *Midnight in Paris*, and Jackie Robinson is hired by the Dodgers in *42*. The Big Event for Paul Edgecomb (Tom Hanks) in *The Green Mile* is when John Coffey heals him.

In *Up*, Carl is about to lose his house, which represents his life with Ellie, so he uses balloons to literally uproot the house and head up and out to Paradise Falls. But he has a stowaway! Russell, a wilderness explorer, is on the front porch.

The Big Event is the clincher in setting up your story and audience. They're now prepared for the long haul through the second and third acts. They want to know what happens next.

Crisis management

Now let's look at an example of the Crisis, or second major turning point, the one that moves the story from its middle to its end.

In *E.T.* it is the moment when E.T. is dying, and the scientists converge on the house. Everything looks bleak. It is the moment when it looks least likely that E.T. will ever get home. This is the Crisis. What follows is the final struggle to get home.

You have a similar low point in *Thelma & Louise*. How will they ever escape the law now? In *The Incredibles*, how will the Incredible family defeat Syndrome when he has apparently defeated them? The low point in *Avatar* is when the Na'vi homeland is about to be wiped out. That leads to the final battle.

When you watch *Sleepless in Seattle*, you feel pretty low when Annie (Meg Ryan) announces that Sam (Tom Hanks) is history and that she's finally decided to marry Walter (Bill Pullman).

In *Titanic*, the central character is Rose. The Crisis is precipitated by the separation of the lovers. Jack is arrested for stealing the Heart of the Ocean. (Is he stealing Rose's heart as well?)

Trouble in Cairo

The Purple Rose of Cairo is about movies and their effect on people. Cecilia has a crummy life, a crummy husband, and a crummy job, and lives during the Great (or Crummy) Depression. For relief, she goes to the local theater where, this week, *The Purple Rose of Cairo* is playing. She's seen it four times already, and at the fifth showing, one of the fictitious characters in the movie notices her in the audience and walks right off the screen and into her life. The Big Event—right?

Let's take a closer look at this clever flick. In the beginning, we are introduced to reality (Cecilia's husband and life) and then to fantasy (the fictitious character and movies in general). So what will happen next—in the middle? Can you guess? We'll have a rising conflict; in this case, fantasy vs. reality. This conflict will build to the Crisis. What's the Crisis going to be? It's the point when Cecilia has to choose between her husband (reality) and the fictitious character (fantasy). Just as Cecilia returns to reality in the end, so must we when we leave the movie theater.

The Crisis in this film is not just a low point, but an event that forces the central character to make a crucial decision. Once she decides, she can then move into the final act, the *Showdown* (or climax) and resolution of the story.

The crisis decision
As with *The Purple Rose of Cairo*, the Crisis often forces the central character to make a tough decision.

In *The Green Mile*, Paul learns that John Coffey is innocent. What will he do now? Will he lead him to the chair so he can "ride the lightning"?

Walt, in *Gran Torino*, really gets himself and his neighbors into a fix. As a result of his actions, Sue is raped and Tao's house is shot up. What can Walt do now to defeat this gang?

In *Aliens*, the Crisis is precipitated when the little girl is kidnapped by the alien creatures, and the planet is about to explode. Ellen Ripley (Sigourney Weaver) must make a crucial, life-or-death decision. Will she abandon the planet and save herself? Or will she return for the little girl? She demonstrates her choice by igniting her flamethrower.

The perfect drama
Many years ago, I discovered the perfect drama: Charles Dickens's *A Christmas Carol*. We meet Scrooge, Tiny Tim, Bob Cratchit, and others. Each has a problem. Scrooge's problem, which he doesn't realize he has, is that he lacks the Christmas spirit. The Big Event is the appearance of Marley's Ghost.

During the middle of the story, three more spirits appear to Scrooge, but the Crisis comes when Scrooge sees his name on a tombstone, and he asks the crisis question: "Is this fate or can I change?" The story ends with Scrooge getting the Christmas spirit and helping the others solve their problems.

We are allowed to catch our breath after each apparition. In other words, this story is well paced. Excitement and action are followed by reflection and reaction, and each major and minor turning point creates even more anticipation for the next, so that the story's high points get higher and higher until the end.

In terms of dramatic tension and conflict, *your* story also needs peaks and valleys. Remember that the peaks (the turning points) should get generally higher as the story progresses.

Of mints and men
I'll take a moment here and offer a letter from a student who thanked me for bringing candy mints to class and demonstrated her clear understanding of basic story structure. She writes:

It was ironic that I met another writer who shared my addiction to Starlight Mints. In my case, it began as an innocent habit. I would keep a jar of mints beside my computer so I could have a little pick-me-up at any time during the day. THE SETUP. Then a trip to the dentist revealed I had my first cavity in 12 years. BIG EVENT. Things went from bad to worse as I missed dentist appointments, spent the housekeeping money on Starlight Mints, and couldn't even kiss my husband because of all the mints crammed into my mouth. PLOT COMPLICATIONS. Until the CRISIS MOMENT, when my husband told me that I had to choose between Starlight Mints or our marriage. I made the agonizing decision to give up mints. I'm happy now and my marriage is stronger than ever. RESOLUTION.

Comedy and story structure

Does comedy use story structure? Yes. Effective comedy is built on the same principles as effective drama. *Airplane!* is the story of a man who has lost his nerve to fly and who must regain it to save the people on the airplane. Here's a quote from the writers of *Airplane!* and the *Naked Gun* series, David Zucker, Jim Abrahams, and Jerry Zucker:

> The movies appear to be a kind of screen anarchy, but believe me, the process of getting it up there is much different. I mean, we're not maniacs, we don't bounce off the walls when we write. It gets to be a very scientifically designed process, actually. We spend a lot of time . . . marking off the three acts, concentrating not on the jokes but on the structure and sequence of the story. It's a very dull first couple of months, but that's how we spend them (*Hollywood Scriptwriter*).

Situation, conflict, and resolution—the flow of the story

MAKE A GOOD FIRST IMPRESSION

The first thing your script should be concerned with is hooking the reader and setting forth the rules or parameters of your story. If the opening scene captures the reader's interest in some unique way, it is called the *hook*. Otherwise, it's just the opening scene.

Obviously, the opening image—the first thing we see—makes your first impression. It implies something about your story—the location, the mood, or even the theme.

The screenplay *Body Heat* opens with these words: "Flames in the night sky."

Little Miss Sunshine opens with Olive's eyes. She's watching a beauty pageant. Her eyes reflect the desire that will drive the movie.

Argo opens with the American flag burning at the embassy in Iran.

Apocalypse Now opens with a jungle aflame and the surreal sounds of helicopters. Superimposed over this is the face of Captain Willard (Martin Sheen) watching a ceiling fan that reminds him of helicopter rotors. He is recalling his last mission. The writer/director is setting the standards by which we'll measure the rest of the story. He is defining the context of his story.

What is the context of your story? It will include the atmosphere or mood, the location, the emotional setting, and the genre. *Genre* (in this book) refers to movie type: for example, action, adventure, Western, thriller, romantic comedy, sci-fi, family drama, zombie-revisionist history-comedy, and so forth.

Communicate something about the rules, parameters, nature, and culture of the special world you have created in the first ten pages or so. You set the tone. For example, Don Corleone teaches Bonasera about friendship, loyalty, and the patron-client relationship in *The Godfather*'s opening.

In *Signs*, first we see the farm; then we see the central character wake up. There's a sense that something is wrong. And then we see the crop circles in the corn. (Although crop circles are normally found in wheat fields and similar grains, Shyamalan used corn because it is "scarier.") From this quick opening, we get an idea of who the story is about, where they live, the fact that they have a mystery at their farm, that there's something otherworldly afoot, and the film's genre.

O Brother, Where Art Thou? opens with a Depression-era chain gang. *Seabiscuit* opens with photos of Depression-era cars and assembly lines: "It was the beginning and the end of imagination all at the same time."

In *Spider-Man 2*, Peter Parker is late delivering pizzas. He's fired. And then it's one problem after the other: he has money problems, he's late for class, and so on. Peter's situation is well established, and we feel for him early on.

In *Ghostbusters*, we see a librarian scared by a ghost and we laugh our heads off. Supernatural comedy. Then we see Dr. Venkman (Bill Murray) hitting on a coed. There are probably a thousand ways to portray this, but the writers stay in the genre. Venkman pretends the coed has ESP and that she needs his tutelage and support to understand her gift.

In *L.A. Confidential*, we meet two Los Angeles police officers in the 1950s. The first few scenes define the story's tone, time, and location. And we see a particular police officer dispensing "justice" before an arrest.

Blade Runner opens with a "guided tour" of a definite future place while setting the mood of the story. *Jerry Maguire* opens with an introduction to the world of sports agenting.

Scream begins with a long sequence of Casey Becker (Drew Barrymore) at home alone. Someone calls her, terrifies her, and asks her questions about horror movies. The caller tells her the consequences are deadly if she answers the questions incorrectly. She answers incorrectly. This interchange and resulting carnage establish the film's genre as well as its hip style.

In Episode IV of *Star Wars (A New Hope)*, the "rules of the game," the nature of the weaponry, the limits of the technology, and the two conflicting sides are all established early.

YOUR TWO KEY CHARACTERS

Early in your script, you'll want to introduce us to your *central character*, sometimes called the *pivotal character*. Often this person will appear in the opening scene. Obviously, the primary *opposition character* must be introduced as well. This person does not have to appear as early, but could. It's your dramatic choice.

We generally think of the *protagonist* as the good guy or hero, while the *antagonist* is the bad guy. I recently heard someone arguing that the protagonist can be antagonistic, but isn't that a contradiction in terms and maybe a little confusing? In creating a story, I think it is helpful to think in terms of a central character and an opposition character. Usually the protagonist is also the central character, but sometimes the role of central character goes to the antagonist.

In *Amadeus*, Salieri, the bad guy, is the main cause of action and, therefore, the central character around whom the story is built. His opponent is Mozart, the good guy.

The same holds true for the Joker in *The Dark Knight*. The Joker is the main cause of action, the central character and the antagonist. And certainly in *The Ladykillers*, the central character is Professor G. H. Dorr (Tom Hanks), and he is definitely the lead antagonist.

In *The Hand That Rocks the Cradle*, Peyton, the nanny, is the central character because it's her goal that drives the action of the story. Claire, the wife, is the primary opposition character, even though she is the protagonist (good guy). Marlene is a secondary opposition character.

In both *Falling Down* and *Chronicle*, the protagonist becomes the antagonist in the end. You can see why I believe it is helpful to think in terms of a central character and opposition character(s).

One key to making a story dramatic is to create a strong central character with a powerful goal, and then provide a strong opposition character who (consciously or subconsciously) tries to stop the central character from achieving that goal. This assures us of conflict. And *conflict is drama*.

Can there be more than one central character? Of course, but ensemble pieces like *The Breakfast Club* and *Best Exotic Marigold Hotel* are difficult to write, as are parallel stories such as *The Godfather: Part II*, *Pulp Fiction*, *Crimes and Misdemeanors*, and *Julie & Julia*. Students often present examples of dual central characters in a movie, and in most cases, the reality is that there is just one central character.

For example, Butch Cassidy is the central character and the Sundance Kid is the sidekick (in *Butch Cassidy and the Sundance Kid*). That's true for most buddy movies, including the old Bob Hope and Bing Crosby road pictures—only one (Bing Crosby, in this case) is the central character. In *The Hurt Locker*, we have three main characters, but the central character is Sgt. William James, who happens to enter the story later than the other two, but who is most prominent in the end and carries the theme about addiction to war. Mike is the central character in *Monsters University*.

Recently, I reviewed *Best Exotic Marigold Hotel* a second time because I liked it so much. There are three characters that are candidates for the central character—Muriel (the hotel's problem-solver in the end played by Maggie Smith), Evelyn (the narrator played by Judi Dench), and Sonny (the hotel owner played by Dev Patel). In truth, this is a genuine ensemble piece with no clear central character.

I see four reasons for the film's artistic and commercial success: 1) Each of 10 characters has a goal, desire, need, or intention; 2) Those goals or intentions complicate those of other characters; 3) The characters' past histories (backstories) motivate present actions; and 4) The movie ends with a clear and emotionally satisfying ending. All loose ends for all 10 characters are cleaned up nice and tidy.

Ensemble films are certainly a valid form. Even so, they are usually difficult to write and sell; thus, I recommend that you build your story around one central character in your first screenplay.

A DYNAMITE EXPERIENCE

My introduction to *Napoleon Dynamite* came at the urging of my 17-year-old nephew. "Uncle Dave, it's great. It's totally unique, and it doesn't even have a plot."

I watched it and loved it, especially the classroom "happy hands" scene, but I had "bad" news for my nephew. I said, "I hate to tell you this, but the writers used classic romantic-comedy structure for their story." He looked shocked. "Let me take you through the main turning points," I said. "A drama begins with things more or less in balance, and then the *Catalyst* upsets the balance and gets the story moving. The Catalyst is when Deb meets Napoleon at his doorstep, where she tries to sell him beauty aids."

"But *Dynamite* is a comedy, not a drama," Taylor said.

I explained that comedy has its roots in drama and then continued with the lecture. "The Big Event is when Deb sits down next to him in the cafeteria. And this is a big event if girls don't usually like you."

Even though my nephew didn't have girl problems, he understood, having read previous editions of *The Screenwriter's Bible*. Encouraged, I blabbered on. "The *Midpoint* is usually the moment toward the middle of the movie when the character becomes more committed, involved, or motivated. In *Napoleon Dynamite*, it's the dance. And who does Napoleon end up with at the dance?"

"Deb," Taylor said knowingly. And then he put the rest together. "The *Crisis* is when the two are pulled apart by a misunderstanding. She calls Napoleon a 'shallow friend.'"

"But the big guy bounces back," I interrupted. "He dances at the election assembly demonstrating his skill. Remember what he said earlier about girls liking boys with skills such as 'nunchuk skills' [referring to *nunchakus*]?"

My nephew laughed, recalling the moment, and then resolved the story for me: "So Deb returns to the tetherball court, where Napoleon delivers his immortal romantic line, 'I caught you a delicious bass,' and asks, 'Wanna play me?' So she plays him. That, combined with his earlier dazzling footwork, is the *Showdown* or climax."

"A dynamite experience," I quipped. "But it's not the whole story. Napoleon has not one but two goals that drive this movie. Remember, he's trying to help Pedro win the election for student body president. In fact, that's the only reason Napoleon dances at the end, to win the election for Pedro. So his dancing is not only the *Showdown* for the get-Pedro-elected action plot, it also sets up his climactic meeting with Deb at the tetherball court (resolution of the relationship plot). That's when Napoleon realizes he's got himself a babe; I call that the *Realization*."

"Hey, don't forget the other romantic subplot of Kip and La Fawnduh," Taylor added proudly, emphasizing the syllable "duh." My nephew scratched his head, thinking. "I guess the flick seemed plotless because the structure was handled in a fresh and original way."

"Exactly," I said, and then I put my hand on his shoulder and said, "Hungry?" He was. "I know a place that serves a delicious bass."

• • • • •

Let's review those key turning points, one by one.

THE CATALYST AND BIG EVENT

You've heard the horror stories of agents and executives reading only the first few pages of a script and then tossing it on the dung heap. One way to avoid that is for something to happen in the first 10 pages. It pains me to be so pointed, but I do so for your own good: Readers need to know right from the get-go what kind of story they're reading, who to root for, and where the conflict may be headed.

I recall how delighted my agent was when he told me about a script he had just read, *Regarding Henry*. "He's shot on page seven! Imagine, shot on page seven!" He emphasized "page seven" for my benefit because I was late getting things moving in the script of mine he was representing at that time.

Somewhere in the first 10 or 15 pages of your script (or earlier), something should happen to give your central character a goal, a desire, a mission, a need, or a problem. I like to call this event the *Catalyst*, although it's often referred to by others as the *Inciting Incident*. Yes, it is a turning point. No, it's not usually the same as the Big Event, although it can be. This term and many other terms are used in a variety of ways by industry people. One person's Catalyst is another person's First Major Turning Point. For example, many writers and writing gurus think of the Big Event as the Inciting Incident. Defining the terms is less important than understanding the principle. I use terms that I believe will be the most helpful and least confusing to understand.

Here's the principle: When a story begins, life is in balance. Yes, your hero may have a problem, but it's a problem he's always had—his status quo. Then the Catalyst kicks things out of balance and gives the central character a new problem, need, goal, desire, or mission. The central character spends the rest of the movie trying to get things back into balance.

For Mark Zuckerberg in *The Social Network*, life is in balance. Yes, he'd like to get into a Final Club, but that's an issue he had before the movie began. Then, on page eight, his girlfriend dumps him; that's the Catalyst. The Big Event is his creation of the precursor to Facebook. That's what changes his life in a bigger way. In this case, the Catalyst motivates or leads naturally to the Big Event.

In *Witness*, an Amish boy witnesses a murder. It feels like the Big Event, but it can't be because it doesn't happen to the central character, Detective John Book (Harrison Ford). Rather, it's the Catalyst. It creates a problem or desire for Detective Book. Now he wants to solve the murder. Now the movie's moving. In other words, the Catalyst begins the movement of the story. But the Big Event in *Witness* occurs later.

The little boy peers through the trophy case at the police office and spots a picture of the killer. Book realizes that the murderer is on the police force. He goes to the chief and reports this. The chief asks, "Have you told anyone else?" Book says, "I haven't told anyone." Then when Book goes home, he is shot. He knows they'll attempt to kill the boy next, so he rushes to the boy and his mother and together they escape to Act 2 and the world of the Amish.

Do you see that the Big Event is bigger than the Catalyst?

Moss's theft of the money in *No Country for Old Men* is the Catalyst of that story. The event that changes his life, however, is when he returns to the scene to bring water to a dying man (the only humane act in the movie). He is now pursued until he is finally killed.

In *My Big Fat Greek Wedding*, Ian Miller enters Toula's restaurant. That's the Catalyst. She decides that the only way to land a hunk like Ian is to get away from her family and improve herself. The Big Event is when Ian walks into the travel agency where she works.

In *Toy Story*, the arrival of Buzz Lightyear (Catalyst) creates a lot of buzz in the toy community. And now Woody has something of a problem to solve. But it's not until Buzz tumbles headlong out the window (Big Event) that Woody's life really changes.

Pretty Woman Viv (Julia Roberts) and Edward (Richard Gere) meet: the Catalyst. He pays her to stay with him at the hotel: the Big Event.

Jerry Maguire sees his client in the hospital, then writes a mission statement: the Catalyst. He is fired: the Big Event.

Independence Day. The aliens arrive: the Catalyst. They attack and blow up the White House: the Big Event.

Thelma & Louise. They leave town to go fishing: the Catalyst. Louise shoots Thelma's attacker: the Big Event.

You may ask, Can the Catalyst also be the Big Event? Sure. *Ghost* and *Regarding Henry* are two examples, as is *Juno* (the pregnancy). Keep in mind that I am presenting guidelines in this book, not hard-and-fast rules.

The Central Dramatic Question
A good Catalyst and/or Big Event, besides giving the central character a new problem or desire, will often reveal something of the main conflict or story premise. It may raise *the central dramatic question* (or obligatory question) for that film.

For example, will John Book (in *Witness*) catch the killer? Will E.T. get home? Will Toula attract Ian (in *My Big Fat Greek Wedding*)? Will Kowalski and Stone return to earth in *Gravity*? What was Citizen Kane referring to when he said, "Rosebud"? Will Police Chief Martin Brody (Roy Scheider) get Jaws? Will Edward and Viv find true love in *Pretty Woman*? Will Pi Patel survive his adventure in *Life of Pi*? Can J. C. Wiatt (Diane Keaton) have it all—a family and a career—in *Baby Boom*? Will Chuck Noland in *Cast Away* survive and return home? Will the Americans escape from Iran in *Argo*?

Often, a situation in a film can create a relatively minor obligatory question. The shallow granddaughter in *Gran Torino* wonders who will inherit the Gran Torino when Walt dies. That's the obligatory question. The answer comes at the end: Tao gets it.

FORESHADOWING

Because Act 1 is primarily devoted to setting up the story situation, foreshadowing becomes a vital tool. In the first act of *Aliens*, we establish early that Ripley (Sigourney Weaver) can operate a combination loader/forklift. This large contraption is literally an extension of her arms and legs. That's the setup. At the end of the movie, she uses it to fight the big mama alien. That's the payoff.

Incidentally, we see a version of that contraption in the movie *Avatar*. Fairly early in Avatar, we see a creature called the hammerhead titanothere (or *angtsik* in the Na'vi language). We soon forget about it until it is skillfully used at the end of the movie to defeat the really bad military guy, Colonel Quaritch.

The tetherball court is established in the first act of *Napoleon Dynamite*. Napoleon asks Summer Wheatley, "Wanna play me?" She rejects him. The payoff is the final scene when Napoleon asks Deb, "Wanna play me?" And she does. This new response is the measure of how things have changed for Napoleon.

You can get away with almost anything if you set it up, or foreshadow it, early in your story. Much of screenwriting is setting things up for a later payoff.

In most James Bond movies, Q gives James the gadgets he'll use later in the movie. They can be pretty ridiculous, but as long as they are established early, we accept them. However, if at the end of the movie James saved himself with a gadget that was not given to him, perhaps a tiny missile that carried a 100-megaton nuclear warhead, we'd say, "Where did that come from?" And we'd feel ripped off—right? The payoff for skillful foreshadowing is that it satisfies an audience's need for completion and lends your story a sense of unity.

18

Look at all we learn in the first scenes of *Raiders of the Lost Ark*. The story is about lost artifacts, archeology, and high adventure involving World War II Nazis. We learn that both Belloq and Indiana are resourceful, that Indiana hates snakes, and that he must recover the lost Ark of the Covenant.

Early in *A Beautiful Mind*, John Nash (Russell Crowe) witnesses the "presentation of the pens." This is the ceremony at which each professor in a department gives his or her pen to a member of the department in recognition of a lifetime achievement. When we see this presentation again, Nash is the recipient.

High Noon is a wonderful example of foreshadowing. The audience is made aware of the terrible thing that might happen at high noon. This foreshadowing helps motivate conflicts between Marshal Will Kane (Gary Cooper) and his wife, and with certain town folk.

In an early scene in *Ghost*, Sam Wheat (Patrick Swayze) watches an airline disaster on the news and comments about how quickly life can end. Later he confides in Molly (Demi Moore) that he is afraid—every time something good happens in his life, something bad happens. This is a foreshadowing of his imminent death. There is also a suspenseful moment when a statue of an angel is moved into the apartment. Can you guess what this foreshadows?

Here's a partial list of foreshadowing elements in *Titanic*. Most are introduced early in the story.

- The sunken ship, rooms, fireplace, safe, Rose's comb, the nude drawing
- The automobile where they later make love
- How the *Titanic* would sink
- Heart of the Ocean necklace
- How freezing the water is (Jack points this out in the "suicide" scene)
- Spitting lessons pay off later when Rose hocks one up on her fiancé
- The number of lifeboats
- The gun
- Jack: "You jump, I jump."
- Jack: "You'll die warm in your bed." This foreshadowing comes late.
- The whistle. This is also introduced appropriately late, and its payoff is powerful.

A more sophisticated use of foreshadowing can be found in *Slumdog Millionaire*. Early in this tale of two brothers, young Jamal is willing to jump into a pool of excrement to get what he wants—the autograph of movie star Amitabh Bachchan. This is really a microcosm of the entire story. Jamal is willing to go through crap for his love, Latika.

Just as his brother, Salim, steals Jamal's autograph of Amitabh, he later steals Latika. But Salim has a good side: He saves his brother from blindness and slavery, and at the end he frees Latika from slavery.

Early in the script, a teacher asks the boys who the third musketeer is in the novel *The Three Musketeers*. Jamal doesn't know. Later, after they are orphaned, they see little Latika standing in the rain. Jamal tells his brother, "She could be the third musketeer." At the end of the screenplay, Jamal is asked by Prem, the game show host, "Who is the third musketeer?" Jamal is allowed to place a call to his brother, but it is Latika who picks up the cell phone. Well, she is the third musketeer.

This kind of inventive foreshadowing creates a sense of unity in a story, even when the audience may not be consciously aware of the foreshadowing and payoff. It also becomes a tool of economy, providing more than one use for an object, story element, character, or line of dialogue.

A word of caution on the first act taken as a whole: Don't provide too much background information or exposition at once. Only give the audience what they need to understand the story and its special world without confusing them. We'll discuss *exposition* at length in the dialogue chapter.

UP AND AWAY WITH MY BEAUTIFUL BALLOONS

In terms of setting up a story or situation, it will be hard to find a better example than the opening sequence of *Up*, the marriage montage in particular, which I suspect will soon be declared a classic. (Actually, in the screenplay, it's a series of short scenes presented in the film as a montage.)

As children, both Carl and Ellie are inspired by Professor Charles Muntz (who later, with his dogs, becomes an opposition character). However, it's Muntz's "Adventure is out there" attitude that brings the two kids together. As they become acquainted we see the following visual moments (among others):

- Ellie's house (which will become *their* house and a symbol of Ellie)
- The grape soda pin—"You're in the club now"
- Ellie sends a balloon trailing a note through Carl's window
- Carl crosses his heart
- Ellie's *My Adventure Book*, including additional blank pages she's saving

Next is the marriage montage. It contains no dialogue; many small, touching moments; and the following visual elements:

- Handprints on the mailbox
- Carl sells balloons that lift his balloon cart (and will later lift his house)
- Ellie can't have kids, so Carl shows her *My Adventure Book*
- Carl crosses his heart—he'll take her on an adventure
- They save their money in a jar labeled "Paradise Falls"
- Later, Carl looks at his photo of Ellie as a child (he wants to take her to Paradise Falls, but now she is dying)
- Carl sends a balloon trailing a note through Ellie's window
- Ellie gives him her *My Adventure Book* as a farewell

Not only is the audience hooked, but the story is *set up*. Most everything that follows derives from the above. Ellie and the house that symbolizes her become the motivating force of what Carl does thereafter. We see all of the above visual elements repeated later in the movie, including the grape soda pin. Each "payoff" is touching, dramatic, funny, or some combination thereof.

The above opening sequence is a wonderful example of foreshadowing, but it additionally illustrates the importance of establishing emotional, motivational, and visual elements early. The screenplay as a whole is a lesson in economy. The writers use objects and characters (in this case, Muntz) more than once, which lends the story a sense of unity. This is cinema at its best.

THE MAGNIFICENT 7 PLOT POINTS

Thus far, we have discussed the Catalyst, Big Event, and Crisis. There are four additional major turning points that you'll want to apply, making seven major plot points in all. I call these The Magnificent 7 Plot Points. They are the Backstory, the Catalyst, the Big Event, the Midpoint (sometimes called the Pinch), the Crisis, the Showdown (also called the Climax), and the Realization.

The Backstory
The Backstory is an event that generally occurs before the movie begins. It is usually some definitive past trauma that affects the character's attitude and behavior throughout the movie. On occasion, writers present the Backstory as the first scene and then cut to "years later" when the present-day story begins. Other times it is revealed through flashback. Most often, it emerges through dialogue. We'll discuss this plot point in detail in the "Story layering, plot, and genre" chapter and the chapter "Ten Keys to Creating Captivating Characters."

The beginning (Act 1) of a screenplay ends with the Big Event. The middle focuses primarily on the conflict and complications. The central character emerges from Act

1 with a desire to do something about the difficult situation created by the Big Event. Her action will likely fail, forcing her to take new actions. There will be many setbacks in Act 2, as well as some breakthroughs or temporary triumphs.

The long middle section (Act 2 of a three-act structure) usually focuses on a *rising* conflict (rising action). Your reader will lose interest in a conflict that is merely repetitive: for example, when the central character and opposition character fight, then fight again, then fight again, and so on. Strong subplots that crisscross with the main plot will help you avoid repetitive conflict because they will create more complications that ratchet up the main conflict. Thus, the conflict builds or intensifies.

The Midpoint

At the *Midpoint* (or *Pinch*) of the story, about halfway through, another major event occurs. The central character often becomes fully committed. I sometimes think of it as the Point of No Return. *Gone with the Wind*'s midpoint is when Scarlett O'Hara makes her famous vow before intermission: "I'll never go hungry again."

The Midpoint can also be the moment when the motivation to achieve the goal becomes fully clear, or the stakes are raised. In *Ghost*, this is when Sam, as a ghost, learns that his best friend is the one who had him killed.

In *Dave*, the Midpoint is when Dave defies the chief of staff and acts as president. This is truly a *point of no return* for Dave, the point when he becomes fully committed. There is no turning back now!

In *Titanic*, the Midpoint comes when Rose decides to jilt her fiancé and go with Jack. Once she makes this decision to leave her social world, there is no turning back. She has reached the Point of No Return. Shortly after her decision, the ship strikes an iceberg.

From the Midpoint on, the central character takes stronger actions, perhaps even desperate actions that threaten to compromise her values. One or more temporary triumphs by the central character arouse the opposition, who now shows his true strength. There may be a major setback, followed often by a new revelation or inspiration.

This is when Charlie Babbitt (in *Rain Man*) discovers that his brother Raymond is the Rain Man of his childhood, and that his dad protected Charlie as a baby by putting the Rain Man (Raymond) in an institution.

Notice the rising action in the second half of *Gran Torino*. After spending his birthday with his Hmong neighbors, Walt (Clint Eastwood) puts Tao (the boy who tried to steal his car) to work in his yard. Tao has gang problems, so Walt gets Tao a job. Smokie and the gang destroy Tao's tools and burn his neck with a cigarette. Walt reacts by beating Smokie and telling him to lay off Tao. The gang rapes Sue and shoots up Tao's house. That's the Crisis.

As a story's conflict intensifies, its pace quickens until the worst thing that could happen happens. This is the Crisis, the point when all seems lost, or when the central character faces a crucial decision. The worst thing that could happen to Indiana Jones is to be locked in a tomb with thousands of snakes while his enemies get away with the world's most important artifact. What's the worst thing that could happen to your character?'

The Showdown
As you know, the Climax or Showdown follows on the heels of the Crisis. Often, some-one or something spurs the character on to the Showdown. The goal is on the line, including the theme or movie message (discussed later) and/or some important value.

In *Independence Day*, the crisis is very dark, but a new revelation provides a glimmer of hope that moves our heroes to take one last gamble. Basic American values and global unity are at stake.

The same is true in *Gravity*. At the Crisis point when Stone (Sandra Bullock) turns off her oxygen so that she can die, she sees Kowalski who scolds her for giving up. When she realizes that Kowalski's appearance was not real, she vows to fight on.

There's something you should know about your movie's end: It's not mandatory to have car chases and explosions in it. In *Moonstruck*, everyone simply gathers around the breakfast table. It's the big scene at the end—the biggest scene in the movie. It's the point when everything comes together. It's the Showdown, which is even bigger than the Big Event.

Although Hollywood loves a happy ending, some of the most effective and affect-ing stories are bittersweet or end in some sadness: e.g., *Cast Away, My Best Friend's Wedding, Up in the Air, Philadelphia, Gone with the Wind, The Social Network, Sling Blade*, and *Casablanca*.

Avoid the *deus ex machina* ending (literally, "the god from the machine"). In ancient Greece, at the end of a play, the gods would enter in some sort of a contraption and solve all the mortals' problems. Easy solutions are not dramatic; better that your central character do his own rescuing in the end. An exception to that "rule" is apparent in the movie *Captain Phillips*.

In the end, Captain Phillips does not save himself, but is rescued by secondary characters (the SEALs). How does the writer compensate for this? First, this is apparently a true story, and that is one reason we "accept" the ending. Secondly, the pirates (the teen pirate in particular) elicit some sympathy or interest as desperately poor pawns of a warlord. Thirdly, the resolution is not easy, but is dramatic with plenty of conflict. The most important reason the ending works is the high level of emotional involvement we have with the captain, including the story's denouement of his being treated for shock.

It's not that the captain is inactive in the third act. He isn't. One of my favorite moments is the captain's desperate search for a pen and paper. At first, we don't know what he is up to plus we worry that he might get caught, so suspense is created in two ways. We finally realize that he simply wants to write a last note to his family; he thinks he's going to die. A lesser writer might have handled this with an overwrought line of dialogue: "I'm gonna die here, and I wanna to tell my wife that I love her!" You can see in this instance how much better show is than tell.

I further suggest that you don't end your screenplay by essentially saying, *"It didn't really happen."* That type of ending seldom works dramatically. Bring closure to your story's end; don't leave its ending open or ambiguous. I realize there are exceptions to these guidelines. After all, the events in the magical land of Oz were part of a dream and the animals in *Life of Pi* were just representations of people—and I love those movies. And apparently, everything in *The Usual Suspects* except the heist itself was made up by Verbal under interrogation.

Does the unclear conclusion of Hitchcock's *The Birds* work for you? How about the ambiguous ending of *All Is Lost*—does it frustrate you or lead you to some kind of statement (or theme) about life and death? In any case, I suggest you don't take these types of artistic risks in your first script; but of course, that's totally up to you.

The Realization

During or just after a screenplay's climactic scene or sequence of scenes, the central character realizes something new about herself, or we're shown some visible or spoken evidence of her growth. The central character has emerged from a crucible, has shown great courage—physical, emotional, and/or moral—and now the final result must be revealed to the audience and understood by the central character. This is a story's moment of *realization*.

In *Ghost*, Sam's growth is demonstrated at the end when he's finally able to say "I love you" to Molly, instead of "Ditto." Sam grows in another way—from mortal to guardian angel to heavenly being. Beginning, middle, end.

In *A Christmas Carol*, Scrooge needs the Christmas spirit. His attitude toward Christmas is neatly summed up in two words of dialogue: "Bah, humbug." The story is about transforming his attitude. In the end, the change in Scrooge is revealed through his charitable actions and words.

In *City Slickers*, after Mitch Robbins (Billy Crystal) battles the river, he declares, "I know the meaning of life. It's my family."

William James, in *The Hurt Locker*, comes to realize his one true love as he's talking to his baby about all the things his baby loves. "That bobba is one day just going to look like an ordinary plastic bottle to you. And the older you get, the more this happens and the fewer things you love. And by the time you get to be my age, sometimes you only love one or two things." And then he pauses and adds, "With me, I think it's one." The next shot reveals he has returned to the war.

Neo in *The Matrix* realizes that he can view the matrix as software code. Thus, he is able to destroy the antivirus code (Agent Smith). In this case, the realization is what gives the central character the ability to defeat the opposition.

Jerry Maguire brings many elements together in the Realization. At Rod's interview after the game and on television later, he expresses gratitude to Jerry. It's then that Jerry realizes he has achieved his mission statement about integrity and providing personal attention. This realization is never directly stated, but the audience recognizes it when Rod thanks Jerry in the interviews. The audience also realizes that Jerry has succeeded with his outside goal when the terms of Rod's new contract are announced in the interview. Finally, during all this, Troy Aikman, quarterback for the Dallas Cowboys, mentions to Jerry that he likes his "memo," referring to the mission statement. Is Troy going to let Jerry represent him now? Looks like it to me.

In *Mr. Holland's Opus*, Mr. Holland (Richard Dreyfuss) is rewarded for his years of dedication to teaching when all of his students return and play his composition for him. He realizes that he has touched all of these students.

In *Groundhog Day*, Phil Connors (Bill Murray) goes through the five stages of grief— denial, anger, bargaining, depression (the Crisis), and acceptance—and then is presented to us at the town dance and bachelor auction. The town likes him, Rita likes him, and (at long last) he likes himself.

In the beginning of *Falling Down*, we identify with William Foster (Michael Douglas) but soon lose affection for him as he declines. Detective Martin Prendergast (Robert Duvall), however, grows. So our affections shift to him. At the end, these two characters square off, both realizing what they've become. Prendergast has become a good cop and a man. Foster has a different realization. He says, "You mean I'm the bad guy?"

Sometimes, the Realization can be thought of as a "resurrection" of the hero. Oskar Schindler is presented with a ring at the end of *Schindler's List*. He realizes the good he's done (though he regrets not doing more) and that maybe he is a good man after all. He has grown from sinner to saint.

In *A Beautiful Mind*, the hero not only is recognized by his colleagues in a "presentation of the pens," but is awarded the Nobel Prize.

The realization of growth can be negative. At the end of *The Godfather*, Michael is able to lie to his wife while a patron kisses his ring. We realize that he truly is the Godfather.

The overall realization for you as a writer is this: All of these examples provide an emotional pay-off to the reader of your script and to your audience.

• • • • •

Finally, we have the *Denouement*, which is not a plot point, but is the final brief section after the Showdown where all the loose ends are tied together and any remaining subplots are resolved. Usually, the Realization is part of the Denouement. In *Back to the Future*, we see how Marty's family turns out, and the professor returns from the future with a stunning new outfit.

In summary, the Magnificent 7 Plot Points are:

1. The **Backstory** usually happens before the story begins. It motivates or haunts the central character.
2. The **Catalyst** kicks things off. It's part of your story's setup.
3. The **Big Event** changes your character's life. We move to Act 2.
4. The **Midpoint** is a major moment in your story's middle; it's often a point of no return or moment of deep motivation for your central character.
5. The **Crisis** is the low point, or a moment that forces a decision that leads to your story's end. We move to Act 3 (the end).
6. The **Showdown** or Climax is the final face-off between your central character and the opposition.
7. The **Realization** occurs when your character and/or the audience sees that the character has changed. The Realization is usually part of the denouement.

Note: For a summary review of the function of each of these key turning points, see "Step 3—Develop your core story" in Book II.

FORMULAIC WRITING

There is a moment in *Pirates of the Caribbean: The Curse of the Black Pearl* when Elizabeth, aboard the *Black Pearl*, demands that Barbossa return her to shore. She then cites the pirate code, the "rules of the Order of the Brethren." Barbossa responds, in part: " . . . the code is more what you'd call guidelines than actual rules." The same holds for this book; I present **guidelines** rather than rules. Please don't internalize the above guidelines as a formula. This book is not intended as a write-by-the-numbers text. It is your handy guide for a successful writing journey. In reality, you can do anything you want . . . as long as it works.

Almost every guru and teacher has his or her model or paradigm for structuring and outlining a screenplay. Among them are the following (in no particular order): Michael Hauge's "Six Stage Plot Structure," Robert McKee's "The Quest," Linda Seger's "Story Spine," John Truby's "Twenty-Two Building Blocks," Syd Field's "Paradigm," Blake Snyder's "Beat Sheet," Christopher Vogler's "The Hero's Journey," and my own "Magnificent 7 Plot Points." All of the "great eight" paradigms named above are loosely compatible and present different ways to look at the same thing—basic story structure.

They are provided by master teachers and are all worthwhile . . . as guidelines, but not as jackhammered-into-granite rules. Precisely imitating someone's surefire model without a strong application of creativity may result in a formulaic screenplay. And you can name a few classic and successful movies that do not exactly follow anyone's paradigm.

Movies such as *Shrek*, *Napoleon Dynamite*, *Gravity*, *Being John Malkovich*, *Spy Kids*, *Sleepless in Seattle*, and *O Brother, Where Art Thou?* are fun to watch partly because they are so fresh and original. They use classic dramatic structure in inventive ways, in a few cases bending the framework.

In the case of Joseph Stefano's *Psycho* (directed by Alfred Hitchcock), the framework is broken when the protagonist is killed before we are halfway into the movie. The tactic shocks the audience so forcefully that a tremendous amount of suspense is created, enough to carry us through the second act.

Quentin Tarantino's *Pulp Fiction* tells two stories. One is about how Jules (Samuel Jackson) comes to believe that God has a mission for him. At the Showdown, he doesn't shoot the robber because he's going through a "transitional period." In the other story, Butch (Bruce Willis) refuses to throw a prizefight and comes to terms with his boss while escaping with his life. Each of the two stories has a beginning, a middle, and an end, but the events are not presented in exact chronological order. I wouldn't try something as tricky as this for my first script, but it illustrates an unorthodox and effective use of dramatic principles.

Perhaps the most traditional and rigid of paradigms is the love story or rom-com (romantic comedy) basic structural model. The two lovers generally meet at the Catalyst and are thrown together by the Big Event. But the Backstory gives rise to a flaw which interferes with love. Even so, they fall in love at the Midpoint (or at least one does), and are separated at the Crisis. In the Showdown, one or both overcomes the flaw and they come together. In the end, the Realization comes that they will live happily ever after.

Please note the creative use of the "Magnificent 7 Plot Points" in *Sleepless in Seattle*, where Annie (Meg Ryan) "meets" Sam (Tom Hanks) via a radio program, and by the Midpoint the two are interested in each other—all without either saying a complete sentence to the other. The classic Crisis separation is manifested by the great gulf between the Empire State Building and the Rainbow Room, where Annie dines with her fiancé. Whom will Annie choose, a guy she has not spoken two words to or her sweet-as-sugar fiancé? Annie makes the Crisis decision by racing to the Empire State Building where she finally connects with Sam. This can be seen as the Showdown or Climax, and it's without an opposition character or antagonist. In fact, much of the interpersonal conflict in *Sleepless* is provided by Sam's son, Jonah, plus there is a lot of inner conflict, some of it motivated by Sam's backstory—his wife's death. Thank you, Nora Ephron, David Ward, and Jeff Arch for your inventive approach.

A Beautiful Mind is an episodic story that deals with a man's entire adult life. As with *Pulp Fiction* or *Sliding Doors*, the story doesn't precisely follow anyone's paradigm. At a key point during the second act, John Nash faces a crisis decision: He must choose between his wife Alicia and his imaginary life. It is here he realizes that his imaginary friends do not age; he now believes he has found the key to solving his schizophrenia problem. This leads to the main Crisis that determines his fate. Instead of placing that main Crisis in the hands of the central character, as I would normally recommend, it's Alicia who must make the key decision to sign (or not sign) the commitment papers. This is followed by a longer-than-normal final act. I have no quibbles with any choices made because they worked wonderfully! It's a beautiful and dramatic film.

Dramatic structure is at once firm *and* flexible. There are many ways to tell a story. In fact, I maintain that structure is not the same things as formula. Your basic structure may change or evolve as you write, so be open to new, creative insights. As Paul Haggis, who wrote *Crash*, put it, "Subvert people's expectations." Avoid clichés of structure, character, and dialogue. Every story has its own structure, its own life, its own way of unfolding. Let your story and its characters use you, the writer, to express itself and themselves.

The lowdown on high concept

A TITILLATING TITLE

In the marketplace, a screenplay or teleplay will benefit from an attractive title. Of course, from the very beginning you'll want a working title to inspire you. The title you choose for your completed work should be short enough to fit on the marquee. Ideally, it conveys something about the concept (*Cast Away*), character (*Mall Cop*), genre (*Star Wars*), event (*Date Night*), theme (*To Kill a Mockingbird*), location (*Monsters University*), or main action of the story (*Finding Nemo*). Like the headline in an ad, the title must stop the reader and pull him into the story.

Spy Kids has a direct appeal to its primary audience. The premise is clearly implied: What if James Bond were a kid?

Scream is almost as good as *Psycho* as a title for a horror movie, and *Toy Story I, II, and III* identify its market as well as the story concept. *Die Hard* and *Dirty Dancing* were considered "million-dollar titles" at the time of their conception because they were so provocative.

Super Size Me was enough to grab my attention. That expression is well known by most people. The title *The Sixth Sense* clearly communicates the genre and main idea of the story. Although a little long, *Honey, I Shrunk the Kids* is a superb title. It effectively conveys the idea of a fun sci-fi family comedy.

An example of an ineffective title might be *Raiders of the Lost Ark*. I heard Sydney Ganis, the marketer of this project, explain how much he worried about this title. Is this the football Raiders? Is this Noah's ark? How is this title going to fit on the marquee? Not to worry. The movie had good word-of-mouth and a heck of an advertising budget, so it didn't matter. The same is true for *Argo*; that title only makes sense after one has read the script.

Nevertheless, in almost every case, an effective title can make an important first impression for your script, especially if it hints of a high concept.

IT'S GOTTA BE BIG

Jeffrey Katzenberg, in his now-famous and still relevant internal memo to Disney executives (published in *Variety*, January 31, 1991), preached the following:

> In the dizzying world of moviemaking, we must not be distracted from one fundamental concept: the idea is king. If a movie begins with a great, original idea, chances are good it will be successful, even if it is executed only marginally well. However, if a film begins with a flawed idea, it will almost certainly fail, even if it is made with "A" talent and marketed to the hilt.

According to Robert Kosberg, "Screenwriters usually focus on the craft of screen-writing . . . plot, developing characters, but these all fall aside if the initial concept is not clear. Find great ideas. Keep asking yourself, Do you have a good idea here?"

These quotes should not surprise you when you consider that producers, distributors, and exhibitors need a simple, easy way to sell the movie to their audiences. The concept sits at the core of every pitch, regardless of who is pitching to whom. So let's discuss what makes a good concept. Here are a few clues I've gleaned from Hollywood pros:

- Easily understood by an eighth-grader
- Can be encapsulated in a sentence or two with a clear, visible goal for the hero
- Provocative and big
- Character plus conflict plus a hook (the hook is often the Big Event)
- Sounds like an "event" movie with sequel potential
- Has legs—it can stand on its own without stars
- Will attract a big star
- A fresh and highly marketable idea
- Unique but with familiar elements

May I summarize all of that? *When I hear a good concept, I immediately see a movie that I can sell.* Does your concept say, "This is a movie!"? I realize there is an element of subjectivity here, but that should come as no surprise. And as we will discuss later, most script deals are development deals in which your ability to execute an idea into a great script is paramount. Even so, look for great ideas.

There is an *implied structure* in strong concepts. For example, here's the concept of *Homeboy*, a spec script that Fox Family Films paid $500,000 for: *Two black brothers are out to adopt a younger brother to mold into an NBA player and get rich. They find only a white country bumpkin, then bring him to their neighborhood to make him a star.*

You can almost see the beginning, the middle, and the end. You see the conflict. You see the fun. It's a subjective evaluation to be sure, but that's a good movie concept.

Concept comes in many forms. For example, it can be presented as a *premise question:*

What if Peter Pan grew up? (Hook)

What if the devil had a son? (Rosemary's Baby)

*What if superheroes were forced out of action due to lawsuits? (*The Incredibles)

The concept can be expressed as a *logline*. The logline is a one-sentence summary of the story or story concept.

Terrorists hijack Air Force One. (Air Force One)

Have you noticed that the logline, hook, or concept statement often centers around the Big Event, the first major turning point in the screenplay. In the case of *Air Force One*, the hijacking is the Big Event. Here's the logline for *Chain Letter*, a spec script sold to Touchstone for around a quarter of a million dollars:

A legal secretary, after being fired and getting dumped by her boyfriend, receives a chain letter, then sends it to the people who wronged her, only to find them dead the next morning.

You know it's a movie. It grabs you—hook, logline, and sinker. Most importantly, you (as a producer) know just how to sell it to the public. And that's the key. You know you can sell it to your particular market. You see the theater ad in the paper. You see the DVD jacket. In this case, a movie with that title was made years later with the following updated logline: *A maniac murders teens when they refuse to forward chain mail.*

The following logline became *The Kid*:

A 10-year-old boy time-travels 30 years into the future to save the overly serious man he will become.

The concept is always a *hook*, which is any brief statement, premise, or logline that hooks someone into the story.

> *What's the worst thing that could happen to a babysitter? Lose the kids.* (Adventures in Babysitting)

> Top Gun *in a firehouse.* (Backdraft)

> *A man dies and becomes his wife's guardian angel.* (Ghost)

> *Your girlfriend is able to have all memory of you blotted from her mind. What do you do?* (Eternal Sunshine of the Spotless Mind)

These are very briefly presented concepts, but they grab your attention enough to make you want to get to the substance behind them.

Considering the large number of teenagers who go to movies, here's a strong concept:

> *A teenage computer hacker breaks into the Pentagon computer system. In the end, he prevents World War III.* (War Games)

Or how about this one:

> *A spoiled teenager realizes too late that she has wrecked everyone's life and jumps off a cliff.* (I'm sorry, but I couldn't resist sharing my wife's reaction to *Crouching Tiger, Hidden Dragon*.)

The concept statement is important for another reason. It's what you lead with when you pitch your script or write a pitch letter. We'll cover all of that in Book V. What's important now is this: The concept is what hooks—or fails to hook—the agent or producer. It's also important that you understand what your story is at its core.

Some of the best concepts present something extraordinary happening to someone who is ordinary—someone just like us. That something extraordinary is often—you guessed it—the Big Event.

A radio talk-show host is out to redeem himself after his comments trigger a psychopath's murderous act. This is the intelligent, character-focused *The Fisher King*.

The fish-out-of-water concept is always popular—a character is thrown into a whole new situation or lifestyle, as in *Beverly Hills Cop*. *Splash*, for example, is almost literally about a "fish" (mermaid) out of water.

As I mentioned earlier, successful concepts often combine something familiar with something original. The following concept helped sell *The Rottens* for $150,000 to Avnet-Kerner.

When the most rotten family moves into a small town and wreaks havoc, the family's youngest son starts to break his parents' hearts when he realizes that he wants to live a life of goodness and virtue. Instead of the familiar black sheep of the family, we have the white sheep of the family. It's a twist on an old idea.

Speaking of a twist on an old idea, a high school version of *My Fair Lady* sold for low six figures. It was produced as *She's All That*.

Can you see why this next concept sold? *A teenager is mistakenly sent into the past, where he must make sure his mother and father meet and fall in love; then he has to get back to the future.* It presents a clear beginning, middle, and end. It's about a character with a problem.

Keep in mind that most scripts sold are not produced. In fact, only about one in 10 of the scripts purchased and developed are ever produced. Even million-dollar scripts are sometimes not made: e.g., *Jackson* (sold for $2.5 million, and written by Brandon Camp and Mike Thompson) and *The Cheese Stands Alone* (which made Kathy McWorter the first woman to be paid a million dollars or more for a screenplay). But the money still changes hands.

Of course, not all production companies are looking for high-stakes action. You would not pitch the concept *"Die Hard* in a mall" to a producer of art films. But regardless of the company, they all are looking for an angle they can use to sell the kind of movie they want to produce.

One of the many pluses of having a powerful concept is that the execution of the concept into a screenplay does not have to be superior. In other words, the higher your concept, the more forgiving producers will be with your script. Of course, you don't want it to be rewritten by another writer, so make that script the best it can be.

But what if you're writing a sweet little character-driven story with no car chases and bombs? Don't despair! *Look Who's Talking* is just a simple love story, but the premise is, *What if babies could talk?* And that's intriguing. Also, many of the loglines, hooks, and concept statements in this section are for character-driven stories.

Also, keep in mind that stories are about characters with problems. For example: *A starving sexist actor masquerades as a woman to get a role in a soap opera.* As you can see, high concept does not necessarily mean high adventure. *Tootsie* is neither, but the concept is strong, and the character growth arc is implied.

The same is true for *Philadelphia*. Here's the IMDb tagline: No one would take on this case . . . until one man was willing to take on the system. It's great for the one-sheet (movie poster), but I think it's a bit vague for a pitch. I suggest something like this: *A black attorney prejudiced against gays gets one as a client who himself is the victim of prejudice.* Do you see the unique character hook in that pitch?

There are two reasons you should clearly understand your core story concept. First, you need to know what your story is about, what makes it special or unique. Second, someday you'll pitch that story. A student asked me in class about *A Beautiful Mind*, saying it's not a high concept movie. My response was, "You have to find that concept or hook in your own work. After all, many (if not most) of the great movies of all time are character-driven. In this case, I might opt for something like this: *What if you learned that your friends and work only existed in your imagination?*"

Stories that are offbeat or provocative stand a chance of being purchased if they're easily visualized and encapsulated in a few words. Regardless of how mainstream or non-mainstream your story is, ask yourself these questions as you begin the writing process:

What is at the core of my story?

What makes my story stand out?

What is the concept that will help the people understand what it's about?

Keep in mind that there are numerous markets for screenplays besides the big-budget Hollywood scene. We'll get into that in Book V. Also, the above section is written more from a marketing viewpoint than an artistic viewpoint. That's because I suspect you eventually want to sell your script

ADAPTATIONS

Don't adapt it until you own it. This is one of my few carved-in-stone rules. Don't adapt a novel or stage play unless you control the rights to the property. We'll discuss the acquisition of rights to true stories, books, and plays in Book V. There are three basic steps to writing an adaptation:

1. Read the novel or play for an understanding of the essential story, the relationships, the goal, the need, the primary conflict, and the subtext.

2. Identify the five to 10 best scenes. These are the basis for your script.
3. Write an original script.

Adaptations are not as easy as that, of course; they're difficult assignments. In fact, Linda Seger has written an entire book on the subject. A script cannot hope to cover all the internal conflict that the novel does, nor can it include all the subplots that a long novel can. Novels often emphasize theme and character. They are often reflective, but movies move. These are all reasons why novel lovers often hate movie versions. But Hollywood thrives on adaptations.

When you adapt, you must decide how faithful you want to be to the original book. Some adaptations reinvent the story. For example, *Apocalypse Now* is adapted from *Heart of Darkness*, which is set in a different continent and in a different century.

Jurassic Park is a novel that was adapted for the screen. The book's central character is the billionaire, with the mathematician as the opposition character. The book is science-driven, an intellectual experience as much as an emotional experience. Spielberg saw the high concept: *What if you could make dinosaurs from old DNA?*

It's interesting to note the changes that transformed this book into a movie. First, the central character becomes the paleontologist. This provides a more youthful hero. Our paleontologist is given a flaw he didn't have in the book—he doesn't like children. He grows to like them by striving for his goal. There is no love interest in the book, but Dr. Ellie Sattler (Laura Dern) fills that role in the movie. Although the character development in the movie is thin, the above changes make for a more visual and emotionally accessible film. The focus of the movie, of course, is on the dinosaurs, the T-Rex in particular. Hey, movies are visual.

My favorite scene in the book—the moment at the end when the paleontologist realizes that the velociraptors want to migrate—is simply not visual enough or emotional enough for the movie; plus, it doesn't have a strong bearing on the main action plot. I think the right choices were made.

Story-layering, plot, and genre

Now that we have a basic understanding of how a story works, let's expand on that and deepen the story.

GOALS AND NEEDS

In virtually every story, the central character has a conscious goal. The goal, as defined here, is whatever your central character outwardly strives for. Of course, opposition makes it *almost* impossible to reach the goal. That opposition usually comes in the form of a person who either has the same goal or who, in some other way, opposes your central character's goal.

Beneath it all lies a (usually) unconscious or subconscious *need*. The need, as defined here, has to do with self-image, or finding love, or living a better life—whatever the character *needs* to be truly happy or fulfilled. This yearning sometimes runs counter to the goal and sometimes supports or motivates it. The Crisis often brings the need into full consciousness.

Usually the need is blocked from within by a character flaw. This flaw serves as the inner opposition to the inner need. This character flaw is obvious to the audience, because we see the character hurting people, including himself. The flaw is almost always a form of selfishness, pride, or greed.

Where does the flaw come from? Usually from the character's past. Something happened before the movie began (or sometimes in the first scene) that deeply hurt the character. That Backstory haunts the character enough that he acts in inappropriate or hurtful ways. In other words, the character is wounded in the Backstory and carries the wound or the wound's scar until he is finally healed in the end. Let's see what we can learn about goals and needs from *Twins*.

Vincent Benedict (Danny DeVito) is the central character. His conscious, measurable goal is $5 million. There is a strong outward opposition to this goal—a really bad guy wants the money as well. Vincent also has a need of which he himself is unaware. He needs the love of a family. Blocking him is his own greed and selfishness—he's out for himself. This is the character flaw, and it is motivated by his Backstory. His mother abandoned him, and he learned early that all people are out to get him, so he'd better get them first. Vincent can never have what he truly needs until he gives up his selfish and self-pitying point of view.

This is a neat little story because the goal and the need happen to oppose each other at the Crisis. Vincent must choose between the two. He can escape with the money (his goal), but someone holds a gun on his brother (his need). What will Vincent decide?

At this crisis moment, he finds himself unable to leave his brother. Why? In a later scene, we learn that he really cared but didn't fully realize it until the Crisis. That's why he turned around and willingly gave up the money to save his brother's life. Vincent reformed. He gave up something he wanted for the sake of his brother. Fortunately, in the end, he gets both a family and the money. And his wound is healed. The writer gives the audience what they want, but not in the way they expect it. Don't you love those Hollywood endings?

TWO STORIES IN ONE

Screenplays often tell two main stories. The *Outside/Action Story* is driven by the goal. It is sometimes referred to as the spine or the external journey.

The *Inside/Emotional Story* or Relationship Story usually derives from a relationship and is generally driven by the need. It is sometimes referred to as the *heart of the story* or the *emotional through-line* or the internal journey.

To find the Inside/Emotional Story, look in the direction of the key relationship in the story and/or the character's growth arc. Sometimes there is no inside story, no backstory, no flaw, and no need, as in many thrillers, action/adventures, and horror movies. In most James Bond films, 007 has no flaw or need, only a goal and an urge.

Each story—the Outside/Action Story and the Inside/Emotional Story—has its own turning points and structure. One is the main plot, the other a subplot. Hopefully, the two stories are intertwined synergistically.

Again, *Twins* serves as a good example. The Outside/Action story is driven by the $5 million goal, and the Inside/Emotional Story is driven by his need for a family. The action is what keeps us interested, but the emotion is what touches us. Although there are exceptions, the Inside/Emotional Story is what the movie is really about. The movie is really about a relationship.

The action plot in *The King's Speech* is focused on overcoming stammering, while the relationship plot involves the relationship between Bertie and his therapist. When Bertie was a small child, he was teased by his brother and denied food by his nanny; this is the Backstory. This wound expresses itself in the form of stammering. The stammering is a physical flaw with moral consequences: A voiceless king cannot adequately serve his people in their time of need. The crisis comes when Bertie learns his therapist has no credentials. He feels betrayed. This event forces the crisis decision to retain the therapist or not. This happens to be the crisis for both the action and relationship stories. In the end, the wound is healed. Bertie becomes a good king and his therapist a trusted friend.

In *Gone with the Wind*, Scarlett has several goals. She wants to be seen by all the boys. She wants to get married. She wants never to eat radishes again. She wants to save Tara. And she wants Ashley, which is probably her main goal. Rather complex. It may even sound confusing until you realize that the story is really about what she needs—Rhett Butler. Scarlett is outwardly striving for all the things just named, but she is not consciously after Rhett. Nevertheless, the movie belongs to Scarlett and Rhett.

In *Romancing the Stone*, what is Joan Wilder (Kathleen Turner) outwardly striving for? She wants to find the stone so she can save her sister. Is this a clear and visual goal? Yes. Is she consciously aware that this is what she's after? Yes. Is her goal opposed by anyone? Yes. Zolo wants it, as do the kidnappers. And Jack Colton (Michael Douglas) wants the stone so he can buy a boat and sail around the world.

What does Joan Wilder need? Romance. Is she striving for romance? No. She writes out her fantasies in her romance novels. Her flaw is simple indifference—she won't try. In this story, she gets what she needs by striving for the goal and overcoming her flaw. The stone is the external journey; the romance is the internal journey and character arc.

In my script-consulting work, I receive many scripts that are completely missing a goal. To illustrate, let's pretend I was a consultant for Diane Thomas when she first started writing. She tells me she has a script about a woman who goes on vacation to South America and falls in love with an adventurer. Sounds interesting, but it's not compelling enough. So I ask Diane about the goal.

"Happiness is Joan's goal," she responds.

"Happiness is not a goal. It's too vague."

"Well . . . romance is her goal. That's it."

"That feels more like a need than a goal. It's actually part of your Inside/Emotional Story. You need an action track for this inside story to roll on."

"Well, vacationing is her goal. She consciously wants to have a good vacation. She deserves it after all that writing."

Diane relaxes. It appears as though she has a complete story now, but I disappoint her. "Technically, vacationing is a goal," I say, "but it does not stir my heart, nor does it set up strong opportunities for conflict. Something specific has to *happen*."

"I know!" Diane states triumphantly. "What if her sister is kidnapped and she has to save her?" Now Diane has a strong Big Event and a story.

This problem is so common that I strongly urge you to stop and examine your story. Are you missing a specific goal and an action track for your wonderful inside story to roll on?

Variations on the action and emotion tracks
In *Back to the Future*, the outside story plot, as you would expect, is action-oriented. It is driven by Marty's goal to get back to the future. So far so good. The inside story plot, however, is driven not by a need, but by a second (relationship) goal: Marty wants to get his mom and dad back together again.

This results in twin crises at the end of the story, side by side. First, can Marty get his parents to kiss before he disappears into oblivion? This is the Inside/Emotional Story built around a relationship. Once it is resolved, Marty races from the dance to the Outside/Action Story: Can Marty, in the DeLorean, hit the wire at the same moment that lightning strikes the tower?

Is there an inner need in this movie? Yes. Marty needs a better family, and that's just what he gets in the end.

In *The Sixth Sense*, two characters go through a mutual healing. Dr. Malcolm Crowe wants to help Cole, but needs to communicate with his wife and accept his separation from her. His Backstory is the first scene of the film; he is shot by a former patient. His flaw is that, like other dead people in this film, he sees only what he wants to see. He achieves his goal of helping Cole and meets his need by communicating with his wife and seeing the truth.

Cole wants to stop being scared by dead people, but his need is to communicate with them and also with his mother. Cole's flaw is that he won't share his secret with his mother for fear she'll think he's a freak. In this case, his flaw is not motivated by a specific backstory. What's interesting is that Cole's goal is achieved by satisfying the need. In other words, once he communicates with the ghosts, he's no longer afraid of them. We'll discuss this story in more depth in the chapter on "Theme."

Moonstruck: Loretta's goal is to marry by the book. This relationship goal is represented by Danny. She was married once before and it was unlucky because they didn't do it "right," so "this time, Danny, you've got to have a ring and get on your knees and propose, and we're going to a priest." She's doing this marriage by the book.

Loretta *needs* to marry for love. This need is represented by Ronnie. This is not fully in her consciousness until she goes to the opera with Ronnie. Blocking her need is her character flaw—she's going to marry someone she doesn't love. This character flaw is motivated by her Backstory of having an unlucky marriage. At the breakfast table scene in the end, she admits that the need is more important to her than the goal.

In *Spider-Man 2*, the hero's main goal is to defeat Otto. He has a goal/need to find his identity. Underneath it all, there is a need for Mary Jane. His flaw is that he's too passive with Mary Jane and won't communicate with her because he wants to protect her.

Home Alone's Kevin strives to protect the house and himself from the Wet Bandits. That's the main action plot. The emotional plot? He needs his family's acceptance, his mother's in particular. Two flaws block him: One, he's a brat; two, he is incompetent— he can't even tie his shoelaces. These are subplots. The first flaw hooks the parents in the audience—he becomes a son who learns to appreciate his mother and family. The second flaw hooks the kids—he becomes competent when fighting the adult bandits. This is a coming-of-age subplot.

The mother's goal is to get home. Her need and her flaw are similar to those of her son. In fact, they are mirrors of each other. Another subplot involves the man with the shovel who wants to become reconciled to his son. It's not hard to see that the underlying theme of this flick is family reconciliation.

My Best Friend's Wedding: Julianne wants to break up her best friend's wedding, but needs to accept it and let life go on.

Kramer vs. Kramer: The goal? Custody. The need? To be a loving father. In this screenplay, the goal and the need oppose each other, creating a crisis. Ted Kramer (Dustin Hoffman) loses custody in a court battle and wants to appeal. His attorney tells him, "It'll cost $15,000." No problem. Ted wants to go ahead. "You'll have to put Billy on the stand." Well, to put Billy on the stand could deeply hurt him. Ted loves him too much. He chooses to give up custody rather than hurt the child. He overcomes his selfishness and abandons his goal for custody.

There's another way to look at this. Think of yourself as the next great screenwriter creating this story from scratch. You know the story is going to be about Ted Kramer becoming a father, learning to love his son. So you, the writer, give Ted goals, behaviors, and desires that are flawed. You give him a main goal of gaining custody because you know it will eventually contrast with what he really needs, which is to unselfishly love his son. So Ted's goal in this story is flawed—seeking custody is not the best way to love his son or satisfy his inner drive to be a father. In the end, he becomes a father by giving up custody, by giving up the goal.

In *The Wizard of Oz*, the main goal is Kansas; the need is to realize there's no place like home.

Pretty Woman: Two prostitutes need love (Edward could be characterized as a business prostitute). Their behavior does not harmonize with their need. In the end, they give up their old ways and thus fill their needs. They grow.

My favorite romantic comedy is *Some Like It Hot*. Joe (Tony Curtis), posing as a millionaire, uses Sugar Kane Kowalczyk (Marilyn Monroe). He's after her body, but he *needs* to love her in the full sense of the word. Sugar's goal is to marry a millionaire. She chases after Joe because she thinks he is one. Her unconscious need, however, is to marry for love. The Crisis comes when Joe is forced by Spats Columbo, a gangster, to leave Sugar. At that point, Joe realizes he is actually in love with Sugar. He realizes what a jerk he is and vows to get out of her life. He'll do what's best for her and leave without her. Sugar, however, realizes that he's the one, even though he's not really a millionaire. She chases after him. Together for the right reasons, they sail off into the sunset.

In love stories (and even buddy movies such as *Midnight Run*), one or both of the characters is usually willing to give up something in the end for the sake of the other. That something is often a goal related to their flaw. In *Pretty Woman*, Edward not only gives up his questionable business practices, but he also overcomes his fear of heights. Love stories are essentially about two people transforming each other and learning to love each other. *Pretty Woman* is pretty good at doing just that.

Jerry and Juno
Jerry Maguire wants a big contract for his only client, Rod. In the process of working with Rod, he manages to accomplish his mission and even finds intimacy with his wife.

Let's take a closer look at this story, since it has not one but two flaws and two growth arcs. (Naturally, the flaws are related.)

	Action Story	Emotional (Relationship) Story
Flaw	Self-doubt.	Can't love and be intimate.
Catalyst	Client suffers in hospital.	Meets woman who believes in him.
Big Event	Fired.	Goes on a date.
Midpoint	Jerry accuses Rod of playing without heart; Rod accuses him of marrying without heart.	Proposes marriage.
Crisis	After refusing contract, Rod is apparently injured.	Wife separates from Jerry because he doesn't love her.
Showdown	Rod plays well, gets interviewed, and gets big contract.	Jerry returns to his wife.
Realization	At the two interviews, Rod recognizes Jerry: Jerry has fulfilled his mission, no longer doubts himself.	He wants to be with his wife.

The screenplay *Juno* focuses on relationships, so even the Action Story involves a close relationship between birth mother and adoptive mother. In fact, both storylines blend to show Juno coming of age to some degree.

Juno is independent and intelligent, but somewhat immature and maybe a little too smart for her own good. The pregnancy (the Catalyst and Big Event) is a bit overwhelming. In fact, she confesses to her Dad that "I have no idea what kind of girl I am."

The Action Story involves what to do about the pregnancy. She tries an abortion clinic, but decides on adoption. She chooses Vanessa Loring as the adoptive mother and shows her full commitment by bringing her ultrasound pictures. But Mark seems a bit too friendly with Juno and Vanessa a bit too uptight. Is this going to fall apart? The Crisis is when Mark leaves Vanessa. What will Juno do? In the end, she gives Vanessa the baby. The note written on the back of a Jiffy Lube bill adds a nice touch.

The Emotional Story is the love story, which is also kicked off by the pregnancy. What is Juno going to do about the father? At the Midpoint, we see that both she and Bleeker miss each other, but their quarrel puts the relationship in question (Crisis). After a conversation with Dad in which he unintentionally helps her realize whom she loves, she initiates "making up" with an avalanche of orange Tic Tacs. She confesses her love on the track field.

In the process of the above, Juno becomes more mature, in contrast to Mark, who remains rather juvenile. As you can see, both the Action story and the Emotional story are relationship bound.

THE STRUCTURE OF THREE MOVIE CLASSICS

Star Wars, Episode IV, A New Hope

Star Wars opens with a war amid the stars. We soon get a sense of the parameters of that faraway galaxy. And it's handled visually. Luke Skywalker is the central character.

His Backstory is this: Luke's father was once a Jedi knight who was killed by Darth Vader . . . or so he was told. Likewise, Obi-Wan, Darth Vader, Princess Leia, and Han Solo all have Backstories. Even though Star Wars is essentially a cartoon on the screen, these Backstories give the film a richness it would not otherwise have.

Luke Skywalker wants to become a pilot, but he's stuck on the farm. It's a problem he's always had. Life is in balance.

For Luke, the Catalyst happens when he tinkers with R2-D2 and accidentally triggers a holographic image of Princess Leia saying, "Help me Obi-Wan, you're my only hope." Now Luke has a desire to help the beautiful Princess Leia. He begins a search for Obi-Wan.

The Big Event is when Luke returns home and discovers that his aunt and uncle have been slaughtered. Now he joins with Obi-Wan to fight the empire. He enters a whole new world and is trained by Obi-Wan to join the fight against the Empire. As you can see, the Big Event is bigger in Luke's life than the Catalyst. The Catalyst upsets the normal equilibrium and gets the character moving.

At the Midpoint, a tractor beam pulls him (and his friends) into the Death Star. This can be seen as the point of no return. There's no going back to the farm now.

The Crisis is the death of Obi-wan. Without his mentor, all looks lost for Luke. This is particularly powerful because the key relationship is Luke and Obi-Wan—that's the dominant emotional through line in this sci-fi action movie. There are others between Luke and Han Solo and Princess Leia.

The Climax or Showdown is the battle that leads to the destruction of the Death Star.

At the end we enjoy an awards ceremony—this is the Realization or acknowledgment that Luke and Han have become heroes. Luke's life is now at a new and higher level of equilibrium.

Chinatown

The Backstory in *Chinatown* is supremely important. You see, Jake Gittes used to work in Chinatown for the district attorney. While there, he tried to keep someone from being hurt, and—in that effort—ended up making sure she was hurt. The wound has never healed. Now Jake is sensitive about being embarrassed or looking like a fool. The past hurts.

As the movie opens, Jake now works as a detective who deals with extramarital affairs. A woman claiming that she is Mrs. Mulwray hires him to spy on her husband. The Catalyst, right? Jake goes to work. He takes some photographs of Mrs. Mulwray's husband with a girl. These are published in the local paper, and his job is done. He celebrates at a barber shop, where he hears a dirty joke. He's feeling good.

Cheerfully, he returns to his office and tells his operatives the joke, but they try to stop him. He doesn't see the beautiful high-class woman standing behind him. The tension increases as Jake tells his joke because we know he's going to be embarrassed when he finally notices the woman. That's the suspense. Jake delivers the punch line and turns. Surprise! The woman informs him that her name is Mrs. Mulwray and she certainly didn't hire him to spy on her husband. She says, "I see you like publicity, Mr. Gittes, well you're going to get it."

Jake has big problems now. If this woman is the *real* Mrs. Mulwray, who was the *first* Mrs. Mulwray? Who set him up and why? And how is he going to save his reputation? We're all set up for Act 2 where Jake gets on the case.

The Midpoint occurs after Mr. Mulwray's body is found. The police question Mrs. Mulwray who is evasive and who gets Jake to cover for her. Now he's fully involved with the case and with her. You could say, he has passed a point of no return.

In fact, Jake is attracted to Mrs. Mulwray, who notices that he doesn't like to talk about Chinatown. In the love scene, he finally confesses this past event to her, how he tried to save a woman once and inadvertently made sure she got hurt. This painful confession not only foreshadows the resolution of the story, it reveals the Backstory. In a different scene, Mrs. Mulwray reveals the Backstory that haunts her—her daughter is also her sister.

Later, Jake finds the necessary clue that implicates Noah Cross (Mrs. Mulwray's rich father) as the murderer, but Noah Cross takes Jake prisoner. That's the Crisis. Cross drives Jake to Chinatown where Mrs. Mulwray is waiting. Thus, the action story (the case) and the emotional story (Jake and Mrs. Mulwray) come together.

At the Climax, the result of Jake's trying to help Mrs. Mulwray results in her being killed. The Realization is summed up in one unforgettable line: "Forget it, Jake. It's Chinatown." Once again, Jake feels like a fool, and, in this case, his wound is deeper than ever.

Meanwhile, back in *Casablanca*

Casablanca is considered by many as the best movie ever made and the best screenplay ever written. The Relationship Story is about Ilsa (Ingrid Bergman) and Rick (Humphrey Bogart). It's the love story. And, in this movie, it's the main plot.

The Action Story is about how Ilsa and her husband Victor Laslow finally escape from Casablanca (with Rick's aid) to help the Allies win World War II. It's the main subplot. In this case, the action story is not driven by Rick's single-minded goal; he doesn't have an action goal. Instead, Ilsa has the goal that drives the action story to get her husband out of Casablanca. I've never heard anyone complain that this story breaks one of the "rules."

Does Rick have a flaw? Yes, he is a bitter and cynical isolationist. "I stick my neck out for nobody." How did he get that way? His Backstory. He once loved Ilsa in Paris, but she left him, disappeared without a trace. Rick has been a "walking wounded" ever since. What is Rick's unconscious inner need? To put aside his own bitter feelings and help Ilsa and Laslow escape. In other words, become a patriot.

As the movie opens, the city of Casablanca is visually portrayed as a huge prison, complete with searchlights and guards (the police) making sure no one escapes. That's the opening image system. The place is corrupt and life is cheap. When Prefect of Police Louie can't find a criminal, he simply "rounds up the usual suspects." By the way, that line foreshadows a wonderful moment at the very end.

Rick runs a saloon and casino. Before we are 10 minutes into the movie, a man named Ugarte (played by Peter Lorre) asks Rick to hide two stolen Letters of Transit. Think of these as free passes out of prison. That event is the Catalyst.

Later, Ilsa enters Rick's place and recognizes the piano player. She says, "Play it, Sam." Sam recognizes her and tells her that she's bad luck to Rick, but plays "As Time Goes By" anyway. Then Rick enters and tells Sam, "I thought I told you never to play that—" And then he sees Ilsa. Ouch, the wound! His angry look and the entire scene imply that there's a lot of history between these two people. This is the Big Event. It's so big that no one dares leave the movie theater for popcorn again until the movie's over.

That night, Rick drinks . . . and recalls how Ilsa loved and left him in Paris. This is a flashback to the Backstory. Notice that the flashback is motivated—the audience is dying to find out what happened between these two. And the flashback ends with a mystery, moving the present day story forward.

After the flashback, in present time, Ilsa comes to Rick to tell him what happened in Paris, but he is so drunk and abusive, she leaves. The next day, Rick tries to make up, but Ilsa tells him she is married to famous Nazi-fighter Victor Lazlow, and she was married to him even in Paris. SLAP! This is the Midpoint for the Relationship Story. And it deepens Rick's bitterness.

A moment later, Ilsa learns that Rick has two letters of transit. This is the Midpoint for the Action Story. Ilsa must get the letters of transit from Rick. It's the only way she and her husband, Victor Laslow, can escape from the Nazis.

One night, Rick returns to his room, and Ilsa is waiting for him. She pleads with him for the Letters of Transit, but he will not give them to her. He's getting even with her. Finally, she pulls a gun on him. He says, "Go ahead and shoot, you'll be doing me a favor." But can Ilsa shoot him?

She can't, and her crisis passes; Rick realizes that she must still love him. They have their moment together. She says she can never leave him again. This is a wonderful, romantic moment, and it doesn't feel like the Crisis at all. But it is. Let's see why.

Ilsa says, "I don't know what's right any longer. You have to decide for both of us, for all of us." Please allow me to translate this: "Rick, there are three key people in this movie and only two Letters of Transit. You have to decide who gets the Letters of Transit. I am just the love interest. That's why I don't know what's right any longer. But you are the central character and the person who has to be the most active character in the final act. Therefore, you must make the crisis decision as to who leaves Casablanca for both of us, for all of us."

Rick says, "All right, I will." So this romantic moment forces Rick to make the Crisis decision. But we don't know for sure what that decision is. That creates suspense.

At the airport, we have the Showdown. Rick shoots the Nazi major and makes sure that Ilsa and her husband escape. As the police arrive, Rick expects to be arrested by Louie, but Louie is inspired by Rick. Louie says to the police, "Major Strasser has been shot." Then he exchanges glances with Rick. Will he arrest Rick? He says, "Round up the usual suspects." That pays off the earlier foreshadowing.

A moment later, Louie observes, "Well, Rick, you're not only a sentimentalist, you've become a patriot." This is the moment of Realization. Rick has reformed, overcome his flaw. He's no longer an isolationist. He sacrifices what he loves most (Ilsa) and gets involved in the fight. In other words, he sacrifices his flaw for two things: a higher value and Ilsa (the relationship)—"We'll always have Paris." His wound is healed.

The movie plays at another, more philosophical level. Rick is a symbol of America that does not want to get involved in the war, but that makes the sacrifice and eventually does.

YOU GOTTA HAVE HEART

Relationships. We often look at movies in terms of individual characters, but the relationships those characters have with each other are vital. I think of the key relationship or dominant relationship as the *heart of the story*. We can certainly see that is the case with Casablanca.

The Usual Suspects is a wonderful script. In fact, the Writers Guild of America rated it the 35th-best screenplay ever. The movie is well acted and won awards. However, with all that movie had going for it, it made only $23 million domestic gross at the box office. Perhaps one reason is, it doesn't have heart. The dominant relationship is between Verbal and the Customs Agent, and there is not much going on in emotional terms. The movie is rather intellectual in that regard. It appeals to the mind, but not as much to the heart.

King Kong, on the other hand, has a big heart (literally). Ann and Kong are the heart of the story, even though neither is the central character. We care about both characters. I realize that special effects help this movie, but it's the heart that makes both the original and the most recent *King Kong* films tick.

I realize that commercial appeal does not necessarily equal artistic quality. That's a separate issue. I'm only pointing out that screenplays with heart might have a better shot in the script marketplace than those without it. *World Trade Center* did more than twice the business of *United 93* (and both are based on the 9/11 tragedy), and *Juno* more than doubled the gross of *No Country for Old Men*. Obviously, there are many reasons for a film's commercial success, and I understand that the comparisons above are unfair. But could at least one reason that one film did better than another be that it had more heart?

I think that even Ryan (*Up in the Air*) would agree that relationships are more important than he once thought. And it's easy to see how the heart of *A Beautiful Mind* carries that story. The central character chooses a real life over an imaginary life because of the love of his wife. And I'm sure Bertie and Lionel (from *The King's Speech*) would say it's all about the relationship.

I notice in *Little Miss Sunshine* that the six main characters are paired. We actually have three couples: Frank and Dwayne, Grandpa and Olive, Richard and Cheryl. Do you think that helps move this story along?

My suggestion for your consideration is this: Keep in mind this idea of "heart" and relationships as you work through your Inside Emotional/Relationship Story. And in terms of character goals, desires, and needs, don't just think in terms of what your character wants, but what she wants from others. It is just as important to develop a relationship as it is to develop a character. A relationship can have an arc just like a character can.

Up where we belong

Consider the movie *Up*. It's the relationship Carl once had with Ellie that motivates his actions. Early in the story we see how she inspires him, how their opposite traits become complementary. Visually, she is connected with the house and the things in it. The Action Story is driven by the goal to take the house to Paradise Falls, while the relationship story (with both Ellie and Russell) is driven by the unconscious need to let go of the past, have a new adventure, and connect with people again.

Carl wants to preserve the house, which represents his deceased wife, and take it to Paradise Falls. He's single-minded about that. What he needs to do is to let go of the past (but keep the memories) and begin a new adventure with someone else (another relationship), but he clings to the house. Throughout the movie, his companion, Russell, has been trying to help Kevin the exotic bird. The Crisis comes when Kevin is taken by Muntz (the old adventurer).

So what does Carl do? He reaffirms his goal of Paradise Falls, the place that he and his wife wanted to go to when they were children and during their marriage. Kevin is not his concern. And when he achieves his action goal of arriving at the Falls, he's done . . . and a bit unfulfilled.

He opens his wife's adventure book and sees those additional pages that were once blank. They are now filled with photos of their marriage. And then he sees her message to him for the first time: "Thanks for the adventure. Now go have a new one." Inspired, he begins to throw furniture out of the house so that they can go save Kevin (his new action goal). He's letting go of the past adventure and moving forward to a new adventure with Russell.

Notice how the relationship with Russell is developed. Carl first sees him as a nuisance, later as a helper to put up with, and finally as a surrogate grandson.

PLOT

Up until now, we've discussed the Outside/Action Plot and the Inside/Emotional Plot. *Plot* is the structure of action and emotion. The verb *to plot* is a creative process that uses character development and story structure. When all the plotting is over, you end up with the main *plot* and several *subplots*.

Plot comprises the important events in a character's story. The words *plot*, *structure*, and *story* are often used interchangeably. Plot grows from character because everything starts with a character that has a goal. Since the goal is opposed, the character takes action. The resulting conflict culminates in a crisis. Will she win? Will he lose? Will he grow? Will she decline? The answer to those questions determines the kind of story—the kind of plot—you're writing.

There are basically two kinds of stories: plot-driven stories (which I prefer to call goal-driven stories) and character-driven stories. In goal-driven stories, the focus is primarily on the character's goal and the action—the spine of the story. In character-driven stories, the focus is primarily on character dynamics, a need, and a key relationship—the heart of the story. First, let's look at some examples of goal-driven stories.

The character wins
In this plot model, the character strives for a goal and wins. Very simple and very common. Examples include *Monsters University*, *Argo*, *Slumdog Millionaire*, *Shrek*, *Independence Day*, *Rocky* (Rocky achieves his goal of going the distance), *Die Hard*, *Avatar*, *42*, *The Fugitive*, *Men in Black*, *The Silence of the Lambs*, *Rudy*, *National Treasure*, and *The Karate Kid*. In *Saving Private Ryan*, Captain Miller achieves his goal, even though he dies. *Napoleon Dynamite* not only succeeds as a campaign manager, but he gets the girl, too.

The character loses
With this plot, a moral victory of some kind often results despite the failure of a very sympathetic character. *Spartacus* fails to achieve his goal for the slaves and is crucified, but he sees his wife and child escape to freedom. *Thelma & Louise* never get to

Mexico, but in the attempt they achieve a certain freedom. In *O Brother, Where Art Thou?* Everett (George Clooney) never gets his wife back, and there's not much of a moral victory either, except that he has a job with the governor, and that ain't bad in Depression-era Mississippi.

Other examples are *Braveheart, One Flew Over the Cuckoo's Nest, From Here to Eternity, The Mission* (here, they flat-out lose), and *JFK* (the Jim Garrison character).

The character sows the seeds of his own destruction

What Goes Around, Comes Around. Examples include *The Ladykillers, Frankenstein, Dangerous Liaisons, Moby Dick,* and *Scream* (the perpetrators). In Episode III of *Star Wars* (*Revenge of the Sith*), the Emperor molds Anakin Skywalker into Darth Vader; in Episode VI, it is Darth Vader who kills the Emperor.

The following plot models seem more focused on character dynamics, and on the Inside/ Emotional Story.

The character grows by doing the right thing

Here, the character is about to do the wrong thing, but transforms into someone who overcomes his or her flaw and does the right thing. This is very popular everywhere. In *Casablanca*, Rick wants to get even with Ilsa; in the end, he does the right thing and helps her and her husband escape. Charlie (Tom Cruise) in *Rain Man* wants his inheritance; in the end, he tears up the check and does the right thing for his brother.

An ideal example is *An Ideal Husband*, in which at least three characters grow by doing the right thing. Other examples include *Hitch, Gran Torino, Emma, Up, On the Waterfront, A Beautiful Mind* (both John Nash and his wife, Alicia), *My Best Friend's Wedding, Les Misérables, Jerry Maguire, Saints and Soldiers, Scent of a Woman, Big, An Officer and a Gentleman, Groundhog Day,* and *Schindler's List*.

Romantic comedies usually fit this plot model because one or more of the lovers gives up something (the flaw or the goal) for the other. In *Pretty Woman*, both characters give up their careers. In *Some Like It Hot*, the lovers stop using each other. *Midnight Run* is a love story without the romance—both Jack Walsh (Robert DeNiro) and Jonathan Mardukas (Charles Grodin) give up their goals for each other in the end.

The character grows up

Here the character comes of age while striving for one or more goals that are either achieved or not achieved—it doesn't matter which. We don't really care whether the boys are first to find the body in *Stand by Me*. What we care about is the relationship and growth of the boys. The goal is only there to give the relationship a track to roll on. In some character-driven stories, the goal may change. And that's fine as long as the conflict intensifies and rises to a crisis and showdown.

Here are more examples of characters growing up: *Good Will Hunting*, *Juno*, *Risky Business*, *Hook* (Peter Pan grows up), *Breaking Away*, *Platoon*, and *American Graffiti*. Tao in *Gran Torino* comes of age. In *Unbreakable*, David Dunn grows from mere mortal, bad husband, and not-so-great father to a somewhat-super hero.

In a sense, Peter Parker, the central character in *Spider-Man 2*, comes of age by affirming his identity as Spider-Man. However, this could also be seen as a "character learns" plot. Let's look at that next.

The character learns

Here, the character learns what he or she needs to be happy. George Bailey (Jimmy Stewart) realizes he has a wonderful life in *It's a Wonderful Life*. Bishop Henry Brougham (David Niven) learns what's important in life in *The Bishop's Wife*—that the people in the cathedral are more important than the cathedral itself. Harold, in *Harold and Maude*, discovers that life is worth living. In *The Sixth Sense*, Cole and Malcolm learn to communicate.

In *The Green Mile*, Paul learns that "everyone must walk his own green mile." This knowledge does not necessarily make him happy, but it deepens his character and his appreciation for life.

Gil learns in *Midnight in Paris* that he and most everyone else thinks of a past epoch in time as the most romantic or desirable. While visiting a past era, he realizes, "These people have no antibiotics." Maybe modern-day Paris is more desirable than he had once thought.

In *The Wizard of Oz*, Dorothy finds out there's no place like home. She also achieves her goal of returning to Kansas. (An argument could be made that the main plot is a Character-Wins Plot and that the realization of her need is merely a subplot that supports the goal.) Notice in this instance and in many other instances that the realization is the same as or closely related to the theme.

Other examples: *The Hurt Locker*—in the end, Sgt. James realizes what his only love is. *The Prince of Tides*—Tom Wingo (Nick Nolte) learns he wants to live with his family. In *City Slickers*, Mitch Robbins (Billy Crystal) finally figures out the meaning of life. In *Finding Neverland*, little Peter tells James Barrie that he (Barrie) is Peter Pan.

The character fails to learn

Here, the character fails to learn what he or she needs to learn to be happy. In this plot, the character does not grow, but the audience learns the lesson. Examples include *War of the Roses*, *Goodfellas*, and *Raging Bull*. In *Butch Cassidy and the Sundance Kid*, Butch and Sundance never figure out that they are in the wrong line of work and need to change with the times.

I suppose you could argue for *O Brother, Where Art Thou?* After all, even at the end, Everett (George Clooney) still wants to print up a dentist diploma and just get any old wedding ring for his wife. He's not very bright for someone who uses Dapper Dan pomade.

The character declines

T. E. Lawrence in *Lawrence of Arabia* declines while striving to achieve a worthy goal. That's common for this particular plot category. Here are other examples: *Unforgiven*, *The Social Network*, *Citizen Kane*, and (if I may) *Super Size Me*.

In the beginning of *The Godfather*, Michael (the central character) is something of a patriot who doesn't want a part of the family business. In the end he *runs* the family business, but his rise is also his decline, which is demonstrated in the final scene where he lies, straight-faced, to his wife.

In virtually all stories, there is one main plot. Everything else happening in the character's life is a subplot. In addition to the central character's plot and subplot, each of the other characters in the screenplay has his or her own plot with a goal, action, crisis, and resolution. These are all subplots.

Furthermore, each character's crisis may come at a different juncture in the script, or may converge at the same crisis moment, depending on the story. The great secret to master-plotting is to bring the various subplots and main plot into conflict. In other words, most or all of the subplots should cross the central character's main purpose, creating complications. One purpose of the step-outline (described in Book II) is to accomplish this. You should find the Character/Action Grid in Book II to be helpful as well.

GENRE

Another element to consider in plotting is genre. Each genre carries with it certain characteristics.

Love stories

In a rom-com (romantic comedy), the lovers meet (Catalyst), are forced to be together or willfully choose to be together (Big Event), fall in love (Midpoint), are separated (Crisis), after which one or both will change in some way, reform, and return to the beloved (Showdown). Most often, this results in a Character-Grows-by-Doing-the-Right-Thing Plot.

This category includes "date movies," a term popularized by Nora Ephron's *Sleepless in Seattle*. In fact, in the film itself, *guy movies* are distinguished from *chick flicks*. A date movie is a movie that appeals to both guys and chicks. In the case of *Sleepless in Seattle*, women presumably see this as a love story, while men see a widowed father getting a second chance.

What I find most interesting about the film is that it follows the "standard" plot progression, but does so without the characters being together. For example, Annie meets Sam over the radio rather than in person. There are other films with notable twists on (or exceptions to) the standard rom-com structure, including *(500) Days of Summer*.

Action adventure

These stories usually open with an exciting action sequence, followed by some exposition. Although these can be suspenseful, the key to this genre is exciting action. Make sure there is plenty of it. These stories generally follow a Character-Wins Plot and usually end with a chase and/or plenty of violence.

William Martel, quoting Shane Black in *Scriptwriters Network Newsletter*, writes the following:

> The key to good action scenes is reversals. . . . It's like a good news/ bad news joke. The bad news is you get thrown out of an airplane. The good news is you're wearing your parachute. The bad news is the rip cord breaks. The good news is you have a backup chute. The bad news is you can't reach the cord. Back and forth like that until the character reaches the ground.

Love stories and action stories are probably the most consistently popular movies over time. I interviewed a successful children's book writer who told me that there are really only two basic stories: "Cinderella" (love story as in *Pretty Woman*) and "Jack the Giant Killer" (action story as in *Die Hard*).

Thrillers

Thrillers focus on suspense more than on action. In a thriller, an ordinary man or woman gets involved in a situation that becomes life-threatening. The bad guys desperately want the *MacGuffin*, a name Hitchcock gave to the plot-device or object that often drives the thriller. In *North by Northwest*, the MacGuffin is government secrets. In *Charade*, it's $250,000 in stamps.

Although the characters are after the MacGuffin, the audience generally cares more about the survival of the central character than the MacGuffin. This is because she cannot get help, has been betrayed in some way, and cannot trust anyone. The primary motivation is one of survival, so there's not much of a Character Realization in the end.

Many thrillers don't have a MacGuffin, but most feature a character who is betrayed, isolated from help, and in grave danger. That helps us identify with her fears.

Traveling angel

This is a story about a character who solves the problems of the people around him. He doesn't grow much himself because he's "perfect," but other characters do, and once they have done so, the angel rides off into the sunset. *Mary Poppins* (who is practically perfect in every way), *Shane*, and *Pale Rider* are examples. Percy in *The Spitfire Grill* redeems virtually everyone. In the case of *The Bishop's Wife*, the traveling angel actually is a traveling angel.

In a way, Seabiscuit (in *Seabiscuit*) qualifies as the only horse to be a traveling angel. The other characters in the story heal because of Seabiscuit, although you could argue that Seabiscuit himself "grows," too.

Detective-mystery

The murder mystery opens with a murder. Then the police officer, private detective, or retired novelist solves the case. Since solving the case is primarily a mental exercise, there is often a voiceover narration so we can be privy to the central character's thoughts.

If this central character is a private detective, he will usually be portrayed as one who operates on the fringes of the law, such as Jake Gittes in *Chinatown*. Often, detectives uncover a small corruption that leads to a larger one. Many detective stories, like *Chinatown*, contain elements of "film noir."

Film noir

Film noir (literally, "black film") describes both a genre and a shooting style—shadowy, cynical, and realistic—as well as a storyline that features ordinary people in over their heads, no heroes and villains per se. In fact, there is usually a moral ambiguity, even though there may be a struggle between good and evil within the central character. Stories often end unhappily. *L.A. Confidential*, *The Usual Suspects*, *Touch of Evil*, *D.O.A.*, *Basic Instinct*, *Pulp Fiction*, *Fargo*, *The Postman Always Rings Twice*, *Double Indemnity*, and its offspring *Body Heat*.

Fish-out-of-water

This is a popular genre because it creates so much potential for conflict and fun. A character is abruptly taken out of her element and forced to adjust to a new environment. Thus, Detective John Kimble (Arnold Schwarzenegger) becomes a kindergarten teacher in *Kindergarten Cop*, and Detective Axel Foley (Eddie Murphy) goes to 90210 in *Beverly Hills Cop*. In *Three Men and a Baby*, three Peter Pans suddenly must care for a baby. *Private Benjamin* could be pitched as "Jewish American Princess joins the Army."

Horror

Scary movies differ from the thriller in that the opposition is a monster, or a monster-like human or a supernatural force. This genre leans heavily on shock and surprise. Examples include *Jaws*, *The Conjuring*, *Scream*, and *The Ring*. The horror film *Alien* relies heavily on surprise, but its sequel, *Aliens*, was wisely written as an action/adventure story, not another horror movie. Instead of scaring us, James Cameron thrills us with exciting action. Naturally there are horror elements in *Aliens*, but the focus of the movie is on action.

Science fiction

Yes, *Alien* and *Aliens* are science-fiction movies, but the horror and action-adventure genres dominated in each respective case. Thus, we have hybrid genres: horror/sci-fi and action/sci-fi. *Back to the Future* is a fantasy family drama, or a sci-fi comedy, or a combination of all four. For purists, we have *Star Wars*, *Star Trek*, *Ender's Game*, and a host of others. The point is that many science fiction movies take on the characteristics of another genre and move it to another world or time.

Combos

In many films, there is a secondary genre, such as some of the science-fiction films named. Some are combination genres such as horror/comedy (*Zombieland*), Western/sci-fi (*Cowboys and Aliens*), and Historical/horror (*Abraham Lincoln, Vampire Slayer*). I suppose you could say that Marty in *Back to the Future* is a fish-out-of-water when he drops into 1955 culture. So maybe that film is actually a sci-fi/fantasy/fish-out-of-water/family comedy.

Obviously there are many genres, combinations of genres, and genres I haven't named: revisionist ecological Western (*Dances with Wolves*), screwball comedy (*Bringing Up Baby* and *What's Up, Doc?*), historical epic (*Seven Years in Tibet*, *Lawrence of Arabia*), buddy picture (*Midnight Run*), milieu (*Alice in Wonderland*, *Midnight in the Garden of Good and Evil*, and *Lord of the Rings*), action/romance (*Romancing the Stone*), and on and on.

Once you choose your genre, watch several representative films. This is not to research your story but to learn more about what makes that genre work.

MYTH

Beyond genre and plot is myth. In any story you write, it may help you to understand the mythological journey. The Hero's Journey, as presented by Joseph Campbell and explained by Christopher Vogler, follows a particular pattern that may be woven into the fabric of any story, regardless of its genre. Many stories contain elements of this mythological journey, while a few, like Episodes IV through VI of *Star Wars*, *The Polar Express*, and *The Wizard of Oz* can be called myths because the central character passes through each stage of the Hero's Journey. Briefly, these are the stages in the Hero's Journey:

The hero lives amid ordinary surroundings. The Catalyst is actually a call to adventure, but the hero is reluctant to heed the call. This could be the moment when the hero receives her mission.

She is given an amulet or aid of some kind by an older person, a mentor. For example, Dorothy is given the ruby-red slippers by a good witch. Luke is given the light saber by Obi-Wan. Bertie is given a recording of his voice in *The King's Speech* by his speech therapist. Many stories feature mentors, e.g., Sean Maguire (Robin Williams) in *Good Will Hunting*, the train conductor in *The Polar Express*, and Agent K (Tommy Lee Jones) in *Men in Black*. In *Lord of the Rings*, Frodo is mentored by Gandalf.

The central character crosses the threshold to the extraordinary world. This is followed by a series of tests and obstacles. The hero often undergoes a death experience and enters the secret hideout, the witch's castle, the Death Star, the belly of the whale, the speaking booth (*The King's Speech*) or the innermost cave.

Finally, the hero seizes the treasure and is chased back to the ordinary world, where this treasure blesses the people. The Grail heals the land. In *The Polar Express*, the little reindeer bell confirms the spirit of Christmas to all who hear it ring.

The hero may be resurrected in some way. Luke and Han are honored at an awards ceremony. Dorothy returns to her family. *The Last Starfighter* is transfigured in front of the townspeople. Oskar Schindler is honored in a ring ceremony. And the king (in *The King's Speech*) is congratulated by all and appears to his people on the balcony. The resurrection almost always corresponds to the Realization, the last of the Magnificent 7 Plot Points.

Years ago, I read *Archetypes and the Collective Unsconscious* by Carl Jung. I didn't pay the book much heed until I became acquainted with the Hero's Journey. I looked at a script I had written before I studied Jung and realized that my hero followed the steps of the Hero's Journey. Many of the archetypes were there. Wow, obviously there was something to this collective unconscious.

As a writer, you may have heard or felt a call to action, a call to write, but hesitated. You must heed the call. As you struggle, as you learn, and as you write, you may very well walk the path of the hero, overcome obstacles, gain allies, and become the next great screenwriter. The Hero's Journey may very well become your personal odyssey.

Note: This is a good time to do Steps 1, 2, and 3 in the workbook (Book II).

Ten keys to creating captivating characters

Plot generally derives from character, and not the other way around. Screenplays may be structure, but that structure develops from your characters. In fact, structure and character often develop together. However, it's easy for developing writers to get over-involved with their structure, while their characters emerge as colorless pawns of the writer's will.

I have often found science-fiction writers so wound up in the world of their story, the cool gadgetry, and their carefully conceived plots that I am forced to ask, "What do you love most about *Star Trek*?" And almost always, they start talking about Kirk, Spock, Bones, Uhura, Scotty, and others. Special effects are wonderfully helpful, but audiences generally fall in love with characters more than they do events and effects. Indeed, it's the originality of the characters that gives meaning to the events and effects.

Your central character requires 10 things from a writer. Keep in mind as we review these that virtually all of them apply to supporting characters, and even minor characters, as well as to your main characters. Also keep in mind what we discussed earlier about the importance of developing relationships as well as characters.

1. A GOAL AND AN OPPOSITION

Your character wants something. A dramatic goal is specific and measurable. Dealing with life is not a goal. Happiness is not a goal. Seeking $10 million worth of doubloons on an old Spanish shipwreck off the Florida Keys is a goal. Winning the Pan American Ballroom Dance Competition is a goal. Getting the broomstick of the Wicked Witch in order to return to Kansas is a goal. The nature of the goal reveals a lot about your character.

Whatever the goal is, it should not be easy to attain. There must be opposition to the goal. Opposition creates conflict, and conflict makes drama. Conflict reveals character and motivates people to learn. Ask yourself, *What does my character want and what does she most fear?* The opposition will force her to face her fear in some way.

Cole in *The Sixth Sense* is afraid of being seen as a freak, especially by his mother. The worst thing that could happen to Andy in *The Shawshank Redemption* is to be unable to prove his innocence and remain a permanent slave to the warden. In *Liar, Liar*, the worst thing is to tell the truth, and that's funny because the central character is an attorney. The worst thing that could happen to a babysitter (in *Adventures in Babysitting*) is lose the kids. In some stories, like *The Hurt Locker*, the worst thing is to be killed.

In most screenplays, the main opposition will be an individual. If it is an organization, let someone represent that organization. In *Ghostbusters*, the Environmental Protection Agency is represented by a man who makes it his personal business to bust the Ghostbusters.

Billy Wilder and I. A. L. Diamond had a huge problem while writing *Some Like It Hot*. They had a funny idea of two men joining an all-girl band. They weren't able to develop a story from it because they didn't have a motivation for the two men to join the band, and they didn't have an opposition.

One day, Diamond walked into the office they shared on the studio lot to find Wilder waiting for him. As soon as he entered the office, Wilder shouted out, "St. Valentine's Day Massacre!" Diamond shouted back, "That's it!" They made the two men accidental witnesses to the famous gangland killing. Now, in order to escape from both the law (represented by one individual cop) and the mob (represented by one individual mobster), they become cross-dressers so they can join an all-girl band. Once on the road with the band, they become opposition characters to each other (they both want the same woman). That's characters developing the plot.

When possible, personalize the opposition. That will create greater drama and will elicit the audience's sympathy for the central character. The hero is often defined by his opposition. And that opposition need not be evil; you just need someone who has a good reason to block your hero's attempt to achieve his goal, even if she is doing so subconsciously (as with the overprotective mother controlling her adult son's life "for his own good").

It is possible to have a nonhuman opposition, such as the forces of Nature, or even a monster (such as the Great White in *Jaws*). If you do have such an opposition, consider adding a human opponent as well. In *Jaws*, the mayor of Amity serves as a secondary opponent to Police Chief Brody.

In *The Hurt Locker*, the greatest opposition is the unknown—bombs, bomb tripwires, a faceless enemy that wants to kill you. To supplement that, the three members of the team are often at odds about procedure or something else.

In addition to the goal, you may wish to give your character some related inner drive or yearning that either supports the goal or is in opposition to the goal. This inner need may be inwardly blocked by some character flaw. This was discussed more fully in a preceding section.

Can the goal change? Of course it can. It generally will not in action-driven stories, but may in character-driven stories. In *Up*, the goal is to reach Paradise Falls, but that changes to save Kevin. Sometimes the main goal is met by achieving milestones (little goals) along the way, as in *The Wizard of Oz*.

The Unity of Opposites

When two characters are at clearly motivated cross-purposes, you have a *Unity of Opposites*. To ensure a conflict right up to the story's end, you need a unity of the central character's goal or need and the opposing character's goal or need. The unity exists when the two are in direct opposition to each other, and compromise is impossible because both characters are strongly motivated. That ensures a struggle to the end.

For example, in *Fatal Attraction*, a married man has an affair with a beautiful woman and wants to terminate the relationship with her, but he can't because she carries his baby and is fixated on him. There exists a *unity of opposites*. He wants to end the relationship; she wants the relationship to grow. Both are clearly motivated. Compromise is impossible. The motivation is the key.

2. MOTIVATION

Your character must be motivated. Ask yourself this question: Why does my character want what he wants? The answer to that question is the motivation. And the more personal, the better. That's because the more personal it is, the more the audience will identify and sympathize with the character. It's the emotional touchstone between your audience and your character. It's the character's motivation that makes the audience care.

What is Rocky's goal in the first *Rocky* movie? His goal is very specific. He wants to go the distance with the champ—15 rounds. It is not to win. He knows he can't win. So why is "going the distance" so important? Why do we care? Because his motivation is *to prove he's not a bum*. It's the personal motivation that gives the story its power. Personally, I hate boxing. I couldn't care less who won the "Thrilla in Manila." And yet I've watched four of the Rocky movies. Why? Well, it's not for the boxing scenes. It's for the motivation *behind* those boxing scenes.

In the second *Rocky* movie, the boxer's wife goes into a coma. Then she blinks her eyes open and says, "Win." Now Rocky has a motive for winning.

In *Rocky III*, Clubber Lang (Mr. T) has a tiff with Rocky's manager, Mickey (Burgess Meredith). Mickey suffers a heart attack and dies. Does Rocky want to clean Clubber's clock? Absolutely, and so does everyone in the theater.

Another boxing movie, *Million Dollar Baby* (which is actually more of a character drama than a "boxing movie"), goes deeper. Frankie Dunn (Clint Eastwood) is motivated by guilt and by the fear of getting close to someone. He is lonely. Maggie Fitzgerald (Hilary Swank) grew up believing she was "trash." She wants to escape the past. She needs someone to believe in her. Boxing gives her life meaning. It's easy for people to identify with her personal motivation and with Frankie's; thus, people get "emotionally involved" with these characters.

Love is behind the desire to get well in *A Beautiful Mind*. John Nash is motivated to give up his imaginary life for a real life with his wife. Her love is his motivation. The love of Ellie (*Up*) is behind Carl's goal of Paradise Falls. And in *The Sixth Sense*, Dr. Malcolm (Bruce Willis) wants to help Cole because he was unable to save Vincent. He has a personal reason for wanting to achieve his goal.

Think of Bertie's motivation for wanting to stop his stammering. First is his horrible humiliation of stuttering at Wembley Stadium. At the Crisis moment, he wrongly accuses Lionel; listen to the fear behind his words: "With war looming, you've saddled this nation with a voiceless king. . . . It'll be like mad King George the Third, there'll be Mad King George the Stammerer, who let his people down so badly in their hour of need."

In *Rain Man*, Charlie Babbitt's perception of his father's past harsh treatment of him motivates his goal of collecting the inheritance. In other words, he wants the inheritance to get even with his father.

Jaws is a horror movie complete with body parts and a monster. The only personal motivation needed here is survival, but the writer adds something very personal. When Brody fails to close the beach, a boy is eaten by the Great White. At the funeral, the mother slaps Brody's face in front of the entire town and says, "You killed my son." Now Brody wants not only to protect the town but redeem himself.

In *Jerry Maguire*, our character is fired and humiliated. He is also motivated by his employee/wife, who is the only person who supports him.

Like Jerry Maguire, Rose in *Titanic* is motivated by two things: She is imprisoned by a lifestyle in which no one sees her as she is, and Jack is the only person who really does "see her." This is why she literally reveals herself to him.

The motivation usually grows with the conflict. It becomes stronger as the story progresses. Often, the motivation deepens or becomes most evident at the Midpoint of the story.

In *Amadeus*, Salieri has many reasons for disliking Mozart. It seems that whenever they are together, Mozart finds a way to insult Salieri, even if it's innocently done. These accumulate over time. The clincher, however, is when Mrs. Mozart visits Salieri. She brings her husband's work with her and confesses that they need money and wonders if Salieri will help them. Salieri scrutinizes the manuscripts and sees that these are "first and only drafts of music," and notices no corrections. From Salieri's point of view, Mozart must simply be taking dictation from God. Salieri takes it personally. He goes to his private room and throws his crucifix into the fire. "From now on we are enemies," he says. Why? Because God chose a degenerate like Mozart over him, Salieri, whose only wish had been to serve God through music. So here, at the Midpoint or Pinch, we have the goal (to fight God by killing Mozart) and the motivation (because God is unjust).

3. A BACKSTORY

In the words of Oscar Wilde, "Every saint has a past, and every sinner has a future." Before page one of your screenplay, something significant happens to your central character that gives him "a past." As discussed earlier, that singular event is called the *Backstory*. Sometimes the Backstory is an overall situation that has always existed in the past, but usually it's a single representative event. In some movies, there is no Backstory.

In *Ordinary People*, the Backstory involves two brothers, teenagers, boating on a lake. A storm capsizes the boat and one drowns. The other blames himself and tries to kill himself. The script begins when he returns from the hospital.

In *Sleepless in Seattle*, the Backstory is the death of Sam's wife.

In the above examples, we are given quick glimpses of the Backstory. Most often, the Backstory is not seen by the audience, but it is there, haunting the central character and affecting his actions. In *Thelma & Louise*, Louise was raped in Texas. That's what makes it possible for her to shoot Thelma's attacker. This Backstory is not revealed to Thelma or the audience until much later in the story.

Hana in *The English Patient* is troubled by the notion that everyone she loves dies, and Jake is trying to deal with his paralysis in *Avatar*. In *Unforgiven*, Bill Munny (Clint Eastwood) was a killer before his wife reformed him.

In *The Spitfire Grill*, Percy is haunted by her dark past, which involved the death of her baby and a five-year prison sentence.

Talk about haunted! Fox Mulder, in the *X-Files* television series, is haunted by a single, traumatic event: When he was young, his sister was (apparently) kidnapped by aliens. This event deeply affects his actions and personality. He's not just your run-of-the-mill FBI man, but a person with a life and a past.

Sometimes only the screenwriter knows the Backstory (as in *As Good as It Gets*), but because he knows it, the characters seem fuller on the page. Not every character has a single past event that haunts her, but every character has a past that influences that character's actions and dialogue.

Backstory, flaw, and need

The Backstory can be subtle. For example, in *Foul Play*, Gloria Mundy (Goldie Hawn) was once in love and it ended badly. It's as simple as that. At the beginning of the movie, we see a cautious Gloria, a person not quite ready for a new lover, particularly if it's Tony Carlson (Chevy Chase). It's easy to see how the Backstory gives rise to the flaw that blocks the need. In the case of Gloria, she needs to feel safe with a man. She's not approachable because she's afraid. That's the essence of the Backstory of main love stories—the character was burned in the past and is afraid of "fire" in the present.

In *Ordinary People*, Conrad's need is to forgive himself for his brother's accidental death. His flaw is that he tries to control his feelings too much and is self-accusing. This all emerges from his Backstory.

Del Spooner (Will Smith) in *I, Robot* hates robots. This is because of his Backstory: A robot saved his life instead of that of someone more deserving. He needs to stop blaming robots and overcome his bias.

The Silence of the Lambs: When Clarice (Jodie Foster) was a little girl, her dad, a police officer, was killed. She went to live on a ranch. One night they were slaughtering lambs and the lambs were crying. She picked up a lamb and ran, but she wasn't strong enough. They caught up with her and slaughtered the lamb. The need of her adult life was to silence those cries. When a woman is captured by Buffalo Bill and placed in a pit, that woman becomes a crying lamb that Clarice wants to save. But is she strong enough? She is. After she saves the woman, she gets a call from Dr. Lecter. "Well, Clarice, have you silenced the lambs?" That's the *Realization*. We know she hasn't. They'll always be crying, but now she is strong enough to save them. (Some of my students dispute this, maintaining she *has* silenced the lambs of her past. What do you think?)

Showing the Backstory

Occasionally, the audience is actually shown the Backstory. In *Flatliners*, we see each main character's Backstory at the appropriate moment in the script. The films *Contact*, *The Philadelphia Story*, and *Backdraft* open with a Backstory.

Theoretically, each quiz show question Jamal is asked in the film *Slumdog Millionaire* is linked to a past event that shows (in flashback) why he knows the answer. In *Casablanca*, the Backstory is revealed in a flashback, as is the case in many films. In *Nuts*, attorney Aaron Levinsky (Richard Dreyfuss) must unravel the Backstory of his client Claudia Draper (Barbra Streisand) to win the case.

4. THE WILL TO ACT

How do you judge a person? By words or by actions? Don't actions weigh more heavily than words for you? As the saying goes, "What you do sounds so loud in my ears, I cannot hear what you say."

Action reveals character, and crisis reveals a person's true colors, because he does what he does because of who he is. Problems and obstacles reveal what he's made of. Drama is a character's reaction to an event, and that reaction helps define him.

A house is on fire and there are children inside. Outside is a gardener, a nun, a 12-year-old paper boy on a bicycle, a housewife, and a well-dressed businessperson. What will each do? We don't know for sure from the characterizations I just gave you. It's the character within that determines what each will do. So pressure and opposition not only reveal character, they provide the opportunity for the character to grow; in other words, they can help build character.

Since actions speak louder than words (and outside characterizations), your character will generally reveal more of his character through action than through dialogue. Yes, dialogue can tell us a lot, particularly about what is going on inside, but actions show us. Even old Carl in *Up* is willing to act. In some cases, dialogue can be action. When Darth Vader tells Luke that he is his father and that he should join him, that can be seen as an action.

Running Bear is a Sioux hunting buffalo on the wide prairie. This is interesting action. The buffalo are the opposition. But how can we make this more dramatic? Suppose the white settler's son is in the buffalo's path. The white man is Running Bear's enemy, but now Running Bear must make a decision that will reveal his true character. He decides to save the boy. Now he has an action—to save the boy from the herd.

Okay, let's take this one step further. The boy's father looks through the window and sees his son and the buffalo; then to his horror, he sees his enemy, Running Bear. He thinks Running Bear is trying to kill his son. He grabs his rifle and races outside. Now we really care about the outcome. This is drama—characters in willful conflict, reacting to events and complications of events. Note that each character has a different view of the facts. That leads us to our next point.

5. A POINT OF VIEW AND ATTITUDES

How does your character see dragons? Are they to be feared as destructive enemies or can they be trained to be pets, as Hiccup learns in *How to Train Your Dragon*? After all, maybe the dragons are attacking in self-defense. Once we see them in a different light, our view of them might change as well.

Everyone has a belief system, a perception of reality that is influenced by past experience, a point of view that has developed over time. Our current experience is filtered through our past experience. This means that two people may react in totally different ways to the same stimulus. It depends on their perception. Their point of view is expressed in attitudes.

Some time ago, I was in a department store. I found a little two-year-old who was alone and crying. I tried to calm her down so I could find her mother. The problem was that her mother found me, and guess what she thought I was? That's right, Chester the Molester. Her perception was understandable, given the times we live in, but it was not reality. We don't see reality the way it is; we see it through the filter of our past experience.

Your character also has a past. We're going to discuss how to create that past shortly, but for right now realize that your character has a point of view expressed through attitudes. What is your character's point of view about life? What is your character's concept of love? How does he or she view the opposite sex? What is your character's attitude toward growing old? Sex? Falling rain? Grocery shopping? Dental hygiene and regular professional care? Is happiness a warm puppy or a warm gun?

Sol Stein recommends that you "give each character a separate set of facts. Don't give them the same view of the story." With different views of things, your characters will also have different attitudes. Your character will act from his or her point of view or belief system, regardless of how that point of view squares with reality. Salieri believes that great music comes from God. Therefore, Mozart must be God's creature on Earth.

The Hurt Locker features three characters with three different views of the war and how to survive. James is addicted to war (he loves it) and is rather cavalier about survival. He doesn't think about survival. Eldridge thinks about it all the time, is sure he nearly dies every day, and is trying to figure out how he's going to survive. He looks to the other two for clues. Between the two extremes is Sanborn, who sees the danger realistically and tries to take a rational approach. But it wears him down, until at the end he says, "I'm ready to die."

One thing I like about *The Dark Knight* is the competing philosophies or points of view. The Joker (the black knight) is a moral philosopher who believes people will only be as good as society allows them to be, and he converts the DA (the white knight) to that view. Batman (the dark knight) believes people are "ready to believe in good." So the Joker, who is obviously versed in game theory, presents a "prisoner's dilemma" to people on two ferries to prove his point. When the people fail to blow each other up, they apparently prove Batman is right. However, Batman feels he must take the blame for the white knight's murders, so that people will have a hero to believe in (the white knight). It's the opposing philosophies that make the story work.

Notice in *A Beautiful Mind* that the writer gives the audience the same point of view as John Nash. That leads to a wonderful movie moment when we (the audience) realize that John Nash is imagining things. And that, in turn, helps the audience get emotionally involved with John Nash. How else can a writer get people to identify with someone who sees things that don't exist?

In *Up in the Air,* Ryan (George Clooney) has a completely "rational" view of life—get rid of the excess baggage, physically and emotionally. This counters Natalie's philosophy, which creates conflict between the two when they travel together to inform people that their "position is no longer available." Ryan's unique viewpoint, represented visually by a backpack, motivates his attitude, and, thus, his actions.

A summary from the Starman

In *Starman*, an alien creature crash-lands in Wisconsin. He is a being of light who floats over to Jenny's house. Jenny has withdrawn from life because her husband was killed. The alien finds a lock of her husband's hair and uses it to clone himself a body. Now he looks just like her husband. He then makes her drive him to Arizona, which is where his mother ship will pick him up. The alien's motivation for this goal is to get home. (This is "*E.T.* meets *It Happened One Night*.") His point of view of life happens to be that *life is precious*.

Jenny's goal is to escape. Her motivation is to be safe from the alien and also to be safe from her past. And the alien looks just like her past. The writer has taken her inner problem and put it on the outside to make it visual. Jenny's point of view of life or belief is that life is scary: Husbands die (the Backstory) and aliens kidnap you (the action story).

At the Midpoint, Jenny observes the alien bringing a dead deer to life. This action emerges from his belief that life is precious. Touched by this action, she finds her goal of escape replaced by a desire to help Starman. This new goal is motivated by his inspiring action. Her point of view of life changes as well: Life is not so scary.

This story uses the deer as a metaphor. Jenny is the dead deer that Starman (an apparent Christ figure) brings back to life (the emotional story). Her perception of life changes, and that's the key. When a character's point of view changes, that's character growth.

6. ROOM TO GROW

Your central character also has a point of view of himself. This point of view of self is called "self-concept." *I'm a winner, I'm a loser. I'm clumsy, I'm graceful.* All of us act from this point of view of ourselves, and so do your characters. Here's what happens in the well-written story:

Metaphorically speaking, your character is a fish. The Big Event pulls him out of the water. He tries to swim. It's worked in the past, but it doesn't work now, and so he is forced to take new actions, different actions. But things get more and more difficult, right up to the Showdown. Mustering all the courage and faith he has, he takes the final action. Then he emerges from the climax with a new self-concept—he's a fish no longer.

This moment is the Realization—the character realizes a change has taken place. Usually the Realization follows the Showdown (or climax), but it can take place during the Showdown or just before. It's a key emotional moment for your audience. We discussed the Realization at length in the second chapter, but here are a couple of additional examples:

Michael Dorsey (Dustin Hoffman) states his realization in *Tootsie* as follows: "I was a better man as a woman with you than I was as a man. I just have to do it without the dress." He has grown or changed.

In *The Wizard of Oz*, Dorothy is asked point-blank, "Well, Dorothy, what did you learn?" And then Dorothy tells us all the ways her perceptions and attitudes have changed. Most important, her attitude toward home has changed. She realizes now that there's no place like it.

How does growth come about? Only through adversity and opposition, and through striving for some kind of goal. Only through conflict, making decisions, and taking actions. "True character is revealed," the proverb goes, "when you come face-to-face with adversity." Part of the excitement of reading a script or viewing a movie is identifying with someone who grows and learns in the face of adversity.

The goal in *Galaxy Quest* is to save the Thermians from the reptilian race that wants to destroy them. In the process of striving for this goal, the TV show actors become the characters they portrayed on the TV show.

In *Gran Torino*, Walt is a racist who is not at peace. In the end, he finds peace and gives his life for people of another race.

In defining your character's arc, ask yourself how your character grows or learns or acquires new skills or knowledge. Often, your character will grow from some form of slavery to some form of freedom (*Titanic*, *Argo*), but it can be from death to life (*Starman*). A character can learn to love (*Rain Man*) or overcome pride (*Driving Miss Daisy*) or become more principled (*An American President*) or become a good king who is on his way to overcoming a disability (*The King's Speech*). As already stated, all growth can be defined as a changed perception of self, life, others, or something else. Often that change is gradual. Often it comes with breakthrough events.

Sometimes change doesn't occur at all (*Butch Cassidy and the Sundance Kid*). A character does not necessarily need a growth arc to be interesting or for a movie to succeed. Just ask James Bond, who doesn't grow at all . . . except in *Casino Royale*. In that movie, he becomes James Bond, which is why it is the only movie that *ends* with him saying, "My name is Bond. James Bond."

Let the sunshine in

Little Miss Sunshine presents six characters, at least five of which are losers. Each adjusts to his or her loss in a negative or unproductive way, and then begins to make a positive adjustment by the movie's end. However, we don't see anyone succeed at anything except to come together as a family in the end. It's a completely different kind of growth arc. Let's look at each of the six characters.

Richard wants to be a winner and get a book deal. His adjustment to his failure is at first denial. Eventually he starts getting over it, but not completely.

Dwayne wants to fly for the Air Force, but can't because he is color blind. When he learns that fact, he has an emotional breakdown, but he also starts talking again.

Grandpa was kicked out of Sunset Manor. How does he adjust to his failure? Drugs. But he also trains Olive for the beauty pageant.

Sheryl wants to hold the family together. She sees the family fall apart like the van falls apart (a visual way of showing something that's somewhat abstract). She mentions divorce. But she sees the family come together at the end and abandons the idea of divorce.

Frank wants love and the MacArthur Grant. When he fails, he chooses suicide. But eventually he starts to become peaceful and happy. Notice that Frank's failure is his backstory. The same is true for Grandpa.

Olive fails to win the Little Miss Sunshine beauty pageant, but her dancing is the thing that brings her family together.

Another interesting arc is presented in *The Color Purple*. Sophia is a strong woman who is beaten down by her husband and others until she is essentially a broken woman, but she gets her strength back and returns to her former feisty self in the end. This is a story of decline and ascendance.

Some characters grow negatively (Michael in *The Godfather*), and as mentioned, some don't grow at all, as in some action/adventures, thrillers, and similar stories. Jamal (*Slumdog Millionaire*) doesn't reform or grow. He is honest from Day One to Day Last—his basic nature doesn't change. In fact, his honesty is puzzling to most of the other characters he comes in contact with, such as Prem the game show host and the Inspector of Police. But his life circumstance change greatly.

However, in most stories, character growth of some sort is desirable, even essential. One reason I enjoyed the original *Die Hard* was that the writer gave action hero John McClane (Bruce Willis) room to grow in his relationship with his wife. That added more heart to the story than it would otherwise have had.

7. BELIEVABILITY

One reason dramatic characters are interesting is that they are generally single-minded and focused. Humans, on the other hand, have many things going on in their lives and tend to run off on tangents. Your job as the next great screenwriter is to make your dramatic and comedic characters seem as human as possible. In other words, your job is to make us care about them. Here are some ways to accomplish that.

Give them human emotions

As you know, people watch movies to feel emotion vicariously. Whether it is love, revenge, fear, anticipation, or what-have-you, you can only touch these moviegoers if they are able to relate to how your character feels. This doesn't mean that your character should blubber all over the place. Don't overdo it. It means that we need to see your character frustrated, hurt, scared, thrilled, in love, etc.

Often, we empathize with a character more when she fights what she feels than when she expresses it. We see that more than once with Leigh Anne (Sandra Bullock) in *The Blind Side*. And that's precisely what happens in *The Hurt Locker*. Sgt. James likes the kid that sells DVDs. Then he finds what he thinks is that kid's body. What follows is Sgt. James fighting his emotions. And he does it with no one else around, which gives the audience a moment alone with James. Moments alone with a character are truthful moments.

Rain Man is a remarkable film because one of the main characters is incapable of emotionally connecting with another person. I admire the writers, who dealt with this problem by giving Raymond (Dustin Hoffman) a desire to drive a car. "I'm an excellent driver," he would say. If your eyes ever became misty, it was at the end, when Charlie (Tom Cruise) lets Raymond drive the car on a circular driveway.

Give them human traits

Spider-Man 2 succeeds largely because the focus of the story is more on Peter Parker the human being than on Spider-Man the superhero. Peter has human emotions, traits, values, and dimension. And that's why we love him. In *The King's Speech,* we love Bertie the future king because he is so believable as a human.

When *Snow White and the Seven Dwarfs* was being developed, the dwarfs were seven old guys who looked alike and acted the same. Then Walt Disney decided to give each dwarf a human trait and to call him by that trait. What a difference a trait makes. We're actually discussing personality; does your character have a fascinating or unique personality?

In creating characters, first focus on the core of your character—her soul. Who is she? What is her strongest trait? We'll call this her dominant trait. Look for a couple of other traits. Then look for a flaw that might serve as a contrast. That flaw, if it exists, may create an inner conflict.

Finally, determine if your character projects a façade. That fake persona is an element of the character and can be thought of as a trait. In *The Pink Panther* series, we all love Inspector Clouseau's presumed competence. Children who watch *The Polar Express* gradually learn that the train conductor is not nearly as mean as he first seems. In *As Good as It Gets*, Melvin Udall's (Jack Nicholson) articulate attacks and obsessive-compulsive behaviors are part of the scary façade he uses to fend off what he perceives to be a scary world. Once he learns to deal with his fear, his hidden compassion begins to emerge and his obsessive compulsions become less intense. That is what is at the core of his growth arc.

In all, identify three to five specific traits for each of your characters, including a possible flaw, façade, or imperfection.

You don't have to reveal a character's traits all at once. Ideally, each scene reveals something new about your central character. Each contact with a new character sheds new light until the central character is fully illuminated. You will want to introduce your central character in normal circumstances before the Catalyst upsets that balance, so that we have a feel for who this person is. Occasionally, this is done by other characters talking about the central character. For example, in *Casablanca*, everyone talks about Rick before we meet him.

It is also important to include characteristics, problems, and imperfections that are familiar to all humans. He's a grouch. She can't deal with people until she's had her morning coffee. Inconsequential human imperfections will make your dramatic or comedic character more believable and more human. An opposition character's imperfections might be more irritating than endearing.

Some writers determine their characters' astrological signs for them. You could give your character one of many psychological and personality tests. Is your character primarily visual, auditory, or kinesthetic? Since you want difficult people in your story, you might avail yourself of a copy of *Coping with Difficult People*. The book describes certain difficult personality types.

Centuries ago, some writers used the four body humors (liquids) for help in characterization. The sanguine character (for whom blood is the humor) was courageous, active, extroverted, and creative. The melancholic character (black bile) was depressed, ponderous, and often considerate; Hamlet is your classic melancholic. The choleric character (yellow bile) was ill-tempered, but also charismatic and ambitious. The phlegmatic (phlegm) was more calm, accepting, and consistent.

Give them human values

Now let's take a moment to consider the Corleone family. It's doubtful that you'd invite these guys over for dinner in real life. And yet, in the *Godfather* movies, you actually root for them. Why? Well, for one thing, these guys are loyal. They have a sense of justice. They have families and family values just like most of us. We like people with positive values.

If your central character happens to be a *bad guy*, make sure he's morally superior to the others in the story. If your character breaks the law, make him less corrupt than the law. The Corleones had a code of honor—they didn't sell drugs. Sure, extortion, protection rackets, murder, prostitution, and gambling—but hey, they didn't sell drugs. In fact, they are morally superior to most of the other people in the movie.

Other ways to create a little sympathy for your character is to give her a talent for what she does, and/or an endearing personal style in how she does it. Give her a moment alone to reveal her goodness. In such a moment, Rocky moves a wino out of the street and talks to a puppy. An audience (and the reader is your audience) needs to bond with your character.

Confront your character with an injustice, or place him in a difficult situation or in jeopardy. Be careful not to make him too much of a victim. In *Godfather II*, the Corleones are immigrants in an unfair situation. We sympathize. They take action. We may not agree with their choices, but we admire their fortitude.

In stories where the central character is unsympathetic, the story will succeed if that central character is fascinating, and it helps if there is some other person in the story that we like. The Queen in *The Queen* is fascinating and we like Tony Blair. The Joker in *The Dark Knight* is fascinating and we like Batman (and a few other people). The same is true of Mark Zuckerberg in *The Social Network*; Mark is fascinating and we like his betrayed partner Eduardo.

Give them human dimension

Your characters, and particularly your central character, should have dimension. Avoid cardboard characters and stereotypes. In *Juno*, we see the following transformations from the typical to the unique:

> What we initially think is the evil stepmother is revealed to be a rescuing guide—
> "Would you give my kid the damn spinal tap already?"

What initially appears to be the hip, cool husband becomes an immature dreamer more interested in comic books and horror films than in becoming a father.

What we initially perceive as an uptight, controlling wife is revealed to be a caring, responsible mother.

These are not growth arcs, but each character is a metaphorical onion that is peeled until we get to the truthful center.

Occasionally a stereotype works, particularly in a broad comedy or sometimes in an action script, but your main characters will play better if they have depth. No one is totally evil or perfectly good. The bad guy loves his cat (and may even "save the cat"), while the good guy kicks his dog once in a while.

Speaking of "saving the cat," notice how Ryan, the consummate isolationist in *Up in the Air*, does a favor for his sister. Not only does this act of carrying around a cardboard poster of his niece and fianceé give the audience hope that he can have "feelings" for others, it foreshadows his later doubts about his own philosophy and point of view.

Writers have a tendency to make their favorite characters flat, lifeless, and passive. We're afraid to bloody their face or to give them flaws. Don't fall into that trap. By and large, the most-loved characters in film have depth and dimension. Yours should, too. Even sitcom characters tend to have some dimension to them. They may not be terribly deep, but you'd be hard-pressed to name a favorite TV character that is not flawed. The old TV show *Family Ties* was designed to feature two liberal parents with a conservative son, but because the parents were near perfect (and, thus, flat), the flawed son became more interesting and stole the show.

Heroes and villains

Depending on the nature of your story, your character probably lies somewhere between real life and a cartoon. Some heroes are swashbucklers with hardly a flaw. And some villains are bad all the way through. Often, that works for special-effects movies. (I say that without any intent to denigrate such movies. Each movie should do what it does best.)

Other films go deeper. In such stories, the hero is often an ordinary man or woman who becomes a hero on his or her way to something entirely different. An ordinary person becomes an extraordinary person, or an extraordinary person comes to realize who he really is or finally finds his way.

Likewise, the opposition character does not need to be a classic villain. Who is the villain in *As Good as It Gets*, *Good Will Hunting*, *Up in the Air*, *Juno*, and *Kramer vs.*

Kramer? Yes, there is plenty of opposition and conflict, but no villain among the main characters, just people.

Generally, the best villains or opposition characters believe they are doing the right thing. In other words, they wouldn't characterize themselves as a villain. In fact, often the opposition character has difficulty recognizing another person's view of reality or her needs. I have noted with interest that each opposition character in the Pixar movies has a motivation for his bad behavior.

8. CHARACTERIZATION TOOLS

Specific details are the little things that can mean a lot. They are characterization tools that can define a character's personality and even reveal aspects of inner character. Idiosyncrasies, habits, quirks, imperfections (as discussed), and other characterizations will round out a character. They help make the character a distinct individual. Who would Columbo be without his crumpled overcoat? Who would Melvin Udall (Jack Nicholson) be (in *As Good as It Gets*) without his door-locking procedure or avoidance of stepping on a line in the sidewalk? Even when he's under pressure to get a coat so he can have dinner with Carol (Helen Hunt), he cannot bring himself to step on a line.

Personal expressions can make a difference. The Emperor in *Amadeus* concludes his pronouncements with, "Well, there it is," and Raymond the Rain Man says, "I'm an excellent driver." Jane Craig (Holly Hunter) bursts into tears periodically in *Broadcast News*, and Paul Bleeker in *Juno* says "Wizard" when he is astounded or excited.

In *When Harry Met Sally*, Sally orders her food in a certain way, and she drops letters into the mailbox one at a time. These are tiny characterizations that add to the believability and definition of a character.

If it seems right for your character, give him a specialized knowledge or skill, such as Hiccup's tinkering skills in *How to Train Your Dragon*, David Lightman's computer-hacking skill in *War Games*, Sgt. James's bomb-defusing skills in *The Hurt Locker*, and Luke's knowledge of The Force in Episodes V and VI of *Star Wars*.

In *Three Days of the Condor*, Joseph Turner (Robert Redford) is a full-time reader for the CIA. It's easy to believe in his intelligence and knowledge when he's forced to the streets.

One of my personal favorite characterizations comes in *O Brother, Where Art Thou?* Everett (George Clooney) is obsessed with his hair. He wears a hair net at night, says "My hair" when he wakes up in the morning, and uses Dapper Dan pomade in the daylight hours. Nothing else will do; it has to be Dapper Dan. You can see how original, specific details can make a character memorable.

A prop becomes a character in *The Ladykillers*. A portrait of Irma's husband seems to have a different facial expression each time Irma looks at it. And she takes guidance from it.

When a prop takes on special meaning, it becomes especially effective. That is true for a beautiful detail in the movie *A Beautiful Mind*. Alicia gives John Nash her handkerchief for good luck. We see that prop on two other key occasions in the film, the latter on the occasion when he declares his love to her at the Nobel Prize ceremony.

Props have been used to good effect: Melvin's plastic baggies in *As Good as It Gets*, Captain Queeg's ball bearings, Anton Chigurh's cattle gun (*No Country for Old Men*), Captain Hook's hook, the Joker's makeup and cards, James Bond's gadgets, and the weapons in *Men in Black*.

Some objects and some character traits can be seen as *lifelines* because the character uses them to save himself or rescue others later on. For example, whenever Indiana Jones gets into trouble, he has his whip. (The whip, of course, does not save him. He uses the whip to save himself. That's an important distinction.)

It follows that coincidences should generally work against your central character. Make it increasingly difficult for her to achieve her goal. Don't bail her out at the end. She should be the most active character in the final act.

9. A WRITER WHO CARES

Every character hopes for a writer who cares. Your central character must have a life and a voice of his own. He can only get that from a writer who cares. You show that you care by researching.

The main purpose of research is to come to really know your characters. Once you know who they are, you can observe them emerging on the page as real. One of the most beautiful experiences you can have is when your characters take over your story and tell you what they want to do.

Research is observing people, taking notes in your little writer's notebook or smart phone when things occur to you. Research is searching your mind, your own experience, people you've known who can serve as character prototypes, places you've seen, and so forth.

Research is investigating, exploring, and creating your character's background. For instance, your character has an educational background; ethnic, cultural, and religious roots; a professional (or work) history; past and present social connections; and a family of some kind. Your character also has a particular way of speaking.

What kind of character would Forrest Gump be if little thought were put into his background, psychology, traits, imperfections, idiosyncrasies, and moral character?

Research means Internet searches or trips to a place of business to understand your character's occupation. Research is interviewing someone of a particular ethnic group, or even visiting a neighborhood. Don't assume you can get by because you've seen other movies that have dealt with the same subject matter. Remember, you are writing an original screenplay.

It's easy to get interviews. Some time ago, I interviewed a petroleum geologist. I told him I'd buy him lunch if he'd let me ask him some questions. He was thrilled for several reasons. One, he could tell the guys at work, "Hey, I can't go to lunch with you tomorrow. I got a writer interviewing me for an upcoming movie." Two, he was getting a free lunch. Three, he's proud of the job he does. The benefit to me was that I learned many unexpected things that I could use in my screenplay to lend authenticity and authority to it. For instance, the oil reserves in Southern California rival those in Kuwait. In the 1920s, California supplied much of the world's oil, and there are still over 30,000 active wells.

A struggling student on the East Coast tells me that she didn't really understand her story until she interviewed a blackjack dealer in Las Vegas. Another from the Heartland benefited immensely investigating fencing and other kinds of sword fighting.

A client informed me that most private investigators are employed in family and marital disputes, and by insurance companies. They use clipping services. They sit on the passenger side of the automobile because there's more leg room. He also learned that it's legal to go through someone's garbage.

Research is writing a character biography or completing a detailed character profile. Of course, much of this information will never make it into your script, but since your character will be alive to you, he or she will appear more fully drawn on the page.

Although your character's physical description is very important to you, it will usually be of little importance to the script. All actors want to see themselves in the part, so only include physical details that are essential to the story. When you describe a character in your script, it will be with a few lines or words that really give us the essence of the character. Something the actors can act. We discuss character introductions in Book III.

However, you, the writer, the creator, need to see this person in detail, because a person's physiology affects his psychology. What kinds of emotions does your character have? What is her disposition? How does he handle relationships?

Identify complexes, phobias, pet peeves, fears, secrets, attitudes, beliefs, addictions, prejudices, inhibitions, frustrations, habits, superstitions, and moral stands. Is your character extroverted or introverted? Aggressive or passive? Intuitive or analytical? How does he solve problems? How does she deal with stress? In what way is he screwed up? And so on. Have fun with this!

Research is reflecting, and asking questions.
- What are my character's values?
- What does my character do when she is all alone?
- What's the most traumatic thing that ever happened to my character?
- What is his biggest secret?
- What is her most poignant moment?
- What are his hobbies?
- What special abilities does she have?
- What is his deepest fear?
- What kind of underwear does she wear?
- Which end of the toothpaste tube does he squeeze?
- What kind of car does she drive?
- What is the worst thing that could happen to my character? (Maybe this will be the crisis.)
- What is the best thing that could happen?
- What is my character doing tonight?

Research is creating unique aspects to your character that make her stand apart from all other movie characters. Part of this may consist in giving your character a contradiction or traits that exist in opposition, such as the beautiful woman who's as clumsy as an ox, or brave Indiana Jones's fear of snakes. You may wish to identify one or more lovable imperfections as well.

As this research progresses, certain things will stand out. After all, in the actual script, you will only be able to emphasize certain aspects of your character, so you will want to select those that say the most about your character and best relate to your story. The work you've done will reveal itself in the unique and multifaceted character that you have created from the dust.

When do you do this research? Some writers like to do it early in the process; others prefer later in the writing, so that the characters can be created to fit the demands of the script. Whenever you choose to do it, it's important to be thorough. A thumbnail sketch of the main characters is seldom sufficient. On the other hand, in the writing process, it can be helpful to think of your character in terms of a descriptive label, such as "control freak" or "nitpicker" or "magnanimous."

10. A STRONG SUPPORTING CAST

A screenplay is a symphony and a symphony requires orchestration. Your character is just a lonely solo without other characters. In the well-written story, relationships are emphasized. Some relationships work because of opposite personalities. *The Odd Couple* is an excellent example. Some relationships work because each character can fill the other's need and they transform each other. Others work because the characters are rivals. Still others work because of similar interests or goals.

Create contrasts. Opposites attract in rom-coms; for example, the innocence and faith of the princess contrasts with the cynicism of the divorce attorney in *Enchanted*. Look at the differences in the two brothers in *Slumdog Millionaire*. The differences between characters help define both characters. The same is true of the three suitors in *Mamma Mia!*

Contrasts within a character can be useful. The gentle giant has become something of a cliché. However, Hagrid in the Harry Potter movies has a variety of traits that make him a unique gentle giant; he is much different from Sgt. Schultz in *Hogan's Heroes*. In *Slumdog Millionaire*, Salim is a devoted Muslim and a hit man. Walt (Clint Eastwood) in *Gran Torino* is both a racist and a basically decent man. It's a wonderful contrast.

You can contrast characters on many levels—from attitudes to methods to social statuses. As you create your story's characters, remember that each one must perform a specific function in moving the story forward.

In your cast of characters, you want one central character, at least one opposition character, and a confidant (or sidekick) your central character can talk to. This is one way to reveal your central character's thoughts, feelings, and intentions. The confidant sometimes performs the additional function of lending contrast to your central character. In dramas, the confidant sometimes creates necessary comic relief, although this function (if needed) can be performed by another character. It goes without saying that your confidant should have a life of her own; she's not just there to be a sounding board to your principal character.

Roy O'Bannon (Owen Wilson) is a superb sidekick and comic-relief character in both *Shanghai Noon* and *Shanghai Knights*; he also serves as a clear contrast or foil to Chon Wang (Jackie Chan). In the *Star Wars* movies, R2-D2 performs important duties while also serving as a comic-relief character and a sidekick to C3PO. Are these two robotic versions of Laurel and Hardy?

You may want a love interest, who may function in another role as well, the way Eric Matthews (Benjamin Bratt) is both love interest to Gracie Hart (Sandra Bullock) and leader of the police investigation in *Miss Congeniality*.

Occasionally, you see a thematic character, someone who carries the theme or message of the story, such as Uncle Ben in *Spider-Man 2*. We'll discuss this in more detail in the upcoming chapter on "Theme."

Sometimes a shapeshifter adds a twist to the story. For example, the central character's friend betrays her. In *The Matrix*, Cypher betrays his fellow crewmembers to Agent Smith. In *The Verdict*, one of attorney Frank Galvin's aids works for the opposition. In *Minority Report*, John Anderton's mentor/boss turns out to be the bad guy. You have a similar shapeshifter in *L.A. Confidential* when Captain Smith shoots one of his own police officers. Alex (Vera Farmiga) leaves Ryan (George Clooney) "up in the air" when she instantly changes from an unattached fun-lover to a family woman; it feels like a betrayal.

Make sure your other characters have a goal, desire, intention, or need. Avoid creating characters as furniture, just to be in the scene. In *Gran Torino*, Fr. Janovich is not there just to be the family priest. He promised Walt's wife that he'd get Walt to confession. The goal drives an important subplot.

Note: This is a good time to do Step 4 in the workbook (Book II). You will find plenty of character-building tools there. You will also find Step 7 on revising your script to be helpful.

Theme

Did you know there is something inside you that is motivating you to write? There is something that you want to say. This thing inside you is not a little alien creature; it is the *movie message*, sometimes called the *premise*, sometimes called the *theme*. I realize that Samuel Goldwyn reportedly said, "If you want to send a message, use Western Union." He may have been speaking of the supremacy of story and character; I don't know. What I do know is, an underlying theme tends to deepen the impact of the screenplay.

Regardless of what it is called, think of it as the *moral* or meaning of your story. This moral is not a sermon and it is not preached. Often, you don't know what this special meaning or point-of-the-story is when you start scripting your story. Not to worry—you'll know before you're through. Just keep writing. CAUTION: There is a danger in overfocusing on the theme. You run the risk of writing a preachy script with poorly developed characters.

The resolution of your story will make the point and verify the acceptability of your underlying message. This theme could be expressed as a universal statement that could apply to anyone. It's the subtext of the movie. It's something you've wanted to say. For this reason, it can also be thought of as the *point of view* of your story.

Witness has a point of view: *Love cannot bridge the gap between two different worlds.* In *The African Queen*, the opposite is true: *Love **can** bridge the gap.* As you can see, the movie message isn't necessarily true in real life, just true in your story. And it should never be communicated in a heavy-handed way. It's the subtext of the movie, not the text, although the theme itself may be stated by one of the characters, as is the case in *The Usual Suspects*: "The greatest trick the devil ever pulled was convincing the world he didn't exist."

Speaking of love, *A Beautiful Mind* proves that *love can overcome mental illness*. Or in the words of John Nash, as he addresses his wife at the Nobel Prize ceremony: "It is only in the mysterious equations of love that any logical reasoning can be found. I am only here because of you."

War is addictive is the clearly communicated controlling idea of *The Hurt Locker*. In the end, Sgt. James has just one love.

The message of *Chinatown* is this: *You can get away with murder if you have enough money*. The last act demonstrates just that.

In *Little Miss Sunshine* the point is, Life is one beauty contest after another. You need to forget that and do what you love.

After Chuck Noland (Tom Hanks) is cast away on a deserted island and returns home (in *Cast Away*), he finds that he has lost the love of his life. He tells his friend that at one time on that island he wanted to kill himself. When that failed, he realized that he had to stay alive. And then the tide came in and gave him a sail. Then he explains to his friend that now that he has lost Kelly (his love), he knows what he has to do. He has to stay alive because *who knows what the tide could bring*. And that's the point.

In *My Big Fat Greek Wedding*, the controlling idea is, *My family may be obnoxious, but they're my family and they'll always be there for me*.

Times are a-changin', and you have to change with them if you want to survive. This thematic statement, or movie message, suggests characters who are fighting time (the conflict) and who will not succeed. Can you name the movie? *Butch Cassidy and the Sundance Kid*.

In *The Spitfire Grill*, Percy is an apparent Christ figure who gives her life in the end. The theme is, *Christ redeems and heals*. Notice how most of the characters have biblical names. And the name of the town is Gilead, from the Bible passage that asks, "Is there no balm in Gilead?" The Balm of Gilead is what heals, and that is what Percy becomes—a healing balm.

Seabiscuit's theme also sums up the story: *Everyone thinks we found this broken-down horse and fixed him, but we didn't . . . he fixed us*. Of course, the theme does not have to be directly stated, it can be communicated visually, as is the case with the rebirth theme of *Gravity*.

John Truby suggests that theme is the writer's view of how people should act in the world. For example, in *Ghost* and *Romeo and Juliet*, *Great love defies even death*. And in *Casablanca*, *Self-sacrifice for the right cause gives life meaning*.

Theme is what your movie is about. According to Patrick Sheane Duncan, "A movie is generally about one thing, one theme or idea, and every scene and every character is formed from that fountainhead" (*Screenwriter Quarterly*). In *Mr. Holland's Opus* (written by Duncan), *Life is what happens when you are making other plans*. Each scene, and the conclusion in particular, points to that idea. In Duncan's *Nick of Time*, it is simply, *How do I save my daughter?* That dramatic question is the controlling idea. And *Life goes on* in *My Best Friend's Wedding*.

The Sixth Sense

M. Night Shyamalan called *The Sixth Sense* a "writer's final cut." He explained that he avoided using anything that he had already seen in another movie. That may be why I like it so much. It's a writer's movie about characters that *need* to communicate. Once they learn that, they are at peace.

Malcolm (Bruce Willis) wants to help Cole because Cole reminds him of another child that he was unable to help. So he seeks redemption. He has a second, lesser goal, which is to save his marriage. His unconscious need is to communicate with his wife and accept his separation from her (his death).

Cole wants the ghosts to go away. His driving desire is to stop being scared. His need is to communicate with his mother. But he won't, because he is afraid she'll think he's a freak. That's his worst fear. So he has nowhere to go emotionally until Malcolm comes to him.

Things get scarier and scarier until Malcolm has a breakthrough and tells Cole that maybe the ghosts want something. Essentially, he tells Cole to try to communicate with them.

Along comes a very scary Kyra. Cole finds the courage to say, "Do you want to tell me something?" In other words, he opens the lines of communication. Once he does, everything goes well for him. The final two sequences serve well the theme of *Communication overcomes fear*.

In the first of these sequences, Cole finally tells his mother his secret, risking the relationship. Will she think he's a freak? It's an emotional, cleansing scene that is very touching. It is successful not just because it is a great scene, but because of what preceded it in terms of character development and story.

In the final sequence, Malcolm communicates with his sleeping wife. It is then that he realizes he is dead, but now he is able to accept it. The characters are healed and at peace.

Thematic material and thematic characters

A few stories may lack a theme. Some others deal with *thematic material*. For example, *Witness* explores themes of violence and nonviolence (represented by Eli). *Broadcast News* discusses substance versus style. *Babe* presents issues of self-worth, class structure, and personal identity. *Unforgiven* compares false reputation (Bob and the kid) with true reputation (Will and Bill). *The Adjustment Bureau* contrasts control with free will.

In a few stories, it may be effective to create a thematic or symbolic character, someone whose purpose is to carry a theme, a value, or even the story message. This character is seldom the central character, but can be, as in *The Hurt Locker*.

The mathematician (Jeff Goldblum) in *Jurassic Park* and Libby Holden (Kathy Bates) in *Primary Colors* are both thematic characters. They also serve as moral consciences. The same is true of Uncle Ben (Cliff Robertson) in *Spider-Man 2*, who says, "With great power comes great responsibility."

Dialogue, subtext, and exposition

WHAT DIALOGUE IS

Dialogue is not real-life speech; it only sounds like it. It is more focused, less rambling than real-life speech. Yes, it contains fragments and short bits, but anything extraneous is pulled out, including the *ahs* and *uhs*. You might say that dialogue is *edited* speech. It is organized and has direction, but it retains the style of real-life speech. It doesn't have to be realistic, just believable.

Dialogue should be lean. Avoid long speeches. Try to keep to one or two lines. Naturally, there can be many exceptions. However, remember that in a movie, people have to understand what's being said the first time through. In a novel a passage can be reread, but a movie keeps "reeling" along. Avoid monologues. Dialogue should "sound" conversational. Allow characters to interrupt each other on occasion. Let them lie to each other. Let them misunderstand each other. Avoid having your character say the other person's name he is talking to. Dialogue is often characters in competition; there is some level of conflict in the exchange. Think of the motivation behind the speeches.

Don't think too hard when writing dialogue. In fact, don't think at all. Write from the heart. You can always return to it later, read it out loud to hear how it sounds, and make adjustments. Take a look at your words and ask yourself: Is there a better, more original, and/or leaner way to say this? Am I writing more but the audience is enjoying it less? I'm not saying you can't write long speeches; I'm only saying they must be justifiable.

Be patient in writing dialogue. Sometimes it takes a while for your dialogue to break through. With many professional writers, dialogue is often the last thing that "comes through," so don't panic if your dialogue isn't working at first. The key here is to know your characters well enough that they speak with a voice of their own. That voice consists of eight elements:

1. The text, or words
2. The subtext, or the meaning of the words
3. Grammar and syntax
4. Vocabulary
5. Accent and/or regional or foreign influences
6. Slang
7. Professional jargon
8. Speaking style, including rhythm and sentence length

THE 7 DEADLY DIALOGUE SINS

After decades as a teacher and script consultant, these are the dialogue errors I see over and over again:

1. Obvious exposition

```
                MAUREEN
     We've been married ten years now, honey.


                GILBERT
     Yes, I recall. We were married under the
     great oak in the backyard, the one that
     your mother cut down a year later.
```

When your characters seem to be speaking more to the audience than to each other, you are being obvious. When two characters tell each other things they both already know, that's almost always "obvious exposition." Allow exposition to emerge naturally in the context of the story; don't force anything.

2. Overwriting

This is simply using more words to say something than is necessary for that character. In such situations, the cure is often to make the exchange more back and forth between the characters—that is, more conversational—rather than one character "making a speech" followed by the other. On occasion, let one character interrupt the other, talk over the other, or complete the other's speech. Avoid question-and-answer sessions except in courtroom scenes, police interrogations, and similar situations.

Sometimes, screenwriters try to cover too many ideas in one speech. As a general guideline, limit one idea per speech. I've read speeches where a character has asked four questions before concluding the speech. That might be a sign that the speech is too long and will not "sound" conversational.

Another example of overwriting is when one line is followed by the subtext. For example, "The sound of her voice takes the sword out of my hand. I love her." "I love her" is the subtext or underlying meaning of the first line. Thus, omit the second line ("I love you").

3. Exaggeration

I recently read a script where every single character used the F-bomb in most of their speeches. It gave me the impression that the screenwriter lacked imagination and/or did not understand his characters enough to know how they talked and/or was exaggerating the emotions of the characters to compensate for weak motivation or story context.

Oh, and by the way, just one exclamation point is plenty; and you may not need the one. In *The Shawshank Redemption*, the warden approaches Andy, who is in solitary confinement. He tells Andy that the man who could prove his innocence is dead. Andy tells the warden to have H&R Block do his taxes; he's done with the warden's scams. Then, in the screenplay, the warden yells at Andy, but in the movie, the warden's speech is whispered with intensity. The movie version is much more effective.

Most writers have a tendency to exaggerate character emotions. I remember recently explaining to a writer that five of her characters sobbed at various times in the script. That's overwriting. Sometimes, trying to control emotion has more impact than actually expressing emotion.

4. Everyday pleasantries

Sue: "Hi!"

Bill: "How are you?"

Sue: "Fine."

Bill: "How's the dog these days?"

Sue: "Getting along great."

That's boring. Avoid chitchat and introductions, unless they are original and interesting. On rare occasions, there can be a dramatic purpose for such talk. Recall the scene in *Fatal Attraction* when Dan Gallagher (Michael Douglas) walks into his home and sees his wife talking to Alex (Glenn Close), his lover. At this point, his wife does not know about his affair with Alex. Then, his wife makes formal introductions. Dan says, "I don't believe we've met." Alex responds, "Oh, we've definitely met." This is one of the rare instances where chitchat is dramatic and suspenseful.

5. Unnecessary repetition

Repeating a particular phrase or line can be effective, as with "Here's looking at you, Kid" in *Casablanca*. One instance sets up the next.

The kind of repetition that seldom works dramatically is repeating information the audience already heard a couple of scenes ago. It creates a sense of stasis, and the story feels like it is dragging.

6. No room for subtext

This is obvious writing, but in a different sense than with #1 above. Here we have characters saying precisely what they are thinking or feeling. In other words, the subtext is stated rather than implied.

Generally, you're best off having characters beat around the bush, imply their meaning, speak metaphorically, say one thing by saying something else, or use double entendre.

No, you don't need room for subtext in every single speech. We'll discuss subtext again a little later in this chapter.

7. Derivative dialogue and other unoriginal speeches

Avoid clichés and lines we've heard in other movies. An occasional allusion to another movie or literary work can be effective, but I've already heard "We're not in Kansas anymore" at least a hundred times (or so it seems). "May I buy you a drink" only tells the audience that the character is unoriginal, and it may work as such. However, I suggest you find a better line that derives not from another movie but from your character's unique personality.

When a character's speeches could be delivered by any character in the screenplay, you may have a problem. I am referring to typical, ordinary, expected lines that virtually anyone could have said and that have little originality.

In most fight and swordplay scenes, the opponents shout typical epithets. In *The Princess Bride*, they compliment each other's technique. How refreshing!

Incidentally, when your characters speak far too often in complete sentences, they are likely saying your words rather than their words. Giving your characters their own voices will strengthen your voice as a writer.

WRITING BETTER DIALOGUE

Here's a technique that will improve your dialogue: Read it out loud, record it, and then listen back to it, or have members of your writers group or a few actors read it to you. With the spoken word, it's easier to detect errors. You will better hear what works and what doesn't. Is the dialogue too *on the nose*, too direct? Does it have an implied meaning or subtext?

Also be aware of the rhythm. Some characters are terse and staccato; some are lyrical and elegant. Each character has a style of speech. If a character speaks with a dialect or accent, just give us a flavor of it.

If you're having difficulty, consider this approach. Tag each of your characters with a label, such as "sports nut," "sex maniac," "nervous," "control freak," "bully," and so on. Then, with each speech of that character, try to capture that trait.

Avoid voiceover narration. Narration works when it adds another layer of meaning or humor or drama, or when it contradicts what appears on the screen, or when it foreshadows in a clever or interesting way. Such is the narration with *The Shawshank Redemption* and *Sunset Boulevard*. Sometimes, an end-of-story summation (or a combination setup and end-of-story voiceover) can be effective.

Narration doesn't work when it says the obvious, presents boring exposition, or reveals the thoughts of the character. In the last instance, voicing over the thoughts of a character may work only in a broad comedy.

Likewise, avoid breaking the fourth wall. Don't allow a character to speak directly to the camera unless you have a doggone good reason.

Dialogue should also move the story forward, just as scenes do, and reveal something about the character's attitudes, perceptions, traits, and values. When there's sufficient intention behind a speech, the speech is an action. Every dialogue scene should involve some conflict, even if it is just passive resistance. Back and forth, like a contest or competition.

The diner scene from *Five Easy Pieces* illustrates the essence of dramatic writing. Robert Dupea (Jack Nicholson) stops at a diner. He wants toast, he orders toast, but the waitress won't give him toast because it's not on the menu and she doesn't "make the rules." He tries several approaches. She fends him off every time, each time the tension building, the conflict escalating. Finally he orders a chicken salad sandwich, toasted. And he tells her to hold the butter, lettuce, and mayonnaise, and to hold the chicken between her knees. She kicks him out, so he clears everything off the table and onto the floor. The exchange of verbal blows creates the rising tension of this classic scene. The theme underneath the dialogue has to do with "the rules." This scene, in effect, is a mini-movie.

GREAT DIALOGUE IS LIKE RICE KRISPIES

Movie dialogue should snap, crackle, and pop.

Snap is the crispness of the dialogue. In *The Fugitive,* when Lt. Gerard corners Dr. Richard Kimble at the top of a cliff, Kimble says, "I am innocent." Gerard doesn't come back with a long explanation; he just says, "I don't care." It's one of the strong moments in that film.

An exchange between Warden Charley Butts (Larry Hankin) and Frank Morris (Clint Eastwood) in *Escape from Alcatraz* is instructive.

```
                    WARDEN
          What kind of childhood did you have?


                    CHARLEY
          Short.
```

Crackle is the freshness of the dialogue. Which speech is better? "Young lady, you're definitely pregnant," or "No doubt about it, Mama Bear, your eggo is prego." The latter is from *Juno*, and it's the one you picked. Favor original expressions over cliché or standard expressions.

Years ago, I was playing monster with my four-year-old daughter. I chased her upstairs, telling her how hungry I was for little princesses. I caught her, wrestled with her, and growled, "I'm hungry." She looked straight at me and said, "Daddy, you shouldn't play with your food." That not only leaves room for subtext, but it is original—and that's why it's funny.

Penny (Holly Hunter) in *O Brother, Where Art Thou?* doesn't say, "My mind is made up," when she closes an issue. Rather, she says, "I've counted to three." Find original ways of saying things.

Pop is the subtext.

Mama was right—it's not what you say, but how you say. The **subtext** (how you say it) has more impact than the text (what you say). Of all the elements of dialogue, subtext is the one that gives writers the most fits, and yet it is a key principle.

What is subtext? Subtext is what's under the text. It's what's between the lines, the emotional content of the words, what's really meant. Dialogue is like an iceberg. The text is the visible part. The subtext is below. The text implies the subtext lying below. Audiences seldom want to see the whole block of ice. Likewise, your characters should seldom say exactly what they feel. When an actor wants to know her motivation in a scene, she wants to understand the emotions going on within the character. She wants to know the subtext.

In *Double Indemnity*, Neff (Fred MacMurray) tells Phyllis (Barbara Stanwyck) he's not sure if he likes her name: "I'd have to drive it around the block a couple of times," he says. She picks up on the metaphor.

```
              PHYLLIS
        There's a speed limit in this state.
        Fifty-five miles per hour.


              NEFF
        How fast was I going, Officer?


              PHYLLIS
        I'd say about ninety.
```

They're not really talking about traffic laws, are they? The subtext is steaming off the words and the exchange heats up from there. Of course, she's pretending to be offended; she's actually setting the hook. When the text is a lie, the truth (the subtext) will/should be understood by the audience.

Usually, the dialogue's context in the story suggests the subtext. For example, in the "fireworks" scene of *To Catch a Thief*, Frances Stevens (Grace Kelly) seduces John Robie (Cary Grant), a reformed jewel thief. That's the context. Does she talk about sex? Does she say, "Come on, John, let's go for a roll in the hay"? Of course not. This moment requires a little more finesse. She talks about her jewelry, and wouldn't he do anything to steal such beautiful works of art? "Hold them," she says, "the one thing you can't resist." Clearly, she's not talking about jewelry here. The subtext is, *I'm the jewelry; you're the thief—take me*. She says one thing by saying something else. The subtext is always obvious to the audience.

In a previous section, we discussed goals and needs—your character not only has an outside goal but some inner need. The goal is the *text* of the story and the need may be thought of as the *subtext* of the story, or emotional through-line, often leading to the them. It follows, therefore, that the subtext of the dialogue in a scene will often derive from the character's underlying need or desire in the scene. Here's an example:

Late in *Spider-Man 2*, Spider-Man tries to convince Otto Ottavias to give up his dream. Here's the text: "Sometimes we have to give up the thing we want the most—even our dreams." The context of the scene makes the subtext clear: *To be Spider-Man, I am going to have to give up the thing I want the most, my dream of being with Mary Jane.*

Subtext has to do with the true intention of the character. *The Princess Bride* is, in part, the story of a grandfather who wants to get his young grandson to appreciate a "kissing book"—a book in which the boy and the girl actually kiss in the end—yuck! The grandson is sick in bed and is forced to listen to his grandfather read him this book. The grandfather begins reading. I will summarize:

"Once upon a time, there was a girl named Buttercup and a farm boy. And Buttercup used to torture the boy by asking him to do things for her, and every time the girl asked the boy to do something for her, he would say, 'As you wish.' One day, Buttercup realized that whenever the farm boy said 'As you wish,' what he really meant was, *I love you*."

I can't think of a better explanation of the relationship between the spoken word and the subtext than this grandfather's explanation.

At the end of this movie, the grandson has learned to enjoy this "kissing book"—and as the grandfather leaves, the boy asks him if he could . . . well, maybe . . . come by tomorrow and read it again. And the grandfather says, "As you wish." Wouldn't you agree that this indirect statement, loaded with subtext, is much more powerful than the more direct *I love you*? And it's a lot more fun as well.

Here's a dramatic situation: A cop confronts a robber, who holds his gun to an innocent woman's head. Which line works better? "If you shoot her, I'll be real glad, because I'm gonna enjoy killing you." Or: "Go ahead, make my day." In this case, less is more. Thank you, Dirty Harry.

Not long ago, my wife asked me if I was feeling tired in my "old age." I responded with my best Indiana Jones impression: "It's not the years, Honey, it's the mileage."

Another angle at subtext is having a character project her situation on another character, so that in talking about that other character, she's really talking about herself.

How do you show that someone's parents don't understand their teenage daughter? One client handled this with the following simple exchange.

```
                    GIRL FRIEND
          Did your parents like your poem?


                    SUZANNE
          They don't understand poetry. They think
          it's dumb.
```

When writing dialogue, keep in mind the character's attitudes, point of view, feelings, thoughts, and underlying need or drive. Try to say one thing by saying something else. Anytime an emotional current runs under or through a conversation, the dialogue will be deeper and more interesting if there is room for subtext.

This does not mean that every line of dialogue must leave room for subtext. Most speeches don't require subtext. However, most beginning scripts have too little subtext. Likewise, not every speech needs to be short or completely original.

EXCITING EXPOSITION

Another purpose of dialogue is to communicate the necessary facts and background information of the story. These facts are called *exposition*. Your job is to make the exposition exciting.

Much of the exposition comes out in the beginning of the story. For example, the audience needs to understand how Indiana Jones's mission will benefit the world. Don't give the audience any more information than is necessary to understand the story. Be careful not to reveal too much too soon. Let your characters keep their secrets as long as they can. Often, saving up exposition and using it in crucial moments will make it more exciting, and even transform it into a turning point. At the same time, don't hold back so much exposition that the audience is confused rather than intrigued.

Speaking of intrigued, that describes me when I saw Nietzsche's image on a sheet pinned to the wall of Dwayne's bedroom in *Little Miss Sunshine*. About seven or eight pages later in the script, I learned with Uncle Frank the following.

```
                    FRANK
          You can talk. You just choose not to?


Dwayne nods. Then he points to the bed-sheet painting of
Nietzsche hanging on the wall. Frank turns and looks.


                    FRANK
          You don't speak because of Frederich
          Nietzsche?
```

Later, we finally learn that Dwayne has taken of vow of silence until he can become a test pilot at the Air Force Academy. In this case, exposition is revealed piecemeal to create a little mystery with clues along the way.

Some exposition can be creatively planted in love scenes, action scenes, or comedy scenes, because at those moments you already have the audience's attention. I love the sword fight scene in *The Princess Bride* for that very reason. You learn a lot about both characters in the dialogue that accompanies the thrusts and parries of their swords.

Be careful not to get *too* exciting. In the second *Indiana Jones* movie, the main exposition is presented through dialogue at a bizarre dinner. The food is so disgusting that the audience's attention is diverted from the characters' dialogue.

In the first *Indiana Jones* movie, the exposition is handled more effectively. The opening sequence is so exciting that we are riveted to the screen for the succeeding sequence, where most of the necessary information about the lost Ark of the Covenant is communicated through dialogue.

Another way to make exposition exciting is to have characters argue over it. Some exposition can be handled without dialogue. In the opening scene of *Unbreakable*, David Dunn (Bruce Willis) sits on the train looking rather morose. A pretty woman sits next to him and he removes his wedding ring. That's exposition. It tells us he's unhappily married.

Often in sci-fi and other screenplays involving a world the audience may not be familiar with, I see a lot of exposition via dialogue. Consider the opening sequence in *The Hurt Locker*. We learn a lot about the world of an Explosive Ordinance Disposal (EOD) team with very little dialogue.

Note: There are many sample scenes containing dialogue in Book IV.

How to make a scene

Screenplays are composed of acts, acts break down into sequences, sequences into scenes, and scenes into beats. A scene is a dramatic unit consisting of the camera placement (INTERIOR or EXTERIOR), a location, and time. When one of these three elements changes, the scene changes as well. In this discussion, I am using the term *scene* loosely. The points that follow could apply to any dramatic unit consisting of one or more scenes.

Each scene should move the story forward in terms of both plot and character
In other words, the scene you are now writing should be motivated by a previous scene, and it should motivate a scene coming up. One creates anticipation for another in a cause-and-effect relationship.

If the central character gets more involved in some way, that means your scene is probably moving the story forward. All scenes should direct us to the Showdown at the end, which is the biggest scene, or sequence of scenes, in the movie.

Ask yourself: What is the payoff for this scene? Why do I need this scene? What is my purpose for this scene? Does the scene reveal something new about a character and/or the story? At the end of this scene, does the audience want to know what happens next?

Do not tell what you can show
Be as visual as possible. Rather than two ladies at tea commenting on the fact that Darla skydives for relaxation, *show* us Darla actually jumping from a plane, or (for a low-budget production) show her coming home with a parachute and trying to stuff it into the closet.

There are only a couple of lines of dialogue in *All is Lost*. The entire movie is made of visual images, but perhaps that is an extreme example.

Do you recall the barn-raising scene in *Witness*? When the workers pause for lunch, the eyes of the elders are on Rachel Lapp (Kelly McGillis), who is expected to marry an Amish man but who likes John Book (Harrison Ford). Without a word of dialogue, she makes her choice by pouring water for John Book first.

One sequence in *Seabiscuit* presents a key episode in the life of Charles Howard, the central character. We first see his young son reading *Flash Gordon*. Charles tells him to go fishing. That's about the only dialogue in the entire scene.

The sequence continues with his son seeing his father's car. He gets his fishing equipment. He starts the car, and notices the birds and trees. He drives erratically; he's too young to be driving. We see another car approaching going the opposite direction. We sense there could be a collision.

Back at the house, the phone rings. Charles picks up the phone. We cut to the car; there's been an accident. Charles drives. Charles runs. Charles holds his dead son MOS (without any sound).

We cut to the graveside, then back to the house, where Charles plays with his son's Flash Gordon puzzle. He cries. He locks the garage.

In *My Best Friend's Wedding*, Julianne (nicknamed Jules) and Michael (her best friend) have a moment together. The setting is visual: A boat on the Chicago River (not a couch in an apartment). They both want to tell each other how they feel about each other, but they fight it (which makes the audience empathize with their feelings more strongly than if both characters just blurted out what they were thinking).

Jules wants to tell Michael that she loves him. As they both approach the moment where they might say what they feel, they approach a bridge. The dialogue continues as follows:

```
                    MICHAEL
         Kimmy says, when you love someone, you
         say it. You say it out loud. Right now.
         Or the moment...
```

He pauses. Jules wants to say it. They are under the bridge, silent for a long moment, and then past the bridge. She's misty-eyed.

```
                    JULIANNE
            ... passes you by.
```

That visual cue of passing under the bridge tells us that the moment has passed for her to say that she loves him. The visual cue brings the message home and makes for a stronger moment.

Avoid talking heads

John and Mary argue over breakfast. One head talks, then the other. Make this more interesting by beginning the argument at breakfast, continuing it while in the car racing to the club, and concluding it during a tennis match. Each statement a character makes is punctuated by the whack of the racket. Now the action complements the dialogue, plus you give yourself the opportunity to characterize your characters by how they play tennis, how they drive, what they drive, etc.

Recently, a screenwriter asked me in a challenging voice, "Well, Mr. Screenwriter's Bible, how do you explain the eight-page talking-heads scene that opens *The Social Network*?" I smiled sweetly and responded: "It was written by Aaron Sorkin." In other words, he could pull it off. Add to that the fact that it superbly sets up the remainder of the story, that it clearly characterizes Zuckerberg, and it makes the audience want to know more. It also proves that my suggestions are guidelines and not rules.

Every dramatic unit has a beginning, a middle, and an end

Ask yourself, "What does my character want in this scene at this moment? Each dramatic unit should have its own central character who has some goal, desire, need, or intention. In effect, a scene is a mini-movie with its own central character. The same is true for a sequence of scenes with the same focus.

Look for twists and reversals

If most scenes are mini-movies, look for opportunities for a twist, turning point, or reversal. William Goldman is a genius at setting up an expectation and then subverting it in a surprising and entertaining way. In *The Princess Bride,* Inigo is about to lose the sword fight when he announces that he is not left-handed, and he switches his sword to his right hand; later in the same scene, the Man in Black does the same thing.

Later in the same movie, The Man in Black outsmarts Vizzini in a "battle of the wits," but he doesn't do it the way we think he does. As we understand it, there is iocane powder in one of the goblets. They both drink and Vizzini dies. The princess asks the Man in Black how he knew which goblet the poison was in. Then comes the shocking twist that ends the mini-movie. The poison was in both goblets; the Man in Black had gradually developed an immunity over the last several years.

In *Marathon Man*, Janeway (William Devane) "rescues" Babe (Dustin Hoffman) from former Nazi dentist Szell (Lawrence Olivier), who has been torturing Babe while asking him a single enigmatic question: "Is it safe?" Falsely believing that Janeway is a good guy, Babe talks openly with him while the two ride around in a car—until Janeway brings him right back to Szell's hideout. Reversal: Babe is back in Szell's hands, where he overhears Janeway tell the dentist that he doesn't think Babe knows anything about Szell and his plans. That gives Babe hope. Reversal: Szell doesn't care, and he resumes torturing Babe.

Start the scene as close to the end of the scene as possible

In other words, once your scene is fleshed out, evaluate it and lop off anything at the beginning that is unnecessary. (In fact, cut the fat anywhere you can.)

Imagine a cowboy riding up to a log house in the middle of the prairie. There's no one for miles around. He quietly dismounts, grabs his rifle, and gingerly approaches the cabin. He peeks through the window. There she is: young, beautiful, and alone. Inside the cabin, the woman turns. The door is kicked in. The cowboy steps inside and points his rifle right at the woman. He wants the money and he wants her. She reaches behind for a knife and throws it at the cowboy.

Does the above description remind you of the opening scene of *Romancing the Stone*? It is, except that the final version of the scene begins at the moment the door is kicked in. Everything preceding that moment was cut. The writer wisely started the scene as close to the end of the scene as possible.

In terms of scene length, challenge any scene that runs more than two pages. Many great scenes are long, and some scenes should be long. Nevertheless, if you challenge your long scenes, you may find ways to improve them and shorten them. This will strengthen the pace of the story. You may even find scenes that should be a little longer, and that's okay, too.

In *The Hurt Locker*, there is a long scene of a group of soldiers pinned down by snipers. Then we the cut to the EOD team horsing around in the barracks, getting drunk. A lesser writer would have opened that scene with the men entering the barracks and talking about what happened or what they are going to do, and then they would start horsing around. We simply don't need that introduction. I also like the fact that they are engaged in action rather than just getting drunk (a cliché) and talking.

Pace your scenes

Provide peaks and valleys of emotion and tension, with the peaks ascending toward a climatic conclusion. Follow action scenes with dialogue scenes. Contrast heavy scenes with light scenes. In *Home Alone*, we have the reflective scene in the church just before the madcap slapstick sequence at the house. Make sure the pace quickens as you close in on the Crisis and Showdown. What happens next should be more interesting that what just happened.

Pacing does not need to focus on action and events, such as in *Lethal Weapon*; it can focus on details and emotional beats as in *Steel Magnolias*. *Lethal Weapon* is plot-driven and must move fast, while *Steel Magnolias* is character-driven and more leisurely paced; you can stop and describe the roses.

Scenes should culminate in something dramatic

This could be a decision or an imminent decision. It could be a reversal, a cliffhanger, a punch line, or a revelation—something that makes us want to see what's going to happen next. Scenes should end with a punch, with some kind of tension that leads us to another scene. For example, in *Titanic*, Rose's mother orders her to never see Jack again. Throughout the scene, Rose's mother tightens Rose's corset, visually adding tension to the scene. It's a visual subtext. The pressure is tightening around Rose in more ways than one.

In *Good Will Hunting*, Will (Matt Damon) confronts a college kid who is hitting on a coed (Minnie Driver). After the long scene, Will flashes the coed's phone number at the college kid, showing he has won. It punctuates the scene. It brings the scene to a conclusion, but it also creates anticipation that more is to come. And what comes next should be more interesting than what just happened. The story must build.

In dialogue scenes, generally the last line should be the strongest line. In the very last scene of *Some Like It Hot*, Jerry (Jack Lemmon), posing as Daphne, must convince Osgood Fielding III (Joe E. Brown) that she (Daphne) can't marry Osgood. The wonderful conflict is created by Osgood's subtle resistance to Jerry's attempts to achieve his goal of getting out of the wedding.

First, he tells Osgood that he can't get married in his mother's dress because they aren't built the same way. "We can have it altered." Then Jerry (still posing as Daphne) confesses that he is not a natural blonde. "Doesn't matter." Then Jerry admits that he smokes all the time. "I don't care." Jerry tries another angle: He tells Osgood he's been living with a saxophone player. "I forgive you." With feigned remorse Jerry announces that he can never have children. "We'll adopt some." Finally, Jerry removes his wig, speaks in his male voice, and admits that he is a man. The response? "Well, nobody's perfect." And that's the *punch* line that ends the movie.

Strive to create effective transitions between scenes

I'm not referring to tricky cuts and arty dissolves—leave editing directions to the editor. Find ways to fit certain scenes together. For example, one scene ends with a roulette wheel spinning. The next scene begins with a car wheel digging into the mud.

Early in *2001: A Space Odyssey*, a prehistoric man throws his tool into the air. It's a bone that becomes a spaceship, a tool of modern man.

Here's an effective transition from Bruce Joel Rubin's *Jacob's Ladder*. In it, Rubin uses sound and images to move us from Vietnam to New York.

```
As he spins around, one of his attackers jams all eight
inches of his bayonet blade into Jacob's stomach. Jacob
screams. It is a loud and piercing wail.

From the sound of the scream, there is a sudden rush through
a long, dark tunnel. There is a sense of enormous speed
accelerating toward a brilliant light.

The rush suggests a passage between life and death, but the
light ahead reveals this is actually a subway far below the
city of New York.
```

This would be followed by INT. NEW YORK SUBWAY, and the scene would continue.

This kind of transition is the exception rather than the rule. It is important in this screenplay because of the theme. This is the story of how a man comes to accept his own death, very much like Rubin's prior screenplay, *Ghost*.

You are not required to link your scenes with transitions. You do this occasionally, when appropriate. The important thing is how the content of the scene leads naturally to something later. Transitions can be visual, verbal, thematic, and so on.

Is it okay to sharply contrast scenes? Absolutely. If your idea moves the story forward, use it. Keep in mind that a straight cut from one scene to the next is not only correct, but the norm. The object is not to get fancy but to give the story cohesion.

Each scene should contain a definite emotion or mood
Focus on that emotion as you craft the scene. Ask yourself: What is my character's intention or goal in this scene? What is my character's feeling? What is my character's attitude? Asking this will help give the scene direction and the dialogue subtext.

Focus the scene on a well-motivated conflict
Even in less dramatic scenes, a conflict should exist, regardless of how minor or how subtle it is. Often, two people with the same goal will disagree over methods or procedure, or just get under each other's skin: Bones and Spock, James Bond and Q, Butch

Cassidy and Sundance, Mr. and Mrs. Incredible, and Mr. and Mrs. Smith (in *Mr. and Mrs. Smith*). Even in love scenes, there may be some resistance at the beginning. Conflict is one of the tools you can use to build suspense.

Flashbacks

About 95% of the flashbacks in unsold scripts don't work. That's just a guess, of course. Usually, the flashback is used as a crutch, a cheap way to introduce exposition. This has given rise to the industry bias against them in spec scripts. Seldom do they move the story forward. And that's the key: Use a flashback only if it moves the story forward. And, yes, it's definitely okay to use as many flashbacks as you want . . . if they work. Look at all the flashbacks and flashforwards in *Slumdog Millionaire*; they all work dramatically.

You'll see dozens of flashbacks in *The Fugitive*, and each pushes the story forward or makes you want to know what's going to happen next. Don't reveal exposition in a flashback unless it also motivates the story, as in *Julia*, *Memento*, and *Casablanca*. Generally, do not take us to the past until we care about what's happening in the present. Otherwise, a flashback becomes an interruption.

Generally, avoid long flashbacks and dream sequences. They are high-risk. If you must have a flashback, use a transitional device: an object, place, visual image, color, phrase, or incident. Quick flashes are the safest, such as the momentary glimpses of the Backstory we see in *Ordinary People* and *The Blind Side*.

One approach to flashbacks is to find a more creative way to communicate exposition. To illustrate, put yourself in the place of the writer of *Star Trek II: The Wrath of Khan*. You have a story problem: Khan, the opposition character, is Kirk's superior physically and mentally. How can you make it believable that Kirk can defeat Khan?

One solution is to *flash back* to the days when Kirk was a cadet. He takes a field test called the Kobiashi Maru, which presents a no-win scenario. Kirk, however, beats the no-win scenario by reprogramming the test computer so that he can win. (This is the same field test referred to in the 2009 release of *Star Trek*.)

You, however, reject this idea of a flashback for one that is more creative. You decide to open the story with a starfleet captain on a ship that is in trouble. Soon we learn that this captain is really a cadet and that she is taking a field test called the Kobiashi Maru. She is bothered by her performance. Kirk tells her not to worry, that there is no correct solution—it's a test of character. So she asks Kirk how *he* handled it. He won't tell her.

You have successfully made it a mystery that is touched on throughout the story—how *did* Kirk handle the Kobiashi Maru? The audience wonders. You, the next great screenwriter, have created suspense.

CUT TO: Late in the story. It appears as though Kirk and his friends are trapped in an underground cavern with no way out, and with no apparent way to contact Spock, who is somewhere out in the universe. At that moment, the female cadet once again asks Kirk how he handled the Kobiashi Maru. Bones tells her that Kirk reprogrammed the computer. "You cheated," someone says.

Then Kirk surprises everyone by pulling out his communicator and contacting Spock: "You can beam us up now," he says. Ah-ha, so Kirk had it all prearranged (reprogrammed), but to do it, he and Spock broke Federation rules. He has cheated Khan and has surprised everyone else. That's when Kirk explains: "I don't believe in the no-win scenario. I don't like to lose." Not only have you explained how Kirk could defeat a superior being, you have also given us the *key* to Kirk's character. And this particular solution plays better than a flashback.

For examples of scenes, see Book IV.

Suspense, comedy, and television

Building suspense is the art of creating an expectation of something dramatic that is about to happen. Since we go to movies to feel vicarious emotion, putting us in suspense simply builds emotion as we anticipate the outcome. Here are 10 tools to thrill and manipulate us.

TOOLS FOR BUILDING SUSPENSE

Evoke emotion
Create characters we like. They must be believable, since they act as a conduit through which emotion can pass to us. We need to sympathize with them and feel what they feel.

Create conflict

As mentioned earlier, rising conflict creates suspense. Since conflict is drama, two committed forces in conflict will always heighten suspense. Remember grade school? Two boys would start fighting and everyone would make a circle around them. No one tried to stop the fight. (This is very irritating if you're the smaller boy.) No one stopped it because we were all in suspense, wondering if blood would squirt out someone's nose, and betting on who would win.

Provide opposition

Give your central character a *powerful opposition*; then force your character to battle this foe. The opposition should be in a position of strength, capable of doing damage. In *Star Trek II*, Khan serves as an excellent example, because he is superior to Kirk physically and mentally. We all go through the extreme mental duress of wondering how Kirk is going to survive, let alone defeat, this "giant."

The "giant" in *Fatal Attraction* is Alex (Glenn Close), the lover. She is in a position to do damage to Dan (Michael Douglas). The "giant" in *Gravity* is the space debris and the situation it creates.

The formidable foe in *My Best Friend's Wedding* is Kim, the fiancée. She has the emotional leverage on Michael, Julianne's best friend. Besides, she's adorable. How can Julianne compete with that?

In *The Sixth Sense*, the dead people seem infinitely more powerful than little Cole. Since we know so little about the aliens in *Signs*, they seem formidable. And Otto Ottavius is made more powerful when Spider-Man appears to be losing his powers. It creates an expectation of trouble, our next point.

Build expectation

Create an *expectation of trouble*. Do you recall the baby carriage in *The Untouchables*? In this scene, Elliot Ness must face off with Capone's boys at the train station. He's ready and in position, but a woman is having difficulty moving her baby carriage up the stairs. We get nervous—we just "know" she is going to get in the way. The suspense builds, just as it did in the baby carriage scene of *The Battleship Potempkin*.

Consider also the scene from *Fatal Attraction* where Dan Gallagher (Michael Douglas) returns home and finds his wife conversing with his lover. There is an expectation that the wife might realize that this blonde she is talking to is having an affair with her husband. In this case the jeopardy is emotional, not physical. When the wife introduces the lover to Dan, the subtext is powerful because they have already met. The lover says such lines as, "Don't I remember you?" "We've definitely met." "I never forget a face." The scene's subtext is, *You're not getting away from me. I'm going to make you pay.*

At the Showdown of *Ghostbusters*, our heroes confront the goddess Gozer. Gozer tells them that the Destructor will come in whatever form they choose with their thoughts. Dr. Stantz (Dan Aykroyd) has obviously thought of something, and the other characters try to figure it out because they, and the audience, know the Destructor is coming, but they don't know what form it has taken. Comedic suspense builds as Stantz points to his head and says, "It just popped in there." What just popped in there? We catch glimpses of something huge and white moving past the buildings, but we still don't know what it is. Stantz babbles, "It can't be, it can't be." The anticipation peaks and finally Stantz admits, "It's the Stay-Puft Marshmallow Man." And then we see the huge figure lumbering down the avenue.

Increase tension

Put the audience in a *superior position*. Take, for example, a couple we care about. While they are out to dinner, someone sneaks into their apartment and places a bomb under their bed. Later, our happy couple returns and they hop into bed. The danger is there, and we're "in on it." We, the audience, are in a *superior position* in the sense that we know the bomb is there, but they don't.

Imagine a small child playing in the yard. The mother steps inside the house. The child wanders toward the busy street. We are in a superior position to the child and to the mother. We are the only ones who are aware of the danger, and that builds suspense.

In *The Green Mile*, a tremendous amount of tension is created when Percy purposely doesn't wet the sponge prior to the execution of an inmate in the electric chair. We know the sponge is dry, but no one else in the movie realizes it until it is too late.

Use surprise

Throw in an occasional nasty twist, or sudden turn of events. The first surprising appearance of a dead person in *The Sixth Sense* creates a great deal of suspense. The sudden collapse of the house in *Lemony Snicket's A Series of Unfortunate Events* puts us on edge.

In *Psycho* (the classic 1960 version), Norman Bates kills the protagonist, Marion Crane, in the now-famous shower scene. This nasty twist serves the purpose of creating an expectation of *more* violence. Indeed, Hitchcock once remarked, "At this point I transferred the horror from the screen to the minds of the audience." Interestingly enough, there is only one more violent act in the entire movie, and yet we are held in suspense throughout.

Create immediacy

When *something vital is at stake* for the character, that *something* becomes vital to us, the audience, as well. It can be the physical safety of the world or the moral redemption of a juvenile delinquent. It can be the emotional fulfillment of two lovers who find each other, the protection of a secret document, or the triumph of a value. In *Spider-Man 2*, it is the safety of both Mary Jane and New York. The higher the stakes, the more intense the suspense.

Establish consequences

Closely related to the above is the establishment of terrible consequences if the central character does not achieve her goal. When the *Challenger* space shuttle exploded, there was a lot of grief and sadness. A couple of years later, we sent up another shuttle. Do you recall the suspense you felt as the countdown proceeded on this later shuttle mission? That heightened suspense was due to the prior establishment of terrible consequences.

In *Inception* it's the possibility of entering and being trapped in limbo. In the last major scene of *The Hurt Locker*, Sgt. William James has just a couple of minutes to disarm a bomb locked as a steel vest around an innocent man. We know what the consequences will be if James fails. This is also an example of how a deadline of some kind can create suspense.

Limit time

Put a ticking clock on it. "You have only 24 hours to save the world, James. Good luck." Deadlines create suspense because they introduce an additional opposition—time. You can probably think of a dozen movies where a bomb is about to explode, and the hero must defuse it before the countdown reaches zero. What I love about *The Hurt Locker* scene described above is we never see the bomb tick down to zero, but we know it is ticking. It's handled realistically rather than stereotypically.

The torpedo-firing sequences in *The Hunt for Red October* were particularly thrilling because of the element of time adding pressure. The same is true with the limited oxygen supply in *Gravity*. Will she have enough? When will she run out?

Likewise, when the Wicked Witch in *The Wizard of Oz* captures Dorothy, she turns over the hourglass. "This is how long you have to live, my little pretty." Although we are never told how Dorothy is going to die, we still worry. Apparently, Hitchcock was right when he said that "the threat of violence is stronger than violence."

You can easily create an artificial deadline. The damsel is tied to the railroad tracks. Can Dudley Do-Right save the damsel before the train runs over her? Here you have an implied deadline. Other effective examples of the ticking clock include *High Noon*, the rose petals in Disney's *Beauty and the Beast*, and the prediction that John Anderton (Tom Cruise) will murder someone in 36 hours in *Minority Report*.

Maintain doubt

Finally, if there is a reasonable doubt as to how the scene or movie is going to end, the suspense is intensified. How is Cole going to get away from his "dead people" problem in *The Sixth Sense*, especially if Dr. Malcolm stops trying to help him (as he decides to do in one scene)?

In the opening scene of *The Untouchables*, one of Capone's boys leaves a briefcase full of explosives in a store. A little girl picks it up and it explodes. At this point, we realize that anyone in this movie can die, and we fret over Elliot Ness's little girl and wife for the entire movie. Why? Because this scene has left us in genuine doubt about their safety. The same is true with the opening sequence and later scenes in *The Hurt Locker*—anyone can die at any moment.

LEAVE 'EM LAUGHING

Have you ever watched a comedy, laughed for about 20 minutes, and then grown restless? The probable reason for this is that the comedy had a weak story structure and poorly drawn characters. The comedy may have relied more on gags than on character and story. Virtually all of the humor in *Shrek* flows from the characters and the situation, which is one reason the story is so effective.

Comedy is drama in disguise

There is no comedy without conflict. This means that virtually everything in this book applies to comedy as well as to drama. Start with a goal and think of all the ways to screw it up. I'm often asked about comedy story structure and story structure in general. I enjoy referencing the Pixar movies as excellent examples of both. You won't go wrong studying those films.

Comedy benefits from a skewed viewpoint

Comedy generally takes an unusual point of view through use of exaggeration, deception, overstatement, understatement, contrast, parody, a ridiculous point of view, escalation, competition, or obsession. The goal in a comedy can be ridiculous or insignificant—that's what makes it funny. The character may get excessive about it. This is especially true in a broad comedy like *What's Up, Doc!*, where most all of the characters go to extremes to achieve their goals.

There is much we can learn from *The Odd Couple*, which features a slob and a neat freak, each with traits slightly exaggerated. We can understand why both were divorced, and the contrasts assure us of conflict. Woody and Buzz Lightyear are both heroes in *Toy Story*, but they are very different in personality.

Clever character combinations create conflict in comedy

As you look at the three principals in *Ghostbusters*, note the contrasts and opportunities for comedic conflict:

Stanz (Aykroyd) — spontaneous "child" — overstates — is very emotional

Venkman (Murray) — "animal" (focused on physical needs) — understates — is cool

Spangler (Ramis) — "machine" or rational "adult" — does not emote at all

The TV show *Golden Girls* is set up similarly, with Rose (Betty White) as the "child," Blanche (Rue McClanahan) as the "animal," and Dorothy (Bea Arthur) as the "adult."

In *Bridesmaids*, you have a loser (Annie), a cynic (Rita), an idealist (Becca), a Queen Bee (Helen), and a wild card "animal" (Megan). One of the funniest scenes in *Bridesmaids* is the competition and escalation that takes place in the "toast scene." Helen and Annie just have to outdo each other at all costs.

In one of my favorite episodes of *Monk*, Monk competes with another character as to who has a worse life. It's completely within character for Monk to look at this negative side.

Comedy thrives on readily identifiable, personal situations and fears

Love situations and other personal situations are easy for us to identify with and are ripe for comedy. That's one reason the family situation comedy has done so well. As psychologist Abraham Maslow stated, "That which is most personal is most general." Comedy reveals our secret desires and yearnings so that we can laugh at them.

Comedy is often more truthful than drama. Comedy makes good use of surprise and reversals, in revealing the truth about people, personal situations, and life.

Comedy provides psychological shifts, twists, and deception

For example, two male musicians disguise themselves as women in *Some Like It Hot!* In *Ruthless People*, two perfectly nice kidnappers expect to get a ransom from a husband for his kidnapped wife. He won't pay; they can go ahead and kill his wife. So what do they do now?

While You Were Sleeping is a light comedy without a lot of interpersonal conflict. So what makes it work so well? It is built on one single deception: Lucy (Sandra Bullock) goes along with the assumption that she's the fiancée of the man in a coma. There is a strong inner conflict that makes this movie work as burden after burden is laid on her, all stemming from the initial deception. For example, if she told the truth, it would hurt the family. Besides, it would wreck Christmas. I count eight burdens in all that serve as the rising inner conflict in this movie, until the Showdown, when the truth is finally told.

In *Bridesmaids*, you expect Megan to be wrong when she asserts the guy next to her is an Air Marshall. Actually, she is right. And in *Toy Story*, you don't expect a toy to talk directly to a human, but that's what Woody does in the end.

Comedy utilizes the Rule of Threes

Things seem to feel right when they come in threes. It's true in art as well as comedy dialogue. The first line is the setup line, the second establishes a pattern, and the third breaks the pattern with a twist. "I'll have four chili dogs, three jalapeno tortillas, and an Alka-Seltzer." The third line is the punch line.

In *The Shawshank Redemption*, which is no comedy, the Rule of Threes is brilliantly applied to three scenes that bring a laugh with the third (punch line) scene. Red (Morgan Freeman) appears before the parole board three times. On the first two occasions, he makes an excellent case for granting parole. In both of those instances, his paperwork is stamped "Rejected." The third time he's indifferent and talks honestly about the stupid kid he once was. His speech ends with this zinger: "Rehabilitated? That's just a bullshit word, so you just go on ahead and stamp that form there, Sonny, and stop wasting my time. Truth is, I don't give a shit." The paperwork is stamped "Approved."

Comedy presents façades and pretenses, and tears them down

One scene from *Play It Again, Sam* features Allan Felix (Woody Allen) preparing for a blind date (a situation most of us can relate to—right?). He goes to extremes to impress her. He thinks he can score the first night, and that's his pretense. He impresses her, all right, but not the way he had hoped. It's a reversal of what he expected. He's brought back to earth. His "walk of shame" is hilarious.

Another example of two characters with a pretense appears in *Celebrity Wedding*, a screenplay by Yours Truly and Greg Alt. Sam and Natalie pretend not to like each other (that's the pretense). They have just seated themselves on a plane, thinking they have escaped from the bad guy, Novaks.

Immediately, Sam spots Novaks, who hasn't yet spotted them. Somehow, Sam must find a way to hide Natalie's face so that Novaks doesn't recognize her. They have to act quickly. Watch how the pretenses are removed and the truth of their feelings for each other are revealed.

(As you will read in Book III, the dash is normally used for interruptions of speech and the ellipsis for continuation of speech. An ellipsis at the end of a sentence normally means the character did not continue her thought. When an ellipsis ends a sentence, add a period.)

106

INT. PLANE - DAY

Sam and Natalie throw themselves into two back seats.
Sam leans into the aisle and spots Novaks headed their
direction, searching the passengers.

                    SAM
          He's coming.

Sam turns to Natalie. Gets eye contact. She gasps just as he
kisses her long and hard, hiding her face from Novaks.

Novaks glances at them in disgust, then turns back.

Sam releases Natalie, who is momentarily paralyzed.

                    SAM
          Ah sorry. I -- ah, couldn't think of
          anything else.

                    NATALIE
          Right -- I mean, I mean under the
          circumstances it was good. I don't mean
          good good, I mean, well....

                    SAM
          We really didn't have any other --

                    NATALIE
          -- Exactly. And if we had...

                    SAM
           ... We certainly would've -- or
          wouldn't've....

                    NATALIE
          Absolutely.

```
                    SAM
              (overlapping)
         Naturally.


A brief, unbearable silence. Face to face. Instantly, they
both reach for the same in-flight magazine.


                 SAM AND NATALIE
              (simultaneously)
          Go ahead.


Disgusted with himself, Sam rips the magazine from the seat
pocket and buries himself in it.


Natalie pulls out the emergency flight card and fans herself.
```

In this scene, the kiss comes as a surprise. The situation is readily identifiable in the sense that we've all embarrassed ourselves at one time or another in the presence of someone we were interested in. The scene ends with a visual subtext that implies Natalie is "hot."

TELEVISION

As you can imagine, television situation comedy writing is less visual than screenwriting, with less action. There may be only one or two locations. And so the emphasis is on interpersonal conflict and dialogue. The best situation for a sitcom is one that forces the characters to be together. They live together, work together, or belong together.

Sitcoms thrive with a *gang of four*, four main characters where each can easily be at cross-purposes with any of the others, creating more possibilities for conflict. In other words, they can play off each other.

Structurally, the sitcom opens with a teaser that says, "Boy, this is going to be really funny. Don't change the channel during the next two minutes of commercials!" Act 1 introduces the secondary storyline and the primary storyline in succession. (Sometimes one of these is introduced in the teaser.) Act 1 ends on a turning point that is either the most hilarious moment in the episode or is very serious. The second act resolves the primary story, then the secondary story. This is followed by a tag at the end that usually comments on the resolution. Some sitcoms present three stories or plotlines.

The hour-long TV drama or comedy also opens with a teaser or prologue. Act 1 establishes what's going on, Acts 2 and 3 develop it, Act 4 pays it off. (Note: Many shows have more than four acts.) Most shows add an epilogue. If the show is relationship-driven, an arena or setting is created in which the story can play. For example, the arena for *House* is a teaching hospital.

The best way to break into television of any kind is with a feature script or pilot script that you can use as a sample. It shows that you can create characters from scratch and write a story around them. Being the next great screenwriter, it's a challenge you can meet.

It goes without saying that the principles of screenwriting that we have covered up until now apply to writing teleplays as well.

Note 1: For more on television writing, see "How to format TV scripts" in Book III and "Television markets" in Book V.

Note 2: This is a good time to do "Step 5—'Step-out' your story" in the workbook, Book II. Next, read the formatting and style guide (Book III and Book IV). Then do "Step 6" and "Step 7" in the workbook. Finally, use the marketing plan in Book V to sell your screenplay.

7 STEPS TO A STUNNING SCRIPT

BOOK II

A Workbook

About this workbook

This workbook takes you through the seven steps of the writing process. I've tried to make it simple and easy to follow.

Each step is marked with checkpoints to keep you on track. In all, there are 26 checkpoints and more than 150 key questions to help you evaluate your progress. Not every question needs to be answered. Not every checkpoint needs to be reviewed in the order it's presented. These are not hard-and-fast rules, but fluid guidelines to help you craft a stunning script. In fact, many writers like to begin the process by developing their characters; if you are one of those, you may want to do Step 4 before Steps 2 and 3. Some writers allow the steps to overlap. Adapt the process to your needs.

This workbook becomes a more effective tool if you've studied the primer (Book I) first and have the nascent concept for your script.

Take a moment now to congratulate yourself. You are embarking on a great journey. I hope you enjoy the adventure of creating movie people and plotting the events of their lives. May success be yours.

Step 1—Summon your muse

At the start of the workshop, two writing students were arguing. Sheila insisted that writing was purely a creative endeavor, while Sam argued that screenwriting was an analytical process. Back and forth they went. Finally, Robert, my teacher's pet, chimed in. "Stop! You're both right. Screenwriting is both an art and a science. The professional writer uses the head as well as the heart." Both wondered how Robert could possibly be right. But he was, and here is why.

The writing process begins with the creative urge, a desire to express something. Like a tiny seedling, an idea emerges from your heart and pushes its way through the soil of your conscious mind. Often, several ideas will sprout. Like any birthing process, this can happen at any time and any place. And with the emergence of your idea comes that wonderful creative feeling.

How do you nurture that young seedling of an idea? What makes it grow? Thought and hard work make it grow. You think about the possibilities. Then, you blueprint the core story, which consists of a beginning, a middle, and an end. All this head work will act like a shot of adrenaline to your heart. More ideas will flow, and the story will emerge and evolve until it matures.

Every writer has two natures: the heart and the head. The heart is the passionate creator, the emotional artist, the child, the intuitive subconscious. The head is the detached critic or editor, the parent, the logical and analytical scientist or surgeon. And quite conscious of the "rules."

Good writing utilizes both natures, but often operates like an alternating current between the two. When you're in the creative, artistic mode, you shut off the head. You encourage the creative flow. You don't correct the spelling or improve the grammar. You just play in your sandbox. There are no rules or restrictions. It is imperative that

114

you remain in a relaxed state of mind; you cannot write when you're uptight. Relax and have fun!

How do you get into that relaxed state of mind? You try by not trying. It's a lot like falling asleep. How do you fall asleep? You place yourself in a position where you can fall asleep, and then you don't try. Trying to go to sleep is the definition of insomnia. So it is with drafting from the heart. Stop thinking and relax. Enjoy those childlike feelings and intuition. Once that creative energy is expended, your parental side takes over and cleans up the mess. After all, admit it; some of what you've written is nonsense.

Back and forth you go. You write from the heart. You edit from the head. Back and forth until the head and heart agree (or you've become a schizophrenic).

The good Lord gave our brain two hemispheres. Both are important. Sheila is "right-brained" and focuses on the intuitive, artistic side of creativity. Sam is "left-brained" and focuses on the analytical, scientific side of creativity. Each should use his or her greater talent without abandoning his or her lesser talent.

I sometimes worry about writers who search for formulas, who want to make writing purely a science so that they can write by the numbers. They may want inflexible rules so they can be in control of the process. This is to be expected. Our educational system inculcates this into our minds. The secret to great writing is to be part of the *process*. You can't control it. In truth, the story knows from the beginning where it's going. There is no sweeter moment than when your characters take over and tell you what they want to do and say.

I also worry about the purists who may insist that anything written from the heart is perfect just the way it comes. That which comes easily is not necessarily good. They may be loath to edit their work for fear of breaking some divine law or harming their baby. If it were true that everything pouring from the heart is perfect, no one would ever revise anything. There would be no second drafts, no rewriting. Just because it felt good when you wrote it doesn't mean that it is ready for market.

Writing is an evolutionary process that must be trusted. You must believe that there is a story within you. You must believe that it will find its way out. And you must believe in your talent to nurture it into a stunning script. If you believe, and act on your belief, your muse will come to you.

Now, let's discuss the above process in a different way.

THE WRITING PROCESS

Becoming part of the writing process is like "getting religion." For some writers it is almost a mystical experience. Let me provide a suggested framework for this process.

First you start off with a creative jolt, an idea that's about a 7.0 on the Richter scale. Then you do a lot of hard thinking—hammering out a good dramatic premise—beginning, middle, and end. You write the logline in terms of character, action, opposition, and resolution. What's the concept?

Then, on wings of song, your muse comes down from Mt. Parnassus and whispers sweet things. You write all these gems down.

You visualize the one-sheet, the poster that will adorn the movie theater walls in just a couple of years or so. You ask: Do I have a story? Do I have an original concept that will pull people in? If everything feels right up till now, you begin your research.

You develop your characters using both sides of your brain. Remember, even though your characters are within you before you ever begin, once they emerge, they must take on a life of their own.

With some level of understanding of your story and characters, you now construct the all-important story outline. This outline, sometimes called a step outline, is usually made up of paragraphs, one paragraph for each scene, anywhere from 30 to 100 steps in all. (This figure can vary, depending on genre.) Many writers use 3"×5" cards, a card for each scene, and pin these cards to the wall; or they use a software application for the same purpose.

Some writers need only a bare-bones outline while others prefer a detailed outline. Whatever your method, chart the sequence of your story, alternating between your creative/intuitive nature and your evaluative/practical nature. Whenever you think you're getting off base, you write a short synopsis—about three pages—to get back on track.

By now, your creative pump is primed. As instructed by Sean Connery in *Finding Forrester,* write your first draft from the heart. Some of these scenes are already written from previous bursts of creative joy. Intuitively, creatively, the draft takes shape. Write the second draft from the head, analytically.

Even as you approach the end of the process, the story is fluid, evolving into what it eventually wants to be. Don't force the process by being too rigid about scenes you have fallen madly in love with. Don't feel confined by your original outline. Remain open to your Muse.

This is just one of many ways to approach the writing process. With experience, you will find the way that works best for you. Some writers prefer to just write and allow things to manifest themselves in the writing. The most important thing is to trust the process, relax, and believe in yourself. The story is inside you; you must let it out one way or another.

So what are you waiting for? Come on. Let's create a masterpiece!

Step 2—Dream up your movie idea

What if you don't have any ideas? Here are a few tips that will help you get those creative juices flowing.

1. Put your mind in a relaxed state through meditation or deep breathing. Visualize a natural setting where you feel safe, or drift off to the setting of your script. The right brain, the Inner Creator, always works best when the left brain, the Inner Critic, has been tranquilized.

2. Rely on the Inspiration Cycle: Input, Incubation, Inspiration, Evaluation. After a few days of jamming your brain, relax and tell yourself that you need a breakthrough; then incubate. In other words, wait. It may take a few days. Soon enough, while falling asleep or taking a shower—Eureka!—the inspiration comes. You're flying. It may continue to flow for some time. But don't stop when it does. Evaluate it (the Inner Critic has been waiting for this moment) as a means of bringing on the next cycle of inspiration.

3. Stimulate the senses. Engage in a physical activity such as gardening, chopping wood, sewing, shoveling snow, fishing, dancing, aerobics, kneading clay, washing the dishes, tinkering with the car, and so on. "Mindless" physical activity not only relaxes you, but it stimulates the senses, and sensory details will stimulate your writing. It also keeps the left brain occupied, freeing your childlike right brain.

4. Stir your creative desire by inventing writing rituals. Acquire a baseball cap and imprint or embroider the word "writer" on it. Whenever it's time to write, you can tell your loved ones, "I'm wearing my writer's cap tonight." I know a writer who begins every session with an herb tea ceremony, instructing her "analytical brain to sleep so that the creative brain can come forth with a masterpiece." Speaking of ceremonies, why not conduct opening and closing ceremonies for the Writer's Olympics, starring you? Writing should be fun, so have a good time.

When I need to drop into the creative mode, I sometimes play stimulating music, usually soundtracks and classical music, because they stir my emotions and imagination. You may find it helpful to look at a painting, photo, or object that suggests theme, character, or location to you, something that pulls you into your story. I know a writer who closes her eyes and types as she visualizes.

5. Reflect on and dip into your past. The research has already been done on your life and your world. It's all inside you. You can draw from this well, especially when you need to feel the emotion your characters are feeling. But beware: There are pitfalls in autobiographical writing.

I'm often asked: Is it true I should write what I know? Can I base my script on something that happened to me years ago? How true to life should my characters be? Can I use myself and people I know? The general answer is you need just enough distance from these characters and incidents that they can take on a life of their own.

Writing that is too autobiographical is usually flat, with the central character often becoming an observer of life instead of an active participant. Once I read a script about a wife who was abused by her husband. The wife did nothing but complain for 90 pages. On page 100 a neighbor rescued her. The only reason I read this all the way through was because I was paid to evaluate it. I thought to myself, "This is often how real people behave, but movie people are more willful and active."

The writer had painted herself into a creative corner. She was too close to the truth. She needed to use the energy of her personal experience and create a drama with it. Even with "true" stories, writers will combine characters and condense time for dramatic purposes.

A possible problem with autobiographical writing (and all writing, of course, is partly autobiographical) is that we usually love our central character. So we protect her. Solution? Use yourself and people you know as a basis for the fictional characters you create. Be as autobiographical as you want—you need that energy—but create enough distance to be objective. It's a razor's edge that every writer must discover.

6. Carry around a recorder or notebook, or use a smart phone app. (There's scarcely been a writing instructor or adviser who hasn't recommended this helpful tip.) When you carry around a notebook or recording device, you are asking your subconscious to

find ideas for you. Armed with one of these tools, you'll be more observant and open to wandering ideas looking for a home. Write down, or record, these ideas and bits as they occur to you.

7. See movies in your genre. In fact, see eight good films and two dogs. Read a screenwriting book. Read screenplays—yes!—*read* screenplays, even though virtually all of them are shooting scripts replete with camera directions and lots of CAPS. Page through old movie books or books of foreign films. Attend a seminar or workshop. Remember, don't stop learning in order to write, and don't stop writing in order to learn. Subscribe to my newsletter at www.keepwriting.com.

8. Read and steal. Shakespeare did. Are you greater than he? Look to the classics for plot and character ideas. Creativity is not creating something out of nothing; it's a new twist on an old idea. It's making new combinations of old patterns. It's converting the Big Dipper into the Little Ladle. Creativity is disrupting the regular thought patterns to create a new way of connecting. Gutenberg took the wine press and the coin punch and created the first printing press.

Read fairy tales, folklore, mythology, and history. Many classic plots can be easily adapted. *Romeo and Juliet* became *West Side Story* and *Titanic*. *Faust* became *Damn Yankees*, *Rosemary's Baby*, *Wall Street*, and *Blue Chips*. Homer's *Odyssey* became *Falling Down* and *O Brother, Where Art Thou? The Tempest* has been transformed into several movies. *Pygmalion* became *My Fair Lady*, which became *She's All That*. *Moby Dick* became *The Life Aquatic with Steve Zissou*.

How many *Frankenstein* plots can you identify (including a subplot of *Spider-Man 2*)? How about "*King Midas*," "*Jack the Giant Killer*," and "*Cinderella*"/*Pretty Woman* plots? Maybe it's time for your character to take the Hero's Journey (see "Myth" in Book I). Try variations and twists of plots. How about a modern update of *Lord of the Flies* or some other classic? Just make sure that any work you adapt is in the public domain. (Refer to the index for more on adaptations.)

9. Visit parks, airports, parties, courtrooms, crisis centers, or other places where people are likely to congregate or be in some kind of transition. This will help you look for character and story details. You may even find someone to be a character in your script.

10. Read the news. "Giant White Caught Off New England Coast" was the headline that inspired *Jaws*. "80-Year-Old Widow Weds 17-Year-Old Boy" inspired *Harold and Maude*. TV and radio talk shows can give you ideas for topics that are current. A bulletin board at work inspired *The Usual Suspects*.

If you are aware of a true story that would work for a TV or cable movie (and if it's not a big story that has already attracted producer-types), then buy an option to the story's rights and write the script. (See Book V for more on true stories.)

11. Understand dramatic structure. This needs to be emphasized. Sometimes you're stuck because you've violated some principle of dramatic structure. Use this in connection with #7 above. I've heard many writers credit a book or seminar for helping them work through a writing problem.

12. Be open to radical change. Be flexible. I once changed the gender of my central character to energize a tired story. Maybe you should open your story on your current page 30 instead of page 1. Ask questions. Ask the "what if" question. What if an earth child was accidentally left behind on another planet? What if my central character's mother is a jackal? Be open to any ideas, and any criticism. Everything goes. Nothing's written in stone until the shoot wraps.

13. Write what you care about, what you have passion for. What type of movie do you like to watch? That may be the type of movie you ought to write. Discover and follow what fascinates you.

14. Use the energy from pet peeves and gripes. Writing what you feel strongly about will help you keep going when the going gets tough. And keep in mind that the process of writing one script will generate ideas for other scripts and will grease the works for future creative success.

15. Try clustering. It's a technique that naturally summons your creativity and eliminates anxiety. Get a clean sheet of paper and write your story problem, concept, or character about halfway down the page. Draw a circle around it.

Now brainstorm, using free association. Whatever comes to mind, write it down, circle it, and connect it to its parent (or simply make a list). Go with any ideas that float by, regardless of how bizarre or strange. Keep your hand moving. If you have a moment when no idea comes, doodle in the corner until it does. Within about five minutes, you'll have a feeling of what you're supposed to do. An insight will come, the solution will be revealed, or a new idea will leap into your mind. If nothing happens, just stay relaxed. This is something that can't be forced.

16. Interview. Interviewing experts in specific fields can result in ideas. One client emerged from an interview with his grandfather (an expert on life) with three story ideas. Another client was blocked about certain characters—who they were and how they talked. He solved the problem by interviewing each of his characters (in his imagination) and asking them the questions listed under "Checkpoint 11" in this book. Out came history, attitudes, goals, and so on. Review the section on research ("9. A Writer Who Cares" in Book I).

17. Confront your blocks. List all your barriers to writing and communicate with them; that is, turn your barrier into an object or person and write a dialogue. In this free-writing exercise, an insight will come to you. Yes, you can overcome the barrier.

Keep in mind that the master key to overcoming writer's block is to realize that it's no big deal, just an occupational hazard. The real problem is when you panic. Blocks are just part of the writing process. In fact, a block is a blessing in disguise because now that your "head" is stymied, your subconscious is free to break through. So relax. Have fun. Trust the process.

18. If you have been hired to develop a screenplay for a production company or have received "notes" on your own script, don't be afraid of constraints. They will actually help you be more creative. For example, Joseph Stefano and Alfred Hitchcock had so many constraints when writing and directing *Psycho*, they were "forced" to be creative in the now classic shower scene. There is no nudity, no knife appearing to penetrate a body, and no gore in that scene; it's all implied.

I was hired once by a producer to write a low-budget script; she gave me a list of about 20 parameters. I could light one guy on fire; I could include a crash of two late model cars; I could only have one outdoor set; I could only have five characters; and so on. At first I was chagrined, but I reframed the situation. It was a lot of fun figuring out how to work within my constraints. In such situations, I suggest you set your emotional resistance aside and embrace this paradox of creativity.

Once you have a hat full of story ideas, you can search for the nuggets, the genuine movie concepts, the premises that have commercial potential. Consider reviewing the chapter, "The lowdown on high concept" in Book I.

What follows is the first of many checkpoints in this book; all are intended as guidelines or indicators you can use to evaluate your script.

CHECKPOINT 1

- How solid is your story idea, premise, or concept? Is it naturally intriguing, or just average, requiring perfect execution in the script?
- Will it appeal to a mass audience? Or is it just right for a niche market?
- Is it fresh? Original? Provocative? Commercial?
- Does hearing it make people say, "I want to see that!"?

- Is it large enough in scope to appear on the silver screen?
- Does it have "legs"—stand on its own as a story without big stars?

CHECKPOINT 2

- Do you have a working title that inspires you?
- Will this title titillate the audience? Is it a "grabber"?
- Does it convey something of your story concept or theme?
- Does it conjure up an image or an emotion?
- Is it short enough to appear on a marquee (not always necessary)?

CHECKPOINT 3

Imagine how your movie will be advertised. Then, on a sheet of paper, sketch out the one-sheet (movie poster) for your movie. What is the tagline or logline?

- Is there a striking visual image that will stop passersby?
- Is there a headline that plays off the title or conveys a high concept?
- Will people (in a general market or niche market) want to see this movie?

Step 3—Develop your core story

What is your story about? You need to know this and you need to know it now. There are producers who believe that if you can't tell them your story in a sentence or two, there isn't a story. They may be right.

A story presents a character who wants something and who is opposed by at least one other character. This opposition causes conflict and a series of critical events, all leading to the Crisis and Showdown at the end. What follows is a quick review of the critical events (plot points) in virtually all dramas and comedies. (See Book I for a complete explanation of each.) As you know, not all movies follow this exact pattern, and yours may not as well. The point is to create a brief sketch of the main events of your story. Although outlining is the fifth step in the process, it could certainly be done at this point if you prefer.

BACKSTORY

This is an event that happens before the movie begins. It's usually traumatic enough that it haunts the character throughout the story, often giving rise to a character flaw (as in *Casablanca*). In some cases, it's an overall situation from the past (as with Hiccup in *How to Train Your Dragon*, who has always been an embarrassment to his father, the village chief). In some movies, there is no Backstory (as in *Psycho*). Sometimes the backstory is shown as the first scene in the movie and is generally followed by a jump in time to the "present day" story (as in *Vertigo* and *The Sixth Sense*). On rare occasions, it involves the historical past (as in *Argo*).

CATALYST

Your story starts out in balance, but the Catalyst upsets that balance (usually around page 10), giving the central character a desire, problem, need, goal, mission, or something to do. The story now has direction and movement. In *How to Train Your Dragon*, the Catalyst is when Hiccup makes a dragon-killing weapon because he is told he must capture a dragon.

BIG EVENT

This is an event that changes your central character's life in a big way, thus the Big Event. It comes in around pages 20 to 30. This is when Hiccup shoots down a Night Fury and is unable to kill him in *How to Train Your Dragon*.

MIDPOINT (OR PINCH)

About halfway through the script, there is another major plot twist. It is often a point of no return for the central character, or the moment when the character becomes fully committed, or when the motivation is strengthened or becomes clear. In *How to Train Your Dragon*, It's when Astrid discovers that Hiccup his trained Toothless, the Night Fury he earlier shot down. This is a point of no return for Hiccup.

CRISIS

This is an event that forces a crucial decision. Often it is simply the low point in the story, the moment when all looks lost (as in *Avatar*), or when the lovers are separated (as in *Pretty Woman*). It's when Benjamin Franklin Gates is abandoned underground by Ian in *National Treasure*. In *How to Train Your Dragon*, Hiccup is stuck in the village while Vikings take Toothless to the dragon lair.

SHOWDOWN (OR CLIMAX)

This is when the central character and opposition character square off. It's the final battle or fight in each of the *Star Wars* movies, and the final struggle between the Incredible family and Syndrome in *The Incredibles*. In *How to Train Your Dragon*, Hiccup and Toothless defeat the monster dragon.

REALIZATION

Just after the Showdown, or during it, or occasionally before it, the audience realizes that your central character has grown, changed, or figured something out. In *Little Miss Sunshine,* it's at the end of the dance, when the family admires how important the family is; and of course, with *How to Train Your Dragon*, Hiccup understands that he is useful and that he has changed his village's view of dragons.

Let's look at a few other examples.

DAVE

Backstory:	Not great at finding jobs for people; divorced.
Catalyst:	Dave is asked to pretend he's President.
Big Event:	The real President becomes comatose; Dave "becomes" President.
Midpoint:	Dave acts as President and defies the Chief of Staff.
Crisis:	The Chief of Staff implicates Dave in a scandal.
Showdown:	Dave defeats the Chief of Staff at a joint session of Congress.
Realization:	I can help people find jobs—Dave runs for office.

TWINS

Backstory:	Vincent abandoned by his mother.
Catalyst:	Vincent meets his brother Julius.
Big Event:	Vincent is saved by his brother, so he takes him in.
Midpoint:	Vincent meets the scientist, believes Julius really is his brother.

Crisis:	Vincent must choose between his brother and $5 million.
Showdown:	Together, Vincent and Julius trick the bad guy.
Realization:	I'm not genetic garbage—Vincent finds his mother.

THE KING'S SPEECH

Backstory:	Bertie is teased by his brother and denied food by his nanny.
Catalyst:	Bertie's disastrous speech at Wembley.
Big Event:	Bertie meets Lionel, the speech therapist.
Midpoint:	The King dies; Bertie opens up to Lionel.
Crisis:	Bertie learns that Lionel has no credentials.
Showdown:	Bertie's first wartime speech as king.
Realization:	I have a voice and will be a good king; Lionel is a good friend.

NOTE: Screenwriter David Seidler outlined backwards: "I knew my final piece was going to be the speech…. So I knew what I was headed for. It was just working out how to get there." Reportedly, Francis Ford Coppola wrote from the final scene backwards.

THE HAND THAT ROCKS THE CRADLE

	Peyton (Central Character)	Claire (Heroine)
Backstory and Catalyst:	Hub's suicide; no family.	Molested by doctor.
Big Event:	Gets Claire to hire her.	Hires Peyton.
Midpoint:	Gets Solomon kicked out.	Fires Solomon.
Crisis:	Kicked out of the house.	Asthma attack.
Showdown:	Battle with Claire.	Battle with Peyton.
Realization:	None.	I trust my instincts (trusts Solomon w/child).

CHECKPOINT 4

Write the logline or concept statement for your story.
- Who is your central character?
- What is his/her main goal? (This is the goal that drives the story.)
- Why is the goal so important to him/her?
- Who is trying to stop your character from achieving the goal?

CHECKPOINT 5

Identify the parameters of your story.
- What is the genre (action, adventure, thriller, romantic comedy, etc.)?
- What is the time and setting?
- What is the emotional atmosphere, and the mood?
- What, if any, story or character limits exist?

CHECKPOINT 6

- What is the Catalyst that gives your central character a direction?
- What Big Event really impacts your character's life?
- Is there a strong, rising conflict throughout Act 2?
- Does the conflict build? Or just become repetitive?
- Is there a pinch, a twist in the middle, that divides Act 2 in half and more fully motivates your character?
- What terrible Crisis will your character face?
- Will the Crisis force a life/death decision, and/or make the audience fret about how things will turn out in the end?
- How does your story end? What is the Showdown?
- In the end, does your character learn something new?
    Or is his/her growth (positive or negative) made apparent?
    Or does he/she receive any recognition in the end?

CHECKPOINT 7

Now write out your core story in three paragraphs, one for the beginning, one for the middle, and one for the end. Paragraph 1 will end with the Big Event, paragraph 2 with the Crisis. Obviously, you cannot include all of the characters in this brief synopsis. Once this is done, reevaluate your story.

Step 4—Create your movie people

Your central character wants something specific. That something is the goal. The character, who is conscious of this desire, strives for it throughout most of the story. Of course, the character is opposed by at least one other person.

In most stories, the character also has an inner need, something she may not be consciously aware of until the Crisis. This need is a yearning for the one thing that will bring true happiness or fulfillment to the character. The need is blocked by a flaw, usually a form of selfishness or hubris. The flaw emerges from a past traumatic event—the Backstory.

The main plot of most movies is driven by the goal. It's the Outside/Action Story.

The main subplot is driven by the need. It's the Inside/Emotional Story. It is usually focused on the primary relationship in the story. It's concerned with character dynamics.

The Outside/Action Story is the spine; it holds things together. The Inside/Emotional Story is the heart; it touches the audience with the key relationship. To make the Outside/Action Story and Inside/Emotional Story work, you need to understand your movie people and how they function. (See "Two Stories in One" in Book I for a detailed explanation.)

CHECKPOINT 8

Does your central character have the following?
- An outside goal (or series of goals) that the audience will care about?
- A powerful, personal motivation for achieving the goal?
- An opposition character in a position of strength, capable of doing great damage?

- The will to act against opposition, and to learn and grow?
- Human emotions, traits, values, and imperfections that people can identify with?
- A particular point of view of life, the world, and/or self, giving rise to attitudes?
- Details, extensions, idiosyncrasies, and/or expressions that are uniquely his/hers?
- A life and voice (dialogue) of his/her own?
- A key event from the past that has given rise to a character flaw?
- An inner need that he/she may be unaware of at first?

CHECKPOINT 9

Evaluate your other main characters (and especially your opposition character) by the criteria of Checkpoint 8. Each should have at least a goal or intention in the story. The more depth you can give them, the more interesting they will appear.

CHECKPOINT 10

Your movie people have sociological, psychological, and physiological characteristics. Use the following to provoke your creative thought.

Sociology		
Occupation	Education	Criminal record
Birthplace/upbringing	Ethnic roots	Religion
Past/present home life	Political views	Social status
Hobbies	Affiliations	Private life
Work history	Work environment	Personal life

Physiology		
Height/weight	Build or figure	Attractiveness
Appearance	Hair/eyes	Voice quality
Defects/scars	Health/strength	Complexion
Clothing	Physical skills	Athletic ability

Psychology		
Fears/phobias	Secrets	Attitudes
Prejudices	Values/beliefs	Inhibitions
Pet peeves	Complexes	Addictions
Superstitions	Habits	Moral stands
Ambitions	Motivations	Temperament
Personal problems	Imagination	Likes/dislikes
Intelligence	Disposition	

CHECKPOINT 11

These are questions to ask of any of your movie people:
- How do you handle stress, pressure, relationships, problems, emotion?
- Are you extroverted or shy? Intuitive or analytical? Active or passive?
- What's your most traumatic experience? Most thrilling experience?
- Essentially, who are you? What is at your core?
- What is your dominant trait?
- What do you do and think when you're alone and no one will know?
- How do you feel about yourself?
- How do you feel about the other people in the story?
- Who are the most important people in your life?
- How do you relate to each?
- What's the worst (and best) thing that could happen to you?
- What are you doing tonight? Tomorrow?
- Where do you want to be 10 years from now?

CHECKPOINT 12

- How does your central character grow or change throughout the story?
- Did any of your characters suffer a traumatic event or "emotional wound" before the movie begins that expresses itself as a moral flaw or special attitude or perception?
- How is your character different at the end of the story?
- What does he/she know at the end that he/she did not know at the beginning?
- What is your character's perception of reality?
- Does that perception change by the end of the story?
- What is each character's perception of the other characters in the story?
- Is your central character likable? If so (or if not), what skills, sensibilities, values, or human traits will make her fascinating?

- Will the audience identify with your central character on some level?
- Does your central character have depth, with both strengths and weaknesses?
- Does each of your characters have a specific idiosyncrasy, habit, quirk, imperfection, lovable indulgence, self-defeating behavior, or prop that helps define them?
- Does each minor character (such as a confidant) have his own life?
- Most movies feature five to seven main characters. If you have too many, can two similar characters be combined? If too few, do you have enough subplots to sustain a long second act?
- Will either of the two key roles attract talent?

CHECKPOINT 13

- What is the theme or message or meaning or point of your story? What are you or a key character trying to say?
- Will the end of your story say it for you without being preachy? (The theme may not be evident to you until later in your writing.)

CHECKPOINT 14

Revise your three-paragraph synopsis to incorporate any changes to your story.

Step 5—"Step-out" your story

Outline your story. This is where you find out if your story is going to work or not, or at least get a good idea if it is. For many writers, the outline is their first step after they get an idea. This outlining effort will make the actual writing much easier than it would ordinarily be. Of course, an outline is never written in stone and may be very simple or complex, depending on what works better for you. What follows is an outline of *The Mission* in its eight main beats.

1. The Cardinal writes a letter to the Pope, explaining what has happened.
2. The Man of Peace, a Jesuit priest, replaces a murdered priest and converts the Guarani tribe.
3. The Man of War enslaves the Guarani and kills his brother for sleeping with his fiancé.

4. The Man of Peace oversees the penance of the Man of War and ordains him a priest.
5. The Cardinal must endorse the Treaty of Madrid by vacating the missions; he announces this to the Guarani converts at the missions.
6. The Guarani choose to fight rather than vacate the missions. The Man of War vows to help. The Man of Peace will stay but not fight.
7. The Guarani and the priests are slaughtered.
8. The Cardinal concludes his letter to the Pope: "Thus, we have made the world."

The above outline emphasizes story, but could have been written more from a character viewpoint. Again, outlining is a tool for you to use as you see fit.

CHECKPOINT 15

Plot the action of your story. Identify your central character's action plot and emotional subplot. Look at your other movie people; identify their goals. Their goals will drive their individual plots (actually subplots). Do these various plotlines intersect, resulting in adequate conflict for drama or comedy?

CHECKPOINT 16

If appropriate for your purposes, write a four-page synopsis or treatment (double-spaced). Summarize the beginning of your story in one page, the middle in two pages, and the end in one page. Focus on two to four main characters, the key events (plot points), and the emotional undercurrent of the story. Although somewhat difficult, this exercise will help tremendously in laying a strong foundation for your story. Now answer these questions:

- Is the central conflict of the story clearly defined?
- Are the character's goal and need clear?
- Are the stakes of the story big enough for a commercial movie?
- Does the story evoke an emotional response?
- Will the audience cry, get angry, laugh, get scared, fall in love, get excited, etc.?
- What makes this story unique, fresh, and original?
- Is your story too predictable? Have we seen this before?
- Are the facts of the story plausible? (They don't have to be possible, just plausible.)
- Will people be emotionally satisfied at the end?

CHECKPOINT 17

Step-out your script. Traditionally, the step outline consists of a series of 3"×5" cards, one card for each scene or dramatic unit. Consider attaching these cards (or Post-it Notes) to a wall, table, or corkboard to see the entire story at once. My personal preference is to do this on a computer, using one of the two formatting software programs or some other application.

Continuing with the traditional method: At the top of each card write the master scene heading; then summarize the action of the scene in a sentence or short paragraph, emphasizing the essential action and purpose of the scene. Some writers like to list the characters appearing in the scene in the lower left-hand corner of the card. That way, they can see who is where at a glance.

You can use the lower right-hand corner for pacing and tracking plots. Some writers use a highlighter and identify plots by color: Blue is the action story, red is the love story, and so on.

You can identify scenes as fast or slow, action or dialogue. If you discover that you have four dialogue scenes in a row, all with the same characters, you can adjust this pacing problem by moving scenes around, crosscutting with action scenes, condensing, or even omitting an unnecessary scene.

If additional ideas come to you, jot them down on blank cards. You'll end up with 30 to 100 cards (or more), depending on the nature of the story.

As mentioned, you don't have to use 3"×5" cards. You can step-out your story on your computer—whatever works for you. Once completed, your step outline will become the basis for writing your script.

CHECKPOINT 18

Now that your step outline is complete, ask yourself these questions:
- Are your scenes well paced?
- Do the major turning points come at about the right time?
- Do things just happen, or is there a cause-and-effect relationship between character actions?
- Do the subplots intersect with the main plot, creating new complications?
- Are your characters' actions motivated, or do they exist just to make the story work?

- Do action, conflict, and dramatic tension build, or just repeat and become static?
- Are your central and opposition characters forced to take stronger and stronger actions?
- Does the conflict rise naturally to a crisis/climax?

Step 6—Write your first draft

Write your first draft from the heart. Keep your head out of it as much as possible. It's okay to change the outline. It's okay to ignore the outline. It's okay to overwrite. It's okay to include too much dialogue. It's okay to do this step first and then go through Steps 1–5. Anything goes, everything flows. If you are writing full time, you can knock this out in a week or so. Essentially, you are a story sculptor molding your clay into basic shape.

CHECKPOINT 19

Consider doing the following upon completion of the first draft:

1. Take at least two weeks off from your script. Let it ferment for a while. You will be much more objective for the pre-revision analysis (Checkpoints 20 through 24). During this time you may want to read a book, go to a seminar, see movies of the same genre, or read scripts, or turn your attention to other things.
2. Reward yourself in some way that makes you feel good about being the next great screenwriter.

Step 7—Make the necessary revisions

Writing is rewriting, so let the rewriting begin. Here, you become a script surgeon or your own script consultant. Use your head as well as your heart during the remaining drafts. Whittle down the dialogue; remove unnecessary narration, flashbacks, dream sequences, and so on. You become an analyst in every way you can define that word and you remain open to inspiration. Once this work is completed, polish your script until you are ready to present your wonder to Hollywood. The following checkpoints will help you evaluate your revisions.

CHECKPOINT 20

Review Checkpoints 1 through 19. The checkpoints are intended to help you evaluate your script. Not all may apply to your project.

CHECKPOINT 21 (the script itself)

- Is your script too technical, too complex, or too difficult to understand?
- Will your script require a huge budget requiring extensive special effects, period settings, exotic locations, too many arenas or locations, a large cast, water, and live (non-CGI) animals.
- Is your script's budget about right for its market?
- Have you followed the rules of formatting and presentation as described in Book III?
- Have you written as action the thoughts, feelings, or memories of any characters, or anything else that cannot actually appear on the movie screen?
- When you read your script, do you stop reading for any reason? That is usually an indicator that there is a problem on that page.

CHECKPOINT 22 (dialogue)

- Are there any speeches that are too "on the nose" (obvious)?
- Have you allowed room for subtext when possible?
- Does each character speak with his/her individual voice, vocabulary, slang, rhythm, and style?
- Is the dialogue crisp, original, clever, compelling, and lean? Does it snap, crackle, and pop?
- Are individual speeches too long or encumbered with more than one thought?
- Does the story rely too heavily on dialogue?
- Are your dialogue scenes too long?
- Are there too many scenes with talking heads?
- Are you telling when you could be showing?
- Is the comedy *trying* to be funny, or is it naturally funny; that is, flowing from character, plot, or situation?
- Have you committed any of the seven dialogue sins referred to in Book I?

CHECKPOINT 23 (exposition)

- Are you boring your audience by telling too much too soon?
- Are you confusing your audience with too little information?
- Are you giving your audience just enough exposition to keep them on the edge of their seats?
- Is your exposition revealed through conflict or through static dialogue?
- Have you used flashbacks as a crutch or as a means to move the story forward?

CHECKPOINT 24 (character and story)

- Will the reader root for your hero? Why will the reader care about your central character or protagonist? If you central character is a bad guy, is he or her fascinating?
- Will the reader have an emotional identification with the hero or become otherwise emotionally involved in the story? Is there a strong emotion at the center of the story?
- Are your main characters one-dimensional, perfectly good, perfectly evil, flat, or poorly developed?
- Are your characters believable as human beings with dimension?
- Do your characters come across as retreads whom we've seen before?
- Do any of your characters grow or change throughout the story? What's at stake? How does your character's life change (even if she doesn't "grow")? Will the character face her biggest fear?

- Is there a moment at the end when this growth will be recognized by the reader?
- When will the reader cry or feel genuine emotion?
- Does the story deal with the most important events in the lives of the characters?
- Is the story too gimmicky, relying too heavily on nudity, violence, shock, or special effects?
- Is there a clear beginning, middle, and end?
- Will the first 5 to 10 pages capture the reader's interest? What will hook the reader in?
- Do the first 20 to 30 pages set up the central conflict?
- Is the goal specific enough?
- Does the middle build in intensity toward the Showdown at the end?
- Is the end the "biggest" thing in the movie?
- Is the story, plot, or ending too predictable?
- Are all the loose ends tied up in the Denouement (after the Showdown)?

CHECKPOINT 25 - REVISING TIPS

Sometimes it just doesn't work. You have story problems, character problems, and you're not quite sure how to solve them. When you are blocked or you sense something is wrong, what can you do? The following dozen tips are in no particular order.

1. Don't panic. We all go through this. Realize that you have the ability to solve your problems. Relax and call upon your creative muse.
2. Take some time off, go to Disneyland, and let the script breathe. Don't worry about it. You may get inspiration during this period because you are relaxed and having fun. Let go of control. Be open to new ideas.
3. Read a book; go to a seminar; flick-out. A few of my "breakthroughs" have come on a plane while reading a book about writing. Read scripts.
4. Often you actually know where the trouble is. You have a gnawing feeling inside about something in your story, or perhaps a sense that "something" is wrong, but you ignore it because you don't want to do a major rewrite or it's one of your "darling" scenes that needs to be "killed off." In my script-analysis work, I don't know how many times a writer has told me the following: "I kinda knew what was wrong, but I guess I needed you to confirm it." This is Joseph Conrad's "inner voice that knows."

The point is this: You have an inner sense that you must learn to trust, even when it makes the writing process uncomfortable and the rewriting painful. When you read your script through, if you naturally stop reading at some point, it may be due to a problem on that page.

5. Get feedback from other writers, pros, and/or consultants. Look for patterns in the comments you receive. Remember you are not revising for anyone but you and your audience.

6. Revise your four-page synopsis. Get to the core of your story. Write your logline or query letter—what are the script's strongest points? Sometimes these activities help you focus and get back on track.

7. Revise your character sketches. Emphasize contrasts and opposites. For example, these can include the differences between the central character and the sidekick, or contrasts within a character.

8. Look for movie moments, cinematic moments, and emotional moments. Milk them; dramatize them. If you are writing a comedy, have more fun with them. Heighten the conflicts. Is there a strong emotion at the center of the story? For examples, read the section entitled "Dramatizing Cinematic and Emotional Moments" in Book IV.

9. Add visual elements; look for images, objects, metaphors. Since show is usually better than tell, look for ways to show. I love the "mockingbird" metaphor in *To Kill a Mockingbird*, the deer in *The Deer Hunter*, the house in *Up*, and the word "Rosebud" in *Citizen Kane*. In the latter case, Rosebud is the brand of sleigh that is a symbol of Kane's childhood.

10. Ask stupid questions. Don't be afraid to challenge your own ideas. Ask "What if?" Nothing is sacred. Anything goes. Maybe your hero should be the villain. Be creative. While revising, challenge the first thought that comes to mind; it's sometimes not a creative solution or the optimal solution.

11. When revising, if solving one problem also solves another problem, you're on the right track.

12. Create a Character/Action Grid.

THE CHARACTER/ACTION GRID

The Character/Action Grid is essentially a mini step-outline, constructed on a few sheets of paper. Use it to identify each character's purpose and actions in the story. Most writers use it for their five to seven main characters.

On the next three pages you will find worksheets for the Character/Action Grid, developed by Donna Davidson and me. When Donna read the first edition of my book, she expanded my original tool for her own use. Donna has since published five successful novels and used the Grid for each. Feel free to photocopy these three sheets for your personal use, or purchase a PDF of all the worksheets in *The Bible* at my store at www.keepwriting.com.

As you can see, the Character/Action Grid has two sections: 1) Character and Story, and 2) Actions.

Character and story

The first worksheet for Character/Action allows you to develop four main characters on one page. The worksheet on the next page is exactly the same, except it is designed for just one character—it gives you more room to write. Not every cell in the grid needs to be filled. Make this tool *your* tool. Create your own categories. Better yet, create your own Grid.

At the bottom of grid for Character/Action, you have room to think through your main plot points in terms of each character. Obviously, not each character will be involved with each turning point. The Backstory turning point is listed in the "Characters" section of the worksheets.

Actions

You will not be able to plot your entire screenplay on just that third worksheet. You may need two or three of these sheets. In the second row of the Grid, write the names of your five main characters. Then in the remaining rows and columns simply list each action a character takes. Dialogue can be considered action when it constitutes or creates movement.

The Grid allows you to see the entire story on just a few sheets of paper. It helps you notice if a character is static or uninvolved in the action, or if a character's actions are repetitive rather than building. In other words, you can more readily see if you have a rising conflict or a stagnant story.

The Grid helps with pacing and spacing. Is there a major twist every so often? Are the subplots supporting the main plot? Are character actions crisscrossing throughout the story? Are all of your other major characters fully involved in the story? Does a character disappear for half the story? (That can be good or bad, depending on the story.)

I recommend use of the Grid after the first draft or whenever you are stuck. But you are the captain of your ship. Use it when you wish or not at all.

Ferdi Strickler, a Swiss client of mine, told me that he used the Character/Action Grid idea to create a Character/Character Grid. In this grid, "every character says what he thinks about the other characters, and of course, what he thinks about himself." I like this idea and any idea that adapts a tool for your specific purpose.

Below, you will find an example of a partially completed Character/Action Grid.

Character/Action Grid example

I designed the following story idea as a small example of how to use the Grid. I created only three characters. I won't take you through the entire grid with them, nor will I outline the entire story. I just want to give you a feel for the Grid's use. You will want to list every important action of your main characters from the beginning to the end of the story.

CHARACTER/ACTION GRID — Character and Story

Char:	JIM	SALLY	MAX
Role:	Central character/hero	Love interest, 2nd opp.	Main opposition
Occ:	Investigative journalist	Animal-rights advocate	Circus owner
Goal:	Exploit Blimpo the Elephant for a story	Save Blimpo the Elephant from exploitation	#1 Circus Act in U.S.
Motive:	Salvage career	Repay Blimpo for saving her life	Prove he's not a loser
Need:	Be more caring	Trust and love Jim	Respect animals
Flaw:	Anything for a story	Trusts only animals	Inhumane

CHARACTER/ACTION GRID — Actions

JIM	SALLY	MAX
Fired, but then gets last chance		
Dumped by Sally	Dumps Jim; can't trust him	Whips Blimpo
	Kidnaps Blimpo; chased	Chases Sally
	Hides Blimpo in Jim's yard	

Next morning: Finds Blimpo

Continue outlining your characters' actions to the end. When the Grid is completed, you will be able to see your entire story on one to three pages. The structure, pacing, motivation, and plotlines will be easier to work with.

CHARACTER/ACTION GRID — Character and Story				
Title, genre, concept				
Theme or message				
CHARACTERS				
Role, purpose in story				
Occupation				
Conscious goal				
Personal motivation				
Inner need				
Flaw blocking need				
Backstory				
Dominant, core trait				
Other good and bad traits				
Imperfections, quirks				
Skills, knowledge, props				
Point of view, attitudes				
Dialogue style				
Physiology				
Psychology, sociology				
Relationship w/ others				
Catalyst				
Big Event				
Crisis				
Showdown				
Realization				
Denouement				

This grid allows you to see four characters at a glance.

CHARACTER/ACTION GRID — Character and Story
Title, genre, concept
Theme or message
NAME OF CHARACTER:
Role, purpose in story
Occupation
Conscious goal
Personal motivation
Inner need
Flaw blocking need
Backstory
Dominant, core trait
Other good and bad traits
Imperfections, quirks
Skills, knowledge, props
Point of view, attitudes
Dialogue style
Physiology
Psychology, sociology
Relationship w/others
Catalyst
Big Event
Crisis
Showdown
Realization
Denouement

This grid allows you to develop a single character.

CHARACTER/ACTION GRID — Actions				

142   This grid is good for focusing on actions—who does what, and how that influences other characters.

CHECKPOINT 26

Before you submit your script, do the following:
- Get feedback from writers group members.
- Consider hiring a professional reader or script consultant.
- Review Checkpoints 1 through 25 one last time, if needed.
- Make adjustments. Is your script a "good read"?
- Be sure the script looks professional and is formatted correctly.
- Consider registering your script with the Writers Guild of America. We'll discuss copyright in Book V.
- Create a strategic marketing plan (see Book V).

PROPER FORMATTING TECHNIQUE

BOOK III

A Style Guide

How to use this guide to craft a compelling and professional screenplay

This book shows you how to correctly format your *spec* screenplay, teleplay, TV drama, or sitcom script. The word *spec* means you are writing it on *speculation* that you will sell it later; in other words, you are not being paid to write it. This book (and Book IV) also teaches you about writing and spec writing *style*.

Who are you writing for?
Are you writing for the agent, the producer, the actors, the set decorator, or the director? You may say, "Well, Dave, it's all of the above." That's only partially true. The *main* person you are writing for is the *reader* or *story analyst*. After all, when an agent or producer receives your script, she hands it off to a reader. The reader recommends it or not. If he doesn't recommend it, then the agent or producer never reads it. Thus, it is essential to understand that you are writing for a reader.

Properly formatting your script is like dressing your script for its job interview with the reader—you want it to make a positive first impression. If your agent asked you for a piece of cake, would you grab a handful of cake and slap it down on the table, or would you want your presentation to be more professional and enticing?

The script should be written in the language of the reader
Formatting is a key element of screenwriting and is inseparable from it. It is the language of the screenplay writing art. It is what industry people expect to see. In addition, you will find that as your formatting knowledge increases, the quality of your writing will improve. Proper formatting techniques will help you tell your story more effectively.

Rather than viewing proper format as a limiting burden, see it as an integral part of the writing process that frees you to communicate your story clearly to other professionals. Anyone can define formatting "rules," but this book and Book IV go beyond the rules to show you how to apply proper formatting technique to your spec story project.

Recently, a client paid me to review several troublesome sections of his script for formatting; we simply read them together over the phone. As we discussed each section, he became more and more excited for three reasons.

First, he saw how understanding correct format enabled him to write a much more entertaining script. Second, he was happy that his script was more "readable." And third was the big surprise. He had never imagined how flexible formatting is and how there can be many formatting solutions to solve one problem, depending on his objectives. He said, "Dave, this is the best writing experience I've ever had. I can't thank you enough."

Professional scripts sometimes vary slightly in formatting style, and yet they all look basically the same. There are surprisingly few absolutes, and professionals often disagree on this point or that. These formatting guidelines are like accounting principles—they are "generally accepted" by the industry. They will increase your script's chances of being accepted by agents, producers, directors, and talent (actors and actresses). The format of your screenplay does *not* have to be perfect to be acceptable to readers; just don't let errors accumulate to become a distraction.

This book is both a user-friendly guide and a reference book. It contains clear instructions and dozens of sample scenes and other examples. You can easily find information in any of the following ways.

1. Read the entire **Book III** from beginning to end as a style guide. (This is what I recommend.) The book contains numerous instructions, explanations, and clear examples.

2. Read the four-page **sample script** entitled "The Perspicacious Professor," which appears in a few pages. The script contains *codes* identified by letters of the alphabet that refer to explanations and examples that appear later in this book, identified by the same letter of the alphabet.

3. Study specific areas of interest to you. Here is how Book III is laid out:

Sample script (with reference codes)

Explanations and examples
    Formatting in a nutshell (a one-page outline)
    Overall screenplay appearance
    Scene headings (sometimes called slug lines)
    Narrative description (action)
    Dialogue

How to format TV scripts (teleplays)

For ease of use, I suggest you put a paper clip or Post-it "flag" on the first page of the sample script and on the first page of each of the following chapters: Scene headings, Narrative description, and Dialogue. These chapters explain the three parts of a screenplay, and all formatting "rules" and techniques fit into one of those three categories.

4. Check the **Glossary** at the end of this book for terms not defined elsewhere.

5. Use the **Index** at the end of *The Bible* to quickly find any formatting subject or term. Formatting terms appear in all-CAPS in the index.

All sample scenes and excerpts appear just as they would in an actual script, right down to the 12-point Courier New font. The format used for feature-length screenplays is also used for TV/cable movies and hour-long TV dramas. One last thing to keep in mind before going on: You are writing a *spec* script. Let's discuss that in detail.

THE SPEC SCRIPT

The *spec* script is the *selling* script. You write it with the idea of selling it later or circulating it as a sample. Once it is sold and goes into preproduction, it will be transformed into a *shooting* script, also known as the *production draft*. The *spec* script style avoids camera angles, editing directions, and technical intrusions. You may use these tools, but only when necessary to clarify the story. Scenes are not numbered in the spec script; that's done by the production secretary after your script is sold.

All the camera and editing directions in the world cannot save a bad story, but too much technical intrusion can make even the best story a chore to read. The main reason you write a *spec* script is to excite professional readers about your story. So concentrate on the story and leave the direction to the director and the editing to the editor. In this book, and especially in Book IV, I will show you how to direct the camera without using camera directions. That is how you show professionals that you are capable of writing a shooting script version of your spec script.

Virtually every script you buy from a script service or bookstore, or view in a script library, is a *shooting* script or a variation thereof. Many screenwriting books (including *The Hollywood Standard* by Christopher Riley) contain formatting instructions for *shooting* scripts only.

However, the *shooting* script is not a joy to read for agents, executives, and readers who must plow through dozens of scripts every week, week after week. The technical directions clutter the script and intrude on the reading experience. That's fine if the script is about to be produced, but it works against you if you want your story to flow smoothly to the reader, enticing him/her to buy or recommend it to higher-ups.

Both script styles (spec and shooting) utilize the same standard screenplay formatting rules: master scene headings in CAPS, double-space to narrative description, dialogue indented, and so on. And the *spec* script occasionally employs some *shooting* script terms: MONTAGE, FLASHBACK, INSERT for notes and letters, and INTERCUT for telephone conversations.

The essential difference between the two styles is this: The *shooting* script format requires specific technical instructions so that the director, crew, and cast can more easily perform in the shoot. *Spec* script format emphasizes clear, unencumbered visual writing to **sell** agents and producers on a great story. The following two examples illustrate the difference.

Example #1 from a shooting script:

ANGLE ON JIM

He bats his eyes at Alicia.

ANOTHER ANGLE

He winks.

Example #1 revised for a spec script:

Jim bats his eyes at Alicia, and then winks.

Example #2 from a shooting script:

Steve takes a puff from the pipe.

FX. - WE SEE STEVE LEVITATE SLOWLY ABOVE THE FLOOR, STILL IN HIS SQUATTED POSITION.

STEVE'S POV - We SEE the muted COLORS of the room begin to BRIGHTEN intensely.

Example #2 revised for a spec script:

```
Steve, sitting cross-legged on the floor, takes a puff from the
pipe.

Slowly he levitates in the same cross-legged position.

He sees the muted colors of the room brighten intensely.
```

Do you see how much easier the spec examples are to read? In effect, the writer directs the camera without using camera directions and identifies special effects without using technical language. Unless you're being paid in advance by a producer to specifically write a shooting script, use spec style. That's what we'll discuss in this book.

NEW SPEC STYLES

Every so often, a "new spec style" appears and disappears. As of this writing, there is a current fad of bolding and underscoring scene headings. Unless this takes hold and overtakes the industry, I recommend you stick with what has been used successfully for decades. Besides, you should not need to rely on passing fashions. Just communicate with clarity and an entertaining style, and use proper screenplay format. I suspect that if a new style becomes commonly accepted, that fact will be reflected in the two major screenwriting software applications.

SCREENWRITING SOFTWARE

There are two well-established formatting software applications that you can choose from: Movie Magic Screenwriter and Final Draft. Both programs will provide you with all you need to help format your screenplay, and both get the Dr. Format seal of approval.

If you wish to use a word-processing application, I recommend Microsoft Word, because it is universally applicable and you can create a PDF file with it. You can set the margins and tabs yourself; I'll provide the specific information for that later. Do not use Microsoft Works; the files created cannot be read by any other software application except another Works program.

There is another option worth considering at www.screenwritingpro.com. It provides a formatting application that operates similarly to Screenwriter and Final Draft.

Sample script (with cross-reference codes)

Below, you'll find a sample script. It contains *reference codes* identified by letters of the alphabet. The codes refer to corresponding sections in the book where you can find explanations and examples. Since these codes appear in alphabetical order in the body of the text, they are easy to find. In addition, when you read a particular section that's identified by a code, you can return to the same code on the sample script for an additional example.

A personal note on the following sample script: In response to owners of past editions of The Bible *who have written me concerning the content of the sample script that follows, I feel compelled to explain that the scenes romanticize my occasional teaching practice of tossing a candy mint to any student who makes a brilliant comment or asks a profound question.*

LIST OF CROSS-REFERENCE CODES

This chart identifies the following:
- *Each alphabetical **reference code***
- *The page number where an example can be found in the **sample script***
- *The page number where an **explanation** can be found in the text*
- *The **title of the section** where that explanation can be found*

Ref Code	Sample Script	Explanation	Title of explanatory section
A	Page 155	Page 163	The First Page
B	Page 155	Page 166	Master Scene Headings
C	Page 155	Page 167	SAME
D	Page 155	Page 167	CONTINUOUS
E	Page 155	Page 174	Spacing Between Scenes
F	Page 156	Page 175	MONTAGE and SERIES OF SHOTS
G	Page 157	Page 181	INSERT
H	Page 155	Page 183	Establishing Shot
I	Page 155	Page 184	Camera Placement
J	Page 155	Page 190	Character First Appearances
K	Page 155	Page 195	Signs, News Headlines. . .
L	Page 155	Page 195	Sounds
M	Page 155	Page 196	Special Effects
N	Page 156	Page 199	Transitions
O	Page 157	Page 202	POV
P	Page 157	Page 205	Author's Intrusion
Q	Page 157	Page 206	CONTINUED
R	Page 155	Page 208	Character Cue
S	Page 157	Page 212	Continuing and CONT'D
T	Page 157	Page 213	Off Screen (O.S.) and Voice Over (V.O.)
U	Page 155	Page 217	The Telephone Voice
V	Page 155	Page 218	Telephone Conversations
W	Page 156	Page 227	Dialogue Punctuation

THE PERSPICACIOUS PROFESSOR

by

David Trottier

4456 Manchester St.
Cedar Hills, UT 84062
801/492-7898
dave@keepwriting.com

FADE IN: [A]

       [H]
EXT. UNIVERSITY CAMPUS - DAY

A sign on an old ivy-covered building reads: "CINEMA DEPT." [K]
  [E]
INT. SMALL CLASSROOM - DAY [B]

Twenty students sit in rapt attention while the buff DR. FORMAT [J]
scrawls "Formatting" on the board. Slung over his shoulder is a
seal-trainer pouch filled with candy mints rather than fish.
  [J]
CHARLIE kicks back near a window, raises his hand. Two buzzing [L]
flies vie for territorial rights to the chocolate on his face.

              CHARLIE
      How do you handle phone calls?

The professor moonwalks to Charlie's desk carrying a demo phone.

       [R]   DR. FORMAT
      Excellent question, my man.

He tosses the grateful boy a candy mint. Charlie catches it on his
nose and barks like a seal, looking for laughs. [M]

Outside Charlie's window, CALCUTTA COTTER (19) in pigtails and [I]
a pinafore yanks SOMEONE out of the phone booth and steps in.

EXT. PHONE BOOTH - CONTINUOUS [D]

With phone in hand, she turns to the classroom window and frowns at
what she sees -- the professor doing cartwheels down the aisle. [I]

INT. DEAN ZACK'S OFFICE - SAME [C]

DEAN ZELDA ZACK stands at her polished desk, holding her cell.

           DEAN ZACK [U]
      Make him pay, Calcutta.

INTERCUT - TELEPHONE CONVERSATION [V]

           CALCUTTA
      It'll work?

           DEAN ZACK
      Stumps him every time.

The dean chortles. Calcutta smiles; then slams the receiver.

INT. CLASSROOM - DAY
              [N]
The professor's hand slams the receiver of his demo phone.

The students simmer with interest.

The door swings open. Calcutta steps in and shuffles to her desk.

                    DR. FORMAT
     [W]   Remember. It's gotta be lean.
                Description... dialogue.
                     (arching his brow)
                All lean, my pets -- lean!

He pirouettes and clicks his heels, to his students' delight.

Calcutta raises her arm and wags it aggressively.

                    CALCUTTA

          The <u>tabs</u>. Where do I set them?

A hush fades into silence. Dr. format wilts.

The students exchange questioning glances as Dr. F. stumbles
dizzily to his desk. He gazes blankly ahead to a spinning room. [O]

MONTAGE - THE PROFESSOR'S TRANCE [F]

-- The room spins.

-- He jabs at a giant tab key on a keyboard to no effect.

-- Dean Zelda Zack rides up to the window on her swagger stick. She
transforms into a witch, cackles, and rides off.

-- The spinning room slows to a stop. [M]

BACK TO THE CLASSROOM

The students look horrified. Calcutta smiles gleefully.

Dr. Format gazes blankly ahead.

                    CHARLIE
          Our dear professor. What's wrong?

[Q]   3.

Several students clench the edges of their desks. Can he do it?
                              [P]
                    CHARLIE (O.S.) [T]
               He's done for.

Murmurs of agreement. The professor stares at his shoes.

                    DR. FORMAT
               Where to set your tabs. Assume
               a left margin at... um... at fifteen.

The students brighten in their seats. Calcutta frowns.

The professor begins a serious moonwalking stride.

                    DR. FORMAT [S]
                    (the master)
               Dialogue at twenty-five.
               Wrylies at thirty-one...

Calcutta nervously chews a pigtail.

                    DR. FORMAT [S]
               ... And then the character's name
               in caps. At thirty-seven!

Cheers and kudos. The professor's moonwalk has taken him to
Calcutta's desk, where he towers over her limp form.

                    DR. FORMAT [S]
               But why, Calcutta? Why?

                    CALCUTTA
               'Cuz everyone else always gets a
               candy, even Charlie, and I don't.

Her shoulders shake to her heavy sobs.

The professor dips into his leather pouch and deftly snatches a
candy mint. [G]

Calcutta lifts her head just as he flicks the candy into the air.
She catches it on her nose, barks like a seal, and consumes it
greedily. The students cheer.

As the professor pats her head, her pigtails rise as if to extend
her radiant smile.

Formatting in a nutshell

There are three parts of a screenplay: *scene headings*, *narrative description*, and *dialogue*.

1. Scene headings (sometimes referred to as slug lines)
There are three types of scene headings.

    A. Master scene headings, which consist of three main parts:
        1. Camera location (EXT. or INT.)
        2. Scene location
        3. Time (DAY or NIGHT)

    B. Secondary scene headings

    C. Special scene headings for flashbacks, dreams, montages, series of shots, and so on.

2. Narrative description (action)
The word "narrative" loosely means *story*, and it consists of three elements:

    A. Action
    B. Setting and character (visual images)
    C. Sounds.

3. Dialogue
The dialogue block consists of three parts:

    A. The *character cue*, or name of the person speaking, which always appears
       in CAPS
    B. The *parenthetical* or *actor's direction* or *wryly* (this is optional)
    C. The *speech*.

What follows is an example of the three parts of a spec screenplay, the three parts of a master scene heading, the three elements of narrative description, and the three parts of a dialogue block.

```
EXT. FOREST - NIGHT

The moon shines on the pale, serene face of ELEANOR SAWYER.

                    ELEANOR
               (softly)
          Midnight.

She mounts a horse and rides into the darkness, the hoof
beats muffled by the leaves and flora on the forest floor.
```

Overall screenplay appearance

THE COVER, CONTENTS, AND BINDING

Often, a request for a script will come via email, in which case, you can attach a PDF file of your script to your return email. In some cases, you may need to ship the physical script.

Physically, a screenplay consists of a front cover (of solid-color index stock, at least 65-pound, preferably 110-pound), a title page (or *fly page*) on regular 20-pound paper, the pages of the script itself (printed on one side only) on regular 20-pound paper, and a back cover (110-pound paper). The script, 8½"×11" in size, is three-hole punched.

Nothing should appear on the front cover—not even the title. Once an agent or producer receives your script, the script will be placed horizontally on a stack. Someone will write your title on the side binding with a Magic Marker. Don't do it for them.

To bind the script together, use Acco (or similar brand) No. 5 round-head brass fasteners, 1¼" in length (some writers like to use No. 6). It is fashionable to place the fasteners (or "brads") in the first and third hole and leave the middle hole empty. Do not use flimsy brads. You can purchase these at my store (www.keepwriting.com) or from the Writers Store (www.writersstore.com). A very distant second choice for binding is screw-in brads. Do not bind a script in any other way. The above method makes it easy for producers and others to read your script and, if they get excited about your work, to make photocopies to pass around, which is something you want.

SCRIPT LENGTH

Your script should be about 90 to 120 pages—ideally, about 100 for a comedy and 105 to 110 for a drama. Yes, there are many screenplays of completed movies that are over 120 pages, but virtually all of those were developed by studios or production companies; they were not specs.

THE 17 COMMANDMENTS

Certain things turn off most professional readers, agents, and producers. Don't do any of the following unless requested.

1. Don't include fancy covers, artwork, illustrations, or storyboards.
2. Don't number the scenes. This is done after the script is sold.
3. Don't use fancy fonts or proportional-pitch fonts, only 12-point Courier or Courier New.
4. Don't justify right margins. Leave the right margin ragged.
5. Don't bold or italicize.
6. Don't use camera and editing directions unless necessary to move the story forward.
7. Don't date your script in any way. Scripts get "old" fast.
8. Don't write "First Draft," "Final Draft," or any draft.
9. Don't include a suggested cast list or character list with bios.
10. Don't include a list of characters or sets.
11. Don't include a synopsis—you are selling your ability to write a script.
12. Don't include a budget.
13. Don't include a header (such as your name or title) at the top of each page.
14. Don't ignore errors in spelling, grammar, and punctuation.
15. Don't "cheat" by using thinner left and right margins, by squeezing extra lines onto a page, by using a smaller typeface, or by widening dialogue lines beyond the standard 3.5 to 4 inches. Movie Magic Screenwriter and Final Draft provide acceptable methods of cheating; also see "When to break the rules" in Book IV.
16. Don't type CONTINUED at the top or bottom of each page.
17. Don't send out a script that is over 120 pages.

The above rules may seem nitpicky, but they're easy to comply with, and adhering to them places you in the realm of the professional writer in the know, and helps you make a good first impression. Obviously, if your script is wonderful, but breaks one or two of these commandments, it is not going to be rejected. But why not give yourself every advantage to make sure that your script is read in the first place?

In addition, some agents and producers may make a request that violates one or more of these conventions. In such a case, give the agent or producer what she requests.

THE TITLE PAGE

The title page you see for the sample script is correct for a script that has not yet found an agent. You may add quotation marks around the title if you wish, or underscore it, or both. If there are two or more writers and they worked together and contributed equally, use an *ampersand* instead of the word *and*. For example:

```
                "NAZIS IN SPACE"

                      by

          Bart Snarf & Buffy Bucksaw
```

When the word *and* is used, it means a writer was brought in later to rewrite the first writer's script. In other words, they didn't work together.

Your address, phone number, and email address should appear in the lower right corner, where it can be easily seen. Lower left is okay. Nothing else needs to be on the title page. Once your script has found an agent, then the agent's contact information will appear on the title page. Your agent will be able to show you how to do that.

If you register your script with the Writers Guild (WGA), you may indicate your registration on the lower left corner of the title page of your script as follows: Registered WGAw. (Use "WGAe" if you registered with the East Coast office.) However, you do *not* need to type your WGA registration number, *nor* do you need to type a notice on your script to validate your registration rights. Thus, there is no reason to include any WGA information on your title page.

If you register your script with the Copyright Office, then you must place your copyright notice in the lower left corner. (Note: The Writer's Guild registration service and copyright will be discussed at length in the first chapter of Book V.)

TYPEFACE

Always use a Courier 12-point font because it is the industry standard. Prior to the advent of the computer, screenwriters used the Pica typewriter font, which gave each typed character equal width; thus, every ten typed characters always measured one inch. It also helped retain the "one page equals one minute of screen time" industry standard of the time. And Courier 12-point fonts do the same today. And because or Courier, even today's screenplays look like they were typed on a typewriter.

Virtually all other fonts are *proportional* fonts. They compress characters together to get more words on a line. With a proportional font, each character has a different width. *The Screenwriter's Bible* is written in a proportional font, but all of the script examples in it appear in `Courier New` 12-point so that they look exactly the way they would look in a script.

In a `Courier` font, the single "dash" (`-`) is used in master and secondary scene headings. It is made up on a single hyphen preceded by and followed by a space, just as it would've been made by a typewriter. Likewise, the double "dash" (`--`) used in narrative description and dialogue is made up of two `Courier` hyphens preceded by and followed by a space.

MARGINS

If you use screenwriting software, don't worry about margins, tabs, line spacing, and pagination. Skip those sections.

Because scripts are three-hole punched, the left margin should be 1.5 inches, the right margin a half inch to about 1.25 inches. I recommend 1 inch for the right margin. The top and bottom margins should be 1 inch each. Assuming the standard 10 characters per inch (Courier 12-point font), that would mean a left margin at 15 spaces (1.5 inches from the left edge of the paper). The right margin can be anywhere from a half inch to 1.25 inches from the right edge of the paper. As already stated, the right margin should be *ragged*. (If you live outside the United States and use standard A4 paper, configure your software so that you type 55 lines per page.)

TABS

If you do not use Movie Magic Screenwriter or Final Draft, let these standards guide you in setting your tabs:

- Left margin at 15 spaces (1.5 inches) from the left edge of the page.
- Dialogue at 25 spaces (2.5 inches); that's 10 spaces from the *left margin*.
- Actor's instructions at 31 (3.1 inches); that's 16 spaces from the *left margin*.
- Character's name at 37 (3.7 inches); that's 22 spaces from the *left margin*.

Make sure your dialogue does not extend beyond 65 spaces (6.5 inches) from the left edge of the page (in other words, a line of dialogue should be no wider than 4 inches, although many writers limit themselves to 3.5 inches), and actor's instructions not beyond 50–55 spaces from the left edge of the page.

Parentheticals (actor's direction) should not be wider than 2 inches.

```
                    DR. FORMAT
              (spinning around in
               his chair)
         A dialogue block should look like this.
```

The above guides are not written in stone—some writers indent 12 or 14 for dialogue, some indent 7 or 8 for actor's instructions, etc.

LINE SPACING

A script page should contain about 54 to 55 lines. This does not include the line for the page number and the line after the page number. If you add more than that, the page will look cramped. If your software program allows for one or two lines more than the standard, don't be concerned. For more information on line spacing, see "When to break the rules" in Book IV.

PAGINATION

Page numbers should appear in the upper right, flush to the right margin, a half inch from the top edge of the page, and followed by a period. No page number should appear on the first page of the script.

[A] THE FIRST PAGE

(NOTE: The reference code [A] and all future alpha codes refer back to examples on the sample script "The Perspicacious Professor.")

The title of your script may be centered at the top of page, in CAPS, and underscored. This is optional and is seldom used anymore. I recommend that you begin your script as follows:

```
FADE IN:
```

That is followed by a master scene heading or the description of an image, after which normal script formatting rules apply. If you wish, you may begin your script with a master scene heading without the FADE IN.

Some movies begin with a BLACK SCREEN, which is followed by the description of sounds or some superimposed (SUPERed) words or both, which is followed by the familiar FADE IN.

You will not need to use FADE IN again unless you FADE TO BLACK later in your script, after which you will need to FADE IN again. Here's an example:

```
                                        FADE TO BLACK.


FADE IN:
```

CREDITS AND TITLES

Don't worry about where to place your opening and closing CREDITS. They're *not* required for the spec script. Besides, it's very hard to judge just how long it will take the credits to roll. If you have written this beautiful opening segment that is perfect for CREDITS or TITLES to roll over, the reader will recognize that fact without any special notation placed there by you. If you feel strongly about including credits, then use this format:

```
ROLL CREDITS
```

or

```
BEGIN CREDITS
```

And after the last opening credit:

```
END CREDITS
```

In the above example, CREDITS is treated as a "heading." However, it can also be included in the body of the narrative description. The word TITLES is often used in place of CREDITS in a shooting script. Again, I strongly advise against indicating CREDITS or TITLES.

THE LAST PAGE

There are two general ways to end a screenplay. My personal choice is to write THE END at the end. Some writers like to fade out, as follows.

FADE OUT.

or

FADE TO BLACK.

You'll recall that FADE IN appears flush to the left margin and FADE OUT appears flush to the right margin (or at a tab 6 inches from the left edge of the paper). Thus, FADE IN is the only editing direction (or *transition*) that appears flush to the left margin. If your software program places FADE IN flush to the right margin, don't be concerned.

Scene headings (slug lines)

Screenplays and TV scripts consist of three parts: 1) Scene headings, 2) Description (or Action), and 3) Dialogue. This section deals with scene headings.

The most common formatting error

The term *slug line* is often used in reference to scene headings. However, it is a journalistic term. I have no quarrel with the *slug*gish terms used every day by screenwriters and other industry pros, including top writers. They're perfectly okay. My main interest is in helping you clearly understand the elements those terms reference and how those elements are used, which is why I prefer the term *scene heading* over *slug*.

The most common formatting errors I see in developing writers' screenplays are with confusing and improper scene headings. That implies a possible lack of understanding of what they actually are and how they should be used.

Sometimes calling something by its given name rather than its nickname helps us understand its use. I'm sure that is one reason you will find the term *scene heading* rather than *slug line* used in the software applications Movie Magic Screenwriter and Final Draft.

Headings always appear in CAPS. There are three types of headings: A) Master scene headings, B) Secondary scene headings, and C) Special headings. The major formatting difficulty screenwriters sometimes have is in understanding how to use master scene headings and secondary scene headings. The result is often frustrated readers exclaiming, "Where am I?"

(NOTE: The reference code [B] below and all future alpha codes refer back to the sample script "The Perspicacious Professor.")

[B] MASTER SCENE HEADINGS

A master scene heading consists of three main parts, and a rarely used fourth.

1. Camera location

If the camera is located outside or outdoors, then use EXT. for EXTERIOR. If it is indoors, then use INT. for INTERIOR. Please read the brief section "Camera Placement" at Code I; it will provide a helpful example.

Occasionally, the action moves back and forth through a doorway or opening. This can create a large number of master scene headings. Sometimes a scene begins outside, but quickly moves inside (or vice versa). In such cases, the following camera location notation is permissible:

```
INT./EXT. CAR - DAY
```

Now the camera can be placed anywhere that makes sense to the reader (and director).

2. Scene location

The second part of a master scene heading is the master (or primary) location of the scene, the place where everything is happening. Usually one or two words will suffice.

Occasionally, I see incorrect scene locations such as RUNNING or GRABBING LUNCH or CHRISTMAS MORNING. These are not locations. A STREET is a location. A

DINER is a location. SMITHS' HOUSE is a location, and that's where the Christmas tree is.

At code [E] on the sample script, the location is a small classroom. I use the word "small" only because I don't want the reader to visualize one of those large, semi-circular auditoriums. I want a more intimate scene and perhaps a modest budget. Generally, you want master scene headings to be short and specific.

3. Time of day
Most often this will be DAY or NIGHT. Avoid terms like DUSK, DAWN, LATE AFTERNOON, EARLY EVENING, HIGH NOON, GLOAMING, or the time on the clock. Use these only if helpful to the story. Keep in mind that virtually all movie scenes are shot for DAY or NIGHT.

[C] SAME
Occasionally, SAME is used to indicate that the scene takes place at the SAME time as the previous scene. See [C] **on the sample script** for an example. Sometimes the term SAME TIME is used.

[D] CONTINUOUS
As demonstrated at [D] on the sample script, CONTINUOUS is occasionally used for a similar purpose—to show that one scene follows right on the heels of the other, without any jump in time. Here is another example:

```
EXT. BACK YARD - NIGHT

Butch creeps up to the kitchen door. He picks the lock.

INT. KITCHEN - CONTINUOUS

He tiptoes inside.
```

If it is already obvious that one scene follows the other continuously without any time gaps or lapses, then it is not necessary to use CONTINUOUS. This may be the case for the above example. In fact, the time (DAY or NIGHT) would also be obvious, so you could probably get away with the following:

```
INT. KITCHEN
```

When in doubt as to what to do, always opt for clarity. That makes it easy for your reader.

LATER

Sometimes, "LATER" is used to indicate passage of time.

```
INT. DINING ROOM - LATER
```

Or, if you established the dining room in the previous scene heading, you could simply write:

```
LATER
```

Space—the final formatting frontier

If the scene takes place in outer space, then it's neither DAY nor NIGHT, so you may not need to indicate any time of day; just write:

```
EXT. SPACE
```

However, if you have an interior scene, you may want to indicate DAY or NIGHT depending on whether the characters are working or sleeping. Of course, your characters' activity is a clue, so DAY and NIGHT may not be needed even then. The main thing is to not confuse or lose the reader.

4. Special notations

If a scene requires further identification because it is a dream, for example, such a clarification may be added as a fourth part of the master scene heading. Here is an example:

```
INT. ROOM OF MIRRORS - NIGHT - MARTY'S DREAM
```

or

```
INT. ROOM OF MORRORS - NIGHT (MARTY'S DREAM)
```

Suppose your screenplay jumps all over time. In that case, you could additionally indicate the date (or the season) of the scene, as follows.

```
EXT. TOKYO BAY - DAY - 1945
```

or

```
EXT. TOKYO BAY - DAY (1945)
```

If you want the audience to see "1945" superimposed on the movie screen, you will need to use a SUPER.

What if you want a scene to be shot in black-and-white or sepia tone? Use "SPECIAL NOTES" or use a special notation:

```
EXT. ROLLER COASTER - DAY - BLACK AND WHITE
```

Scenes presented out of sequence

If the scenes of your screenplay are not presented in chronological order, as in *Pulp Fiction*, *Run Lola Run*, or *Sliding Doors*, then use the fourth part of the master scene heading ("special notations" section above) to keep the reader oriented. For example, I read a script that alternated between "DREAM STATE" and "REALITY."

What if you jump around geographically? You could add the city of the scene as a special notation:

```
INT. CAFE - NIGHT (PARIS)
```

Scene changes

Technically, if any of the three (or four) elements of a master scene heading change, you have a new scene, and must type in a new master scene heading to indicate the change. Sometimes you don't need a new master scene heading. For example, if the camera location and scene location don't change, but the time does, you could simply type the following:

```
MOMENTS LATER
```

Master scene heading conventions

A master scene heading should appear as follows.

```
INT. CLASSROOM - DAY
```

As usual, variations abound, but the general form remains the same. Occasionally, I have seen some scripts with master scenes bolded. Don't bold or italicize anything in a screenplay (except perhaps foreign words in dialogue). It is not necessary to underscore a master scene heading. A scene heading should not end with a period or other punctuation.

Recently, I saw the following master scene heading:

```
EXT. A DARK, GNARLY AND WINDY FOREST IN ENGLAND - NIGHT
```

Save the description for the description section, and identify the specific location for the scene heading, as follows.

```
EXT. ENGLISH FOREST - NIGHT
```

```
The wind howls through the gnarly trees.
```

SECONDARY SCENE HEADINGS

Master scenes often contain more than one dramatic unit, each of which could require a scene heading. In fact, there can be several smaller or secondary locations that are part of the primary or master location. This is a crucial concept in script formatting, and it's important to understand.

In *Casablanca*, much of the action takes place at Rick's Cafe. These scenes can be quite long unless they are broken up into smaller scenes. For example, the master scene would be written as follows.

```
INT. RICK'S CAFE - NIGHT
```

A few paragraphs into the scene and we go to a specific spot at Rick's Cafe.

```
AT THE BAR
```

or

```
GAMING ROOM
```

or

```
RICK'S TABLE
```

We are still at Rick's Cafe. The bar, Rick's table, and the gaming room are secondary locations that are part of the master or primary location.

If you are so disposed, you could write the first master scene heading of the above example like this:

```
INT. RICK'S CAFE - THE BAR - NIGHT
```

The above heading names the master location first and then one secondary location. Then, later in the master scene, we can go to the

```
GAMING ROOM
```

And so on.

If you wish, you can follow a master scene heading with a secondary scene heading.

```
INT. RICK'S CAFE - NIGHT

THE BAR
```

Once we go outside Rick's Café (that is, an exterior camera position), then we have a new master location that calls for a new master scene heading.

Where am I?

The following example is an incorrect use of a secondary scene heading. It states that there is a library on the beach. What is needed is a new master scene heading: INT. LIBRARY - DAY. Here's the bad example:

```
EXT. BEACH - DAY

Marion runs through the waves.

LIBRARY

Marion reads a book.
```

Directing the camera

Another advantage of using secondary headings is that you can direct the camera without using camera terms. In effect, your goal in spec writing is to direct the mind's eye of the reader. Suppose you want to focus on characters in an intense scene. Instead of the common shooting-script notation ANGLE ON LARRY or CLOSE ON LARRY, you simply write:

```
LARRY

reaches behind his back and produces a dagger.

OLGA

laughs heartily.
```

Now you are using character names as secondary headings, and the story flows easily without being encumbered by camera directions. Keep in mind that when you use a name as a secondary heading, you're communicating to readers that the camera is on that person until the next heading. When the camera is on Olga, we can't see Larry.

Of course, the above could also have been written as follows without the use of secondary headings.

Larry reaches behind his back and produces a dagger.

Olga laughs heartily.

It's all up to you. Here is another example of how to use secondary scene headings. The scene opens with a master scene heading that establishes the master location.

INT. CONVENIENCE STORE - NIGHT

A man wearing a werewolf Halloween mask enters.

AT THE COUNTER

the clerk freezes in fear.

IN THE AISLE

a young couple faints together.

AT THE COUNTER

the masked man opens a large paper sack.

                    MASKED MAN
           Trick or treat.

The same scene could be revised for a cleaner look. That's because, in the above example, the secondary scene headings are not needed to break up the short scene. So even though the above example is correct, the following is also correct and may be preferred.

INT. CONVENIENCE STORE - NIGHT

A man wearing a werewolf Halloween mask enters. The clerk at the counter freezes in fear.

In one of the aisles, a young couple faints together.

The masked man steps toward the clerk and opens a Halloween sack.

                    MASKED MAN
           Trick or treat.

Action scenes
Secondary headings can become especially helpful in action scenes.

EXT. SKY ABOVE THE MEDITERRANEAN - DAY

An enemy plane gets behind Billy's fighter (Eagle One). To his left, Jimmy's fighter (Eagle Two) cruises. Below them is the Mediterranean Sea.

EAGLE TWO COCKPIT

Jimmy glances to his right at Eagle One.

>   JIMMY
>   Look out, Billy!

JUST ABOVE THE WATER

The enemy fighter closes on Eagle One.

>   JIMMY (V.O.)
>   He's on your tail!

Eagle One dodges and weaves while the enemy fires at him, missing.

EAGLE ONE COCKPIT

Billy pulls up on the stick.

>   BILLY
>   Thanks for the tip!

Allow your story to flow
Avoid ending a sentence with a scene heading.

Rick struts into the

GAMING ROOM

However, if you do end a scene with a scene heading, omit the period. Never place punctuation of any kind at the end of a heading. Concerning the above example, my advice is to let your prose flow with something like this:

```
Rick struts into the

GAMING ROOM

where he spots a discouraged young man near the roulette
wheel.
```

Here is one final example:

```
INT. SMITH HOUSE - LIVING ROOM - DAY

John slams the front door and races down the

HALLWAY

and into his

BEDROOM

where he dives on top of his bed and sobs.
```

[E] SPACING BETWEEN SCENES

Do you double-space or triple-space before a master scene heading? I recommend double-spacing unless your script is under 90 pages in length and needs to look longer. Double-space means just one line of space between two elements. For example, if I were using a typewriter, at the end of a paragraphs, I would hit the "Enter" key (or "Return" key) twice. That would leave one line of space between two paragraphs, which is the case for all paragraphs in this book.

Triple-spacing is fine before master scene headings. However, double-space before and after any other kind of heading, including secondary scene headings. Triple-spacing before secondary scene headings looks odd and incongruent because it breaks up the master scene. Imagine an extra space before the secondary scene headings in the above example.

If you have a driving desire to triple-space before each new master scene heading, that's okay, but double-space before all other types of headings, including secondary headings to maintain a natural flow for the eye. If your formatting software makes this cumbersome, then don't be unduly concerned; it is not a script-threatening situation. Maybe you should consider changing the "space before" default to "1" (same as double-space) rather than "2" (same as triple-space). All examples in *The Bible* are double-spaced.

As mentioned in the "17 Commandments," do not number your scenes in a spec script. This is done by a production person after the final draft is sold and the script has gone into production.

It's perfectly okay to end a page on a scene heading, but try not to do that. Unless your script is overly long, move the heading to the top of the next page. Again, your formatting software will handle this for you.

SPECIAL HEADINGS

Other common scene headings are the MONTAGE, the SERIES OF SHOTS, the INSERT, the FLASHBACK, DREAMS, and so on. All follow the same basic formatting pattern, although variations abound.

[F] MONTAGE AND SERIES OF SHOTS

If I didn't use the MONTAGE at [F] on the sample script, I would need more master scene headings than Carter has little liver pills. A MONTAGE is a sequence of brief actions and/or images expressing a single concept or idea, such as a passage of time, falling in love, places within a geographical location, training (as in the movie *Rocky*), or a stream of consciousness. Usually that concept is included as part of the MONTAGE heading, as you will see in the example below.

Montage examples
Here's a common format for the MONTAGE. The concept or main idea is "having fun."

```
MONTAGE - SUZY AND BILL HAVE FUN TOGETHER

-- They run along the beach. Suzy raises her countenance
against the ocean spray.

-- They bicycle through a park.

-- Bill buys Suzy ice cream at a small stand. She stuffs it
into his face. The patrons chuckle.
```

If the MONTAGE takes place within a scene, then return BACK TO SCENE. (In the sample script "The Perspicacious Professor," we return BACK TO THE CLASSROOM.) Otherwise, double-space and type the next master scene heading. It's okay to type END MONTAGE before the next scene heading if desired. For example:

```
END MONTAGE
```

or

```
                                        END MONTAGE.
```

If you wish, include dialogue in a MONTAGE sequence, but generally the focus should be on beats of action or visual images.

If you wish to specifically identify the locations within MONTAGE, use one of the following methods:

```
MONTAGE - SUZY AND BILL HAVE FUN TOGETHER

-- A beach -- They race across the sand. Suzy raises her
countenance against the ocean spray.

-- A park -- They bicycle down meandering paths.

-- An ice cream stand -- Bill buys Suzy an ice cream cone.
She stuffs it into his face. The patrons chuckle.
```

The above locations could be placed in CAPS, as follows.

```
MONTAGE - SUZY AND BILL HAVE FUN TOGETHER

-- EXT. BEACH - DAY -- They race across the sand. Suzy
raises her countenance against the ocean spray.

- EXT. PARK - DAY -- They bicycle down meandering paths.

-- EXT. ICE CREAM STAND - NIGHT -- Bill buys Suzy an ice
cream cone. She stuffs it into his face. The patrons
chuckle.
```

All of the above styles are correct and can also be used with the SERIES OF SHOTS.

Series of shots example

Similar to the MONTAGE is the SERIES OF SHOTS, consisting of a chronology of quick shots that tell a story. They lead to some dramatic resolution or dramatic action, whereas a MONTAGE usually focuses on a single concept. Usually, the main idea of the SERIES OF SHOTS is included in the heading, but not always. Here's an example of a SERIES OF SHOTS:

```
SERIES OF SHOTS - JOHN GETS EVEN

A) John lifts a handgun from his desk drawer.

B) John strides down the sidewalk, hand in pocket.

C) John arrives at an apartment building.

D) Mary answers the door. John pulls the trigger. A stream
of water hits Mary in the face.
```

Those letters numbering the shots could be replaced with dashes, as with the MONTAGE, or omitted altogether.

Montage vis-a-vis series of shots
Generally, the MONTAGE is used more than the SERIES OF SHOTS. Even when the sequence is a true SERIES OF SHOTS, the MONTAGE format is often used. If you wish, you can omit the dashes or alpha numbering. The terms are sometimes used interchangeably.

Generally, a MONTAGE in the script is scored to music in the movie. For example, the above MONTAGE of Suzy and Bill could be lengthened to be accompanied by a love song. Thus, the word MONTAGE often means: *Put the hit song here.* But don't *you* indicate the musical selection you prefer.

FLASHBACKS AND DREAMS

Since the FLASHBACK is often abused by beginning writers, make sure that your use of it pays off dramatically.

In terms of formatting, there are numerous correct methods. The overriding principle is to be clear.

Method 1
In the example below, the flashback is labeled like a montage.

```
FLASHBACK - TRAIN ACCIDENT
```

```
David sees the train coming and jumps on the train tracks.
He laughs; he's playing chicken with the train.

With the train nearly upon him, he tries to leap from the
tracks, but his foot catches on a rail tie.

BACK TO PRESENT DAY
```

The above method is designed for short flashbacks that happen within a scene. For longer flashbacks, consider one of the following methods:

Method 2

```
FLASHBACK - EXT. TRAIN TRACKS - NIGHT
```

Method 3

```
EXT. TRAIN TRACKS - NIGHT - FLASHBACK
```

or

```
EXT. TRAIN TRACKS - NIGHT (FLASHBACK)
```

If you use any one of the above notations, then the next scene heading (let's say it's for an office scene) would follow the same pattern and would look something like this:

```
INT. OFFICE - DAY - BACK TO PRESENT DAY
```

or

```
INT. OFFICE - DAY (BACK TO PRESENT DAY)
```

or, for Method 2:

```
BACK TO PRESENT DAY - INT. OFFICE - DAY
```

Alternate flashback endings for Methods 2 and 3
At the end of a flashback, you can use one of the following alternative methods to end the flashback.

```
                                        END OF FLASHBACK.


INT. OFFICE - DAY
```

Method 4

If a flashback is more than one scene in length, you will use Method 2 or 3 for your first flashback scene heading. Subsequent scene headings will be written as normal scene headings without the word FLASHBACK. The reader will assume that each scene that follows that first flashback scene is part of the flashback until he sees END OF FLASHBACK or BACK TO PRESENT DAY in some form. Here's an example:

```
EXT. TRAIN TRACKS - NIGHT - FLASHBACK

Barry sees the train speeding toward him and leaps from the
tracks, but his foot catches on a rail tie.

INT. HOSPITAL - NIGHT

Barry lies on a gurney. A doctor pulls a sheet over his
head.

INT. OFFICE - DAY - BACK TO PRESENT DAY
```

Method 5

An alternative method is to label the entire flashback comprised of more than one scene as a flashback sequence. I prefer this method to Method 4 because of its clarity.

```
BEGIN FLASHBACK SEQUENCE

EXT. TRAIN TRACKS - NIGHT
```

And then write out all the scenes in sequence, just as you would normally write scenes, and then end the sequence with this:

```
END FLASHBACK SEQUENCE

INT. OFFICE - DAY
```

Quick flashes

On rare occasion, you might have a situation where a character recalls a series of quick flashbacks in succession. Handle that with the same format you'd use for a MONTAGE or a SERIES OF SHOTS.

```
QUICK FLASHES - DUKE'S BASEBALL MEMORIES

-- Duke slides home safe. Jubilant teammates scramble to
congratulate him.
```

-- Duke, playing shortstop, snags a hot grounder, and tosses the man out at first.

-- Duke swings at a fastball and watches it sail over the left-field fence.

BACK TO SCENE

In effect, the above is a FLASHBACK MONTAGE.

If you have just one quick flashback, use the following format:

QUICK FLASHBACK

Duke strikes out.

BACK TO SCENE

Flashbacks, dreams, and daydreams are written in present tense.

Dreams, daydreams, imaginings, mirages, and visions
Handle these events the same way you handle flashbacks.

DREAM - SID IN THE JUNGLE

If your character has a dream sequence, format it as you would a flashback sequence.

If your character has a vision, the formatting is the same:

DAME NOSTRA'S VISION - WORLD WAR FIVE

Label all dreams, visions, daydreams, nightmares, flashforwards, and flashbacks as such. It's not usually in your best interest to hide the fact from the reader to surprise him, although there are exceptions to this advice. And please don't open your movie with a dream and have your character "awaken bolt-upright" in her bed; that has become cliché. If you must use the cliché, give it a fresh twist.

Animated scene
Suppose you have a short animated segment in one of your scenes. Use the same formatting pattern we have been discussing.

ANIMATION - SILLY BILLY MEETS THE MONKEY MAN

or

EXT. PET STORE - DAY - ANIMATION

[G] INSERT

The INSERT (also known as the CUTAWAY in some shooting scripts) is used to bring something small into full frame. This can be a book, news headline, sign, contract, letter, or a leather pouch filled with mints. In the case of the leather pouch on the sample script, I did not use an INSERT. If I had, it would have looked like this:

```
INSERT - THE PROFESSOR'S POUCH

His fingers deftly lift a candy mint.

BACK TO THE CLASSROOM
```

In my opinion, it simply wasn't necessary. Use the INSERT only when it is important to draw special attention to the item you want to highlight. In the case of a letter or a document with a lot of text, you may wish to use the INSERT as follows.

```
INT. LIMO - NIGHT

As Sylvester steps into the limo, the chauffeur hands him a
letter and bats his eyes like an ostrich.

                    CHAUFFEUR
          Your wife, sir.


Sylvester tears the letter open as the door SLAMS shut.

INSERT - THE LETTER, which reads:

          "Dearest Darling Sylvester,

          I am leaving for Loon City to start a
          turkey ranch. Don't try to follow, my
          peacock, or I'll have your cockatoo
          strangled. There's plenty of chicken in
          the refrigerator. I love you, you goosey
          duck.

          Your ex-chick, Birdie"

BACK IN THE LIMO
```

Sylvester smiles like the cat that ate the canary.

>   SYLVESTER
>   So long, Tweetie Pie.

Notice that the contents of the note are indented like dialogue; however, quotation marks are used to quote the letter. To indent notes like the one above using Movie Magic Screenwriter or Final Draft, see the next section entitled "Indenting with formatting software."

Once you have written the INSERT, it is good manners to bring us BACK TO SCENE. In any situation like this, opt for clarity and a smooth flow of the story.

Aside from notes and letters, such as the one above, I find little use for the INSERT these days. Just use narrative description. Here's an example of an *unnecessary* INSERT:

INSERT - COLT .45 ON THE TABLE

BACK TO SCENE

Although the above is technically correct, you can avoid the use of CAPS (which are hard on the eyes) and write the above as narrative description, as follows:

A Colt .45 lies on the table.

It is more important to be readable and clear than to use formatting conventions that might encumber the "read." Besides, the description implies that the gun will fill most of the movie frame, so you have the CLOSE UP you wanted.

INDENTING WITH FORMATTING SOFTWARE

Most formatting software programs will not allow you to indent 10 spaces unless you first type a character cue (character name). Below are instructions on how to indent in special situations such as notes (see previous section), SUPERs, Emails and Text Messages, and similar situations. These instructions are for current versions of the software as of this writing. Check "Bible Updates" at my website (**www.keepwriting. com**) for the most recent information.

If you use **Movie Magic Screenwriter**, make sure the ruler is visible at the top of the document. If not, click on "View" and then "Ruler." Now, click once inside the paragraph you wish to alter and then simply drag the markers on the ruler to where you want them—2.5 on the left and 6.5 on the right.

Here's an alternative method: Select the paragraph you wish to change, and, then from the menus on top, click on Format > Cheat > Element (F3). Then, change the margins to 2.5 on the left and 2.5 on the right, and click "OK."

If you use **Final Draft**, make sure your ruler is visible at the top of the document. If not, click "View," then click on "Ruler." Click anywhere in the paragraph whose margins (aka indents) you want to adjust. Then, with your mouse, drag the square underneath the hourglass at the left of the ruler to 2.5, and drag the margin marker on the right to 6.0.

If you'd like to keep this new element for future use, follow these directions: Click on "Format" and then "Elements." You'll see a list of elements. Below that, click on "New." At the top left, name the new element, for example, "Special indent." Under the "Paragraph" tab, under "Indents," select 2.5 for your left margin and 6.0 for your right margin. Click "OK." To save as a permanent template, click "File" and "Save as." You should be able to find your way from there.

INTERCUT

A full explanation of this special heading plus examples can be found under "Telephone Conversations" in the "Dialogue" chapter. As you view the examples, keep in mind that you can INTERCUT any two scenes, not just two scenes that are part of a telephone conversation.

[H] ESTABLISHING SHOT

Often, at the beginning of a movie, sequence, or scene, there is an establishing shot to give us an idea of where on earth we are. There are two ways to present an establishing shot.

Incorrect:

```
EXT. NEW YORK CITY - DAY - ESTABLISHING
```

Correct:

```
EXT. NEW YORK CITY - DAY
```

Manhattan sparkles in the sunlight.

The second, "correct" example is preferred because it is more interesting, plus it directs the camera without using camera directions. It's obviously a long shot of the entire city that establishes where we are. Also notice that it is not necessary to add the word ESTABLISHING at the end of the scene heading.

[I] CAMERA PLACEMENT

In the scene beginning at reference code [B] in "The Perspicacious Professor," the camera is inside the classroom. We know this because the master scene heading is INT. SMALL CLASSROOM - DAY. The INT. means that the camera is inside the classroom. However, the camera can SEE (at the first reference code [I]) out through the window to the young woman in pigtails and a pinafore.

Likewise, in the scene that follows, the camera is outside the classroom (by virtue of the EXT.) "looking" into the classroom as the professor performs cartwheels down the aisle (at the second reference code [I]). Thus, the window is used as a transitional device between scenes.

Narrative description

A *narrative* is a story, and *description* is that which describes; thus, narrative description *describes the story*. Specifically, it describes the three elements of 1) *action*, 2) *setting and characters*, and 3) *sounds*. We'll break these three down to smaller units for purposes of discussion.

TECHNIQUES FOR WRITING EFFECTIVE DESCRIPTION

Narrative description is written in present tense because we view a film in present time. Even flashbacks are written in present tense. Double-space between paragraphs and do not indent.

Write lean

Keep your narrative description (and dialogue) on the lean side, providing only what is absolutely necessary to progress the story while emphasizing important actions and moments. Be clean and lean.

Limit your paragraphs to a maximum of four lines (not four sentences), although I would strive for paragraphs of one or two lines. Big blocks of black ink can make a reader black out.

You can space once or twice after periods, with twice being the traditional method. In narrative description (and dialogue), make dashes with a space, hyphen, hyphen, space -- like that.

As a very general rule (meaning there can be many exceptions), allow one paragraph per beat of action or image. When a reader reads your paragraph, she should clearly "see" and "hear" what you describe. The result will be that she will "feel" what you want her to feel.

In the paragraph following [B] on the sample script, you'll see a few things that I feel are necessary to set up in order for the sequence to work. First, my professor "looks" different from the stereotypical professor. Second, I establish that this scene is about script formatting. Finally, the professor has a leather pouch filled with candy mints. The pouch of mints is of tremendous importance to the story, so I take two lines to describe it. I could have chosen to give the pouch a separate paragraph, to give it more emphasis and to imply that the pouch deserves a separate camera shot.

Please notice that I describe very little in this classroom. I don't even describe how the professor dresses. In this scene, I don't need to. Generally, physical descriptions of locations and characters should be sparse. In fact, the only physical description I give of the classroom is the fact that there is a window near Charlie. This is mentioned only because of its importance later as a transitional element.

Some visual images need just the briefest of descriptions. For example, I might describe an ordinary conference room as exactly that: "an ordinary conference room." The color of the walls and the number of seats may not be important. However, if, later in the scene, someone throws a TV at the discussion leader, I may describe the room as follows:

```
INT. CONFERENCE ROOM - DAY

A TV sits on a table in a corner.
```

Then again, there may be a lot that is unique about a different conference room that needs to be mentioned. Here's an example:

```
INT. CONFERENCE ROOM - DAY

About a dozen businesspeople sit on leather sofas that form
a circle around a distinguished-looking WOMAN dressed to
the nines. She stands without pulpit or props, and smiles
confidently.
```

Dramatize

If you're writing a dramatic scene, then dramatize it. If two principals are in a fistfight, don't just write *They fight*; describe the action. You don't need to choreograph every move, but you do need to *describe the action*.

In long action scenes, alternate between individual specific actions and action summaries. In the first sword fight scene of *The Princess Bride,* William Goldman does just that. For example, after describing some specific parries, thrusts, and other moves, he provides this summary of what happens next:

```
The two men almost fly across the rocky terrain, never losing
balance, never stumbling. The battle rages with incredible
finesse, first one and then the other gaining the advantage.
```

Use short paragraphs, and emphasize specific images, actions, and emotions. What follows is a partial description of the key moment in a baseball game.

```
Duke sneers at the catcher. Taps the bat twice on the plate
and spits. A brown wad splatters on the plate.

The catcher refuses to notice. Keeps his eyes ahead.

Smiley steps off the rubber. Nervously works the rosin bag.
Wipes the sweat from his forehead with his arm.

Duke leans over the plate like he owns it. Allows himself a
self-satisfied grin.
```

Be choosy on your details

Unless important to the plot, incidental actions—such as *he lights her cigarette, she moves to the table, she stands up*—should be avoided. The actions in the above baseball example—*tapping the plate, spitting*—would be incidental if this weren't the bottom of the ninth, two outs, score tied, and a three-two count.

If your character raises her cup of coffee to her lips, that may not important enough to describe . . . unless there is poison in the cup.

Lean writing is appreciated and expected by Hollywood professionals. The exception is a key dramatic or emotional moment, but in most cases, err on the side of brevity. A key principle of spec writing is, *Less is more.* That means you should say as much as you can with as few words as you can. For example, what follows is an overwritten paragraph describing the setting, a boxing gym:

```
The gym is littered with good wrappers, leftover hot dogs
and tacos, gym clothes, and other debris. It looks like no
one has cleaned it in over a month. It is truly a mess.
There is a push broom in the far corner. The boxing ring is
smaller than normal size, with two wooden stools outside the
ring at opposite corners.
```

The following describes the same gym, and is taken out of the spec script for *Rocky*. As you can see, it's all that's needed to give the reader a visual sense of the setting.

```
The gym looks like a garbage can turned inside out. The ring
is small enough to ensure constant battle.
```

Describe only what we see and hear

It is easy to slip and include information that cannot appear on the movie screen. For example, the following cannot appear on the movie screen, and, thus, should not be included in narrative description:

```
When she saw him, it reminded her of two years ago when they
first met.
```

Memories, thoughts, and realizations cannot visually appear on the movie screen, but you can describe actions, facial expressions, or gestures that suggest them. As a general rule, only describe what the audience can actually see on the movie screen and hear on the soundtrack, such as sounds. (See "Describing what we see and creating mood" in Book IV.)

Use specific words and action verbs

Because a screenplay is written in present tense, it's easy to find yourself writing like this: John *is looking* at Mary. Suzy *is walking* past the cafe. Snake Koslowsky *is seated* on the couch. Replace those passive expressions with sentences written in present-tense active voice: John *looks* at Mary. Suzy *walks* past the cafe. Snake *sits* on the couch.

Now go one step further and create something even more active and concrete: John *gawks* at Mary, or John *gazes* at Mary. Suzy *scampers* down the sidewalk, or Suzy *sashays* down the sidewalk. Snake *coils* on the couch. Now the reader can more easily visualize the action and gain a greater sense of the character as well—and without the help of a single adverb. Use concrete verbs as characterization tools.

Concrete, specific verbs and nouns also help us "see." *He is walking to the boat* communicates less about character and action than *He staggers to the yacht.* And no adjectives are needed in this instance: Instead of *He pulls out a gun*, write *He pulls out a Colt .45 automatic.* Use specific language. As a general rule, write short, crisp sentences. Favor an entertaining style rather than an informative style. The following paragraph is from *The Shawshank Redemption.* Notice the four active verbs.

```
His wingtip shoes crunch on gravel. Loose bullets scatter to
the ground. The bourbon bottle drops and shatters.
```

Action should comment on character

As you can see from the above section, your narrative description should reveal something about character and about the story. For example, don't write

```
Charlie enters.
```

Instead, ask yourself *how* Charlie enters. Make it a *character thing* by being more *specific*. Let every action tell the reader (and the eventual audience) something about the character and/or the story. Here are two examples:

```
Charlie silently slithers in.
```

```
Charlie limps in and, on his third try, kicks the door shut.
```

Avoid redundancies

Steer clear of repetition in your narrative descriptions.

Redundant:

```
INT. CLASSROOM - DAY
```

```
Calcutta enters the classroom.
```

Correct:

```
INT. CLASSROOM - DAY
```

```
Calcutta tiptoes in.
```

Redundant:

```
EXT. OUTSIDE THE SCHOOL - DAY
```

Correct:

```
EXT. SCHOOL - DAY
```

Redundant:

```
He glares at her with anger.
```

```
                    STEVE
              (angrily)
        I feel like breaking your nose!!!!!
```

Lose the exclamation points; you're not writing a want ad. The following is better:

```
He glares at her.
```

```
                    STEVE
         I feel like breaking your nose.
```

. . . And you might not need the glaring.

ACTION STACKING

For action sequences, the following style (called *action stacking*) may be used. The example is from *Wall-E*.

```
Robot and faithful cockroach return home.

Wally stops short of the threshold.

Stares at the ground.

Continues staring.
```

If you decide to use this technique, keep in mind that the sentences must be concise and never over a line in length. Also, you should use the device fairly consistently throughout your screenplay. I worry about writers getting too caught up in stacking actions but losing their story focus. Additionally, most readers are used to seeing the traditional method of writing action. For those reasons, I seldom recommend action stacking. However, I applaud the idea of concise sentences and brief paragraphs when writing action scenes.

[J] CHARACTER FIRST APPEARANCES

The name DR. FORMAT (at the first reference code [J] on the sample script) is in CAPS because this is his first appearance in the screenplay. CHARLIE (at the second reference code [J]) also appears in CAPS because it's the first time he appears in the story. So why wasn't "twenty students" capitalized? Because they are a group and weren't important enough to warrant drawing the reader's attention to them. In fact, as a general guideline, do not CAP groups of people, just individuals. You can break this rule without any consequences; it's not a burning issue.

When a character who is identified only by function or characteristic—BURLY MAN, BELLY DANCER, MUTANT—first appears in a script, then place that nomenclature in CAPS. When a character is mentioned for the first time in a speech, don't CAP the name. CAP the name only when that character actually appears in the story.

When a name in CAPS is followed by a possessive, the *S* is placed in lowercase:

```
PENELOPE's scream shatters the silence.
```

When to withhold a character's name

As a general rule, name your characters at the moment they first appear in the screenplay. Doing that avoids confusion. It's difficult for a reader to keep track of a YOUNG MAN who, pages later, is called JOE. That's partly because someone referred to as YOUNG MAN is obviously not important to the story, or he would have a name. Make it easy on readers; name your characters (those that have names) when they first appear.

On occasion, a character speaks off screen before we see her. In such cases it would be okay to use the following character cue for that first instance and then refer to her by her name thereafter.

```
                    WOMAN (O.S.)
          Hey, Big Guy.


Tarzan turns to see JANE.
```

The following is also correct and is preferred because it is absolutely clear.

```
Tarzan faces a pride of lions and looks scared.


                    JANE (O.S.)
          Hey, Big Guy.


Tarzan turns to see JANE, 25, a beauty wearing a leopard
skin. She tosses him the end of a swinging vine and feigns a
yawn.
```

There may be some situations where it is dramatically effective to withhold the true name of the character, even for several scenes. In such cases, be absolutely clear about who is who when the name of the character is finally disclosed. In the following short example, we initially believe the Shadowy Figure will do harm.

```
EXT. ALLEY - NIGHT

Sandy hurries past a garbage bin. A SHADOWY FIGURE
approaches her from behind.
```

```
                    SHADOWY FIGURE
         Sandy!
```

Sandy nearly screams until she sees that the Shadowy Figure is actually Bob.

CHARACTER INTRODUCTIONS

When a character first appears in the script, you have an opportunity to suggest something of his/her nature. In most cases we do not need to know the character's height, weight, hair color, or the fact that she looks exactly like Cher. Describe these specific physical characteristics only if they are critical to the plot. For example, the lead in *Legally Blonde* must wear blond hair. Do not give a driver's license description of your character, and do not pin the name of a famous actor or actress on your character, because it limits who can star in your screenplay. Your characters should not derive from other movies; they should be original.

Here is how one client describes his contemporary teenage protagonist:

```
Max, 17, is a pirate in ripped jeans.
```

That tells us a lot about Max with just a few words. Notice that Max not only wears certain clothes that comment on his personality or nature or attitude, but he's been somewhere before he got here—he's a human with emotions and a past.

Usually, it's important to include the character's age. Here is a description of a character in *My Best Friend's Wedding*:

```
This is DIGGER DOWNES, 36, kind eyes, an intellectual's
mouth, Savile Row's most unobtrusive and conservative chalk-
stripe suit. He's gay, but you wouldn't guess it. Loyal and
wise, and you might.
```

Notice that the physical description of Digger is qualitative. It characterizes him without forcing an actor to have a certain color hair, eyes, and build. How about the following from *The Social Network*?

```
MARK ZUCKERBERG is a sweet looking 19-year-old whose lack of
any physically intimidating attributes masks a complicated
and dangerous anger.
```

The character description is the one instance where you can provide some information that cannot immediately appear on the movie screen. Here's what *not* to write: *Jenny used to be a cocktail waitress and had an affair with Jane's husband just a year ago, although Jane doesn't know it yet.* You cannot write stuff like that because there's too much that cannot appear on the movie screen. How will the audience get a sense of this? What you can do is say that Mark is Jenny's wife or that Jane is Jenny's sister— you can get away with defining the relationship.

Here's one of my favorite character descriptions from another client's screenplay:

```
ANGIE (45) dresses too young for her age and gets away with
it.
```

The above, in effect, describes character. We understand something about that person. Here's a similar approach:

```
FRAN KOZLOWSKI, 29, enters the room. She's conspicuously
attractive -- like a house about to go on the market.
```

The following from still another client emphasizes the contrasts within his character:

```
WEEF, 30s, half slob, half-connoisseur: he may wear a dirty
beer t-shirt, but it's an imported beer.
```

In *Body Heat*, Teddy Lewis (Mickey Rourke) is described as "a rock-and-roll arsonist." And Alvin Sargent, in *Ordinary People*, introduces Beth by describing her kitchen. Note these words and phrases in the following excerpt: sharply; cold, hard light; perfectly organized; neat as a pin.

```
[Beth] turns away sharply. The refrigerator door opens and
the cold, hard light reveals that it is perfectly organized.
The entire Jarret kitchen is as neat as a pin.
```

Be original in your character descriptions. Rather than "She was the most beautiful babe there," Shakespeare wrote, in *Romeo and Juliet*, she was "like a snowy dove trooping with crows."

Setting descriptions
As with your character descriptions, describe settings briefly to set mood or tone. Do you recall the description of the boxing ring from *Rocky* I provided a few pages back? Here's another example, this one from one of my clients:

```
The room reeks of discount Tiparillos and stale pizza, as
four sleazy-looking Godfather wannabes play poker.

STANLEY BENENATI, 42 and looking about as good as you can in
a mauve polyester leisure suit, throws down his cards.
```

Do we really need any more detail than that to get the picture? And notice that any physical descriptions of the character or clothing serve to comment on the character (or nature) of the character.

VISUAL CHARACTERIZATION

It is often effective to give your character a visual identification, such as Charlie's chocolate-covered face and associated buzzing flies on the sample script. Where would the *Men in Black* (or *The Matrix*'s Neo) be without their sunglasses? And don't *Napoleon Dynamite*'s moon boots and half-opened eyes help make him unique?

CHARACTER NAMES

All of your major characters deserve names, as do your important minor characters. Characters with only one or two lines of dialogue *may* be given names, but usually *aren't* given names so that the reader knows not to focus on them.

When you give a character a name, especially in the first 20 or so pages, the reader believes that that character is important enough to remember. If you present too many characters too fast, the reader can be overwhelmed. For that reason, some minor characters and all characters with no speaking parts should be referred to in terms of their function or characteristics or both. For example, if you have three technicians who only appear in one scene, refer to them as GRUFF TECH, SEXY TECH, SHY GEEK, and so on.

Suppose you have six police officers speaking in a scene. You may choose to refer to them as OFFICER 1, OFFICER 2, OFFICER 3, and so on; but I don't recommend it. First, limit the number of speaking officers to one or two. If any of those six officers is an important character, try to give him most of the lines. If these officers are not important (have no lines, or just have one line, or only appear in one or two scenes), distinguish them in some visual way: MACHO COP, TOOTHPICK, CHUBBY COP. This makes them easier to visualize while signaling to the reader that they are not of major importance.

What about unseen characters?

In the excerpt below, I use sound to communicate audibly that there is an unseen character lurking nearby. The audience will know he or she is in the scene by the sound of the camera.

```
EXT. PUBLIC BUILDING - DAY

James Connors hurries up the cement stairs.

An unseen person clicks the shutter of a 35mm camera.
Another click. And again as James rushes into the building.
```

See "Sounds" below for another version of the same scene.

[K] SIGNS, NEWS HEADLINES, BOOK TITLES, NOTES, AND LETTERS

At code [K] in the sample script, I chose to write the words "CINEMA DEPT." in CAPS and to enclose them in quotation marks. I could have as easily not used CAPS while still using the quotation marks. That would also be proper. However, I wouldn't use italics or bold to set apart anything.

Put quotation marks around any words in narrative description that you want the audience to see and read, including news headlines, nameplates, song titles, book titles, names of magazines, plaques, signs on doors, the time on the clock, etc. Sometimes the contents of notes, letters, or documents need to be shown. In those cases, you may want to use the INSERT as earlier described.

[L] SOUNDS

It is not necessary to place sounds in CAPS. However, if you wish, you may do so. Some writers place only important sounds in CAPS. On page 1 of the sample script, I could have placed the sound BUZZING in CAPS as a matter of preference. I may use CAPS or not, since both styles are correct. Do not use the archaic SFX. BUZZING FLIES.

In the scene above, which takes place in a "public building," I did not place any sounds in CAPS. Of course, I could have, and that would be perfectly fine and may be preferred in this particular instance to emphasize the photographs being taken. Here's an example:

```
EXT. PUBLIC BUILDING - DAY

James Connors hurries up the cement stairs.

An unseen person CLICKS the shutter of a 35mm camera.
Another CLICK. And AGAIN as James rushes into the building.
```

My personal preference is to put only important sounds in CAPS to make them pop out. If you CAP all sounds, the reader may not notice any of them in particular. Besides, CAPS are hard on the eyes.

MOS

Occasionally, characters speak silently, which is to say that we see their lips moving and they are obviously talking, but no sound is heard. Other times, a scene may play in complete silence. In such situations, indicate "without sound" with the term MOS. (The term *MOS* originated with Austrian-born director Eric von Stroheim, who would tell his crew, "Ve'll shoot dis mit out sound." Thus, MOS stands for "mit out sound.") Here's an example of how to use the device:

```
The two lovers flirt MOS in the balcony.
```

You could just as easily write this as follows:

```
The two lovers flirt in the balcony. Their words cannot be
heard.
```

As you might guess, MOS is a useful device. However, don't use it just to use it. Use it only if you have a compelling dramatic purpose.

[M] SPECIAL EFFECTS

A key moment at code [M] in the sample script "The Perspicacious Professor" is Charlie catching a mint on his nose and barking like a seal. In the shoot, this may require a special effect. In the past, this may have been written FX. CHARLIE CATCHING A MINT ON HIS NOSE, but not now. (By the way, FX. and SPFX. both mean Special Effects; SFX. means Sound Effects.) There is another possible special effect at [M] on the second page of the sample script.

Don't use FX. or SPFX, or any technical term. They break up the flow of the read. Besides, most special effects can be described without using technical terms. Here's another example:

```
Suddenly, the room turns green and the walls resemble
mirrors. Sue touches a wall and it is liquid, like mercury.
```

We don't need to type "FX." to signal that the above requires a special effect. The description is adequate for a spec script.

On rare occasions, you may want to MORPH from one image to another, or indicate that the action takes place in SLOW MOTION. Any such technical instructions should be placed in CAPS. (See "When to break formatting rules" in Book IV for an example of how to format time lapse.)

SUPERS

SUPER is short for *superimpose*. Use this device anytime you need to superimpose some words on the screen. For example:

```
SUPER: "Five years later"
```

If you wish, you can place the superimposed words in CAPS:

```
SUPER: "FIVE YEARS LATER"
```

A third method indents the superimposed words. This is mainly used for long super-impositions; however, it's okay to use it for short superimpositions. And by the way, it doesn't matter if you follow the content of a SUPER with a period or not.

```
SUPER:

        "FIVE YEARS LATER."
```

Most SUPERs are used to orient the audience to time or place. Here's an example:

```
EXT. HOSPITAL - NIGHT

EMTs rush a patient out of an ambulance and into the
hospital.
```

```
SUPER: "Bethesda Medical Hospital"
```

```
Scully's car comes to a stop. She steps out with her
cellular.
```

```
                    SCULLY
               (into cellular)
          Mulder? Are you there?
```

Please note that I followed the heading (or slug line) with a sentence of description. I want to first give the audience a visual image before presenting the SUPER that will appear over that image. It would be perfectly okay to follow the scene heading with the SUPER.

Avoid clever alternatives for the SUPER, such as the following:

```
The words "BETHESDA MEDICAL HOSPITAL" spell out across the
lower left of the screen.
```

Although technically correct, the above could be seen as taking liberties. Let other professionals decide where the words will be superimposed.

Suppose you want to superimpose a quote on the screen before the movie begins. This would be the correct format:

```
BLACK SCREEN
```

```
SUPER: "Two can live as cheaply as one, but only half as
long."
```

```
FADE IN:
```

If the quote or text you want to superimpose is very long, you should indent it like dialogue and enclose it in quotation marks.

```
BLACK SCREEN
```

```
SUPER:
          "Two can live as cheaply as one, but only
          half as long."
```

```
FADE IN:
```

For information on how to indent the content of SUPERs using Movie Magic Screenwriter or Final Draft, see "Indenting with formatting software" in the previous chapter.

Scrolls

If you are scrolling words up the movie screen, as in the first six *Star Wars* episodes, you would simply use the word SCROLL instead of SUPER.

Words on TV

What do you do if a character is watching something on TV and words appear on the TV screen? Do you use a SUPER for those? No. Use the TV as a secondary scene heading and write something like the following.

```
Selma turns on the television.

ON THE TV

A city is engulfed in flames. The word "BAGHDAD" appears at
the bottom of the screen.

BACK TO SELMA'S LIVING ROOM
```

[N] TRANSITIONS

On the sample script, the slamming of telephone receivers is a transitional ploy. I am suggesting to the reader (and director) that once Calcutta slams her phone, that we should CUT immediately to the professor slamming his phone. This situation could also be handled with the MATCH CUT, discussed next.

EDITING DIRECTIONS

If I wrote the transition described above to include the editing direction MATCH CUT, I would have written it as follows.

```
The dean CHORTLES. Calcutta smiles; then SLAMS the receiver.
```

                                                    MATCH CUT:

INT. CLASSROOM - DAY

The professor SLAMS the phone receiver.

The MATCH CUT is used to match an object or image from one scene to the next. The above transition of Calcutta slamming her phone receiver to the professor slamming his is an example. However, an editing direction is not necessary here because the transition is obvious. Use the MATCH CUT when the *match* is not already obvious.

It is not usually necessary to indicate transitions (editing directions) in spec scripts. The use of CUT TO is seldom necessary. Obviously, one must CUT at the end of a scene, so why indicate it? Avoid such editing tools as the WIPE, IRIS, FLIP, and DISSOLVE.

Here's my rule of thumb: Use an editing direction (or camera direction) when it is absolutely necessary to understand the story, or when its use helps link two scenes in a way that creates humor or drama, or improves continuity.

The editing direction is placed flush to the right margin. As an alternative, you can place the left margin of the transition at 6 inches from the left edge of the paper.

CAMERA DIRECTIONS

Let's break with current convention and rewrite this section (top of page 2 of "The Perspicacious Professor") utilizing our vast arsenal of camera and editing directions. Note as you read the bad example below how the technical directions detract from the story and slow down the read for the reader. (Note: CU means CLOSE-UP, and ECU means EXTREME CLOSE-UP.)

What follows is an example of poor spec writing.

INT. CLASSROOM - NEAR SUNSET

CU PROFESSOR SLAMMING the receiver of his toy phone.

PULL BACK and BOOM to ESTABLISH classroom.

PROFESSOR'S POV: CAMERA PANS the class.

                                                    DISSOLVE TO:

```
LOW ANGLE of the professor -- confident.
```

```
WIDE ANGLE of THE STUDENTS as they SIMMER with interest.
```

```
ZIP ZOOM TO ECU doorknob opening. PULL BACK TO REVEAL
Calcutta coming through the door. DOLLY WITH Calcutta's
SHUFFLING feet as she makes her way to her desk.
```

```
CLOSE ON the professor expounding.
```

```
SWIRLING SHOT of the professor in increasingly larger
concentric circles.
```

Please, I beg you, don't do this to your script! First, it breaks up the narrative flow and makes the script harder to read. Second, you take the chance of showing your ignorance of shooting script conventions. Third, professional readers are not pleased. So, go easy. Remember, the story's the thing. Concentrate on that. It's true that most shooting scripts (the scripts you buy to read) contain many such camera directions and technical devices. Keep in mind that these directions and devices were likely added *after* the script was sold (if it was a spec script) to prepare it for the shoot, or the script was developed by the production company.

Being fancy is chancy. There is an acceptable way to indicate all the camera directions your heart desires without using the technical terms. Simply be creative and write the script so that they're implied.

For example, at [N] on the sample script, I use the word "hand" to imply a CLOSE-UP or ANGLE of the phone SLAMMING. If Dr. Format "surveys" the class, that might imply a POV (point of view) shot, but certainly it is a MEDIUM SHOT of some kind. The students SIMMERING with interest is a REACTION SHOT of the entire class or REACTION SHOTS of individual students. See how I give the director a choice! If it's tremendously important to the scene that Charlie react strongly, I will write that reaction shot in a separate paragraph, as follows:

```
Charlie leaps from his seat and executes a flawless back-flip.
```

Although correct, avoid headings like the following: ANGLE ON CHARLIE, CLOSE ON CHARLIE, and ANOTHER ANGLE. You may decide to put the camera on Charlie in this way:

```
CHARLIE
```

```
leaps from his seat and executes a flawless back-flip.
```

The *spec* script's emphasis is on lean, visual, and readable writing. Your goal is to create images while avoiding the use of technical terms. Instead of CLOSE-UP OF DARLENE'S TEAR, write *A tear rolls down Darlene's cheek*. (It's obviously a CLOSE-UP.)

In conclusion, use camera directions and editing directions sparingly, only when they are needed to clarify the action, characterize a character, move the story forward, or add significantly to the story's impact.

WE SEE
Some developing writers use the camera directions WE SEE. Avoid this term, and don't place "We see" in CAPS if you do use it. Although correct, it is seldom the most interesting way to convey the action and details of the scene to your reader. However, there may be instances where it is necessary. Likewise, avoid "We move with," "We hear," and other first-person intrusions.

b.g. and f.g.
B.g. stands for *background* and f.g. stands for *foreground*. These terms may be used in your narrative description to clarify action (e.g., The T-Rex moves in the b.g.), but I recommend you use them sparingly. If you must put the T-Rex in the background, just write out the words: *The T-Rex moves in the background*. Or better yet:

```
Behind them lumbers the T-Rex.
```

Dramatize the action. Favor an entertaining style over an informative style.

[O] POV

Many writers use the POV (point of view) device instead of writing creatively. Since the POV is a camera direction, you want to avoid it in your spec script. Sometimes the POV needs to be used for story reasons; that's the case with certain important scenes in *Finding Neverland* where it's crucial that we see the scene from a particular character's view. But how should you format a POV in a spec script?

You can probably get away with the following, although I discourage it:

```
JOJO'S POV - The killer advances toward him.
```

Instead, write this:

```
Jojo watches the killer advance toward him.
```

You're still directing the camera, even though you're not using camera directions. In *Raiders of the Lost Ark,* "What he sees" is used in lieu of the POV. In a spec script, just write, "He sees. . ."

The heading at code [F] on the sample script could have been written THE PROFESSOR'S POV, and that would be technically correct. Instead, I avoided the inclusion of a camera direction, but still made it clear (at code [O]) that the spinning room is seen from the professor's point of view (POV).

At the second code [I] on the sample script, we see The Professor from Calcutta's point of view. This could have been written as Calcutta's POV, but that would interrupt the narrative flow.

Suppose you are writing a funeral scene and your character looks away to see something happening in the background. In a shooting script, that would be a POV shot. Here's the example in spec style:

```
Sharon looks up the

CEMETERY ROAD

where three teenagers break into her car.


                    RABBI (O.S.)
          The Lord giveth and the Lord taketh away.
```

PHANTOM POV

The Phantom POV is used when we don't know the identity of the character sneaking through the bushes toward your unaware hero. Just write: *Someone [or something] pulls away tree branches and moves closer and closer to an unsuspecting Giselda.*

Let's imagine a scene by a lake. Children are playing, and you have a compelling story reason to view this from underneath the water. Since EXT. and INT. refer to where the camera is, we could open with the camera at the lake shore, establishing the children on the shore. We could then cut to the camera underneath the lake. The master location is the lake and the secondary locations that are part of the lake are the Shore and Underwater.

```
EXT. LAKE - SHORE - DAY

The children form a circle.

UNDERWATER

While the others dance, Pam peers down into the lake.
```

Thus, Pam looks right down at the camera. Notice that we signaled that without having to use camera directions.

If you're thinking of the above scene in terms of a point-of-view situation, such as a monster watching the children from deep below the water's surface, just handle the second scene as follows:

```
UNDERWATER

An unseen lake monster watches the dancing children. Pam
peers down into the lake.
```

MUSIC

Don't indicate music in your script unless it is essential to the progression of your story. Yes, if music is an integral part of your story—a movie about a rock singer, for example—then you may wish to indicate music in a general way:

```
A HEAVY-METAL RIFF rips through the silence.
```

or

```
Upbeat ROCK MUSIC plays on the radio.
```

Another way to indicate music generically is to describe the sound of it: The radio BLASTS. Keep in mind that since music is a SOUND, you can emphasize it by placing it in CAPS.

Do not tell the composer where to begin the romantic background music. A more professional approach is to intimate music indirectly by suggesting an emotional mood. You'll manage this through description, dialogue, and character. The director and composer will pick up on your *vibe*, and select or compose music that matches the emotion of the scene.

Regardless of whether you indicate music or not, the one thing you should *not* do (except in rare situations) is pick specific songs. Professional reader Allan Heifetz provides the following bad example:

```
Durden's coffin is lowered into the ground as Poison's "Every
Rose Has Its Thorn" gives the scene a sad, introspective
mood.
```

The above will *not* make a producer drool with excitement. Unless you own the rights to the songs you want used, you are usually creating a difficult situation for yourself and a possible legal hurdle for anyone interested in buying the script.

MOVIE CLIPS

What's true for music is true for produced movies. A producer cannot use a clip from another movie unless he controls the rights to that movie or acquires the rights to that clip. In addition, do not base your screenplay on any work that you do not control the rights to. Do not write the sequel to *Captain Phillips* unless you control the rights to *Captain Phillips*. Just write an original screenplay.

Obviously, you may briefly refer to other movies in a character's dialogue if doing so moves the story forward or adds to character. For example, in *Sleepless in Seattle*, there are references to *The Dirty Dozen* and *An Affair to Remember*. But don't write, "He turned on the TV and the sinking scene from *Titanic* was showing." Doing that will give you a sinking feeling when your script is rejected.

Now all of the above warnings go for naught if you have written a wonderfully commercial screenplay. Many sins are overlooked in such cases, but why tempt Fate.

[P] AUTHOR'S INTRUSION

In virtually every literary form, author's intrusion is unacceptable. In a screenplay, it is only permissible if it helps tell the story or clarifies something. However, don't overdo it and don't get cute. Don't interrupt the narrative flow of the story. When in doubt, stay out. At code [P] on the sample script, I intrude with my sentence, "Can he do it?" I think I can probably get away with that.

Shane Black made "author's intrusion" hip. Here's just one example from page 91 of *The Last Boy Scout*: "Remember Jimmy's friend Henry, who we met briefly near the opening of the film? Of course you do, you're a highly paid reader or development executive." Shane Black can get away with that; you and I probably can't.

In terms of foreshadowing, it's okay to remind us of something we saw earlier, although I suggest that you not be as brazen about it as Shane Black is in the above citation. The following is acceptable.

```
Sheila hands the tiny cedar box to Gwen. This is the same
cedar box that Sheila received from her mother earlier.
```

Obviously, the information in that last sentence cannot appear on the silver screen, but it once did, and it is okay to remind your reader to keep her oriented.

Your personal style

There is a difference between intruding on the story and writing with your own personal flare. Author intrusion calls attention to itself; creative expression contributes to the reading experience. I loved reading *Romancing the Stone*. The first line begins, "A size 16-EE boot kicks through the door. . . ." Notice that Diane Thomas's prose does not pull you out of the screenplay, nor does it call attention to the author. Instead, it enhances the reading experience. The script is a lot of fun to read. Reportedly, one reason Michael Douglas read the script was it seemed apparent that the writer must have had a lot of fun writing it. *Your* personal style has already developed to some degree and will continue to develop naturally.

[Q] CONTINUED

In shooting scripts, when a scene does not conclude at the bottom of a given page, it is customary to double-space and type (CONTINUED) at the lower right (flush right), and type CONTINUED: at the upper left (flush left) of the next page, followed by two vertical spaces, after which the writing resumed. This is totally unnecessary in spec writing. If you own software that writes CONTINUED automatically, I recommend that you disable that function.

WHEN TO USE CAPS

Let's summarize the use of CAPS.

You *must* use all CAPS for the following:

1. Character first appearances.

2. Technical instructions, including camera directions, editing directions, the word SUPER, special effects, etc. These incidents should be rare.

You *may* use CAPS (if you wish) for the following: 1) Sounds; 2) The words on signs, book titles, news headlines, etc.; and 3) Superimposed words. For example: SUPER: "TWO YEARS LATER."

Concerning the words referred to in numbers 2 and 3, make sure you place quotation marks around those words regardless of whether or not you type them in CAPS. Remember, CAPS are hard to read and can slow a reader down. That means you should not CAP anything else in your narrative description unless specifically requested by the person asking for your script. Do not use CAPS for props or other objects that you want to emphasize. That's a shooting-script convention. If you must emphasize any words of narrative description, underscore them, but do so rarely. I would expect to see no more than one or two instances in any screenplay.

In summary, keep CAPS to a minimum. I encourage my clients to CAP character first appearances and important sounds (if they wish). That's about it except for an occasional SUPER or necessary technical direction.

SPECIAL NOTES

Once every blue moon you get a creative idea that does not fit any known formatting guidelines. In these few cases, simply write a note parenthetically in a separate paragraph. Here's another example from one of my old scripts:

```
(NOTE: This scene is shot in BLACK AND WHITE. It should
appear old and scratched as if it originated from a 1950's
public information library. There are intentional JUMP CUTS.)
```

Dialogue

The dialogue sections of a screenplay consist of three parts: 1) Character cue, 2) Actor's direction, and 3) Character's speech (the dialogue).

(Note: The reference code [R] below and all other alpha codes refer back to examples in the sample script.)

[R] CHARACTER CUE

First is the character name or cue, sometimes called the *character caption* or *character slug*. It always appears in CAPS. A character should be referred to by exactly the same name throughout the screenplay, with rare exceptions. In the narrative description and the dialogue speeches, you may use a variety of names, but the character cue for a character should be the same throughout the script.

Do not leave a character cue alone at the bottom of a page. The entire dialogue block should appear intact. For the one exception, see "More," a little later in the chapter.

CHARACTERS WITH TWO NAMES

What if a character changes his name from Tom to Harry? One solution is to refer to him as TOM/HARRY or TOM (HARRY) after the name change.

In the movie *North by Northwest*, we have a case of mistaken identity, but the Cary Grant character is referred to by his true name in each character cue of the entire script. Whatever you decide, make sure you don't confuse the reader.

In stories that span a person's lifetime, you might refer to the adult as JOE BROWN and the teen or child as YOUNG JOE BROWN. That maintains the identity of the character while, at the same time, making clear the approximate age of the character.

What if a character speaks before we see her? What do you call her? You can refer to her in the character cue by her actual name.

PARENTHETICAL DIRECTION (WRYLIES)

Directly below the character name is the *actor's direction*, sometimes called *personal direction* or *parenthetical direction* or the *wryly*. The term *wryly* derives from the tendency in many beginning screenplays for characters to speak "wryly." Here's an example.

```
                TORCH
           (wryly)
      I've had my share of mondo babes.
```

Wrylies can provide useful and helpful tips to the reader, usually suggesting the *subtext* or attitude of the character. However, use wrylies in moderation. Keep in mind that wrylies are not really written for actors—who largely ignore them—but for the readers of your script. In most cases, the context of the situation and the character's actions will speak for themselves. In the case of subtext, use wrylies only when that subtext is not clear. If Chico says "I love you" in a sarcastic way, and we wouldn't guess that he is being sarcastic from the context, then use the wryly.

```
                    CHICO
              (sarcastically)
        I love you.
```

On page 3 of "The Perspicacious Professor," I use only one wryly, and you could argue for its omission on grounds that it is redundant—it is already evident by Dr. Format's action (moonwalking) that he is "the master" once again.

Generally, don't use wrylies to describe actions, unless those actions can be described in a few words, such as "tipping his hat" or "applying suntan lotion to her arms" and if the action is taken by the person speaking while he is speaking. Wrylies should not extend more than 2 inches from the left margin to the right margin. Wrylies always begin with a lowercase letter and never begin with the pronouns "he" or "she."

Describing brief actions in wrylies is not a bad tactic since some executives read dialogue only. A few well-placed wrylies can enhance the value and comprehension of a scene. I hasten to add that an executive seldom reads a script until a coverage is written by a reader (story analyst). Most professional readers read the entire script.

Don't describe one character's actions in the dialogue block of another character, with rare exceptions. The following is *not* proper.

```
                    SHORTY
        What do you mean?
              (Slim pulls a gun)
        Don't shoot.
```

The following would be much better form and more immediately clear:

```
                    SHORTY
        What do you mean?
```

```
Slim pulls a gun and points it at Shorty.

                    SHORTY
          Don't shoot.
```

Generally, don't end a dialogue block with a wryly, as with the following example:

```
                    COQUETTE
          So why did you come here?
                    (raising her lips)
```

Instead write:

```
                    COQUETTE
          So why...
                    (raising her lips)
          ... did you come here?
```

Finally, use a wryly to indicate to whom the character is speaking when that is not otherwise clear.

```
                    MOE
                (to Curly)
          Not you, ya knucklehead.
```

BEAT

What the heck is a beat?
There are three different ways the term *beat* is used by screenwriters:

1. A theatrical term indicating a pause in dialogue or action.
2. The smallest unit of action in a scene. She slaps his face and he kisses her—that's two beats.
3. An important event, turning point, twist, or dramatic/comedic moment when creating a "beat sheet."

An unbeatable strategy for dialogue
Avoid using the word *beat*. It's usually best not to instruct an actor when to pause. If you must indicate a pause, find a more descriptive word than *beat*. Instead, describe

a small action, gesture, or facial expression that accomplishes the same purpose, but which also adds a characterization.

Let's examine the following.

```
               JIM
     You know...
          (beat)
     ... I'll have to kill you.
```

Although perfectly correct, the word "beat" does not tell us much. Is Jim confident or nervous? That could make a big difference in how the scene plays. Granted, the context will tell us something, but why not add a little characterization while still implying the pause? In this case, replace "beat" with something like "nervously," "nearly giddy," "a smug grin," "confidently," or "stroking his gun."

Which of the following three examples creates more interest?

```
               JANE
     Ed Darling, I want you to know...
          (beat)
     ... how much I love you.
```

```
               JANE
     Ed Darling, I want you to know...
          (eyes mist up)
     ... how much I love you.
```

```
               JANE
     Ed Darling, I want you to know...
          (suddenly sneezing
           on Ed)
     ... how much I love you.
```

None of the three examples will win any prizes, but certainly the first is the boring one. The second is dramatic. The third is funny (or disgusting). Here is the point: The word "beat" is the most colorless, lifeless term you can use to indicate a pause. Instead, use specific words that add to the story or help characterize your character. It's an un*beat*able strategy.

SOLILOQUIES

Avoid characters talking to themselves. However, if you have a natural soliloquy or whispered comment, just write "aside" or "to self" as a wryly. You do not need to write "sotto" or "sotto voce." There's no reason to use Italian unless you are a music composer.

[S] CONTINUING AND CONT'D

On page 3 of "The Perspicacious Professor" (the sample script), Dr. Format begins to speak, then stops, then continues. In fact, I interrupt his speech three times with narrative description (each continuation of his speech marked with code [S]). In the long-ago past, this would have been handled in one of two ways:

```
                    PROFESSOR
              (continuing)
          But why, Calcutta? Why?


                    PROFESSOR (cont'd)
          But why, Calcutta? Why?
```

Neither of the above styles is used. Due to the proliferation of screenwriting software, the following is what is now commonly used.

```
                    PROFESSOR (CONT'D)
          But why, Calcutta? Why?
```

Use the above style, or nothing at all (as I did in the same script at code [S]). Either style is correct. If you use Movie Magic Screenwriter or Final Draft, let the software write CONT'D for you.

However, the term CONTINUED should *not* appear at the top and bottom of each page of a spec script.

MORE

When dialogue continues from the bottom of one page to the top of the next, you have four options.

Option 1: Type the character's name again at the top of the next page followed by "CONT'D" in parenthesis, and then continue the speech. You don't need anything more than that.

Option 2: Same as #1, but without the CONT'D. You can probably get away with this, although I would recommend Options 1 or 3.

Option 3: If you use formatting software, let that software type MORE (in parenthesis) centered below the dialogue, and then CONT'D (in parenthesis) next to the character's cue at the top of the next page. Here's how the bottom of one page will look:

```
                    BUGSY
        I am at the bottom of the page, and
        I'm running out of room.

                    (MORE)
```

And then at the top of the next page:

```
                    BUGSY (CONT'D)
        I'd like to continue my speech.
```

Option 4: Ideally, your dialogue should be so lean that you don't have to continue dialogue to the next page at all. Just move the entire dialogue block to the top of the next page, or cheat a little on your bottom margin to get that last line in at the bottom of the page. (Warning: Do not cheat on your left and top script margins or on your dialogue margins. We'll talk about cheating you can get away with in Book IV.)

[T] OFF SCREEN (O.S.) AND VOICE OVER (V.O.)

The term OFF SCREEN, at code [T] on page 3 of the sample script, indicates that Charlie is in the scene—that is, he's at the location of the scene—but that he is not in the camera frame. We hear his voice, but do not see him on the movie screen. Why do I want Charlie OFF SCREEN? Because I want the camera to focus on the Professor, whose back is now to the class.

A voice that comes through a device such as a telephone or radio or that is heard in the mind is "voiced over." For example, if Charlie is not only off screen but also out of the scene (not in the classroom), and the Professor HEARS his voice—say, in his mind or through the phone—then this is a VOICE OVER as follows:

> CHARLIE (V.O.)
> You're done for, old man.

If Charlie is in the scene and hears his own voice in his head *and* his lips aren't moving, that's also a VOICE OVER.

Charlie looks worried. He nods in resignation.

> CHARLIE (V.O.)
> I'm done for.

Narration of any kind is a VOICE OVER. In cases where a character is on screen and we hear his thoughts or he narrates his own story, use the VOICE OVER. In cases when the character is not on screen, but we hear his voice, use VOICE OVER. The VOICE OVER device was used extensively in *American Beauty*. In that film, Lester (Kevin Spacey) narrates. If the person narrating the story is referred to as NARRATOR, you don't have to use the (V.O.) device.

The key to writing effective narration

Do not describe in dialogue what we already see visually. Whenever you use a voiceover narration, let that voiceover dialogue add something that the visual does not already tell us. Don't just describe in your dialogue the same action that you describe in your narrative.

Keep in mind that when you write narration, you take a chance. Most narration that professionals see in screenplays amounts to "obvious exposition" or unnecessary dialogue that simply reveals exposition in a boring or obvious way. Thus, professional readers have a natural bias against the use of a narrator. Narration should comment on the story, or add to it, in a meaningful and/or humorous way. It should add a layer of meaning or humor or drama or all three.

Beginning the scene before it begins

If we hear someone's voice at the end of the scene, but don't actually see her until the next scene, then we have a voiceover, as follows:

> TV REPORTER (V.O.)
> I am standing in front of the White
> House...

EXT. WHITE HOUSE - CONTINUOUS

A huge crowd observes while the TV reporter points.

```
                    TV REPORTER
        ... And, as you can see, it has been
        painted blue.
```

Incidentally, I used the ellipsis to show continuity of dialogue.

Voiceover in phone conversations

In phone conversations in which the person on the other line is *not* "in the scene" but we hear the voice, that's a voiceover. I've recently seen scripts where V.O. is not used in telephone conversations, and that's okay as long as the script is clear and not confusing. I'm not sure I'd be that brave. For more on telephone conversations, see "Telephone Conversations" later in this chapter.

CHARACTER'S SPEECH

The third part of dialogue is the speech itself, the words to be spoken. Because speech is indented, you do not use quotation marks or italics to indicate the spoken word. Avoid hyphenation and maintain a ragged right margin. Do not paragraph a single speech, even if it is long.

Each speech should be as brief as possible and generally convey one thought. One or two sentences are plenty in most cases. Fragments are welcome. Avoid long speeches, although there are times when a long speech is necessary.

Write all numbers out except years: "I've told you twenty-five times now that I was born in 1950." Avoid using excessive exclamation points! One is plenty. Write out all words. Do not abbreviate. Put quotation marks around anything that is quoted.

If you wish to emphasize a word, do not place it in CAPS, italics, or bold; instead, underscore it. Use this practice sparingly.

Acronyms

When a character spells a word, saying each letter individually, use hyphens or periods to separate the characters, as follows:

```
                    DELBERT
        That's Delbert. D-E-L-B-E-R-T.
```

Acronyms that are pronounced as words should be written without hyphens or periods. The following speech is correctly written. The letters F, B, and I are said individually; the acronyms MADD and UNICEF are pronounced as words.

>   DELBERT
> The woman from MADD was thought to
> be F.B.I. until the official saw her
> UNICEF badge.

When working with dialects and accents, sprinkle in bits of dialect and phonetically spelled words just to give us a taste of the accent or regional influence. Make sure the speeches are easy to read. The same holds true for characters who stutter; just give us a sense of his stuttering. In the screenplay *The King's Speech,* Bertie says, "I have received from his Majesty the K-K-K." And then David Seidler, the screenwriter, writes the following:

(NOTE: For ease of reading, Bertie's stammer will not be indicated from this point in the script.)

OVERLAPPING OR SIMULTANEOUS DIALOGUE

Here is the first of five ways to present two people speaking at the same time.

>   SAM AND JO
>   Huh, what?

Or you can add a parenthetical to make it absolutely clear.

>   SAM AND JO
>   (together)
>   Huh, what?

Or replace the word "together" with "simultaneously."

Here's a fourth method that you can use when the two characters say the same thing at about the same time, or when they say *different* things at about the same time:

>   SAM
>   Huh, what?

>   JO
>   (overlapping)
>   Huh, what?

And finally, use the following method only rarely . . .

```
          SAM                JO
Huh, what?      What? Huh?
```

If you wish, you can have three or four characters speaking simultaneously. For another example of simultaneous dialogue and overlapping dialogue, see the "comedy scene" toward the end of Book I.

[U] TELEPHONE VOICES

As mentioned a bit earlier, voices coming through telephones, walkie-talkies, radios, and similar devices are voiced over. Sometimes I see the following: *(on phone)* or *(amplified)* or *(filtered)* typed adjacent to the name. Replace these correct but antiquated notations with (V.O.). In each case, the person speaking is obviously not in camera and not at the scene location.

At code [D] on the sample script, I could have created a voiceover as follows.

```
EXT. PHONE BOOTH - CONTINUOUS

With phone in hand, Calcutta turns to the classroom
window and frowns at what she sees -- the professor doing
cartwheels down the aisle.

                    DEAN ZACK (V.O.)
            Make him pay, Calcutta.


                    CALCUTTA
            It'll work?
```

Television

Treat the television set as a separate character. If there is a specific character who is on television, simply indicate as much in your description and type the character's name as the character caption or cue. If you want to be especially clear, add the following parenthetical: (on TV).

```
                    JOCK JIM (on TV)
            Hi, Mom. We're number one!
```

[V] TELEPHONE CONVERSATIONS

There are essentially four methods for handling phone conversations.

Method 1
Use this method when the audience does not see or hear the other party. This is handled like any other speech.

                              MARY
               He said what?
                     (shaking her head)
               Well, thanks for letting me know.

Notice that I did not use the word "beat" to indicate a pause, although I could have.

Method 2
The second situation is when the audience *hears* the other person, but does not *see* him or her. In that case, the dialogue of the person not seen is voiced-over.

                                MARY
               He said what?

                             JOHN (V.O.)
               He said you're as cute as a cuddle bunny.

                                MARY
               Well, thanks for letting me know.

Method 3A
The third situation is when the audience both hears and sees the two parties. In such cases, use the intercut. You can handle it simply, as with the following example:

INTERCUT - DARIN'S CAR/SUZANNE'S KITCHEN

That would be followed by dialogue written like any other conversation. Please note that when you don't establish the locations prior to the intercut, you must in the intercut heading, as demonstrated above.

Method 3B

Another method of using the intercut is to establish the two locations first. That way you don't have to indicate locations in the intercut heading. That is what I did at [V] on the sample script and in the example below.

```
INT. SUZANNE'S KITCHEN - NIGHT

Suzanne paces nervously; then punches numbers on her phone.

INT. DARIN'S CAR - SAME

Darin drives through the rain, looking depressed. His cell
phone rings.

INTERCUT - TELEPHONE CONVERSATION


                    SUZANNE
          Come back.


                    DARIN
          What? Now?


                    SUZANNE
          Yes. Please.


                    DARIN
          Give me one good reason.


                    SUZANNE
          You forgot your casserole bowl.


                    DARIN
          I'll be right there.
```

The INTERCUT device gives the director complete freedom as to *when* to intercut between speakers (he/she has complete freedom anyway, so why not be gracious?), plus it's easy to read.

Another reason you use this device is that otherwise you would have to write a master scene heading with each change of speaker. This can become laborious and interrupt the story flow. On the other hand, it may improve the scene in a particular situation and give you more dramatic control over which character the camera is on at any point in the conversation.

Method 4

Let's rewrite the sequence that begins at [D] on the sample script without the INTERCUT, using master scene headings.

```
EXT. PHONE BOOTH - CONTINUOUS

The woman in the phone booth is CALCUTTA COTTER. With phone
in hand, she turns toward the classroom window and frowns
at what she sees -- the professor doing cartwheels down the
aisle.

                    DEAN ZACK (V.O.)
              Make him pay, Calcutta....

INT. DEAN'S OFFICE - CONTINUOUS

DEAN ZELDA ZACK stands at her polished desk with a swagger
stick tucked under her arm.

                    DEAN ZACK
              ... Ask him the question.

INT. PHONE BOOTH - CONTINUOUS

Calcutta's excitement is subdued by doubt.

                    CALCUTTA
              It'll work?

INT. DEAN'S OFFICE - CONTINUOUS

Zack's confident smile reveals gold caps over her front
teeth.

                    DEAN ZACK
              Stumps him every time.
```

The swagger stick slashes the desk. The delirious dean
chortles with satisfaction.

EXT. PHONE BOOTH - CONTINUOUS

Calcutta hears chortling through the phone receiver. She
smiles; then slams the receiver down.

(And, of course, you probably don't need to indicate CONTINUOUS at the end of
each scene heading, since it is already obvious that the phone conversation runs continuously.)

Now let's take another tack. Suppose you don't want the camera on Dean Zelda Zack,
nor do you want to hear the dear dean. In such a situation, you would use Method 1,
and the conversation would read something like this:

EXT. CLASSROOM - DAY

With phone in hand, CALCUTTA COTTER turns toward the
classroom window and frowns at what she sees -- the
professor doing cartwheels down the aisle.

                    CALCUTTA
          I'll make him pay, all right --
                    (turns to phone)
          You're sure it'll work?
                    (nodding)
          Beautiful.

Calcutta urges a smile; then slams the receiver down.

This version also works well. The advice and the source of the advice are left out.
Dramatically, that may serve the scene better and create a little suspense. Ask yourself:
What is the best way to make your scene play and move your story forward?

EMAILS AND TEXT MESSAGES

Only words that are spoken should appear as dialogue. That is what dialogue is.
However, if a person repeats out loud what she reads on the computer monitor, then
you could write what she actually says as dialogue. Otherwise, you want to find a clear
way to impart the contents of an email or text message that doesn't confuse the reader

or slow down the read. I suggest you create a variation of the INSERT by using ON THE MONITOR as a secondary scene heading.

```
Sid types on the keyboard.

ON SID'S LAPTOP SCREEN

Sid's words appear:

        "But Renee, they're tapping my phone
        conversations."

BACK TO SID

who waits for Renee's response.

ON SID'S LAPTOP SCREEN

Renee's response appears:

        "You're being silly, Sid."
```

Notice that the words that are typed are indented like dialogue and appear with quotation marks. You could also go to a shorthand version of the above by simply omitting the phrases "Sid's words appear" and "Renee's response appears."

(For information on how to indent the content of emails and text messages using Movie Magic Screenwriter or Final Draft, see "Indenting with formatting software" in the chapter on Scene Headings.)

Perhaps a more readable style is demonstrated below.

```
Sid types on the keyboard. The words appear on his monitor:

        "But Renee, they're tapping my phone
        conversations."

Sid spots Renee's response on the monitor:

        "You're being silly, Sid."
```

The above method is the one I prefer, but the following is also correct:

```
Sid types on the keyboard. The words appear on his monitor:
"But Renee, they're tapping my phone conversations."
```

```
Sid spots Renee's response on the monitor: "You're being
silly, Sid."
```

That certainly takes less space, and may be the best choice unless you want the email or text message to pop out on the screenplay. The key is to be clear and consistent in style. Incidentally, write text messages exactly the way they would appear on the cell phone.

```
Sid smiles at his cell phone. It reads: "FYI I LUV U."
```

Or you could write

```
ON SID'S IPHONE

        "FYI I LUV U."
```

As a general guideline, don't force audiences to decipher a long series of text messages. You're usually better off moving the story forward through dialogue and action.

SPEAKING IN FOREIGN LANGUAGES

In working with other languages, realize there is one general rule: Write your script in the language of the eventual reader so that he or she knows what is going on. In other words, avoid writing dialogue in a foreign language.

If a character speaks in French, do not write out the dialogue in French unless the eventual reader is French, or in the rare case that the meaning of the words doesn't matter. Simply write the lines as follows:

```
                JEAN-MARC
            (in French)
        I will pluck your neck.
```

Instead of having your character speak in French, consider sprinkling his/her dialogue with French words to give us a French flavor. Then everyone knows what is being said.

```
                JEAN-MARC
        Come with me, mon alouette.
```

Now, suppose your character absolutely, positively must speak in a foreign language. Your desire is for something realistic, such as the Italian spoken in *The Godfather*. You have five options, depending on your specific purpose.

1. If it doesn't matter whether the audience understands the meaning of the foreign words, or if you believe the audience will be able to figure out the meaning of the words by their context, then just write them out in the foreign language. For example:

```
Tarzan shouts at the charging elephant.


                    TARZAN
          On-gow-ah!

The elephant turns and stampedes in the opposite direction.
```

Or write the words in English using a wryly to indicate what language the words will be spoken in, as follows:

```
                  PIERRE-LUC
                (in French)
          Imbecile. Idiot. Retard.
```

2. If the characters speak in French throughout an entire scene, then make a clear statement (a "note") in the narrative description that all the dialogue in the scene will be spoken in French; then, write the dialogue out in English so that the reader can understand it. . .

. . . But this raises the question: How will the *audience* know what is being said? They won't, unless they speak French. For that reason, this is seldom a viable option. If your character must speak in French *and* it's also important that the audience understand what is being said, then *subtitles* are the solution.

The last three options below include the use of **subtitles**.

3. If you write a long scene in which French (or any other language) is spoken, and if you want English subtitles to appear on the movie screen while the character speaks in French, then include a special note in the narrative description, as follows:

```
(NOTE: The dialogue in this scene is spoken in French and is
subtitled in English.)
```

Then, simply write the dialogue out in English. After the scene ends, write:

```
END OF SUBTITLES
```

4. Another option for using subtitles is to use a wryly. This is by far the most common method.

MICHELLE
(in French; subtitled)
I spit on your name. I spit on your
mother's grave. I spit on your book.

The spittle flies.

5. There is one other option for using subtitles. Use this device only if the sound of the words in the foreign language is important; for example, in the case of this space visitor's language, the words have a humorous quality.

ALIEN   SUBTITLES
Zoo-BEE, Woo-BEE.   You're cute.

My final advice is to choose English whenever possible and give the reader a sense of a foreign language by including a few foreign words and/or the flavor of a foreign accent.

MUSIC LYRICS

There may be a rare instance when you'll need to include music lyrics in your script because a character sings them. First of all, avoid including lyrics from a song whose rights are not owned or controlled by you. It's usually a negative when a reader sees music lyrics from a popular song in a script. If you are creating a musical, or quoting a poem or song that is in the public domain, or even have a character that is singing nonsense for comedic effect, then you can write lyrics in two different ways. One is to write them as dialogue (since they are dialogue) in stanza form, just like a poem, and the other is to use slashes.

The lyrics quoted below are from an existing song; thus, the quotation marks.

McKAY
"Oh ye'll tak' the high road
And I'll tak' the low,
And I'll be in Scotland afore ye."

An alternative is to use slashes, as follows.

```
                McKAY
     "Oh ye'll tak' the high road/ And
     I'll tak' the low/ And I'll be in
     Scotland afore ye."
```

It's okay to not space after the slashes if you wish.

SOUNDS AS DIALOGUE

Only the spoken word should be written as dialogue. Human screams and dog barks are sounds, and are included in narrative description. Here are two examples:

```
Billy screams.
```

```
Sparky barks.
```

If a character reads someone's journal, those words should not be written as dialogue unless the audience hears them spoken. That could be done with the character reading the journal out loud. Another option is to voice over the voice of the original writer while the character reads.

DEAF DIALOGUE

What if you have a character who is deaf and communicates by signing? Signing is not dialogue since words are not spoken. Of course, general audiences are not familiar with signing, so usually (in a film script) the deaf person's meaning is communicated to the audience either orally (spoken words) or through subtitles. If the deaf person speaks as he/she signs, then simply write the words he/she says as dialogue:

```
                DEAF PERSON
             (while signing)
     Did you understand what I said?
```

If the deaf person is a major character, then indicate once in the narrative description with a special note that the deaf person signs whenever he talks; that way, you won't need to include a parenthetical for each block of dialogue.

If the character signs without speaking, then write out the dialogue as in the example above, except write the parenthetical as follows: "signing; subtitled." An alternative method is to indicate as a special note in narrative description that the mute person signs and that the meaning appears in subtitles. As always in spec writing, your goal is to be as clear and unobtrusive as you can.

TELEPATHIC DIALOGUE

I think we have established that only dialogue is dialogue, but what do you do when people communicate telepathically?

The question to ask here is this: If there is an actual telepathic communication, how will the audience know what is being communicated? In other words, what does the audience see and hear in the movie theater? Whatever it is, that is what you must describe in your screenplay. If the audience hears words *without anyone's lips moving*, then clearly describe that and use a VOICE OVER for the words, although it's probably too hokey to use in a dramatic or serious work.

In some *Star Trek* episodes, I have seen an empath simply state what she is *sensing* or *reading*. Thus, the audience knows what she is picking up.

[W] DIALOGUE PUNCTUATION

The use of the dash (--) and the ellipsis (. . .) has become very clouded in recent years. Usually they are used to make dialogue look like . . . well -- er, dialogue.

There used to be very definite literary rules about these. Today the two symbols are often used interchangeably, and you may use them anyway you like, as long as you are careful not to overuse them and you are consistent. However, understanding their actual use in terms of writing dialogue can be very helpful in presenting a consistent pattern in your written communication.

-- The dash indicates a sudden shift or break in thought, or to show emphasis. It is used when one character interrupts another or shifts his thought, or a character is interrupted by a sound or an action, or a character speaks as if interrupted or with sudden emphasis. The dash is created by typing a space, hyphen, hyphen, space -- like that.

. . . The ellipsis is used for continuity or to indicate a pause. A character will start speaking, then pause, and then continue. When a character stops, and then continues later, the ellipsis is used instead of the dash. When a character finishes another character's sentence, use an ellipsis.

The ellipsis is made by typing three periods (not two or five) followed by a space. If you happen not to space after the ellipsis, the world will not end. When an ellipsis ends a sentence, place a period at the end of the ellipsis (making four dots in all).

Here's an example of both the dash and the ellipsis.

```
EXT. BALCONY - NIGHT

Coquette dabs her eyes with a handkerchief. Suddenly,
Vivi blunders through the French doors. Coquette turns
expectantly; then puts on an angry face.


                    COQUETTE
          Why did you come here?


                    VIVI
          I came here to --


                    COQUETTE
          -- I don't want to know why you came
          here.


He moves earnestly toward her. She softens.


                    COQUETTE
          So why...
                    (raising her lips)
          ... did you... come here?


Vivi's lips are now just a silly millimeter from hers.


                    VIVI
          I came here to...


His gaze fades into a blank stare, then stupefaction.


                    COQUETTE
          You have forgotten --
```

```
                    VIVI
               (recovering)
          But one kiss and I will remember
          why I came here.
```

He lays one on her, then looks joyously into her confused face.

```
                    VIVI
          I came here to kiss my Coquette. You.
```

For another example of dialogue punctuation, see the "comedy scene" in Book I.

How to format TV scripts

This section builds on information in the previous sections of this book. Sample scenes of a sitcom spec script can be found just after this short explanatory section.

TV/CABLE MOVIES

All spec scripts for TV and cable movies should be written as feature film specs. In other words, use standard spec format as presented in this book. Do not delineate acts. This is good news because it means you can market your script as a feature film or TV movie or cable movie or direct-to-DVD movie without adjusting the formatting.

PILOTS AND DRAMATIC SERIES

If you have a hot pilot idea that you believe in, use the same standard spec format that you would use for a screenplay.

The same is true if you write an episode for a one-hour television series—whether drama or comedy—use standard spec screenplay form (as used with feature scripts). You do not need to indicate scene numbers; however, you must designate the acts, teaser, and tag.

Teaser

This is the brief (about one minute or so) initial section establishing the show. Seldom do you find an episodic series anymore that doesn't open with some kind of teaser.

The acts

After the teaser, break to a new page and center ACT ONE at the top of the page, triple-space, and write out the scenes just as you would in a feature screenplay, using standard spec screenplay format.

Many production companies also request that you add END OF ACT ONE at the end of the act (just triple-space and center END OF ACT ONE), after which you break to a new page to the second act, and so on.

Tag

The tag, sometimes called the epilogue, is the brief (about one minute or so, and often less) ending section that ties up loose ends. In some shows, this is "scenes from next week's episode." Usually, the epilogue or tag is identified as such at the top of the page.

Title page and script length

Your script for a one-hour dramatic show will be about 54 pages in length.

The title page for any episodic TV show, regardless of length, is similar to that of a feature script, except that the title of the episode is included along with the title of the series. Here is an example from an imaginary series entitled *L.A. Script Doctors*.

                    L.A. SCRIPT DOCTORS

                 "THE PERSPICACIOUS PROFESSOR"

The titles of the series and episodes may also be underscored if you wish. Also, you can space twice (as I did) or three times between the series title and the episode title.

It will be worthwhile to acquire a script from the series itself as a guide to writing style, number of acts, how acts are labeled, and formatting quirks (keeping in mind that you are writing a spec script, not a shooting script, and that you will avoid camera angles and editing directions in your script.) Also, try to get a copy of the show's "bible" (that contains the show's parameters). Before writing a TV script or pilot, read the section on "Television markets" in Book V.

SITUATION COMEDY

Situation comedies (sitcoms) utilize a mutant variation of standard spec screenplay format because sitcoms are essentially dialogue-driven stage plays with one or two sets. Due to the special format, several pages of explanation plus the sample sitcom script follow.

If you want to write for a specific TV show, obtain a copy of one of their scripts, since each show varies slightly in formatting style. For example, *The Office* used a much different style than most sitcoms. If you use formatting software, check to see which TV templates are included.

Sitcoms are either taped or shot on film or digitally, which is one reason for variations in formatting style. As suggested for the dramatic series, try to get the show's "bible" as well, and read the section on "Television markets" in Book V before writing. A half-hour sitcom script is about 40 to 50 pages, but can be longer depending on the show. This differs from standard spec screenplay form, which is about a page per minute of screen time.

The title page for a sitcom script is handled in the same way as a dramatic series script. See the example above for *L.A. Script Doctors*.

A sitcom is simpler than a screenplay, both in structure and content. Comparing the screenplay scene on the sample script ("The Perspicacious Professor") to the sitcom sample script should prove instructive. What follows applies to sitcom scripts only.

The cast list and sets list
Although these two lists appear in shooting scripts, you will *not* include them in your spec script. They are seldom required. If you are writing a shooting script, the cast list will include any actors already assigned to the series. Usually, the characters appearing every week are listed first, followed by any guest characters. The sets are listed in three categories: exteriors, interiors, and stock shots.

Typeface, margins, and tabs
Like all other scripts, sitcoms are written in Courier (or Courier New) 12-point. Margins for sitcom scripts are at 1.5 inches on the left, 1 inch on the right, and 1 inch at the top and bottom. Tabs from the left margin are 10 spaces for dialogue (although some scripts indent more) and an additional 12 to 14 spaces to the character cue (character's name).

Page numbering

Page numbers are typed at the top right corner of each page and are usually followed by a period. Some shows ask you to indicate parenthetically the act and scene numbers just below the page number. That is what I did in my sample sitcom script. Some shows ask you to indicate only the letter of the scene below the page number (without indicating the act number). Other shows only require a page number at the top right corner of each page.

Acts and scenes

Sitcoms generally consist of a teaser, two or three acts, and a tag. The first act ends on a major turning point, followed by a commercial. Acts are designated in CAPS (for example, ACT ONE) and are centered at the top of the page in the same manner as a dramatic series. If you wish, you may also underscore them. At the end of the act, break with END OF ACT ONE, centered two or three spaces below the end of the act.

In sitcoms, scenes are generally designated with letters: Scene A, Scene B, and so on. Sometimes the word "scene" appears in CAPS: SCENE A, SCENE B, and so on. Often, you see just the letter, without the word "scene": A, B, and so on.

Each time you change to a new scene, you break to a new page, come down about a third or a half of the page, and then center your scene designation and place it in CAPS. On page 2 of the sample sitcom spec script, we have a new scene. At the very top right, you'll see "I-B" in parentheses, which means Act I, Scene B.

End scenes with a CUT TO: or FADE OUT, neither of which must be underscored.

Occasionally, you see a script that includes the designation for an act along with each new scene change, as follows:

```
                         ACT ONE

                         Scene D
```

Only do this if the particular sitcom you are writing for requires it.

Scene headings

Each scene begins with a master scene heading—indicating exterior or interior camera position, location, and day or night—written in CAPS and underscored, as follows:

INT. SMALL CLASSROOM - DAY

In a few scripts, the characters in the scene are included parenthetically, as follows.

INT. JERRY'S APARTMENT - DAY

(Jerry, Kramer, Elaine)

In either case, you will double-space to the description.

Narrative description
Narrative description appears in CAPS and is single-spaced. Because a sitcom is really a TV play, the emphasis is on dialogue rather than on action, so there will be comparatively less narrative description (action) and more dialogue in a sitcom than in a motion picture screenplay.

Entrances, exits, and transitions
In situation comedy, there are very few changes in location (sometimes none). To keep the read from bogging down, all entrances and exits of characters are underscored. This includes a character movement from place to place within a scene. For example:

MICHAEL STEPS OUT OF HIS OFFICE

or

ROZ ENTERS FRASIER'S BOOTH

or

GIBBS CROSSES INTO THE LAB

All first appearances of characters are underscored. Furthermore, at the beginning of each scene, after the heading, establish which characters are in the scene. Do this with the first sentence of narrative description. Note my example on the sample sticom spec script.

Transitions (editing directions) are underscored.

Sounds
Sounds no longer need to be underscored. However, on occasion, there may be a particularly important sound that you want to emphasize. In such cases, double-space and write the sound out as follows.

SOUND: DOORBELL RINGS

Special effects are handled in exactly the same way.

<u>FX: NUCLEAR EXPLOSION</u>

It's hard to imagine much need for a special effect in most sitcoms.

Dialogue
Because there is such an emphasis on the dialogue in television comedy, it is double-spaced for ease of reading. Actor's instructions (wrylies) are used more freely than in a screenplay, and are usually placed within the dialogue block itself. (Sometimes they are brought to the left margin, but they are always enclosed in parenthesis.)

Here's one of my favorite lines from a *Seinfeld* script, in which George pretends he is a marine biologist to impress Holly. Suddenly they come upon a beached whale and a crowd.

```
                    HOLLY

          (BLURTS) Stop! Everyone, this

          is one of the world's foremost

          marine biologists. (WITH PRIDE)

          This... is George Costanza.
```

AS ALL EYES TURN TO GEORGE, A MAN WITH A VIDEOCAMERA BEGINS CAPTURING THE MOMENT FOR POSTERITY.

ACT ONE

Scene A

<u>FADE IN</u>:

<u>INT. SMALL CLASSROOM - DAY</u>

About <u>8 STUDENTS</u> AWAIT <u>THE PROFESSOR</u>, WHO <u>ENTERS</u> WITH
EXCITEMENT. OVER HIS SHOULDER IS A STRAP SUPPORTING A
LEATHER POUCH FILLED WITH CANDY MINTS.

<u>CHARLIE</u> RAISES HIS HAND.

                CHARLIE

    Hey, Mr. Professor, how do you

    handle phone calls in a script?

              PROFESSOR

    (SCINTILLATING) A most excellent

    question.

HE TOSSES THE GRATEFUL BOY A CANDY MINT. CHARLIE CATCHES IT
IN HIS MOUTH AND SMILES BROADLY.

                           <u>FADE OUT</u>.

2.

(I-B)

Scene B

<u>INT. DEAN'S OFFICE - DAY</u>

<u>CALCUTTA COTTER</u> SPEAKS WITH <u>DEAN ZELDA ZACK</u>.

                CALCUTTA

... And then the professor gives

everyone a candy -- all except me.

DEAN ZACK SLAPS HER SWAGGER STICK ACROSS HER POLISHED DESK.

                DEAN ZACK

Make him pay, Calcutta, make him

pay. (PACING) Now do exactly

what I told you. It stumps him

every time.

CALCUTTA <u>EXITS</u> WITH A BOUNCE IN HER STEP.

                DEAN ZACK

Now, Mr. Professor, let's see you

get out of this one.

DEAN ZACK LAUGHS INSANELY.

                                <u>FADE OUT</u>.

Glossary of terms not discussed elsewhere

ANGLE - Directs the camera to a particular person or object. The character's name itself could be written as a heading in CAPS and serve the same purpose. Angles (or SHOTS) can be wide, low, tight, close, high, bird's eye, etc.

AD LIB - This instructs the actors to fill in the dialogue with incidental lines.

ANAMORPHIC LENS - A lens used to shoot a wide-screen film; also, to project it onto the screen.

CRANE SHOT - A moving shot from a camera on a lift.

DISSOLVE - An editing direction where one scene "melts" into another, the former fading out while the latter fades in.

DOLLY or **TRUCK** - Picture this as a camera on wheels. Variations abound: CAMERA IN, PULL BACK TO REVEAL, TRUCK WITH, CAMERA PUSHES IN, etc.

FADE OUT - The image fades to black. This editing direction appears two spaces below the last line, flush right, followed by a period. These days, FADE TO BLACK is more often used.

FREEZE FRAME - The image freezes on the screen and becomes a still shot. Often used with END CREDITS.

O.C. - OFF CAMERA, a term now used only in television. The movie term is off screen (O.S.).

OVER THE SHOULDER - Shooting over someone's shoulder from behind.

PAN - A stationary camera pivots back and forth or up and down (TILT).

Pinks - From the expression *fix it in the pinks*. Revisions of shooting scripts are usually done on colored paper.

REVERSE SHOT - When we're looking over Vivi's shoulder to Coquette, then reverse to look over Coquette's shoulder to Vivi.

SHOCK CUT - A sudden cut from one scene to another. (Also SMASH CUT.)

SLOW MOTION and **SPEEDED-UP MOTION** - You know what these are.

SPLIT SCREEN - The picture is divided into two (or more) sections.

STOCK SHOT - A film sequence previously shot and stored at a film library.

SUBLIM - A shot lasting a fraction of a second.

SUPER - A superimposition—one image (usually words) overlaid on another.

WIPE - An editing direction where one image moves another out of frame.

ZIP PAN - A superfast PAN, creating a blurred image and a sense of quick movement.

ZOOM - A stationary camera with a zoom lens enlarges or diminishes the image.

WRITING & REVISING YOUR BREAKTHROUGH SCRIPT

BOOK IV

A Script Consultant's View

The spec script—your key to breaking in

When a writer breaks into Hollywood, it's with a great *spec script* that helps him find work. When a writer is paid millions of dollars, it's for a *spec script*. Although *shooting scripts* abound and can be easily purchased, *spec scripts* are difficult to find and little is written specifically about them. And yet, agents and producers alike are searching for the right *spec script* that convinces them you are the next great screenwriter.

Virtually every script you purchase from script services or find in screenwriting books is a *shooting script*. And yet, you must write a *spec script* to break in.

READABILITY

We established in Book III that we write primarily for a reader or story analyst who either recommends or does not recommend you or your script to the agent or producer who hired him. A reader wants a script to be readable. *Readability* is the ease with which your script can be read, understood, and enjoyed.

A readable script has five qualities. It is **clear** (you cannot afford to lose or confuse a reader), **attractive** (correct format, punctuation and spelling; lean paragraphs and speeches), **specific** (active voice and specific language), **economical** (says a lot with few words, except in the case of cinematic and emotional moments and scenes), and **entertaining**.

Is this stuff really that important? Allow me to quote just one professional reader: "Oh, the half-baked, recycled concepts. The time and money wasted covering scripts by those who can't spell, can't proof, and who clearly cannot communicate. And the amateurish overwriting! Scene descriptions stuffed like a goose with extraneous character information, set décor, wardrobe design, and camera directions; the failure to edit lengthy and unwieldy dialogue" (Quoted by Ron Suppa in July 2007's *Creative Screenwriting*).

Whew! I think I better stop there, but there's more about sloppy scene headings and on and on. Readers read a lot, so it's a tender mercy when they find something that is readable—fun, fluid, and fascinating.

A SPEC WRITING COURSE

The main purpose of Book IV is to demonstrate effective spec writing. A secondary purpose is to reinforce principles taught elsewhere in *The Bible*. In this book, we will look at scenes from several of my clients' scripts and revise them into the current spec writing style. You will be encouraged to write your own revisions before viewing my suggested revisions. Each example will present new writing problems and provide new insights, from the elementary to the complex.

Revisions of examples do not represent the one "correct answer." Actually, there can be a variety of revisions that "work" marvelously well. The point of this book is to illustrate principles through the revisions. Writing and revising are creative processes as well as deliberative ones.

I will also analyze excerpts from a couple of my scripts that have made a difference in my career, and will conclude with a line-by-line analysis of the first nine pages of a screenplay.

AVOID THIS COMMON TRAP

Many writers make the crucial mistake of assuming that they understand spec format and spec writing. For that reason, some make glaring errors in their scripts that could have been avoided. More importantly, they fail to use formatting and spec writing principles that would improve the impact of their screenplay on readers.

Because the information in this book on spec writing builds on the foundation laid in Book III, I strongly urge you to read (not skim) Book III if you haven't already. *You will find a great deal of direction concerning spec writing, including examples of dialogue, narrative description (writing action), and the effective use of headings.*

KEY REVISING TOOLS

For specific help on how to revise your screenplay, see "Step 7—Make the necessary revisions" in Book II. The next section is focused on writing and revising scenes and sequences in your screenplay.

Key principles and exercises in revising scenes

In writing dialogue and action, clarity is more important than literary quality. Don't overuse the thesaurus, and avoid abstract metaphors. Favor specific language over vague language, active voice over passive voice, and original expressions over clichés. Say a lot with just a few words, but dramatize key moments. In terms of style, write to entertain and excite, not so much to inform and explain.

THE STORY'S THE THING

Many writers who are new to the business believe that they must use fancy formatting techniques in order to get noticed by agents and producers. So they add arty EDITING DIRECTIONS, clever CAMERA ANGLES, truckloads of CAPS, and so on.

I have a copy of the original *Basic Instinct* spec script by Joe Eszterhas—the one he was paid $3 million for. There is not a single DISSOLVE, CUT TO, SERIES OF SHOTS, INSERT, INTERCUT, or fancy technique in his entire 107-page script. Only scene headings, narrative, and dialogue—that's it. His focus is on telling a story through clear, lean, unencumbered writing.

I hasten to add that many screenplays require flashbacks, montages, or what-have-you to communicate the story adequately. Be judicious and keep your focus on the story and characters, as the next section illustrates.

DIRECTING THE CAMERA WITHOUT USING CAMERA DIRECTIONS

What follows are the opening scenes of a writer's screenplay.

```
EXT. HIGHWAY 27 - DAY - AERIAL VIEW

WE SEE the lush Florida countryside until we FIND our
subject, a dark green van.

SLOW ZOOM IN ON VAN

VIEW ON VAN - MOVING

Two characters shout at each other while the CAMERA MOVES
beside the van until we see the child/protagonist looking
out the window at us.

INT. VAN

Everyone is quiet.
```

Try your hand at revising the above sequence. Make any assumptions you wish about the characters, the story, and the vehicle. Naturally, you'll want to use correct spec screenplay format. Once you have written your revision, read my analysis and revision below.

• • • • •

Obviously, there can be many "correct" responses and many revisions that would work beautifully depending on your dramatic goals. Before showing my revision, let me comment on the above sequence.

First of all, I would not call the scene a riveting reading experience. Notice in the scene that the focus is on *how* the story is told, not on the story and characters. What is going on in the van? We don't know. Who are the two characters shouting at each other? Are they parents, kidnappers, siblings? We're not sure. Why is the child looking out the window? What is his or her facial expression? What is the child's name? We don't know because the writer is too involved in *directing* his movie and choosing which technical directions to use.

Of course, we don't need the answers to each of these questions immediately in this opening sequence. Not everything needs to be revealed at once. But we need to know more than is currently being communicated.

Let's try to improve on the original without sacrificing much in terms of the "feel" that the writer wanted to communicate.

```
EXT. FLORIDA - DAY

From the Atlantic shore, the lush countryside extends for
miles.

Below, a black two-lane highway meanders through the spring
growth.

A green van scoots down the highway.

EXT./INT. VAN - DAY

The van rumbles along.

Inside, two twenty-something parents, RALPH and SALLY, shout
at each other, although they cannot be heard.

Ralph shoots an angry look to the back where LISA, age
6, leans away from him and stares out the window at the
beautiful trees and shrubs whizzing by.

The child's eyes look sad. She sits motionless, as if
trapped. One little hand presses against the window.

The parents are silent now -- gathering steam before their
next eruption.
```

In the revision, I have *suggested* almost everything the original writer wanted, but my focus is on the story and the characters, not on fancy ways to tell the story.

The first paragraph describes the aerial shot the original writer wanted. The first three paragraphs are obviously directing the camera to move inland from the shore and down to the highway and finally to the van.

Later in the scene, I direct the camera (without using a camera direction) to a CLOSE UP of the child at the window. In effect, I am directing the reader's eye, and I do it for a *story and character* reason. I want the reader to know that the child is the most important character in the scene, and that maybe she is the central character of the story; and I want the reader (and the movie audience) to emotionally identify with the child's situation. That's the reason for Ralph's look at Lisa. It implies that the child may be the subject of the parents' shouts.

Incidentally, I could have written that paragraph of the parents shouting using the term MOS (which means "without sound," as explained in Book III).

Inside, two twenty-something parents, RALPH and SALLY, shout at each other MOS.

In addition, I *imply* a POV shot of the child staring at the trees and shrubs. If desired, I could even describe the reflection of trees on the window glass (without using technical terms). I identify the child's sex by giving her a name that is definitely a female name. The two adults are parents and they now have names.

I end the scene with a promise of things to come. I am trying to create some interest in what happens next while revealing the emotions of the parents.

In summary, my advice is to focus on story and character; and, while you are at it, use clear, specific language.

• • • • •

I love giving this revision assignment to my students. Here is how one student handled the assignment.

FADE IN:

EXT. FLORIDA - DAY

A seagull flies in circles high above the lush countryside. Diving deep, the seagull soars over a highway towards the windshield of an old multi-colored van.

The collision is imminent when suddenly the seagull elevates.

INT. VAN - CONTINUOUS

A cloud of smoke fills the dirty interior. SLIM and MINNIE, early 30s, loudly laugh while smoking joints.

> MINNIE
> Whoa! Dude, did you see that?

> SLIM
> Awesome! Like an angel gliding over
> electric waves of holistic force!
> > (glancing at the rear
> > mirror)
> Hey, Sweetie, be a good baby and pass
> Daddy a doobie from the box.

SWEETIE, six years old, writes with her crayons over a back
window surrounded by a mess of food wrappers and toys.

> SWEETIE
> Yes, Daddy-O.

EXT. VAN — DAY

As the van meanders away, Sweetie's colorful and childish
writing appears on the back window while she looks to the
sky. It reads: "Take me with U."

The seagull circles above.

EVERY SCENE SHOULD HAVE A SPECIFIC PURPOSE

Here is a short scene that needs a little help. The three children—Jamie, age 14; Billy,
age 10; and Sissy, age 6—stand over the grave of their alcoholic father (Larry). They're
on their own now, and it has been established earlier that Jamie has been taking care
of the family. How would you revise it?

EXT. COUNTY CEMETERY - NIGHT

A soft wind rustles the hair on three darkly dressed figures
standing over an unmarked grave. Eyes fixed on freshly
covered ground. Everyone there who ever cared about Larry or
his family. Jamie, Billy, and Sissy stand alone.

> JAMIE
> We used the last of our savings to put
> Dad here. (pause) There's not much left.

Her conversation is with herself.

> JAMIE
> I guess we'll have to rely on ourselves
> (ironically) We've always had to anyway.

> Not much different now.

She regains some composure.

```
                    JAMIE
                (thinking softly)
            Gotta get some dough. Fast. There isn't
            much time.


She doesn't even have the luxury to allow herself to mourn
for more than a few minutes. It's on to the next crisis to
solve. She has been -- and now certainly is -- the only one
to find the answers to all their worries.


                    BILLY
            We gonna be split up now!
```

Have you written your revision? Okay, let's take a close look at the original again. In terms of formatting, the dialogue lines for Jamie's first two speeches are too wide (more than the maximum 4 inches) and the wrylies are not formatted correctly. You caught that immediately.

What is the purpose of the scene? That's a good question to ask of any scene you write. Every scene should have at least one specific purpose and may have more.

In this case, the purpose is apparently to show Jamie as the new head of the household. A secondary purpose is to show Billy worried about being abandoned—which, of course, adds to Jamie's burden. In your revision, you want to make sure the scene focuses on that aloneness and on that burden (now it's us against the world).

The dialogue is too "on the nose" or obvious. Jamie says precisely what she is thinking and feeling. How can we improve the dialogue?

The exposition about the savings being gone might be worth keeping because it adds to the opposition. But let the line come in response to something Billy says or does. Jamie's last line about needing "some dough" is already implied in the exposition about the savings, so her third speech can be omitted as well.

What does the last wryly, "thinking softly," mean? First of all, how can you think softly? And how can you say a line by thinking softly? So the wryly makes no sense.

The first paragraph of narrative opens with a soft wind. Why do we need the wind? I don't see why, as this is written now, but since the whole world is against these kids, let the whole world come at them like the wind. That might help dramatize their situation. In my revision, I'm going to use a cold wind (not a soft wind) to subtly represent the opposition in this scene. And I'm going to end my revision with Jamie accepting the challenge of that wind. I think that will help move the story forward a little better.

The last two lines of the first paragraph are confusing. Who is everyone? I assume the writer means that the three kids are the only people in the world who cared about Larry. You cannot afford to confuse your reader with general or vague language.

In the third paragraph, Jamie regains some composure. When did she lose it?

The fourth paragraph is an "author intrusion." The writer is including things that cannot appear on the screen. You cannot *tell* us this stuff, you've got to *show* us through action, sound, and images, or reveal it in dialogue.

Once you have written your revision of the above scene, take a look at mine. Remember, there is no one correct way to revise this scene. In fact, I hope your version is better than mine.

```
EXT. COUNTY CEMETERY - NIGHT

Jamie, Billy, and Sissy huddle over a fresh, unmarked grave.
Alone. A cold wind tangles their hair.

Billy crosses his arms over his chest, trying to keep the
cold out. He peers up at Jamie, looking forlorn.

Jamie stifles a sob. Speaks to no one in particular.


                    JAMIE
          Didn't leave us with even a dime.


                    BILLY
              (chin quivering)
          You gonna go away now -- huh?


Jamie pulls Billy close. The three gently embrace.

The wind picks up, but Jamie bravely lifts her countenance
against it.
```

COMMON DIALOGUE PROBLEMS

Dialogue may be the most important element of a spec script. Although professional readers will read your entire script, some producers focus mainly on dialogue. Please review the sections on dialogue in Book I and Book III. And though I've already identified the seven deadliest dialogue sins in Book I, I'd like to share a few more examples that might be helpful.

An unoriginal and colorless dialogue exchange

Kyle is the rooky federal marshal assigned to protect Rebecca/Lauren, the savvy and seasoned Robin Hood type on every hit man's list. She likes to rob the robbers. Rebecca, using the name Lauren, has been giving Kyle a hard time.

> KYLE
> Had I known that you were going to be
> such a pain, I would've been here sooner.
> Are you always this nice to people sent
> to protect you?

> REBECCA/LAUREN
> Oh honey, you aren't the first and you
> aren't going to be the last. Before you
> there was Ryan, Gary, Thomas, Larry,
> John,Malcolm, and Peter. Do you really
> think I don't have experience dealing
> with your kind?

> KYLE
> What the hell does that mean?

> REBECCA/LAUREN
> Macho federal marshals who think they are
> so great.

Do the words "boring" and "obvious" apply here? This is ordinary or typical dialogue that almost any character could say, and I think I've heard the phrase "your kind" dozens of times in other movies. What's needed is an injection of each character's personality into how they speak. In addition, do we really need to name every previous marshal who's been on the job? Since Rebecca dominates the exchange, let's let her interrupt him before he can get started; and let's allow the revelation that he's not the first marshal shock him. Finally, we need a punch line to end the exchange.

                    KYLE
          Had I known that you were such a pain
          in the ass, I --

                    REBECCA/LAUREN
          -- Oh spare me. You sound just like Gary.
                    (off his confusion)
          Your predecessor.

                    KYLE
          You mean there was someone before me?

                    REBECCA/LAUREN
          Seven badass federal marshals in all. I
          think I'll call you Dopey.

Would you agree that the revision is more engaging, better captures the personalities of the characters, and moves faster than the original?

These CIA operatives say too much

Here's an example of a scene that relies too much on dialogue. The three men in the scene are all CIA types. Try your hand at revising it into something more interesting.

Jack is on the speaker phone with Peter.

                    JACK
          Forget that for now, Peter, we have
          something even more troubling. We
          caught a lucky break in tracking that
          Tajik email. It turns out it received
          six encrypted emails over the past
          three years from an email address we
          know Vlad the Russian was using. So what
          do you think about that?

                    PETER (V.O.)
          So who's this Vlad? He is some kind
          of spy?

> JACK
> Perhaps the most notorious arms merchant
> in the world.
>> (semi-sarcastically)
> With his connections he has access to all
> Russian weapon systems, and I do mean
> all, Peter.

> HENRY
> Fortunate for us the Israelis track this
> guy's every move. They say he's in
> Damascus right now. Although who knows?

> JACK
> We need to take him, Peter, and I mean
> now. He's the only target we have that can
> shed light on what's really happening. It
> could cause a diplomatic ruckus though.

> PETER (V.O.)
> I've heard enough, do what you need to
> do, Jack. Run this through Strategic
> Support Branch over at Defense. The
> resources you need are at your disposal.
> Report directly to me. I gotta run now.

How did the revising go? I sometimes find that I like student revisions better than my own. I hope that's the case with your revision, since you are the next great screenwriter. One key to revising is to relax and enjoy the process. Look for opportunities to characterize through narrative description (as discussed in the section on narrative description in Book III) and through dialogue. Write lean; make every word count.

I think you can see that the scene above is overloaded with exposition and is devoid of action or visual input. There is not any differentiation between the characters—they are not characterized. The parenthetical makes little sense—semi-sarcastically? I guess that means he's not fully sarcastic. And where did Henry come from? Shouldn't he be mentioned at the beginning of the scene or at the point he enters the scene? Finally, there is no conflict in the scene.

In approaching the revision, I asked myself, "Who are these guys?" I then created simple characterizations. I think of Jack as someone anxious for action, so I open with him pacing. That's a characterization. I see Peter as rooted, serious, the mastermind, so I open with him riveted, impenetrable, and alert. I like Henry as the opposite of Jack—cautious, calm, and not respected. That contrast will help define both men. I also give Henry a visual prop (a teacup) that I try to use to the max. In addition, I get these men off the phone and into a room together where there can be more interaction.

In view of the above, I decide to inject a little conflict from the start by showing Jack disregarding something Henry says before the scene begins; it doesn't matter what. A little later, Henry is not shown the secret papers. So this is Jack (action) versus Peter (caution). Although Peter is the central character of the movie, Jack is the central character in his scene with Henry as his opposition. A lot is implied by what is said and what is not said, plus, the last speech at the end leaves room for subtext.

Finally, at the end, Peter and Jack are motivated to take further action. We know this dialogue scene will lead to later action scenes. Also, we've foreshadowed possible interference from Henry, who does not like what has happened. Notice that we end with three different reactions to the same event.

```
INT. CONFERENCE ROOM - DAY

Jack paces while Peter sits riveted to his chair --
impenetrable and alert. Henry casually sips his tea.


                    JACK
          Forget that, Henry. We have something
          more troubling.


Jack drops papers on the table for Peter. Peter looks
surprised for only a nanosecond. Henry raises his gaze,
trying to see.


                    JACK
          Picked up a few encrypted emails from
          someone named Vlad.


                    PETER
          The arms merchant?


                    JACK
          Has access to all Russian weapon systems.
```

> HENRY
> Israelis say he's in Damascus.

> JACK
> We need to take him, Peter.

> HENRY
> Could cause a diplomatic ruckus.

Peter waves Henry off. Henry, disgruntled, takes comfort in a sip of tea.

> PETER
> (to Jack)
> Run this through Strategic Support over at Defense...
> (standing)
> ... and report directly to me.

Jack nearly jumps with elation. Peter is emotionless. Henry has a sour look on his face.

> JACK
> Tea not to your liking?

Including the subtext with the text in the same speech

In the above example, the subtext of the last speech is, "Is our decision not to your liking?" It's implied by the text (the actual line).

In the following example, the first sentence says it all, and the second sentence states the subtext, which, of course, should not be stated. I provide this example because I so often see speeches that include the text followed by the subtext in the speech. Here's the flawed speech:

> COOPER
> I should have studied harder in high school. I think I made a mistake.

Since the first line implies the second, omit the second, and you allow the subtext to remain below (sub-) the speech (-text). Remember, the subtext is the unstated, underlying meaning of the text.

                    COOPER
          Should have studied harder in high
          school.

Speaking too often in complete sentences

Let's look at a longer example of an overwritten speech. Try your hand at revising the following speech before reading my comments below.

                    MORGAN
          Have you experienced a lot of violence
          on the job?

                    COOPER
          Not too much, but definitely enough. Plus
          things have been crazy here over the last
          couple of years.

                    MORGAN
          So you couldn't stand it anymore?

                    COOPER
          It was all right. I like my job. It was
          certainly not boring, but my wife
          couldn't stand it. After nine-eleven,
          she didn't sleep much.

Please notice that Morgan and Cooper are mainly speaking in complete sentence, and the exchange feels more like a question-and-answer session than a conversation. The revision below contains fragments of speech.

                    MORGAN
          Seen a lot of action?

                    COOPER
          Plenty.

                    MORGAN
          Couldn't stand it anymore.

                    COOPER
          Wife couldn't. Not after nine-eleven.

As you know, the above is not the only "correct" way to revise the exchange; it's just better than the original. If we understood more about the personalities involved and the situation, we could improve it more. For example, it may be that Cooper is a talker who uses colorful and original phraseology. If that's the case, write on. I loved listening to the long-winded Professor G. H. Dorr (Tom Hanks) in *The Ladykillers*. That's mainly because his character speaks with original phrases and a vocabulary unique to him, rather than delivering derivative or boring speeches.

Overwritten wrylies
There is a growing school of thought that suggests that writers should write actions as parentheticals. If an action can be described in three or four words and seems to accompany the speech, then I think that's fine.

                    TEX
             (tipping his hat)
          Pleased to meet you, ma'am.

However, don't go overboard with this. I consider the following an abuse of parentheticals.

                    JACK
             (grabbing Jill by
             the hand)
          Could sure use some water, my dear.
             (a beat; starts up
             the hill)

                    JILL
             (snatching the bucket
             out of his hand)
          Sounds like a good idea, Jack.
             (swings bucket around
             and around as they near
             the well)

I'm not seeing a major problem with the parentheticals that precede each of the first two speeches. However, try not to end a dialogue block with a parenthetical. Generally, a dialogue block should conclude with dialogue—the speech. Finally, the speeches are rather stiff. Here's my revision.

```
Jack shows Jill his empty bucket.

                    JACK
          Water?

Jill snatches the bucket.

                    JILL
          Race ya.

She swings the bucket around as they gallop to the well.
```

How do I love thee? Let's count the ways

How does your character say "I love you" or show affection? Here's a fun exercise. Think of a character from your screenplay, and have him or her say or do something that communicates love without using the word "love." Here are some examples from successful movies:

"Here's looking at you, Kid" —*Casablanca*

"Shut up and deal." —*The Apartment*

Juno loads her beloved's mailbox with orange TicTacs. When Bleeker asks her why, she says, "Because they're your fave. And you can never have too much of your favorite one-calorie breath mint."—*Juno*

"As you wish." —*The Princess Bride*

"I caught you a delicious bass." —*Napoleon Dynamite*

DETAILS AND ACTION

What follows are the first two paragraphs of a screenplay written by one of my clients before he/she became a client. Rather than overwritten dialogue, we have overwritten narrative description with too many details. The following big blocks of black ink are guaranteed to discourage any reader. Let's see if we can't whittle them down a little while striving to be more specific in describing images and actions. Here's the original:

```
EXT. TRAIN - DAY

We see the skyline of New York from a train. Painted on the
side of it are words that say, Brooklyn Railroad. It's going
very fast and has a gray look to it.

INT. TRAIN - DAY

Inside the train are all kinds of commuters. They are from
every age and ethnic group and they fill the train car clean
up. They are all headed to work in New York City, as can
be plainly seen from their working clothes. A bunch of
them cannot find seats and must stand. One of them is SALLY
STANWICK, who has piercing blue eyes and long, flowing locks
of blond hair. She is in her mid-twenties and is wearing a
silk blouse with a pink sweater over it and a plain black
cotton skirt. She senses someone behind her and turns to see
a young man giving her the eye and smiling at her in a very
peculiar way.
```

Let's critique the first paragraph. To start with, I suggest we avoid using the implied camera direction "We see" and describe the scene in a more interesting way. The second sentence contains the pronoun "it," which could refer to the train or to the skyline of New York. It is unclear. Be specific.

Because no paragraph of narrative description should exceed four lines in length, the second paragraph represents a major violation. We need to condense it or break it up.

Why must this woman's eyes be blue and her hair blond? Unless they are essential to the plot, omit specific physical descriptions. Describing her attire is a good idea, but it would be better if that attire commented on her character.

The writer uses too many words to describe the group and its ethnic diversity.

Finally, what does the writer mean when the man smiles "in a very peculiar way"? That's too general. How can the reader visualize that? What does a "very peculiar way" mean? Be specific. I recall a line of description from a different script that said, "Sally gives him one of her looks." Which look is that? That action is too general.

Our revision should include only what is essential to move the story forward; and since this is an opening scene, it needs to establish a mood, atmosphere, or something about the nature of this story.

As you know from reading Book III, each paragraph of narrative description should, ideally, present one beat of action or one main image. This is not a hard-fast rule, just a guideline. Let's adhere to that guideline in this revision.

Without using camera directions, let's open with a shot of the train in the foreground and Manhattan in the background. In fact, let's handle the scene revision in four brief paragraphs.

1. Our first image will be of the train, establishing departure location and destination (with the train in the foreground and Manhattan in the background).
2. Our second image (and second paragraph) will be of the people in the train car.
3. Our third paragraph will describe Sally and her action.
4. Our fourth will describe the second character.

We will omit Sally's eye and hair color to keep casting options open. The specifics of her clothes are irrelevant in this case, unless we can describe her in something that comments on her character. Why don't we give her a simple cotton dress—this is an uncomplicated young woman. Since this is a character's first appearance, we can get away with identifying a character trait: She's perky.

Let's also make sure that the young man's smile says something about him—I think I'm going to use his smile as an action. And let's use a strong, active verb, like *assaults*. That will imply possible conflict.

Finally, let's make sure that our narrative description is as "lean and clean" as possible and makes the reader ask, "What happens next?"

FADE IN:

A speeding silver train races down the tracks toward Manhattan. A sign on the train reads "BROOKLYN RAILROAD."

INT. TRAIN - DAY

Working professionals crowd the train car. Some stand.

Among them is SALLY STANWICK, 25, perky and pretty in a simple cotton dress. She turns abruptly, sensing someone's stares.

A young man in a suit assaults her with a smug smile.

Look for opportunities to characterize

Watch for vague and uninspired language in your screenplay. I realize I expounded on this earlier, but it bears repeating: We miss so many opportunities to characterize by failing to use specific language and concrete action verbs. For example, the following action looks perfectly okay:

```
Mary drinks a beer.
```

. . . But the two revisions that follow tell us a little more about Mary:

```
Mary meekly sips a Lowenbrau.
```

```
Mary cocks her head, downs a Bud Light, and crushes the can
against her brow.
```

Avoid marking time

The words *when*, *while*, and *as* sometimes slow down "the read." Here's an example:

```
As Suzy steps into the restaurant, she spots Larry on a
stool playing the ukulele to no one's pleasure, so while he
plays, she strides right up to him and when he hits a sour
code, she takes away the instrument.
```

The following revision will communicate more easily and quickly to the reader.

```
Suzy steps into the restaurant. She spots Larry strumming
the ukulele to no one's pleasure. She strides up to him and
snatches the instrument.
```

That doesn't mean you should never use those words. Just focus on action and keep the pace marching forward.

Cut the fat in half

Here's the assignment. Cut the following in half without losing anything that is important.

```
Black smoke billows from a pile of trash at a freeway
construction site. Workers pour concrete into a form that
will become a support for a new freeway overpass. Huge
trucks move dirt and rock from one place to another as
bulldozers level the land. A construction worker uses flags
to direct the flow of the construction equipment.
```

What follows is my shot at the assignment. And, by the way, the fact that this is a freeway construction site already appears in the scene heading, so we don't need to duplicate it here. The reduction is from 58 words to 28.

```
Black smoke billows from a pile of trash. Workers pour
concrete into forms. A FLAG MAN directs huge trucks filled
with rocks and dirt. Bulldozers level the land.
```

For a more complete discussion of writing action and narrative description, see the "Narrative description" chapter in Book III.

START THE SCENE LATER IN THE SCENE

In Book I, I advised you to evaluate a scene to see if starting the scene a little later makes it work better. What follows is a brief sequence from a Western romantic-comedy. The two main characters are James and Margaret. At this moment in time, the two are at odds over a legal issue. He sees an opportunity to embarrass her because he believes she doesn't know how to ride a horse. She doesn't, but doesn't want to admit it. How would you shorten or streamline this excerpt to make it more effective?

```
                    JAKE
          Can she ride?


                    JAMES
          I don't rightly know, but she
          better learn pretty quick if she can't.

James grins mischievously.

INT. KITCHEN - NIGHT

The four men, Sarah, James and Margaret are gathered at the
table. Heads are bowed for prayer. The men are so hungry
there is little talk at first.

                    JAMES
          We'll be going to Ellsworth for cattle,
          day after tomorrow. Jake's going,
          Sarah and Margaret and Billy. I'll ride
          out also. Buddy and Buck will run the
          place here.
```

                    (turns to Margaret)
          Can you ride?

                    MARGARET
          Of course, I can ride....
                    (pauses)
          ... but it's been a long time since
          I've been on a horse.

                    JAMES
          I bet.
                    (looks at Sarah)
          Teach her, but not that sidesaddle stuff
          either. We've got a long ways to go.

Sarah nods.

                    JAMES
          I'll be going into town for supplies first
          tomorrow. Get your list ready.

EXT. HORSE CORRAL - DAY

There is a clue in the above example that helps us to know exactly what to do, and that's the repetition of the line "Can she ride?" In my revision below, I'm going to start the second scene later in the scene for dramatic effect. The context of the scene will communicate that James has just asked her if she can ride a horse.

                    JAKE
          Can she ride?

James grins mischievously.

INT. KITCHEN - NIGHT

                    MARGARET
          Of course, I can ride....

She searches for a vote of confidence from the ranch hands sitting around the table. They silently eat with their eyes down.

```
James allows himself an impish grin.

EXT. HORSE CORRAL - DAY
```

REVEALING EMOTION

When evaluating scripts, I often find myself imparting the following advice: *Describe a character reaction or small action, or describe a facial expression or gesture to give the reader a better sense of what your character is thinking or feeling.* After all, in a normal conversation, about 90% of what is communicated is communicated nonverbally; that is, through voice tone, body language, and the use of objects, space, and time. Nonverbal communication is powerful in real life—ask any baby or toddler—and it can be powerful in your screenplay.

These little "reactions" or "actions" can be as simple as the following:

```
He squeezes her hand.

Anita looks frustrated.

Her face relaxes into an expression of mixed gratitude and
relief.
```

These details invite us into the character's inner life and help the reader to more easily sympathize with the character.

Another problem I often see in scripts is the over-expression of emotion. That can make the emotion seem less real.

MAXIMIZING MOVIE MOMENTS

The following is a description of a family driving home from the airport, and observing a plane that is about to crash. The father of the family is in the plane.

```
INT. CAR - DAY

In the rearview mirror, Lisa sees her children look
terrified by something. Lisa looks out the window and sees
a jet headed toward them, wings seesawing, engines roaring
unsteadily.
```

This is an emotional, cinematic moment, so let's dramatize it. We'll use INT./EXT. so that the camera can be either inside or outside the car at any given moment. The first two paragraphs describe a POV shot. They give us the viewpoint of Lisa, the wife. You'll see in the remaining description a couple of close-ups (clutching her blouse; stomping on the accelerator).

```
INT./EXT. CAR - DAY

In the rearview mirror, Lisa sees her children's faces glued
to the window, looking terrified.

She turns her head to see a passenger jet headed towards
them -- almost upon them. Engines whine loudly.

The children begin to scream. Lisa's hand goes to her mouth.


                         LISA
              Michael.


The jet's wings seesaw. The engines roar unsteadily....

And then the nose dips. The plane appears to be aimed right
at them.

Lisa stomps on the accelerator.
```

And, of course, the action would continue from there. There is a time to shorten scenes and a time to lengthen scenes. In this case, it is a time to lengthen the scene for dramatic and emotional effect.

What happened?

I read four tedious pages of dialogue in a script that was followed by these two sentences:

```
A raging gun battle ensues. Martinelli is eventually killed.
```

This is not an example of "more is less." This is "less is less." In this case, less is almost nothing. Who killed Martinelli? How was it done? How did the action build? And was Martinelli killed over a bottle of apple juice? Dramatize the action; make the reader see it.

Your character's experience is your reader's experience
In the scene excerpt that follows, the patient is the central character. How would you revise the scene to get the reader (and the audience) more involved with him?

```
INT. TRAUMA ROOM - NIGHT

The flight crew enters with a man C-spine/stabilized on a
backboard.

The TRAUMA RESIDENT, appearing like he just got out of bed,
is stationed at the head of the table. The other trauma team
members assume their positions to do their tasks.

The patient is transferred from the backboard to the trauma
table.

The flight nurse commands attention. She fires her report.


                    FLIGHT NURSE
                (announcing loudly)
        We have a thirty-nine-year-old male
        involved in a single-car rollover.
        He was extricated from the vehicle.
        No allergies. No significant history.
        His Glascow Coma Scale is 15.
        PERRLA at three millimeters. He
        complains of pain, nine out of ten,
        in his mid-back and has no feeling or
        movement in his lower extremities.
        All other assessment is negative.
        I gave him a half liter of L.R. in
        flight and twenty milligrams of Decadron
        I.V. He has received no pain medication
        yet. Any questions?
```

Did you have fun with your revision? You guessed right if you thought the above was written by a nurse. Your reader wants the character's viewpoint, not the writer's.

There are two main points I want to make about the above excerpt. First, the focus is on medical procedure, not on the central character. In fact, the writer is so focused on the medical aspects of the scene that she refers to Brad as "patient" in the narrative description. It reads more like a case study than a drama. Second, the Flight Nurse's speech contains too much medical jargon. Just give us a flavor.

One goal that we have as screenwriters is to get the reader and audience to feel emotion and perhaps to bond with the character. People come to movies to feel emotions vicariously through the characters. Readers want to be emotionally affected by what they read. Thus, our task becomes to get our audience involved with Brad. With that in mind, here is one possible revision:

```
INT. TRAUMA ROOM - NIGHT

The flight crew enters with Brad strapped to a backboard.

The TRAUMA RESIDENT, appearing like he just got out of bed,
is stationed at the head of the table. Trauma team members
quickly gather around Brad.

The FLIGHT NURSE fires off her report.


                    FLIGHT NURSE
          We have a thirty-nine-year-old male...

Brad takes a gulp of air, responding to the pain, as he
is lifted from the backboard. He is nearly dropped on the
trauma table -- a sudden throaty yelp escapes him.


                    FLIGHT NURSE (O.S.)
          ... involved in a single-car rollover.
          No allergies. No significant history.

Brad holds a trembling finger to his head, trying to control
the pain enough to hear.


                    FLIGHT NURSE (O.S.)
          He complains of pain, nine out of ten,
          in his mid-back and has no feeling or
          movement in his lower extremities. He has
          received no pain medication yet.

Brad looks helplessly up at the impassive faces of the
professionals surrounding him.
```

In my revision, I keep the focus on Brad and on his situation. I include dialogue that highlights Brad's situation and pain. I include a POV shot of Brad looking up at the medical professionals. The word "impassive" helps the audience sense Brad's aloneness in this scene. Notice that most of the dialogue is spoken off screen (O.S.), so that the camera can be on Brad. That helps the reader and audience better identify with Brad, and it gives the actor something to act. Finally, I removed the unnecessary wryly "announcing loudly."

Wisdom from *Juno*

In the original *Juno* spec script of 94 pages, most everything is summed up in the end on one page. We see Vanessa feeding the baby and hear Juno say in a voiceover, "It ended with a chair." We then see the framed note from Juno on the wall. Then, in voiceover, Juno describes the birth and explains that Bleeker came to the hospital with flowers. But there's a mountain of movie moments missing from this resolution.

For one thing, we don't see Vanessa receive the baby. We don't see Juno in the hospital. We don't have a moment between father and daughter. We're missing a moment in the hospital between Bleeker and Juno. And what about Bren?

All of these lapses are recognized and exploited in the final draft. Diablo Cody does a marvelous job of milking the emotion and dramatizing the drama (and heightening the comedy). In fact, more than five pages are added.

That section begins with the water breaking: "Thundercats are go." At the hospital, Bren rescues Juno by demanding a "spinal tap." Then we see Juno with the baby. Meanwhile, Bleeker wins the track meet and runs off to see Juno. Then the Nurse introduces Vanessa to her son: "I have a son?" Back in the birthing suite, Dad has his moment with Juno: "Someday, you'll be back here, honey. On *your* terms." Then Bleeker arrives to embrace Juno, his dirty track shoes on the bed sheets. Finally, we return to Vanessa, this time rocking her baby: "It ended with a chair." And, of course, we see the framed note from Juno.

In the revision, each character with an important relationship with Juno is given his or her moment with Juno. Some get two. Learn to recognize those cinematic moments in your screenplay and to enhance them.

DESCRIBING WHAT WE SEE AND CREATING MOOD

One problem that I frequently see in scripts that I evaluate is narrative that describes realizations, thoughts, feelings, and memories. These cannot appear on the silver screen. Only describe what the audience will see on the movie screen and hear on the soundtrack. That's it. The following actual examples are all incorrect.

```
When Susan sees his face, she remembers the first pizza she
ever ate.
```

```
Pablo stops walking toward her. He was thinking about how
much he wanted her, but also how much his mother hated her.
He was at a stalemate.
```

```
James feels awful.
```

```
Sigourney knew that this was the last time she would ever
see home again.
```

In each of the above examples, I ask, *How will this appear on the screen?* How will the audience know, for example, that Susan is recalling a pizza, or what Sigourney "knew"?

Let's review these examples one by one and decide how to revise them.

In Susan's case, if this is a comedy, you could describe his face, flash back to Susan's pizza, then describe her shuddering and turning away. You see, you can describe only that which can actually be seen (or heard) to convey your story. Another option is to have her say, after touching or gazing at his face, "I feel like a pepperoni pizza."

In Pablo's case, I think you will have to write some dialogue to convey his indecision, or you might write an earlier scene where he joyfully tells his mother that he is in love, and she expresses her hatred for the girl. Then you could cut to him walking toward his beloved, stopping, looking confused and unsure. Maybe you can think of something better.

With James, describe his facial expression or a gesture that will convey that he feels awful. What do we *see*? *See* is the key word. "James feels awful" is not a visual image. Instead, how about something like this:

```
James drops his forehead into his hand; then gazes up with a
guilty look on his face.
```

That's more "actable," and that's important to remember—describe what is actable, what an actor can act. As with James, you may want to describe Sigourney's facial expression or a gesture. Here's one possible description:

```
Sigourney gazes at the homestead as if memorizing every
detail.
```

For whom the bell tolls
What follows is a paragraph of overwritten narrative description that I'd like you to revise.

```
Matthew's wife, ELLEN, a pretty woman in her twenties, with
red hair, is sitting at a sewing machine making a baby
quilt. There is lots of evidence of the room being made
into a nursery. She HEARS the rain, gets up and goes to the
window. It's evident she's in the early stages of pregnancy.
As she looks out to sea, she HEARS the local church bell
RING, signaling that a boat has been lost. She closes her
eyes.
```

First of all, the scene exceeds the four-line limit for narrative description.

In the second place, you have two visual images here. The first is the image of Ellen in the room. The second is Ellen's looking out to sea and hearing a church bell. Thus, we already know there should be two paragraphs. Since the ringing of the bell is so important, that deserves its own paragraph anyway.

Third, let's only include what's essential in the description. Ellen's hair color is probably irrelevant, so we can omit that.

Fourth, in terms of readability, we should eliminate the present-progressive expression "is sitting" and use an active verb like "sits." As you will see below, the writer also used the active verb "sews" in her revision.

And fifth, the audience can't know what the ringing of the church bell means because that "meaning" (it's a signal that a boat has been lost) cannot appear on the movie screen; thus, we cannot mention the meaning here. It's probably going to have to come out in action and/or dialogue later (or probably earlier).

My client made the following revision.

```
Matthew's wife, ELLEN, 26 and pregnant, sews a baby quilt.
An unpainted crib sits nearby.

Hearing a driving rain, she hurries to the window and gazes
out to sea. The church bell rings. She closes her eyes in
pain, her hand clutching her blouse.
```

In her first paragraph of her revision, the writer provides specific evidence that suggests the room is being made into a nursery.

In the second paragraph, she chooses details that will help create a *mood* and also give a sense that the ringing of the church bell means something painful. She uses the "driving rain," the specific verbs "hurries" and "clutches," and the emotional reaction "closes her eyes in pain" (which is actable). The mood created will suggest possible music to the composer.

CHARACTER MOTIVATION IN A SCENE

Virtually every scene should feature a character with an intention, goal, desire, need, or problem. There should also be some opposition to the central character's actions toward that goal or intention, even if it's subtle. This creates conflict, and conflict is necessary for both drama and comedy. The conflict will escalate if the central character continues to be thwarted in his efforts. The character will be forced to act more strongly until an outcome is determined.

This simple scene is from *The Secret of Question Mark Cave*, a comedy I wrote for children a long time ago in a galaxy far, far away (referring to my mind). It became a sample script that I never sold but which found me work. The children are about 10 years of age. Just prior to this scene, the Red Hat Bandit was about to harm the children because they discovered his hideout. They defended themselves with wood swords, tree limbs, and rocks to render the Red Hat Bandit unconscious. Here is how the scene breaks down dramatically:

Stinky wants to control the group, be the leader, prove he's smarter than the rest. Everyone calls him Stinky because he is likes to cut the cheese. He even woke up his sleeping uncle once that way (established in Act 1). That foreshadows an action in this scene. If I wrote this now, I'd be tempted to cut the farting since I have seen it so much in movies since my little opus was written.

Ralph's primary emotion in this scene is curiosity, which leads him to challenge Stinky. Stinky asserts that the bandit is dead, but Ralph is not so sure. So the primary conflict in this scene is between Ralph and Stinky. Both are motivated in their intentions. Note the differences in their speaking styles.

Glodina's primary emotion is fear. She fuels a secondary conflict with the three boys (the Magnificent Three) because she wants to leave and they don't. Her desire to leave creates a little suspense—we suspect something bad could happen if they stick around too long. In fact, Glodina's line "Let's go then before he wakes up" foreshadows the end of the scene.

Seebee is a big fan of *Zombie Busters*, a TV show in which zombies suck the brains out of their victims (again, established earlier in the screenplay). Although Seebee is the central character of the movie, he is only a minor character in this scene. His purpose is to plant the seed that the bandit might be a zombie. The obligatory question in the scene is this: "Is the Red Hat Bandit dead?"

In my view, this scene accomplishes many things. It serves as a bridge between two action sequences. It plays up the innocence of the children. It moves the story forward— the bandit is more strongly motivated now. After this scene, there is no doubt in the children's minds that he is going to kill them if he can catch them. Plus, we want to know what happens next.

Finally, look at all the white space! The description is sparse, dialogue speeches are short, and the wrylies are useful.

EXT. QUESTION MARK CAVE - DAY

The Magnificent Three plus Glodina stand in a circle gaping at the fallen bandit. They cling to their weapons -- just in case.

                    GLODINA
          Is he dead?

                    RALPH
          Nah, dead people stick their tongues out.
          Like that.

Ralph demonstrates the death tongue.

                    GLODINA
          Let's go then before he wakes up.

                    STINKY
          Don't worry, he's dead.

                    RALPH
          Maybe his tongue don't stick out cuz he
          swallowed it.

                    SEEBEE
          If he's dead, we have to go to jail for
          killing him.

                    STINKY
        Heck no. Self-defense.

                    RALPH
        Yeah, he was going to kill us. Now he's
        a stiff. Wait a minute, is he stiff?
        Dead people are stiff. That'll prove it.

                    STINKY
        Why don't you grab him and see?

Ralph is reluctant to touch the "corpse."

                    RALPH
        He looks kinda stiff.

                    GLODINA
        You guys, let's go.

                    RALPH
        Wait a minute, aren't dead people blue?

                    STINKY
        I say he's dead!

                    RALPH
        He looks kinda blue.

                    SEEBEE
        He looks just like the zombies in Zombie
        Busters.

                    RALPH
                (a victorious smile)
        How can he be a zombie if he's dead?

                    SEEBEE
        They are dead, but then they blink their

eyes open and they suck everyone's brains
out.

Seebee makes convincing sucking sounds. Glodina shivers.

The children shuffle in for a better look at the bandit.

>   RALPH
>   Wait a minute, I heard dead people kept
>   their eyes open.

>   STINKY
>   (the last straw)
>   I'll prove he's dead.

He squats over the robber's face and FARTS.

The Red Hat Bandit's eyes blink open. He grimaces at the
pungent odor.

>   RALPH
>   A zombie! He'll suck our brains out.

The children panic and tear down the trail.

The bandit, angry and groggy, chases after them.

>   RALPH
>   (to Stinky)
>   See, I told you he wasn't dead.

SHOW IS BETTER THAN TELL

Here is one last scene to evaluate and revise. In it, Marilyn tells Helen about her audition. Good luck with your revision.

INT. HELEN'S HOUSE - NIGHT

Helen has torn herself away from her students' papers and is
watching Marilyn pace.

                    HELEN
          Yes... then what?

                    MARILYN
          Then they asked me to sing. It was the
          love song. I belted out the solo part
          without a single problem. I was inspired!
          Then Antonio joined me on the duet and...
          and...

She shudders like a chill just ran up her spine.

                    MARILYN (CONT'D)
               (melodramatically)
          ... the angels wept!

                    HELEN
          That's perfect! Then you got the part!
          It's what you've always wanted! I'm so
          happy for you!

                    MARILYN
               (cuts her off)
          It's not going to happen. They said
          they'd get back to me.

                    HELEN
          What? Why? I don't get it. You said...

                    MARILYN
          I said I did a superb job in the
          audition. That isn't enough on stage.
          They don't like the way I look.

Marilyn drops, dejected, onto the couch.

                    HELEN
          How do you know that?

                    MARILYN
          After the reading and singing, they
          whispered among themselves for a few
          minutes. Then they had me walk back and
          forth across the stage a few times. Then
          they had Antonio stand next to me.

She stands back up again and resumes pacing and gesturing.

                    MARILYN (CONT'D)
          Then they had me walk back and forth with
          Antonio. Then they had Antonio put his
          arms around me. Then they said, "Thank
          you very much, we'll be in touch."

                    HELEN
          Well, that doesn't necessarily mean...

                    MARILYN
          Yes it does. Believe me, I've seen it a
          bunch of times.

She slows her pace and becomes thoughtful. She looks a
little depressed as she walks over and picks up her coat.

                    MARILYN (CONT'D)
          You know it isn't fair. I'm just not sure
          whether to give up, or cry, or just go to
          Baskin-Robbins.

                    HELEN
          Well, whatever you do, don't just give
          up. You have an amazing talent. Sooner or
          later, that will win out.

                    MARILYN
          I hope so. Good night, hon. Don't forget
          we're going to the mall tomorrow after
          school.

Okay, now take a moment to analyze what you've read and revise it into something more interesting, more visual, and more dramatic.

• • • • •

The dialogue is overwritten, too "on the nose," and quite ordinary, with the only action being Marilyn's pacing. There is also too much repetition of the phrase "then they." And both characters speak with the same speaking style.

My first impulse is to take Marilyn's experience and *show* it to the reader, then transition from Marilyn's pacing on the stage to her pacing in Helen's room as she finishes telling Helen the story. Just doing that will give the scene more movement.

In terms of the relationship between Marilyn and Helen, Helen is in the position of nurturing a whiner. Let's revise this so that Marilyn comes off as more sympathetic (not so much of a whiner). Let's allow Marilyn to decide to not give up. And let's give Helen more personality and wit. After all, she's a teacher and knows how to motivate people.

A scene should end on a strong moment. Let's open with a song and close with a song, demonstrating that Marilyn will not give up. And maybe the teacher can give Marilyn an "A," since she's already grading papers. We'll do that indirectly, of course, but it will add a bit of an emotional punch to the scene. In fact, we need to heighten the emotion throughout the scene.

Now let's take a look at some of the specifics of my revision below. We see an empty theater as Marilyn sings. The next image is of Marilyn, who creates a contrast—she's not great looking, but near the angels in her singing. The third image is of two young men, the opposition characters in this scene. Incidentally, even the opposition will recognize her voice, so the reader can be confident that this woman has some talent.

But then the opposition humiliates her. This creates sympathy for her. This moves us into our transition, which we accomplish by putting the camera on Marilyn's face and changing the location. This is easy to do since she is pacing in both places.

Then we have our moment between the two women. We set up Helen with the red pencil so she can use it at the end of the scene. And instead of Helen saying the expected, she tries a more original approach, creating a little conflict in the process.

The laughter releases the tension and sets up the serious moment. Again, we have a contrast. And we get Marilyn to indicate that she won't quit trying without her actually saying any words. Instead, she sings.

• • • • •

Okay, here's our revision, just one of many ways to approach this material:

INT. THEATER - NIGHT

A lovely female voice sings a love song. Her music fills the empty theater.

The voice belongs to Marilyn, looking chubby in her leotards. But her face is angelic -- she is one with her music.

Antonio, slicked back hair and tank top, joins her in a duet.

A YOUNG TURK with a clipboard steps onto the stage.

                    YOUNG TURK
          Enough!
               (circling the couple)
          You'll make the angels jealous.

Marilyn smiles gratefully as Antonio steps away.

Marilyn glances offstage at her image in a mirror. She touches her stomach and frowns.

                    YOUNG TURK
          Gimme a strut. Back and forth.

Marilyn walks across stage -- self-consciously -- then back.

The Young Turk studies her. Antonio steps over to him and whispers something. Looks doubtful.

Marilyn's eyes brim with tears as she paces.

INT. HELEN'S LIVING ROOM - NIGHT

Marilyn paces while Helen listens from her couch.

Homework papers cover the coffee table. Helen fiddles with a red pencil.

                    MARILYN
          ... That's when he said he'd get back
          to me.

                    HELEN
          Well that doesn't necessarily mean --

                    MARILYN
          -- Yes it does. I've seen it.
                    (shaking her head)
          They don't like my looks. That's what
          it is. Always what it is.

                    HELEN
          Well, your voice survived.

                    MARILYN
          The question is... will I?

                    HELEN
          You can always get a tummy tuck.

Marilyn is indignant until she sees Helen's warm smile. Then
her tension releases into sudden laughter. Helen joins in
the laughter.

                    HELEN
          You were made to sing, honey, like a
          big, fat, beautiful bird.

Helen stands and the two briefly embrace.

                    HELEN
          So why don't you fly out of here and
          let me grade some papers, huh?

Marilyn mouths a "thank you." She steps out the door... and
starts singing the love song.

Helen smiles. Writes a big, fat "A" on one of the papers.

When to break formatting rules

As you know, the rules can be bent and even broken. But when? Two conditions must be present. Let's express these conditions as questions.

- Will bending or breaking the rule improve the reading experience? The answer to this question should be "yes."
- Will bending or breaking the rule call attention to the broken rule and create a negative impression? The answer to this question should be "no."

If you have little experience writing, your responses to those questions will necessarily be based on your subjective evaluation. As your experience grows, your assessments will become more objective, but can never be completely objective. But you'll have a better feel for what you can get away with.

SLUGGING IT OUT WITH SLUG LINES

Here is an excerpt from my screenplay *A Window in Time*.

```
EXT. TEMPLE RUIN - DAY

Abu nods gratefully to the Man in Khakis, then rushes to

THE TEMPLE BASE

where a small hole has been cut into the foundation. The Man
in Khakis leads Abu into the blackness.

INSIDE THE CATACOMBS

Abu and the Man in Khakis crawl on all fours toward the
torch light ahead, and finally into

A LARGE CIRCULAR CHAMBER
```

```
where torches illuminate the stoic faces of a dozen workers
standing back against the single, circular wall.
```

In the above scene, I break a rule about scene headings (slug lines). The scene starts outside (EXT.) the temple ruins, then goes inside (INT.). That's a change that requires a new scene heading as follows: INT. CATACOMBS – DAY.

I probably will not be arrested for failing to create a new master scene heading. I don't think the peccadillo would concern a reader. My purpose is to make the scene flow better. In addition, I don't see where someone would become confused. I could make the first scene an INT./EXT. location (which would make all the formatting in the scene correct), but that could confuse the reader: Is Abu inside or outside in the first paragraph?

So—yes!—you can bend or break the rules, but be careful not to get *too* creative. You never want to lose or confuse a reader. Your goal is a clear, unencumbered flow of images, sounds, and actions.

NEVER USE CAMERA DIRECTIONS?

Of course you can use camera directions in a screenplay, but do it rarely and only when you have a good story reason or character reason to do so. I confess that more than once I have used the camera direction PULL BACK TO REVEAL for a comedic or dramatic payoff.

A PROBLEM WITH TIME LAPSE

Throughout Books III and IV, I have emphasized the importance of avoiding technical intrusions. We're going to break that rule here.

Here's a description of a formatting problem as described by my client:

> I want to show a time lapse from day to night for a story reason. A character, Jimmy, parks a Chevy automobile next to a building; someone is locked in the trunk (established in an earlier scene). I want to focus on the Chevy while everything around it changes. Jimmy will stand by the car and then disappear. The sequence will end in a light rain for the next scene. How would you format that?

I suggested she use a format similar to the MONTAGE for the time lapse. Here's the result:

```
TIME LAPSE

The Chevy stays in the same place as everything around it
changes.

-- Jimmy disappears.

-- The day evolves into night as lights go on, then out, in
the building behind the car.

-- Two teenagers gather around the Chevy, then disappear.

-- A light rain drizzles.

EXT. STREET - MORNING

The only sound is the rain on the Chevy. And then the usual
sounds of morning become apparent.
```

CHEATING

If your script is a little too long after all of your excellent revision work and editing, there are little ways you can cheat.

Both Movie Magic Screenwriter and Final Draft provide cheating functions that you can use when necessary. You can use these without concern.

Margins

Do *not* cheat on dialogue margins. Speeches should not extend more than 4 inches across the page. Do *not* cheat on your regular left margin; that should always be at 1.5 inches from the left edge of the paper. Do *not* cheat on the top margin of the page either. The trained eyes that will read your script will readily spot these cheats.

Since the right margin can be anywhere between .5 inches and 1.25 inches, you may set it anywhere within that range. You could go to 1.5 inches and no one would complain.

On some pages, consider changing the bottom margin from 1 inch to .9 or .8 inches, so that you can add another line or keep a speech from continuing onto the next page. However, let me add a word of caution to that suggestion: Some studios and large production companies automatically convert scripts into a "uniform format." This assures them that they are always looking at the same format with each script they get. Of course, in order to do that, they would need an electronic copy of your script.

Line spacing

You may be able to cheat a little on your line spacing. If you are using a word processor like Microsoft Word, adjust your line spacing so that your page holds about 54 or 55 lines, which is standard for a screenplay. Standard for Microsoft Word is 48.

You might be able to make that adjustment with other software programs as well. Most formatting programs give you about 53 to 56 lines per page. If you are not getting 54 to 55 lines, adjust your line spacing so that you do. More than 56 lines per page could look too cramped and may be spotted.

Note: I am not including the page number or the space after the page number in my line counts in the above explanation.

Orphans

Another trick that saves space is shortening paragraphs whose final line contains only one word (referred to as an "orphan"). Thus, if your paragraph contains two lines plus one or two words on the third line, condense the paragraph to two lines.

The same is true of dialogue. If you have just a single line of dialogue that carries over to another page, or a few words of description that carry over to the next page, find a way to move those to the previous page or condense the dialogue or description.

When you force yourself to revise long paragraphs and speeches, the result should be a cleaner, better-written screenplay. I've been able to lose a half-dozen pages in a script just by *tightening up* dialogue and description.

Wrylies

I mentioned in Book III that you can write action in your wrylies (*actor's direction* or *parentheticals*) if that action can be described in no more than two or three lines. As I've said before, think of the rules as guidelines. There may be an instance when a long wryly of four lines works just fine, and saves some space by avoiding breaking to a new paragraph to write action and then double-spacing to write more dialogue.

Naturally, any cheating you do will only be done after the screenplay has been revised and is ready to show. There's no sense in making nitpicky corrections until the script is polished.

Finally, always use 12-point Courier or 12-point Courier New. Do not change the font.

REACHING THE READER

Keep in mind that your primary audience is the reader of your script (not moviegoers), and that he/she is weary of reading scripts. Thus, follow the suggestions for reaching the reader that I have provided throughout *The Bible*, and let the story flow like a river through the mind and heart of those lucky enough to read your script. That river will flow if you use visual, clear, and specific language that directs the eye and touches the heart.

The first 10 pages

The first 10 pages of your script are crucial. They must involve the reader to the extent that she *wants* to know what happens next. What follows are the first nine pages of my action/time-travel/thriller/romance, *A Window in Time*, along with a complete line-by-line analysis of those pages. The Catalyst takes place on page 9, which is why we stop there.

In late 1997, this script was slated for a network movie, but low ratings for time-travel TV shows and movies at that time nixed the production. I chose this screenplay for inclusion in the third edition of *The Screenwriter's Bible* because it was my latest screenplay at the time plus clients and students had requested an example of a successful *spec script*. It still serves that purpose.

In my analysis, I will tell you my reasons for writing this the way I did. I hope that discussing my rationale will prove helpful. In many cases, you may think of a better way to present the same story information. Wonderful! It means you are thinking and learning, and becoming the next great screenwriter.

What are the general strengths and weaknesses of these pages? Overall, the structure is sound and the pacing is fast. Characterization and dialogue are good, but could be stronger. The writing is generally clear and easy to follow. Most importantly, the network people loved it. I have since updated it and made a few minor improvements.

Since *A Window in Time* is primarily an action-adventure story, there are many paragraphs describing the action. One of my challenges was to keep those paragraphs as short as possible while still conveying dramatic action. Although four-line paragraphs are acceptable, I make sure that only one paragraph in the script exceeds three lines.

In today's competitive market, something must happen by page 10. The reader needs to feel that she is into the story by that point. She must want to read more. You will be the judge as to whether or not these pages accomplish that.

Before you jump into the material, you might consider how to proceed. For example, you could read a page of script first, and then my analysis of that page, and so on. Another approach would be to read the entire excerpt first, and then read the analysis. Do whatever serves your purposes.

A WINDOW IN TIME

by

David Trottier

4456 Manchester St.
Cedar Hills, UT 84062
801/492-7898
dave@keepwriting.com

FADE IN:

A window of an ancient Egyptian temple frames the morning sun.

SUPER: "NEAR LUXOR, EGYPT"

It's an archeological dig. At the temple base, a man-sized
hole has been blasted through.

INT. TEMPLE - SAME

Torches illuminate the figures of a dozen motionless workers,
all wearing black headdresses obscuring their faces and heads.

They stand back against the single, circular wall.

At the center sits a four-foot-tall marble pyramid, protected
by Egyptian statues. One is of Thoth, god of magic and time.

A goateed SHEIKH carefully touches the hieroglyphics on the wall,
then gestures to the marble pyramid.

Quickly, several workers pry the heavy marble pyramid from its
foundation and push it over. It CRASHES to one side. Silence.

There, at the center spot, stands the Eye of Ra -- a dark,
metallic pyramid only six inches tall.

Embedded into the top section of each of the four pyramid sides
is a purple glowing crystal.

The sheikh's eyes water -- awestruck. The workers are stunned.
What is this tiny pyramid?

The sheikh carefully picks it up -- almost expecting a jolt --
and examines it with wonder.

A THIEF, disguised as a worker, strides up to the sheikh.

A knife flicks into the thief's hand from under the sleeve, and
quickly slashes the sheikh's throat.

The other hand snatches the Eye of Ra.

A worker attacks the thief, but is repelled by a swift kick to
the face. A flash of the knife severs another worker's windpipe.

The thief dashes through an opening closed by a canvas flap.

BLACKNESS

A foot KICKS open two window shutters.

INT. JAKE'S HOUSE - UPPER ROOM - DAY

Bold beams of sunlight burst through the large window.

JAKE DEKKER, 30, wearing an honest face and a NASA ballcap, and
his best buddy, MARK, are bathed in a shaft of white sunlight.

Mark gazes out the second-story window into the backyard lawn
and beyond to a grove of orange trees, then up to a blue sky.

> MARK
> Beats the hell outa your condo.

The room's walls are covered with posters of military flying
craft of all kinds. Miniatures hang by string from the ceiling.

> JAKE
> And no one knows about it. It's in
> my uncle's name. Got a generator
> downstairs. No mail-man, no sales-
> man, no meter-man...

> MARK
> ...And no wo-man.

> JAKE
> I value my privacy.

> MARK
> If you saw the babe I met last night,
> you'd go public.
> (slugs him in the arm)
> I'll set ya up.

Jake crosses the room and twists the knob of an arching desk
lamp. It hovers over a drafting table like a flying saucer.
Large metal blueprint tubes lie beside the desk.

On the desk is a custom iPad Mini near a computer.

> JAKE
> My one true love. And you're going
> to help me sell her.

His only true love is on the drafting table: The design of a
black and angular helicopter. Mark sighs in amazement as he
turns page after page of blueprint designs.

> JAKE (CONT'D)
> Outside will be Kevlar, carbon fiber,
> and --

                    MARK
          -- Didn't you just present something
          like this to top brass?
                    (sheepishly)
          I heard... a rumor goin' round.

A loud WHACK from behind scares Mark. Jake grins. The wind
has blown the shutter against the wall.

While Mark re-opens the shutter, Jake covertly grabs a small
hand remote. It has a short antenna, control knob, and tiny TV
monitor on its face. He pushes a button and moves the knob.

A miniature helicopter darts up to Mark's face like a hummingbird, and hovers. He jumps back in fright, waving his hands.

                    MARK (CONT'D)
          Hell, Jake....

Jake looks like a teenager operating his remote. This is fun.
Suddenly:

                    JAKE
          Don't move!

Mark freezes and looks a bit scared as the mini-copter silently
orbits his head. His eyes try to follow.

                    JAKE (CONT'D)
          A new concept, Mark. Small, quick.
          Can slip anywhere. For rescue.

Jake lands the thing on Mark's head. Before Mark can grab it,
it darts away.

Jake WHOOPS it up; he's having a ball. He then frowns as he
answers Mark's question.

                    JAKE (CONT'D)
          Yeah, NASA, the military -- they
          rejected it. Don't think it's do-
          able. Besides, they want the big
          gunships. Firepower.

                    MARK
                    (pointing at helicopter)
          Hell, Jake, that's the centerpiece
          of your sales promo right there.

Jake signals Mark over. Mark gazes into the tiny TV monitor.
As the helicopter flits about, Mark views different parts of
the room in the tiny monitor. Jake chuckles, his face aglow.

MARK (CONT'D)
A TV camera. Boy, could I get an
eyeful at the beach.

Mark almost pants. Jake manipulates the knob and the tiny
chopper scoots away and bolts out the window.

EXT. JAKE'S HOUSE

The tiny chopper flies over the Norfolk pine, coconut palms and
philodendron of the Florida countryside, then over the dirt
road leading past the front of the two-story house. Jake's
jeep in the driveway. Miami sits like a jewel in the distance.

Suddenly, the tiny model flits around the house and through the
back window.

INT. UPPER ROOM

Jake maneuvers the remote knob and suddenly Mark is gazing at
himself in the monitor. He lifts his head and the quiet chopper
is an inch from his nose.

JAKE
Silent. Invisible to radar...

It darts out the window and disappears into the blue sky.

JAKE (O.S.) (CONT'D)
... And as free and quick as a
hummingbird.

EXT. ATLANTIC OCEAN NEAR FLORIDA - DAY

A clear, blue sky vaults over a calm, blue ocean. The only
sound is the natural movement of the waves.

SUPER: "THE BERMUDA TRIANGLE"

Then: A low RUMBLE, similar to distant thunder. Strange.
Unworldly. Slowly crescendos into a sharp, deafening CLAP...

... Cutting abruptly to a mysterious silence, and at that
moment...

... A black helicopter bolts from the blue -- suddenly upon us --
as if emerging from a long invisible tunnel.

Small, angular, futuristic. It looks exactly like Jake's
miniature model -- only this chopper is real. Strangely, the
WHOP-WHOP of the rotors is muted.

INT. HUMMINGBIRD HELICOPTER - SAME

KENDALL's nervous hands work the instruments.

A grid appears on her windshield. The seat next to her is empty.

On the far horizon an island jumps into view as the chopper suddenly drops. She is frantic, distraught.

                    KENDALL (O.S.)
          Where's that button?

She sighs in relief, and brushes her hair back behind black sunglasses that contrast silver Egyptian symbol-of-life earrings. She is a lovely 35.

Her futuristic clothes are blood-stained.

Below, the sparkling blue ocean appears to glide silently by.

EXT./INT. COAST GUARD CUTTER - DAY

A COAST GUARD OFFICER spots the erratic movements of the silent and swift helicopter. Dumbfounded, he races to the

RADAR ROOM

and rushes to the radar screen. He looks in vain for a blip.

                    COAST GUARD OFFICER
          Where is it? Where is it?

The TECHNICIAN looks at him like he's crazy.

                    TECHNICIAN
          Where's what?

ON THE DECK

The officer hurries through the door and searches the sky. He sees nothing.

INT./EXT. HUMMINGBIRD HELICOPTER - DAY

Just a few feet below, Florida Bay streaks past at amazing speed.

Kendall lifts her sunglasses slightly, wipes away tears.

She pulls up on the Collective Pitch Lever and suddenly she is a half mile above the water. The Southern coast of Florida ascends on the horizon.

Soon she is over the Everglades, with Miami on the far horizon.

FROM THE EVERGLADES

The chopper silently whisks off into the distance.

EXT. SANDY BEACH - DAY

The blue sky meets a beautiful secluded beach at the horizon.

From ground level, the USA X-1 rocket towers upward, ready to blast off. The gargantuan head of Jake Dekker moves into frame -- ah ha, the rocket is actually a miniature.

Jake lies on his side wearing Levi's and NASA cap. He laughs excitedly and makes room for a kneeling 11-year-old boy to join in the fun. He touches something on the rocket.

> JAKE
> That's it!

Jake jumps up. Holds a megaphone to his mouth. Faces north.

> JAKE (CONT'D)
> Attention. Clear the launch area.
> (facing south)
> Please clear the launch area.

Mark and about a dozen inner-city scouts join Jake. Jake makes annoying emergency siren sounds for effect.

But then Jake spots a small boy (SPORT), who stands apart from the others, looking dejected. The other boys ignore him.

Jake walks over to the boy and squats down, sees the dejection.

> JAKE (CONT'D)
> Hey sport, I need someone with a
> strong voice for the countdown.
> How about it?

Jake hands him the megaphone and a comforting smile. Sport returns the smile. Jake leads Sport to a spot on the sand.

At the same time, Jake nods to Mark who nods to a TALL BOY. The Tall Boy -- intense with anticipation -- holds a hand remote in his hand. The remaining boys stand back with Mark.

Jake winks at an expectant Sport.

> SPORT
> Five-four-three-two-one-zero-Blastoff!

The Tall Boy pushes a big, red button -- FFUSSSH! -- the rocket blasts off.

Jake WHOOPS, and the boys revel in his enthusiasm.

They watch the stage-2 rocket separate and drop to earth while the X-1 continues upward. Finally, it explodes over the ocean.

The boys CHEER when a parachute opens and the small capsule flutters downward. Jake leads the charge into the ocean to recover the capsule. So what if his Levi's get wet.

Without warning, a huge Chinook helicopter -- loud and ominous -- descends. Two boys fall on their backs in fear.

The tiny rocket capsule falls in the ocean, but no one notices.

A few boys run scared. Jake grabs them.

                         JAKE
              Whoa! Take it easy. She's one of
              ours. Isn't she pretty?

Caps fly off, but the boys calm down as the Chinook lands.

Mark looks confused, shaken -- what's this about? Jake shrugs.

Two uniformed airmen approach the group. Jake steps forward.
Holds his arms out asking for an explanation.

                         UNIFORM
              Jake Dekker?

Dekker calmly nods. They escort him to the chopper.

                         JAKE
              What's going on?

The silent airmen usher Jake into the chopper and SLAM the door.

INT. HALLWAY - DAY

A metal door SLAMS shut and ECHOES.

J. C. WARDLE, a sexless woman with an ambitious stride, snatches a paper from the hand of PALMER, her stoic, muscular male aide.

Palmer opens a conference room door for Wardle.

INT. CONFERENCE ROOM - CONTINUOUS

Jake Dekker stands casually at attention. Wardle notices the wet Levi's and bare feet. She's nonplussed and barks an order.

                         WARDLE
              Sit down.

Jake sits. Palmer opens his Tablet. Grabs a stylus.

Wardle slumps into her chair, takes a sip from her coffee cup, and eyes Jake like he's the fly and she's the spider.

Jake turns his head sideways, trying to get a view of a file
that's stamped "Defense Department - Top Secret." She puts her
hand on top of the file.

> WARDLE (CONT'D)
> I just flew in from the Pentagon so
> this better be good.

She pulls something from the file while Jake tries for a little
charm.

> JAKE
> What a coincidence. I just flew in
> from Sandy Beach and --

> WARDLE
> -- Is this your work?

Wardle tosses a drawing of a helicopter labeled "Hummingbird
MG-11" towards Jake.

This subdues him. He's serious now. Wardle allows herself
only the briefest of smiles and takes another sip.

> JAKE
> Yes, I submitted the design to Bates.
> He rejected it.

> WARDLE
> The Coast Guard spotted this less
> than fifty miles from here. In the
> air.

She waits. Jake is stunned, but calm.

Palmer -- face of stone -- nods to himself, takes notes.

> JAKE
> Impossible.

> WARDLE
> Later, two civilians in separate
> incidents. Thought it was E.T.

She taps the helicopter drawing with her finger.

> WARDLE (CONT'D)
> So how did this... get into the sky?

> JAKE
> It didn't. It would take millions
> of dollars to manufacture a proto-
> type --

>   WARDLE
>   Exactly. So who you working for?

Jake is mystified. Casts a glance Palmer's way for an
explanation. Runs a frustrated hand through his hair.

>   JAKE
>   ... NASA.

>   WARDLE
>   Not any more. You're terminated,
>   Dekker, and I'm considering
>   prosecution.

>   JAKE
>   The charge?

>   WARDLE
>   Espionage.

>   JAKE
>   You think I sold the plans to a
>   foreign government?

Wardle stands slowly, glares down at Jake, but he doesn't flinch.

>   WARDLE
>   The helicopter is out there. If
>   you're connected with it, you're
>   going down. Unless you come clean.

Jake's eyes narrow.

>   WARDLE (CONT'D)
>   I want that birdie. And I want it
>   in twenty-four hours. That is all.

Jake -- violated, confused -- staggers out.

ANALYSIS OF THE OPENING PAGES

Page 1 analysis

My opening is thematic. The first thing we see is a window that lets in the light of the sun, and this story is about a window in time that lets in the light of the future, the light of self-knowledge, and the light of love. I'm hoping to create a small sense of mystery right here at the beginning.

There's not a word of dialogue on this page. Makes me shiver. It would be nice to break this action up in some way and create some white space.

In an earlier draft, I described this site at length. It was a gorgeous description, teeming with mysterious images. I could almost hear the orchestra. However, it wasn't necessary to move the story forward, so my wonderful description is gone now. (A moment of silence please.)

We are in a circular room. The torches and the black headdresses add a bit of mystery and mood to the scene.

To complete the scene description, we describe what is at the center of the circle—a pyramid. The four statues mean that this little pyramid is important. In fact, this entire buildup is meant to establish the importance of the "Eye of Ra." Why is it so important? We don't know now, but later we learn that the Eye of Ra (Eye of God) can see you through time. This object is also important to the bad guys. Of course, I cannot explain why the object is important in narrative description, because such an explanation cannot appear on the movie screen. Instead, it must come out later, through action (narrative description) and dialogue. All I can do here is establish the importance of the object and bring in more information later. Besides, I don't want to tell my reader everything at once. In withholding information, I want to intrigue the reader, and take care not to confuse him.

Incidentally, some of the material of this screenplay is old hat now—ancient symbols, New World Order, Ra, etc. Years after I wrote "Window," the book (and later the movie) *The Da Vinci Code* were released, as was *National Treasure. Rats!*

One of the bad guys has disguised herself as a worker. I refer to her as a thief. I hide from the reader the fact that this character is a woman by avoiding the use of pronouns. I also establish the woman's method of operation: a knife under her sleeve. What's the payoff for not identifying the thief? Later in the story, we see a woman, Cherise Joulet, flick a knife into her hand and suddenly we know she is the thief—but our hero does not. This creates suspense because the reader is in a "superior position"; that is, has knowledge that the hero does not have.

Page 2 analysis

We open the second scene with another window. How do you like the transition from the first scene to the next?

Jake is described simply as a NASA employee with an honest face. Jake is an honest man. That's all that needs to be said here because this entire scene comments on Jake. Mark is described as Jake's "best buddy." I wish I had room for a word of characterization for him.

Because so many scenes take place in this room and involve this house, I feel that I must take pains to describe it. So we establish that this room is on the second floor and that there is an orange grove in the backyard. The orange grove, along with the NASA cap, implies that we're in Florida. Also, the grove is where we'll hide a helicopter later.

We'll soon learn that this is Jake's hideout, not his residence, and that he's showing it to his best friend Mark for the first time. Why? Because he needs Mark to prepare a sales presentation for him. Now if we try to reveal all of this in one line of dialogue, it will come off as boring exposition. So we provide our first clue with Mark's first line; obviously, Jake owns a condo. (Incidentally, that first line also indicates that they are in mid-conversation. I started the scene late in the scene.) And then Jake explains, "No mail-man, no sales-man, no meter-man." The subtext is: *This is my secret hideout.* The second clue.

Then Mark helps establish something of Jake's private life. Later, we learn that he's not afraid of anything but women. Mark, of course, is probably a skirt-chaser. Mark's line "I can set you up" is a setup line for the last scene of the movie, when he says, "I told you I'd set you up." The slug in the arm replaces the lifeless words "a beat" that I originally used.

I debated over the two paragraphs describing the desk lamp, drafting table, blueprint tubes, and custom iPad. But I decided to keep them because Jake is an aeronautic engineer and computer whiz who loves miniatures. Besides, he uses the iPad later. The one line you could omit is, "It [the arching desk lamp] hovers over a drafting table like a flying saucer." I'm shooting for mood here, and genre. Technically, this is a science-fiction love story against the background of high adventure.

Jake then declares his love. First we have the declaration, then we show the reader what he loves: his design of a new kind of helicopter. He asks Mark to help him sell it, so now the reader understands the situation before turning the page. *An aeronautic engineer wants his marketing buddy to help him sell his secret helicopter plans, so he brings him to his hideout.*

Jake's last line on page 2 exists to lend authenticity to the story. The materials described were used in stealth bombers at the time this was written.

Page 3 analysis

Apparently, Mark heard something at work that he shouldn't have about Jake's design. He's sheepish about it and feels he has to explain himself to Jake. This short interchange helps establish Mark's employer as NASA or the military. We also get a hint of Mark's dark side. He "hears rumors" he isn't supposed to hear. He interrupts his friend, who is describing his "only true love" and (on page 2) he (Mark) is chasing the babes. At the bottom of page 4, Mark reveals that of all the uses the little miniature could be put to, he'd use it to spy on women at the beach. These little hints do not add up to much now, but they help make Mark believable when he betrays his friend later. We're setting up foils: Jake is straight and serious; Mark is loose and shallow. We're doing this with dialogue that also reveals exposition. This may not be immediately obvious to the reader; but it lays the groundwork so that these characters will seem believable and consistent in later scenes.

We learn a little more about Jake by adding a childlike element to his character. He's both a genius and something of an innocent, though he learns fast.

A loud whack scares Mark. Why do I do this? I want to scare the audience and Mark both. I want to create a sense of unpredictability. I want to show Jake as calm and Mark as skittish. I want to emphasize Mark's little indiscretion. And I need to distract Mark so that Jake can grab a hand remote. Note that I describe the gadget in detail as clearly as I can so that you, the reader, can see it in your head and recognize it in later scenes. This is necessary exposition. The reason I invented this little miniature was because in my first draft the two characters only talked about what the eventual helicopter would look like. I decided I needed a way to *show* people. Finally, this is another example of Jake working with miniatures.

The helicopter is described as behaving like a hummingbird. I settled on that to make it easy for the reader to visualize. Later, I call it the Hummingbird MG-11.

The next thing Jake does is to describe his "new concept." Dramatic characters tend to stick to a single train of thought and an intention. Jake's intention in this scene is to get Mark to help him sell this helicopter design to top brass. At the top of this page, Jake begins to describe the helicopter in order to carry out that intention, but Mark interrupts him, providing subtle opposition. Now Jake must do something to get Mark's attention, so he shows Mark the miniature and then continues describing it as "small, quick," etc., and saying what its purpose is: "For rescue."

And Jake has not forgotten Mark's question (Mark's first speech on this page). Jake answers it by telling Mark that the military has already rejected it. And he tells him why. I think it's important to explain why the military would reject this, because when we see it, we really like it. Why would they reject it? Because it's not big enough. And that, in my view, seems realistic.

Mark has not lost his train of thought either. He's supposed to sell the designs and so he tells Jake that the miniature is his best selling tool. The subtext is *Show them that.*

Page 4 analysis

The chopper bolts out the window for four reasons: 1) to demonstrate its abilities, 2) to demonstrate Jake's intelligence, 3) to establish it as a lifeline that is used later, and 4) to establish more about Jake's house, one of our main sets. I called a client in Florida and asked him what grows in Miami. His answer is in the first paragraph (that's research). That second paragraph (the longest paragraph in the screenplay) fully orients us to the general setting (a suburb of Miami) and Jake's hideaway. Also, Jake—the secretive engineer not interested in women—drives a jeep. That adds just a bit of dimension to his character.

The reader learns that the chopper is silent and cannot be detected on radar. Then the fascinating little miniature chopper darts into the sky, allowing us to transition from blue sky to blue sky. This is a match cut, a smooth transition from this scene to our next scene. Why is Jake's last line spoken off screen? Because we want the camera to be on the blue sky so that we can match-cut to the blue sky of the next scene.

Jake's last line is interesting. He's describing the helicopter, but what's the subtext? Well, *Jake* likes being free and quick.

There is a lot of exposition in this scene. I'm betting (and I won that bet) that the excitement created by the situation, the characters, the motivated dialogue, the hideout, and the cute little helicopter makes the exposition interesting. Now let's double-space to a new master scene and cut to an immediate payoff in the next seven paragraphs:

1. We see the sky and the ocean.

2. A one-sentence paragraph focuses on one image: a superimposition telling us this is the Bermuda Triangle. This will create some anticipation. After all, the Bermuda Triangle has a reputation.

3. and 4. Nothing but sound. Clearly, what is happening is not normal.

5. The helicopter bolts from the blue. Yes, I consciously used that cliché; and, yes, I use the phrase "suddenly upon us." I'm breaking a rule with the word "us" (author intrusion), but I believe it is worth it. Here's what this really says: *This helicopter suddenly fills the movie screen and flies right into the camera.*

6. The next paragraph allows us to see exactly what this looks like. It is absolutely clear that this looks like the miniature but is *real*. Muting the WHOP-WHOP of the rotors reinforces the point that this helicopter is unusually silent.

7. A new character is introduced: Kendall (who is an Egyptologist). I'm hoping these first four pages have already hooked you.

Page 5 analysis

A grid appears on the windshield instead of on some computer screen, adding to the futuristic quality of the helicopter. That was inventive when I wrote it. We also establish an empty seat—that's a setup for a later payoff.

The second paragraph and weak "throwaway" line of dialogue demonstrate that she is having difficulty flying this thing. She is not a Navy flyer, not an expert. The blood-stained clothes indicate that something happened just before the movie began. That something is the Backstory. We won't learn what happened until about page 70. But it prompts several questions: Is she escaping? Did she kill someone? Where did she come from? Why is she here?

The Egyptian symbol-of-life earrings are the first clues (not yet obvious, of course) that Kendall is an Egyptologist and that she brings life and light to our hero, Jake. (Yes, she came through a window in time, and—yes—she is the love interest.)

At this point, while writing the third draft, I wondered if I needed to make this chopper seem "more real" while also showing off its futuristic capabilities. At the same time, I had the problem of creating a way to get our hero into the hands of Wardle (we'll meet her later). The United States Coast Guard came to the rescue. The addition of the Coast Guard Officer solved both problems, as you shall see. I have found in revision work that when the solution to one problem also solves another, you are probably on the right course.

In this little scene, our Coast Guard Officer demonstrates that the helicopter is invisible to radar. The reader will recall Jake's words, "Silent, invisible to radar." We have now *shown* that, which raises the question: Do you need Jake's words? To be honest, that is a good question. We might have an opportunity to shorten that first scene.

Meanwhile, back in the helicopter, we reestablish the Backstory with Kendall's tears. In addition, we add a touch of authenticity to the story with the Collective Pitch Lever. I knew nothing about helicopters until I conducted my research.

A word about the blood and tears: I believe the reader will notice them and conclude, "She is distraught—something has happened." The purpose of the spec script is to communicate the story—make the reader see, hear, laugh, and cry (feel)—not plan the shoot. We only hope other professionals will have the good sense to see the story the way we writers do. Right?

Miami appears to be the destination, and who lives in a suburb of Miami? Jake Dekker. Good. Cut.

Page 6 analysis

Sandy Beach is another important location because it becomes a romantic spot later on. Before we see Jake and his Boy Scouts, however, I have a little fun with perspective. We see a rocket, then realize it's a miniature. I do it to reemphasize that this is another of Jake's miniatures (that later becomes a lifeline) and to change the mood from the serious one in the preceding scene. That's my rationalization.

I hope you've been noticing that each scene has a main story purpose. It's not there just to establish character or mood or location; it's mainly there to *move the story forward*. From here on out, you will see more of the cause-and-effect relationship that should exist between scenes, how one thing leads to another. This is called scene motivation.

The primary purpose of this scene is to get Jake into the hands of Wardle (an opposition character to be introduced later). What motivates that? You will see as you read the remaining pages. The portion of the scene that appears on this page has another purpose as well—to establish Jake as a good guy. Wait a minute! Didn't I just say don't have a scene just to establish character or mood? Yes, but the entire scene itself does more than just establish character, as you'll see on script page 7. In addition, the Boy Scouts play a small role later on, so we need to establish their existence.

Jake is a good guy not just because he is a Boy Scout leader. Yes, his ability to relate to the boys by having a sense of humor, providing a rocket (which is believable because Jake works at NASA), and eliciting their participation is nice; but what moves people is one person relating to another person. We need a personal touch, and that's why Sport is here. (Notice that I don't use a POV shot when Jake spots Sport.) Jake is sensitive, perceptive, kind, and encouraging to a kid who has been rejected by the others. Jake makes him feel important without embarrassing him. If you are a Blake Snyder fan, this is my "Save the Cat" scene.

In review, the scene as a whole (pages 6–7) exists for two reasons: 1) to get Jake into the hands of Wardle, and 2) to establish Jake's service to inner city boys; he's not isolated from the community.

In terms of pacing, this section acts as a buffer. We just experienced some serious action and are about to have storm clouds blow in on page 7. We could use something light and fun here. That's a fourth purpose.

Why is Mark in this scene? To more clearly establish him as Jake's best friend. Obviously, these two see each other a lot. It also gives Mark some dimension. He's apparently a good guy at heart. You see, we planted the seeds of his dark side earlier. Now we show his good side. When the dark side reappears, it will be surprising, but believable.

Page 7 analysis

Speaking of surprise, instead of letting this fun moment play out, we interrupt it with a plot twist. In a previous draft, this scene played out for another page with the boys having fun. In fact, one boy goes out into the ocean to catch the parachute and Jake rescues him. Then Jake goes home and gets a phone call from Wardle. Do you see how this current version is more dramatic? Plus, we lose a couple of pages we didn't need. Also, the surprise of the big Chinook helicopter interrupting all of the fun creates suspense, just like the slam of the window shutter on page 3.

The transition is abrupt. The Scouts cheer and watch the parachute descend. We expect to see the parachute land. Suddenly, the chopper is upon them. Jake, of course, is focused on the boys. I try to create a sense of chaos here with the sudden appearance of the Chinook—the boys running scared, their caps flying off, Mark looking confused, and so on. It's a dramatic moment, so I dramatize it. After all, this chopper will take Jake to Wardle and, as a result, Jake's life will suddenly be in chaos. There's something about that subliminal link that creates a sense of unity.

The dialogue, which in a prior draft went on for an entire page, is just two lines. Jake first speaks with an action, holding his arms out. I believe the uniformed airman refusing to answer Jake's question speaks more eloquently than something like, "Someone wants to see you." Why say that and break the suspense? Keep the audience wondering: Now what's going to happen?

In a way, the Chinook is Wardle, so I try to link the scene of the Chinook with the scene of Wardle. We match-cut from "slamming door" to "slamming door" (without using a CUT TO or MATCH CUT) to link the scenes.

I don't show Mark and the boys reacting to Jake's disappearance, because I want to keep the story moving. Note the nonverbal communication between Mark and Jake in the fourth paragraph; we don't need dialogue.

Consider the description of Wardle. When you describe and introduce your character, do so in a way that reflects on her character and who she is. Wardle is an ambitious, no-nonsense soldier; thus, her first speech is an order. And she dislikes Jake immediately. We take pains in this scene to make her appear powerful, but she is not the main opposition; nor is Cherise Joulet, the woman with the knife, although she becomes a powerful opposition to Jake. It's the man who hired Cherise. And even Kendall, who becomes the love interest, will be at odds with Jake for a while. Why all the opposition? Because opposition creates conflict, and conflict is drama. And adversity is good for revealing character and motivating characters to grow.

In a previous version, Wardle interrogates the Coast Guard officer before questioning Jake. Although there were many advantages to doing that, I ultimately decided to lose the scene because it simply wasn't necessary. This was very hard for me to do, but it helped keep things moving.

In this scene, I also try to reveal more important exposition without being boring. Note that no formal introductions are made and there is no chitchat or small talk. We just get into the scene. Incidental dialogue could be added during the shoot.

Page 8 analysis

Throughout this script, Jake has been presented as calm and steady. Now is the moment to test that. We immediately pit him against Wardle. She flew in from the Pentagon and he tries to charm her. His response might play better if there was a tinge of anger behind it. From his viewpoint, he has reason to be angry. What do *you* think? Should I make an adjustment here?

She asks him if the chopper design is his. We know it is because we saw it earlier. In fact, he told Mark that the military had rejected the design and that he wanted to create a presentation for selling it. Jake's response confirms that. He's telling the truth. The ball is in Wardle's court.

Wardle delivers. She simply restates what she knows to get his reaction. Jake is on trial. The ball is now in his court. Dialogue exchanges are often a competition. Palmer's stoic presence adds additional pressure. (Don't be afraid to run your character through the ringer.)

Jake states the truth as he understands it. After all, he is a Scout.

She brings in new information about other people seeing the helicopter. Her tapping the helicopter drawing with her finger is an unimportant, incidental action. I justify leaving it because the scene is a key scene and I want to dramatize it. But I could easily drop it to save space if necessary.

Wardle's last line is a challenging question, but Jake is equal to it. He confronts her by telling her directly that it didn't get into the sky. He's a reasonable man and explains why. The ball is back in Wardle's court.

Page 9 analysis

Wardle uses Jake's words against him. Because it was in the sky and he can't afford it, someone must have paid him. The conflict escalates. And now we're beginning to see Wardle's point of view. It's generally good policy to give each of your characters a different view of the same facts. And we'll continue to see (later in the script) how she views things differently from Jake. In this particular case, Jake has not seen the facts yet, but *we* have, and Wardle sees this situation differently from us. The result is to create more sympathy for Jake and less for Wardle.

What's the purpose of Jake's action of glancing at Palmer and running his hand through his hair? It is to show his emotion. We need to know what he is feeling, and his action communicates his frustration to the reader. Do not cut off your characters emotionally from the reader.

Jake responds with "NASA"—that's who he works for. I do not instruct the actor how to say this line. It could be a sarcastic answer. A question mark after "NASA" might suggest more of a smart-aleck attitude. Maybe you would advise me to use a wryly here.

The exchange of power between the two crescendos to the moment when Wardle stands up and challenges Jake with her eyes. Standing up puts her physically in a stronger position. But Jake does not flinch. Ah, so he is able to remain calm under pressure.

This is the **Catalyst** of the movie, the event that upsets the equilibrium of Jake's life. There's even a deadline on it, which creates pressure and suspense. How can Jake accomplish this? He doesn't even know where "the bird" is, or even that it exists. We've laid a lot on the shoulders of our hero. Hopefully, the reader wants to read more.

In a previous draft, I ended the scene differently. Wardle slammed her coffee mug on the table before her last speech on the page, and Jake nonchalantly responded, "You should switch to decaf." The producer I was working with dismissed it because it "sounds too much like Mel Gibson." He felt that Jake should be "shaken" at the end of the interview to emphasize the enormous burden he was under, and that Wardle should appear more in control. In the end, I agreed with the producer.

So in this revision, Jake staggers out. That final paragraph is simply an assessment of Jake's emotional state, so that the reader can identify emotionally with him.

• • • • •

Don't be misled by my analysis into thinking you need to be analytical *when you write*. However, you do want to use your reasoning powers in *evaluating* what you've already written. And you don't need to emulate my writing style or anyone else's. A more gifted writer might do a better job of presenting the same material.

Finally, when all is said and done, the real test of your first 10 pages is this: Does the reader want to know what happens next? The Catalyst does not necessarily have to happen in the first 10 pages, but the reader must want to know what happens next after the first 10. If you want to know what happens next to Jake and Kendall, then I have succeeded.

If interested, the entire screenplay *A Window in Time* is available on Kindle for only $2.99. You can download a free Kindle app for any device you own.

HOW TO SELL YOUR SCRIPT

BOOK V

A Marketing Plan

Five steps to selling your work

Congratulations! You, the next great screenwriter, have written a stunning script! You have reached a major milestone. Reward yourself with positive self-talk and a bowl of ice cream.

There are five general steps you should take before you begin to market your screenplay. These steps will be covered in the next five chapters of this book. Additional chapters build on and supplement those first five chapters.

1. Protect your work. Before you send your screenplay out to anyone, make sure it is protected and ready to show.

2. Prepare your screenplay for market. You have a completed screenplay, but is it a "showcase" screenplay? Will it attract a buyer? In this section, we will explore the value of writing groups and script consultants, and conduct an analysis of the marketability of your screenplay.

3. Assemble your selling tools. Before you begin selling, you want to forge the marketing tools that you will need to build a presence in today's marketplace. Don't begin the marketing process empty-handed and empty-headed.

4. Create your strategic marketing plan. In any business, it is important to have a plan of attack. The same is true in the movie business. You not only want to be professional, you want to be effective. You want to nail a deal.

5. Implement the plan. Now the fun begins.

The remaining chapters in this book focus mainly on specific aspects of implementing your plan, such as getting an agent, selling without an agent, penetrating alternative and smaller markets, and moving your career forward. They also provide instruction on developing key selling tools, such as query letters, one-sheets, and treatments.

NOTE: Nothing in this or any other book of The Screenwriter's Bible *should be construed as legal advice. That can only be provided by an attorney.*

1. Protect your work

In Hollywood, no script is sacred. Don't worry; there are ways to protect yourself and your creative offspring. There are ways to protect your rights.

KEEP RECORDS

First, be organized. Life can get very complicated, so write things down. Keep a journal of meetings you have and record what was discussed. Worksheets are provided in Chapter 4 of this book. Keep a log of phone calls, queries, and script submissions. You'll need these if any legal concerns should arise. More importantly, you'll use these records to follow up on contacts and create future strategies for selling your work.

If there's ever any question in your mind that there might be a legal problem, consult an entertainment attorney. You may even want an attorney to review any contracts you're offered, particularly if the offering party is not a signatory to the Writers Guild of America contracts.

COPYRIGHT

There are certain things you cannot protect: ideas, historical facts, plots, titles, phrases, and anything not written down. Here's what you can protect: your original expression of an idea or plot. In other words, your original, spec script is the only thing you can protect.

There are several ways to protect your spec screenplay. Under the current copyright law, you own the copyright to your work even as you write it. You don't even need to use the copyright symbol. To create a public record of your script, however, you may wish to *register* your copyright with the U.S. Copyright Office in Washington, D.C.

It's a simple, painless, and inexpensive procedure. Just contact the Copyright Office in Washington, D.C. Once done, you must display the copyright notice on the title page of your script as directed by the Copyright Office. That notice will look something like this: © 2015 David R. Trottier. Help ensure international protection by adding the phrase *All Rights Reserved*.

My personal observation is that many working writers do not register their scripts with the Copyright Office, presumably because the eventual producer will own the copyright to the completed film, and thus to the script. That doesn't mean that *you* shouldn't. Registering your copyright gives you the best protection available. Throughout my career, I have not registered the copyright of my scripts; however, when I sold my most recent script, my attorney advised me to register my copyright at that time.

Registering one's copyright and displaying the copyright notice on the script's title page is generally no longer seen as something done by paranoid writers. And even though the date of the copyright notice "dates" the script, many writers are now registering their copyright. In fact, I've heard more than one entertainment attorney say that screenwriters should register their copyright once they begin circulating their script. What should *you* do? To know for sure, ask an attorney or agent. Gather opinions from a variety of sources.

THE WGA

The purpose of WGA registration is to establish yourself as the creator of your original work. Most writers register their scripts with the Writers Guild of America. Although WGA registration creates valid evidence that can be used in court, it does not provide as many legal remedies as registering your copyright with the U.S. Copyright Office will, but it does establish a date when a particular work was written.

The Writers Guild maintains two offices. One is in Los Angeles; the other is in New York. The Mississippi River serves as a boundary between the jurisdictions of the east and west Guild offices.

To register your script with the WGA West, simply send your screenplay, treatment, or synopsis to them with $20 and they will hold the copy for 5 years; or register with the WGA East for $25 ($17 if a student) for 10 years. It can be retrieved at any time thereafter. When the registration period has expired, you may renew your registration. You may register your script more than once. Some writers like to register their first draft as well as their final polish. You should register a treatment or synopsis if you are going to present it to others, or if you're going to delay the writing of your script for a long period of time. You may register your script with either office regardless of where you live.

Registering your screenplay with the WGA Registry does not provide evidence for the ownership of registered material, nor determine credits of registered material. Rather, registration with the WGA Registry documents the claim of authorship for a particular version of original work or material. It is completely at your discretion to identify your material as being registered. Doing so has no bearing on your rights to a particular piece of material.

The Writers Guild provides many additional services to writers. You do not need to belong to the Guild to benefit from their services, or to register your script.

WGA services include the following:

- Registration of your script, treatment, or synopsis for a period of 5 or 10 years. You may renew your registration after that.
- Pre-negotiated contracts if you sign with a producer or studio that is a signatory to the Guild or acquire an agent who is a signatory to the Guild.
- Arbitration if a dispute arises regarding credits or for other grievances, such as nonpayment or slow payment of contracted writing fees.
- A list of agencies that are signatories to the Guild. Visit their website at www.wga.org or www.wgae.org.
- A library where you can go and read scripts.
- Information as to who represents a particular writer. This could help in your search for an agent.

Again, you need not be a member to use these services. You may join the Guild once you have the required number of credits. For more information, contact the appropriate office.

OTHER MEANS OF PROTECTION

Another way to protect your work is to have several people read it so that they can testify that you wrote it. Keep records of meetings and phone conversations.

Still another method is the Poor Man's Copyright. Put the script in an envelope, seal it, and send it via *registered mail* to yourself. Don't open it; keep it for the lawsuit later. Although this works in principle, I've always doubted it would protect *me* in actual fact, which is why I always just pay the small fee and register my work with the Guild.

An additional protection

Perhaps your best protection is the completed script itself. If you pitch an idea to a producer who likes it, she'll ask for your script. Why would she steal the idea and pay a working writer $250,000 to execute your idea when she can pay you $50,000 to $100,000 for a script that already exists?

WRITING PARTNERSHIPS

If you collaborate with another writer, first make sure that your goals for the proposed "joint work" are in harmony and that you basically get along with each other. Do you bring different skills to the table that will benefit the project? My co-writer on a script, Greg Alt, once wrote me, "Dave, you flesh it out, and then I'll add the wit, charm, and humor." Well, you need to define your roles in more specific terms. Also, expect a certain amount of clashing, so decide in advance how you will resolve conflict.

Before you do any writing, be sure to have a written agreement, especially if your co-writer is your best friend or a relative. Often, loved ones expect the other to cut them some slack (translated: You do most of the work). The agreement should cover these points:

- Exactly what each will contribute in terms of time and content
- Who gets top writing credit
- What happens if someone drops out or doesn't perform

If your co-writer does not want to sign a contract, then that's a red flag. Just tell that person that this is a normal part of business. You want to be serious about your writing career. You are a writer, not a hobbyist. Even if you have already started a script with someone, stop and create an agreement. An agreement or contract makes the endeavor real.

When two or more writers work together on a project, their names are joined by an ampersand, as follows:

```
Written by


Herman Cappuccino & Mocha Smith
```

When you see the word "and" used on writing credits, it means that the people whose names are joined by that "and" did not work together.

2. Prepare your script for market

There are several markets for scripts, and we will discuss them all. But before you even think of approaching the marketplace, you want to get your ducks in a row. I have watched with sadness many writers who have broken their hearts by approaching the market prematurely. Don't let your passion or the prospect of dollar signs obscure your vision!

Make sure the writing is done before the selling begins. Do not contact producers and agents until you are prepared. Be sure that your script is finished, evaluated, and registered—and your marketing plan is written—*before* you mail that first pitch letter or make that first call. I cannot overemphasize this. I get calls all the time from clients and students who sadly confess that they entered the market prematurely. I worked with one client on a query letter that brought in over 20 requests for the script. The problem was his script needed a polish. It wasn't ready yet, and the opportunity was lost.

There are exceptions. For example, if you are meeting with a producer or agent who asks about your other story ideas, you may want to pitch those, even though their scripts are not quite ready yet. On occasion, the moment may be "right" to talk to an established contact, even though the script may not be quite ready. Be wise.

YOUR CALLING CARD

To break into this business, you need at least one showcase script (preferably two or more) that is proof of your writing ability. If you want to write for television, you will need one feature script and at least one sample television script.

This showcase script (or scripts) should be formatted correctly and should be complete in every way. Do not submit a work in progress. Realize that your script is a prospectus asking for a $10–$30 million investment (more or less). That is why it must be good.

Since Tinseltown is into appearances, it is essential that your script look as good as it possibly can. Make sure you understand spec screenplay writing conventions. I don't know how many times writers have sent me their script for evaluation after it has been rejected all over town, and I find formatting errors, obvious writing mistakes, and easy-to-fix problems whose solution might have made a difference. Please be sure to carefully read, and frequently refer to, Books III and IV; they are your friends.

To further guide you in preparing a professional-looking script, refer to the "17 Commandments" in Book III. Many of the points seem nitpicky. They are, and for good reason. The poor souls who must read dozens of scripts every week are looking for any excuse to eliminate scripts from their reading stacks. Abiding by their simple conventions is an easy way to make a good impression.

Of course, appearance isn't everything, and correct format alone will not save you (just as a few formatting errors will not likely hurt you). Your script must tell an interesting story. It must be well crafted.

Make sure your script is ready. Ask yourself the questions in Book II. When I present seminars, about 80% of the questions I'm asked have to do with selling or formatting the script. I often find these people coming back months later a little beat up, but a little wiser. They want to make sure their next script is well written with a strong story and original characters before they try to sell it. You must write it before you sell it.

Your spec script should provide a smooth, easy *read*. Your narrative description should focus on images and actions; your dialogue should be crisp and allow for subtext. The writing in general should be concise, specific, and clear.

Before submitting your script, you may wish to get feedback. One place for that is through a writers group.

WRITERS GROUPS

Writing can be a lonely job. A writers group may be just the place to turn for comfort, support, and feedback.

I recommend writers groups and associations that meet regularly and provide opportunities to read each other's work. You will get worthwhile feedback and the advice will be free. It's the first place to go for feedback. Likewise, online groups can be just as effective.

Where to find writers groups

Writers groups are everywhere. Here are seven general areas to begin your search:

1. Attend screenwriting conferences, workshops, pitch-fests, and writing classes. Network with fellow writers and ask them if they know of any writers groups.

2. Search writing publications and social media websites such as Facebook and LinkedIn. Use Google Search.

3. Join large, professional organizations such as the Dallas Screenwriters Association, the Wisconsin Screenwriters Forum, and others. Consider online writing communities like Talentville. Some well-established groups like the Scriptwriters Network in Los Angeles may have special requirements.

4. I have created a place at the "Community" page of my website for writers groups and organizations. Look there (**www.keepwriting.com**), or advertise (for free) your writers group.

5. Call your state film commissioner or county film board (if one exists) about possible writers groups in your area.

6. Hang out at film festivals, movie clubs, bookstores, and universities with adult education programs.

If your search for a writers group proves fruitless, there's only one thing left to do— start your own group.

Five ways to find writers to start a group

A. Network with screenwriters at conferences, expos, seminars, workshops, bookstore events, and Internet sites such as those mentioned in #3 above. Trade email addresses. One writer used this simple, proven method to create a group composed of participants of my seminar and Michael Hauge's seminar.

B. In classes, ask the instructor or seminar leader to put your name and phone number on the board because you'd like to start a writers group. That way, interested writers can call you. Distribute flyers or make an announcement to classmates or fellow conferencegoers.

C. Post an announcement in online classes. In most of my workshops and online classes, I have found that the attending writers will form a writers group during the last class or chatroom session. In some cases, the groups are as small as two to three people, and in others they can be quite large.

D. Post a notice on blogs (where permitted), bulletin boards (actual or virtual), and classrooms at screenwriting conferences, asking people to sign up. Ask me to post your writers group notice at my website (**www.keepwriting.com**).

E. Use social media to start a group. "Friend" and connect with other writers.

How to keep the group going

While you're forming the group, you will want to create some rules or guidelines at the same time. Here are some things to keep in mind, whether you are forming an online group or an on-ground group:

1. Include writers who are at basically the same level. One group might consist of people who are just getting started. Another group might set up a requirement of one completed screenplay.

2. Keep the group small at first. Five people may be enough. Seven is an ideal size. If you start with 12 to 15 people, you'll likely end up with seven who are dedicated. Then, you can expand from there.

3. Make it a participative group. You may need a facilitator to head the group, but make sure everyone has an equal say in making rules. You might even rotate responsibilities, such as making reminder emails and assigning refreshments, so that no one is unduly burdened and everyone is involved.

4. Find a place to meet. This will probably be someone's house, or a bookstore. It might be easier to use the same location continuously, but some groups like to rotate. Many libraries, some savings-and-loan associations, and other businesses have "community rooms" that are without cost for noncommercial use. You qualify for these if admittance to your group is free. Finally, you can meet online.

5. Have a regular time for meetings, online chats, TweetChats, and so on. Get people into a routine.

6. Decide on the purposes of the group. For example, here is the stated purpose of a group of my students: "To provide each member with the feedback he or she needs to forward his or her screenwriting career. Group members share screenwriting knowledge and provide constructive critiques of each other's script, treatment, or outline. Members also exchange screenwriting books, magazines, tapes, and their experiences marketing scripts."

Some groups that meet physically together focus on one or two writers per session. Some groups require members to send the work to others in advance of the meetings. It's often profitable to read scenes aloud at the meeting itself and evaluate them on the spot, or discuss writing ideas and specific writing problems.

7. Make sure critiquing sessions do not turn into slugfests. Writers should avoid a defensive posture. Listen carefully, avoid speaking, take the advice seriously (especially if you see patterns in the comments), but remember that you are the writer of *your* script. Criticism should be given constructively. Members should avoid speaking in absolutes, but instead offer their opinions, reactions, observations, and suggestions. Be specific in your comments. Rather than "I liked it," say, "I liked it because . . ." and then name something specific. The more specific your comments, the more useful they will be. If your script or scene is the one being critiqued, wait until the comments are given before you ask your burning questions about concerns you have.

8. Each member should agree to a code of silence. Everything discussed or read is confidential. If people are concerned about theft, suggest that all work be registered before it is distributed. You can even ask people to sign a nondisclosure agreement. Don't get too paranoid about theft. It does happen. Your purse may be stolen at the grocery store, but that doesn't stop you from shopping.

How to creatively maintain your group

After a while, a motivating routine can degenerate into a fatiguing rut. Because all members of the group are *creative*, this problem can be solved by being creative. Here are some ideas to get you started:

- Organize a script-swap night. Read each other's scripts.

- Read the script of a produced movie; then view the movie together (or individually if discussing it online). Read a scene, critique it, and then view it.

- Sponsor a contest.

- Invite a working writer to address the group.

- Compile a collection of query letters or rejection letters.

- Have special awards when a writer passes a milestone.

- Set aside a night just for pitching practice; rotate the roles of writer and producer/executive.

When groups get large, create specialized areas such as the "Comedy Writers" or the "Sci-Fi Chapter" or "Advanced Writers." You can have a short, large meeting for everyone, and then break into the specialized groups (or form subgroups online).

In the best writers groups and organizations, a feeling of camaraderie develops, enabling each writer to root for the others' success. It's an upward spiral of positive energy that revitalizes each writer. This is the fuel each writer needs to keep writing.

GETTING FEEDBACK

Some writers seek out professional readers for a *coverage*. A coverage is what a reader (actual job title is *story analyst*) writes for the agents, producers, and executives who hire her. A coverage usually consists of a two-page synopsis, a brief analysis of the screenplay, and a recommendation. In other words, a coverage "covers" a script. The cost to writers for such a coverage is about $100 or more. You can read a sample coverage in the chapter "How to sell your script without an agent."

More extensive than a coverage is a detailed evaluation provided by professional *script consultants* like myself. That's going to cost you more, but a professional, independent review may be worth it. See my article "How to Get the Most Out of a Script Evaluation" at my website (**keepwriting.com**—click on "Articles" in the left column).

Another way to get feedback is to ask your spouse and friends to read your script. It's free, but may not be entirely objective. Feedback from a writers group might prove more valuable. A few writers contests provide feedback. If you get comments from more than one reader, look for patterns in those comments.

Once you know that the script is ready (and you may not need a consultant to know that), it's time to forge effective writing tools in preparation for your market entrance.

3. Assemble your selling tools

10 KEY SELLING TOOLS

Before you try to sell your script, you need a complete set of marketing tools. Assemble these *before* creating your marketing plan and making your move. Many of the tools listed below are discussed in depth later in this book, but I thought you'd want to see them all in one place so that you can begin to accumulate them at this step in the selling process.

1. A showcase script

You need a great script (preferably two or more) that is proof of your writing ability and can be used as a calling card. If you want to break into television, you will need one feature script and at least one sample television script.

2. A honey of a hook

This will consist of a logline, one-sentence concept, or premise statement that you can insert into a query letter or one-sheet, use over the phone or with an Internet marketing service, or pitch in person. Everything in Hollywood is sold on its premise or hook.

3. A provocative pitch

Actually, you need a handful of these, one for each of your projects. Your short pitch will consist of your hook and story essentials of about two paragraphs in length or more. Think of the short pitch as the hook plus a couple of turning points. Be prepared to go beyond that if asked.

You will carry a copy of your pitch in your head when you go to places where you might meet producers, agents, or other film people. You might meet them at conferences, expos, festivals, or a particular online event. Be ready in case you're asked the golden question: "What else have you done?"

4. A captivating query letter

Never send a script out unannounced. A query must precede it, and this query must convince the producer, executive, agent, director, or actor to request your script. A query letter (or *pitch letter*) is a one-page pitch. It contains the hook, the story core, and your qualifications (if impressive). It's an important weapon in your battle to break through the clutter and get your script read.

5. A scintillating one-sheet

The *one-sheet* is a one-page synopsis that can be handed to or mailed to a decision maker, or it can be left behind at meetings or after other pitching opportunities. (Incidentally, it's important to understand that the term *one-sheet* also means "movie poster.") *Your* one-sheet (synopsis) will open with your logline, hook, or concept, and then the story summary—all on one page.

6. A tantalizing treatment

This is essentially a 3–12 page synopsis or story summary. Like the one-sheet, it is a written pitch. Usually, 3–5 pages are about right. Treatments and synopses are sometimes requested in response to your query or oral pitch. Most often, they are not requested at all.

A bodacious beat sheet (optional)

On rare occasions, you may be asked for a *beat sheet*. A beat sheet usually lists the key events or main dramatic (or comedic) moments of a script. (I did not number this tool because you are unlikely to get a request for a beat sheet.)

7. A convincing telephone script

You will need this next to your phone if you call anyone about your screenplay or TV script, or if you expect someone to call you. Don't be like a client of mine who was called back on a query and who blanked out on the phone. After six seconds of chilling silence, the agent hung up. Quickly, she called me and I told her to call the agent immediately and tell the truth. She did; it broke the ice for both of them and the agent had a good laugh.

The key element of your telephone script is your hook and pitch (Numbers 2 and 3 above). A telephone script is what all professional telemarketers use. It tells you what to say if the person on the other line says "yes" or "no," or makes a particular excuse or objection. It must sound conversational and not read. Here's just one possible example:

> "I'm [name]. I'm a screenwriter with a [name genre, such as action/romantic comedy] that I'd love to get your reaction to?"
>
> (*What's it about?*) [Here you will pitch it, leading with your headline, logline, premise, or concept; then, if you feel encouraged, moving into the story summary.]
>
> (*I'm sorry, we're developing our own projects.*) "Great. Would you like to read this with an eye toward a possible assignment? I'd love to hear what you're doing [or] I loved *Nazis in Space* [or whatever his/her last production was]. [Here you are identifying your script as a mere sample of your work. You hope it will lead to a meeting and a writing assignment. You're not looking to sell the script itself.]
>
> (*Do you have an agent?*) "Actually, I'm making a decision between several agents, so I'm shopping the script now rather than letting it gather dust." [Or] "I'm looking right now. If you have any suggestions, I'd be delighted to hear them."
>
> (*We can't accept a script without an agent.*) "Could you email (or fax me) your release?" [The release is a legal document discussed in the chapter "How to sell your script without an agent."]

(*I'm sorry, we're not interested.*) "Fine. Tell me, is there someone you know who might be interested in this material [or specify the genre]?" [You might just get a referral here.]

The exact words are much less important than your pleasant, respectful persistence. The above is intended as an example in principle. Your telephone script should derive from your personality. Perhaps you won't need one at all.

Keep in mind that you may need to "sell" the assistant first before reaching the party you want. Speak to the assistant as if he is the decision maker. Be professional with all parties that you deal with. Don't engage in "small talk" on the phone. Get to your point immediately. Do not leave voice mail.

8. An inventory of salient strengths and assets

Build on your strengths when you present yourself and your work. Strengths might include your script's genre and market appeal. In fact, you might envision how your movie might be sold to the public through ads and one-sheets (movie posters). Your personal strengths might include your willingness to do assignments, your devotion to a writing career, your passion or enthusiasm, the fact that you've written a half-dozen scripts, and so on. If you have past professional writing experience, that's an asset.

A few screenwriters have created simple websites that pitch their project(s) and provide a way for a visitor to request the script. Some of these sites include cool visuals. Like any website, you must drive traffic to it. One way to do that is to give the hearer of any oral pitch a card containing the URL and then handwrite the password needed to view or download the script.

List any contacts you have in the business, right down to your long-lost friend who is now a key grip. Who do you know who might know someone who could read your script or direct your script somewhere?

In addition, you have many resources available to you on the Internet and elsewhere, including books, classes, software, online communities, and so on. Do you have emotional support from loved ones? That's an asset. Fill your mind with positives that you have going for you.

9. An attitude

Success in the marketplace requires a certain mindset. You want to be professional in your dealings with others. Be confident without being arrogant; be wily without being devious. It's easy to be intimidated by these "glamorous" people, but in reality they are no different from you and me, except that they have a different job.

Today's screenwriter needs to be enthusiastic and pleasantly persistent. I've seen very talented writers fall by the wayside, and mediocre writers make it because they were persistent. Usually the marketing process takes time. You must be committed.

People want to work with writers they can "work with." This is you if you can stand back from your work and be objective about it. It's difficult taking criticism, particularly mindless criticism, but being defensive will work against you whether you are right or wrong. At the same time, you must believe in your work and be excited about it. After all, if you don't believe in it, who will?

Confidence, conviction, and initiative are pluses. Arrogance, doubt, and passivity are minuses.

Don't count on hitting a home run on the first pitch. You are probably not going to get a million dollars for your first spec script, although it has happened. Allow yourself to be realistic without being negative. Be prepared to walk this road one step at a time without appearing too hungry along the way. Someday, you may find what producer Lynda Obst (*Sleepless in Seattle*, *Contact*) calls "a place at the table."

10. The Tenth Tool
Create a *strategic marketing plan*, and get into the habit of using the Weekly Action Plan, both to be discussed next.

4. Create your strategic marketing plan

The movie business is a *business*. To succeed in business, you need to successfully market your product and your service. Your product is your script. And your service is your ability to write. Marketing is not a matter of mass-mailing a query letter and hoping you win the jackpot. And it's not throwing one-sheets against the Hollywood wall to see which ones stick.

Today's market is more closed to outsiders and more competitive than in years past. You need a refined approach, a laserlike focus. You need a strategic marketing plan in which you determine your target market, create marketing strategies that will help you achieve your sales objectives, and position yourself in the market.

You will likely get many ideas while reading through this section, including the worksheets. Write them down as you get them. Once done, read this entire Book V, and then return to the worksheets.

PRINCIPLES

First, let's review a few basic marketing principles that affect all of your marketing efforts.

Two key marketing concepts are *segmentation* and *differentiation*. *Segmentation* is identifying the market segments that seem best for your script. *Differentiation* is how you differentiate yourself from other writers competing for that same market segment. Differentiation has to do both with your product—your script, story, concept—and with your marketing approach. What gives you that competitive edge?

Purpose, audience, strategy

In any persuasive presentation in any business arena, there are three planning steps: purpose, audience, and strategy. First, identify your purpose, then understand your audience (your market and potential buyers), and finally create strategies to reach that audience (market). These steps sound simple enough, but few people apply them.

Purpose has to do with what *you* want to accomplish, what you want to sell. It derives from your point of view. The audience is whom you want to influence. Once you understand your audience—that is, your prospective script buyers plus their market (the ultimate viewers of the movie)—then you will better know what these buyers need to hear.

In my earlier years, I was a marketing executive. I have since become a writer, script consultant, and seminar leader. But I still do a little marketing consulting. I can't tell you how many businesspeople I've given the following speech to: "You cannot say what you want to say; you have to say what they want to hear. They don't care how much your family sacrificed to build your business, they just want to know if the product works." So strategy comes from the point of view of your audience.

Here's an example. You want a raise. That's your purpose. Your audience is your boss. Most people's strategy is to state all the reasons they deserve the raise (using a lot of sentences that begin with "I"). A better strategy is to come from the boss's point of view: "Boss, here is how *you* will benefit. . . ." So strategy is involved with communicating the benefits to your audience. But your purpose should be specific, too. You don't want "a raise," you want a 10% increase over the next two years. There is power in specifics, and the more specific you can be with your purpose, audience, and strategy, the more likely success will be yours.

Your purpose is to sell your script or get a writing assignment. Actually, that's a little vague. You need to identify a *specific individual* you want to sell your script to. Once that's done, you need to understand that person and his or her company. Learn what you can, even if it's just a little. What is their buying history? What are they looking for now? Do they prefer query letters or phone calls? Do they provide an email address? Who is *their* market? In the final analysis, they don't care if you're starving. They don't care that you've been writing scripts for five years. They want to know if *your* ideas can be used to reach *their* market. Or, they want to know if you are the writer who can execute *their* ideas into a script.

Your strategy—therefore—*derives* from their needs. What do *they* need to see in a query or hear in a pitch to interest them in *your* script? How will they benefit from what you have to offer?

This same principle applies to meetings. What is your goal for the meeting? Who are you pitching to? What approach is most likely to succeed with this particular person? We'll discuss how to gather all this marketing information later.

Features and benefits

In any sales situation, the wise salesperson presents features and benefits. *Features* constitute the logical argument; *benefits* are emotional. This ballpoint pen in my hand now features a retractable point. The benefit to you is you don't get ink in your purse or pocket.

Years ago, I was trying to sell my car and an engineer dropped by. I thought this person would be most interested in specific facts about my car. But his reactions were all negative. During the test drive, however, I turned on some music. And he said, "Whoa, what's that?"

I thought to myself, "It's your emotional hot button and I am about to push it as a strategy in presenting an emotional argument (or benefit) for buying the car." Here's how the conversation went. I said, "What kind of music do you like?" He liked classical, so I started the music and said, "Imagine yourself driving through the Irvine hills. Just you, the road, and Mozart." Well, he bought a sound system with a car attached.

In any situation, try to think in terms of how the producer or agent will benefit, and what turns them on emotionally. For example, in a pitching situation, if there are merchandising opportunities that naturally flow from your story, mention them. If your story presents a role that an "A" actor would be interested in, that's a feature that provides an emotional benefit to the producer. Be sure to stress the benefit: "With 'A' talent attached, you know the financing will not be a problem. It's a go."

The "short attention span" obstacle

No one needs to tell you that concept is king in Hollywood. Concept also sells in other industries. Marketers need a handle that buyers can grab and hang on to. In the case of my book, *The Screenwriter's Bible*, the handle or concept is: *Five books in one. Everything you need under one cover* (how-to text, workbook, formatter, spec writing guide, marketing plan, and resource directory—all included).

Agents, producers, and executives have too much to read. That's why it is crucial to find the right concept, those few words in your query or pitch that drive the message home. Be able to tell your story, or present a story hook, in 25 words or less.

But concept is nothing without conviction. Your enthusiasm and conviction about your project are probably your most important assets. The voice of conviction is what sells the concept. Enthusiasm is contagious.

MARKETING RESEARCH

When you sit down and write a script, you cannot know what the market will be when the script is finally completed. You can't outguess the market. Yes, there are some genres and structures that seem perennial favorites. For example, action stories, romantic comedies (date movies), and thrillers are usually in demand. But you don't know specifically what will sell, even though some trends last for years.

However, a study of the market can help you avoid problems. For example, if you are writing a social drama, don't write it for a huge budget. Why? Because it's not likely to become a big-screen movie; it's more likely to become a TV or cable movie.

Depending on the nature of your script, it may also help you if you create a role that an "A" actor will covet. Usually this means that the story revolves around an original character with a great character arc, and that most of the scenes are about that character. In particular, there should be emotional scenes of high drama. Ideally, you want to write a script with a strong growth arc that demands some emotional range. Stars drive this business. Although there are many production companies looking for character studies, most want scripts strong on story with a role that will attract a star.

Four-Quadrant Movies are highly desired. A four-quadrant movie is one that appeals to all four demographic groups—old, young, male, and female. *Up* and *The Incredibles* are examples. It's really nothing new; it's a new name for an old idea. Back in the "old days," *E.T.* was a four-quadrant film. If that's the type of screenplay you want to write, mention that it's a four-quadrant movie in your pitch (but only if it really is).

On the other hand, you may have a small, independent market or avant-garde niche in mind. Perfect. You probably have a better chance with a small market anyway; there are a lot of unproduced and unsold "blockbuster" scripts floating around. Now ask yourself what kind of screenplay will likely meet the needs of that market.

It is true that you want to be aware of your market before you write, but write the story you have a passion to write. In other words, forget about the market once you start writing your script. Remember, you cannot predict the market one year from now. Follow your bliss and make informed choices along the way.

What to do with all of those scripts

From one perspective, you need only three things to break in: connections, concepts, and scripts. As time goes by, and you begin stockpiling unsold scripts (and connections), you will want to use wisdom in managing your inventory.

First of all, don't send a script immediately after you finish it. Let it sit a few weeks and ferment. Some previously unseen problems may reveal themselves and even solve themselves in your head. New ideas may come. On the other hand, don't rewrite it to death. Another reason to let your script lie idle a few weeks is to let your emotions cool. Now you can be objective. In the meantime, you can prepare your 10 marketing tools and create your marketing plan.

If a movie similar to your script is about to be released, wait and see how that movie does. If it succeeds or has a lot of positive buzz before it succeeds, market your script immediately. If it fails, wait about a year. If the word goes out that a producer wants an ecological Western, and you have one in inventory but waited until the market was ready for it, now you're in a position to cash in. Your patience, restraint, and common sense have paid off.

Where to go for information about markets

Read the trades. *Variety* (which leans a bit more toward features) and *The Hollywood Reporter* (which leans a bit toward the world of television) are worthwhile business publications. Weekly editions are also available. They tell you what sold, who sold it, who bought it, when it will be shot, what the logline is, etc.

Both of these publications list films in development and films in production. You will find special focus sections on specific market segments. And there's marketing information on all the players, including the independents. You will even find ads for seminars and scripts.

For example, say you want to sell to a particular company. Would it be worthwhile to know that half their financing comes from foreign sources? That means your project may need to appeal to the foreign market. Now you might say, "Well, that's what I have an agent for." And you're absolutely right. But whether you have an agent or not, understanding the market at some level will help you in pitches, meetings, phone calls, and in planning your next script—for that matter, in planning your career. Believe me, *you* will care more about your career than your agent will.

There are numerous directories, such as the *Hollywood Screenwriting Directory*, published by the Writer's Store. Done Deal (donedealpro.com) provides a database of who sold what to whom and what agent was involved. New resource tools, screenwriting websites, and directories pop up all the time. Industry guidebooks (like this one!) often have accompanying websites that offer supplementary and updated information. See the "Community" page at **keepwriting.com**. Internet Movie Database Pro (IMDb Pro) is an excellent source of industry information. Attend workshops, expos, conferences, film festivals, and seminars, and meet the people there.

There are many other industry publications, and virtually all of them are online, including *Script*. Many organizations publish free newsletters, as do I (subscribe at **keepwriting.com**). Writer's organizations such as Women in Film and Organization of Black Screenwriters can provide information and support. It might even help you to join non-writing industry organizations, such as the Association of Independent Video and Filmmakers.

CREATING THE PLAN

Beginning on the next page, you will find a number of worksheets to help you create a marketing plan and focus your marketing strategies. You have my permission to photocopy the worksheets for your own personal use, or you can purchase a PDF of all the worksheets at the store at **www.keepwriting.com**. Before completing them in full, however, I recommend that you read this entire book. Each worksheet is described below.

Text continues on page 339.

Project Plan

Title _____

Genre/description _____

TARGET MARKET

What is the best market for your script?

❏ Feature film ❏ Indie feature film ❏ TV/Cable movie

❏ TV series (1 hour) ❏ Sitcom (network) ❏ Sitcom (cable)

❏ Interactive, games ❏ New Media ❏ Animation

❏ Reality programming ❏ Direct-to-DVD (feature) ❏ Streaming

❏ Other _____

More specifically, what is the best venue for your project? (This question asks you to look realistically at the market. Where would you find a similar project? A blockbuster summer release? A Fox network weekend one-hour TV series? A woman-in-jeopardy movie for the USA Network?)

_____

_____

_____

_____

_____

List producers or companies that produce for this target market.

_____

_____

_____

_____

_____

If appropriate for your market, list potential talent that could be interested by this project. This means that the actor or actress sees a role in your script that will further his/her career.

_____

_____

_____

_____

_____

_____

List potential directors or other "elements," if appropriate, for your project.

_____

_____

_____

_____

_____

_____

If finding an agent or manager will help you sell this project (and it probably will, although you can sell to some markets without an agent), then list potential agents here (list specific individuals, not agencies).

_____

_____

_____

_____

_____

_____

_____

_____

MAKING CONTACTS

Who in the film business has read your work and responded favorably?

_____

_____

_____

_____

_____

Who do you know in the business (not listed above) who might refer you to someone else or otherwise be helpful? (These people do not have to be in high places.)

_____

_____

_____

_____

_____

List any friends, relatives, acquaintances, business associates who might have industry contacts. (The premise here is that everyone knows someone who knows someone who works in the business. Spend some time with this.)

_____

_____

_____

_____

_____

_____

_____

_____

List places you can go to network. These can be writers groups, professional organizations, social gatherings, clubs, festivals, seminars.

_____

_____

_____

_____

_____

_____

_____

List other marketing research sources (e.g., "the trades," directories, etc.)

_____

_____

_____

_____

_____

_____

_____

List other marketing ideas that might be right for your script, such as contests.

_____

_____

_____

_____

_____

_____

_____

POSITIONING STRATEGIES

Important note: Positioning has to do with creating perceptions in the prospect's mind. The worksheets that follow will provide more detail and support for your marketing strategies and project plan.

How is your project similar to other successful projects in the medium you have chosen? _____

_____

_____

How is your project original? What fresh twists does it add? _____

_____

_____

Draw a picture of a movie poster or a newspaper ad for your script.

Include the ad copy. How will your story or idea be sold?

Which of your script's pluses can you emphasize in the selling process?

_____ A script that can be sold in a brief pitch by you to an agent, by an agent to a producer, and/or by a producer to a studio. Is it a commercial project?

_____ A role that an "A" actor or actress will covet.

_____ A story that is visual, active, and fresh, that doesn't rework other movies.

_____ An ending that is emotionally satisfying.

_____ A character (and characters) that is believable and interesting.

_____ A script that is not too similar to a recent failure.

_____ A script that has something in common with successes within the past five years. This could be a new twist on a past, successful idea.

_____ A script that is in correct spec format, and that reads easily.

_____ A one-sentence concept, hook, premise, or logline that says, "This is a movie. Buy me!"

_____ The 10 marketing tools developed, including a concise, hard-hitting query letter.

_____ The resulting budget is about right for the specific market you have chosen. (Don't be concerned with budget for mainstream movies.)

What personal pluses do you bring to the table?

_____ Enthusiasm—Do you have the "voice of conviction"? Are you confident without being arrogant?

_____ Objectivity—Can you separate your ego from your work, or are you defensive?

_____ Ambition—Do you want a writing career? Do you love the business?

_____ Grace—Do people enjoy working with you? Talking to you? Meeting you?

_____ Other _____

IDENTIFYING PROSPECTS

The next step in your plan—once you have completed the above worksheets and the "positioning" worksheets that follow—is to begin your marketing research and networking. You will also begin to approach people you suspect might know someone in the industry.

Now select your best prospects (producers, talent, directors, agents, and contacts). Generally, you will work with about eight people at a time. You will not contact any of them until you have done your homework (completed the worksheets).

Name _____ Title _____

Company _____

Buying (and/or other) history _____

_____

_____

Budget range (if applicable)_____

Current needs/wants _____

_____

How he/she prefers to be contacted_____

Name _____ Title _____

Company _____

Buying (and/or other) history _____

_____

Budget range (if applicable)_____

Current needs/wants _____

_____

How he/she prefers to be contacted_____

Name _____ Title _____

Company _____

Buying (and/or other) history _____

_____

Budget range (if applicable)_____

Current needs/wants _____

_____

How he/she prefers to be contacted_____

Name _____ Title _____

Company _____

Buying (and/or other) history _____

_____

Budget range (if applicable)_____

Current needs/wants _____

_____

How he/she prefers to be contacted_____

Name _____ Title _____

Company _____

Buying (and/or other) history _____

_____

Budget range (if applicable)_____

Current needs/wants _____

_____

How he/she prefers to be contacted_____

Name _____ Title _____

Company _____

Buying (and/or other) history _____

_____

Budget range (if applicable)_____

Current needs/wants _____

_____

How he/she prefers to be contacted_____

═══

Name _____ Title _____

Company _____

Buying (and/or other) history _____

_____

Budget range (if applicable)_____

Current needs/wants _____

_____

How he/she prefers to be contacted_____

═══

Name _____ Title _____

Company _____

Buying (and/or other) history _____

_____

Budget range (if applicable)_____

Current needs/wants _____

_____

How he/she prefers to be contacted_____

═══

Weekly Action Plan

Main goal _____

Key milestones   1 _____

                    2 _____

                    3 _____

Time commitment _____

What specific actions will you take this week to achieve your milestones?

Marketing research _____

Meetings, pitches, groups, networking _____

_____

_____

Queries and one-sheets _____

_____

Cold calls _____

_____

_____

Follow-ups by mail, email, or fax _____

_____

Follow-ups by phone _____

_____

Contests _____

Other _____

Other _____

Other _____

Notes:

Correspondence Log
(Queries, Treatments, and Scripts)

Date	Q/T/S	Script Title	Person/Company	Comments, response, follow-ups

Meetings, Telephone, and Email Log

Date	Time	M/T/E	Person/Company	Comments, ideas discussed

The Project Plan

The first worksheet is entitled "Project Plan." Let's start there. Your project is the script you wish to sell. After you identify your target market, complete the remainder of the Project Plan (four pages) and focus on more specific possibilities.

Ask yourself, where do you see your project playing? Is it a TV *Simpsons*-type project? If so, who are potential producers of such projects? Is it a summer blockbuster movie? Who produces summer blockbusters? Or who wants to? Is it a teenage horror movie?

Don't ignore the smaller cable markets, reality programming, direct-to-DVD, New Media (web series and online movies), and so on. (See the chapter "Jump-start your career now" in Book V.) If you live outside of California, investigate local production companies. What's happening in your own region? Start somewhere small and work your way to glory.

And don't think you must have an agent to succeed. Most first scripts are sold without an agent. Marketing centers on filling needs. If your script fills a need, then your task is to get the script to the person who can benefit from it. This involves understanding your prospective buyer in order to create an effective strategy; it also entails recognizing obstacles and seeking ways to overcome them.

So be honest in your assessment. Where does your project belong and why? Who produces for that venue? Choose **producers** who have worked on projects similar to your proposed movie. List individual names, not production companies. In a directory, you're usually looking for the V.P. of Development or other creative executive.

As mentioned earlier, the *Hollywood Screenwriting Directory* and IMDb Pro will be helpful, as will other directories and resources. Even the "Film and TV Production Charts" in the trades may be helpful. Keep in mind that sometimes a company grows weary of a particular genre and is ready for something different (but not *too* different).

Now look for potential *talent*. You may ask, *Why look for potential talent if producers are the buyers?* Because many actors and actresses have their own production companies and are looking for projects just for them. The interest of a bankable star can raise your script from obscurity.

Be sensible—you won't likely find Julia Roberts or Will Smith interested in a TV movie about a homeowners insurance adjuster who must learn to cope with shingles. And keep in mind that a star's agent is usually a poor place to send a script. Unless you represent money, the agent may not likely deliver your script to the star. However, a hot query letter might get forwarded to the actor.

What *directors* might be appropriate for your project? If you're writing for television, this may not be applicable. A known TV director may not add that much to the project. But a film director or bankable star, even if they don't have a production company, can add value to a script if they express interest in it. Imagine saying to an agent or producer, "I have a script that Sandra Bullock is interested in."

"Other elements" refers to other creative types. For example, for one particular project of mine, we had interest from a known cinematographer (Vittorio Storaro) and a production designer.

Finally, list the names of potential *agents*. First, try the directories and resources already mentioned. Learn what you can about the agencies through your marketing research, but select individual literary agents to contact. The WGA provides a list of agencies (not individual agents).

Making contacts

It's no secret that the number one way to break into Hollywood is by referral. Many producers and industry people will read a referred script that they would otherwise demand you submit through an agent. As Joan Rivers said, "It's not *who* you know, it's *whom*." This business is built on relationships. Networking is how you find contacts. Contacts are your bread and butter. You need connections. You must meet people and you must nurture the contacts you make.

As you contact people about your script, you will find many who will say no, but who respond favorably to your work. Write down their names along with the names of those who say yes. You will stay in touch with these people once or twice a year. In fact, you can ask them if you may email them every so often. When you complete another script, they might be willing to read it, or refer you to someone it is right for. Don't underestimate the value of someone who has rejected you.

When you attend conferences, pitch-fests, and other screenwriting events, meet people, make friends, and stay in touch.

Very important! List anyone you know who might know someone in the business. That includes any friends, relatives, business colleagues, or acquaintances. Everyone knows someone who knows someone who works in Hollywood or at a local production company. My students and clients are always surprised at the results of this powerful little exercise. Once they mention to friends, acquaintances, and relatives that they have written a screenplay, the windows of heaven often open before them, and blessings pour down on their heads.

You may discover that your Aunt Tilly once dated the head of Castle Rock Entertainment, or that your boss was a fraternity brother of Brad Pitt, or that your friend was a childhood playmate of a principal of William Morris.

Take the time to ask around. This list of potential contacts could include producers, executives, actors, directors, script supervisors, assistants-to-whomever, agents, custodial engineers, gofers, gaffers, and grips. Gofers, gaffers, and grips—oh, my! They are insiders and may be closer to the action than you are.

Once you have a list of names, contact them by phone, text, mail or email. The first words out of your mouth or on the letter will be the name of the person who referred you. Then simply ask this contact to read your script. Tell him you'd love to get his opinion. I am always surprised at how generous people are in these situations. Because producers and agents often receive dozens of scripts a week, it can be difficult getting your script to someone, and yet that same person may readily accept a referred script and place it at the top of their pile.

If your contact enjoys the read, he will know what to do with the script and to whom to give it. If your contact is a producer, she will refer you to an agent so that the script can be "officially" submitted. Sometimes the script will be referred to another Hollywood-type person. I've heard of assistants and mail boys just placing the script on someone's desk. Someone may even want to "discover" you. One surprised student reported that she mentioned her script to a relative who happened to know a TV producer. This TV producer read the script and referred her to an agent. Now she is a working writer.

Don't think that the only possibilities lie in Hollywood. You might have opportunities in your own area. There are many regional production companies, and there are film people in every state and province.

Contests

There must be 100 screenwriting contests available. Some are established and well connected, such as the Nicholl. Others are highly focused on specific genres or film areas. Some are not worth entering. When you evaluate any contest, ask yourself who's running it and why. Who's doing the judging? Some contests are affiliated with agencies and production companies.

On the Community page at my website (**keepwriting.com**), you'll find links to contests I think are good bets. You should be able to find a couple that are excellent for your marketing purposes. In addition, there may be a few contests that are only available in your area. Contact your state film commissioner about opportunities for screenwriters.

Even if you don't win a contest, you may receive helpful "notes" on your script (depending on the contest). Scripts are often judged by, or otherwise find their way to, industry professionals. You might make a contact, get a meeting, or even receive an offer. In fact, entering contests can be done concurrently with your other selling efforts. Many students and clients have "broken in" or have found agents by winning or placing in contests, or making contacts with judges and readers.

In entering contests, be sure to read the rules carefully. Many contests have their own formatting requirements, and some may be looking for specific types of scripts. Most will state their judging criteria. Make sure your script is polished before you submit it. I suggest you choose two or three contests that are suitable for your material or marketing goals.

If you win a contest or place, you can insert this fact in the qualifications section of your query letter. You have more credibility now; plus, you've achieved a milestone that can give you momentum and energy on your upward climb. You may even get discovered.

Positioning Strategies
Positioning refers to how your product is placed in the mind of your prospect. The Positioning Strategies Worksheet and accompanying checklist of questions will help you create a viable positioning and marketing strategy.

Identifying prospects
Okay, you understand the nature of your project, you've targeted your market, and you have identified potential buyers and helpers. Now the fun begins. You match your project to these individuals whose names you have written down. Select at least eight people you think will be most helpful, regardless of their position in the industry, and complete the "Identifying Prospects" worksheets. You can do this for as many as 20 at a time.

List their name, title, and company. What is their buying history? If you don't know already, research it. Your marketing research efforts should continue throughout the selling process. What size projects are they looking for, budget-wise? What are their current needs and wants? And how do they prefer being contacted?

You may not be able to answer all the questions. Don't let that discourage you. Just do your best to learn about your prospects, using the marketing resources discussed. The more knowledge you gain, the more power and confidence you will have. Power? Confidence? Yes. Because these prospects are *real* prospects and *you* know you have something that *they* may want. At the very least, you are likely to find a good contact, a connection you can return to later in your career.

Don't be overly concerned with budget. Most producers want to produce something big. Budget becomes an important issue when your market is small independent producers and other programming where budgets are limited.

Don't rush the process. I've witnessed a lot of heartache from writers who became overanxious and approached the market prematurely, as described earlier.

You don't need to fill in every blank of every worksheet in this book. The worksheets are tools that you use as you need them. They are your servants, not your master.

Weekly Action Plan

You will want to make specific long-term goals, in terms of both writing and selling. (I will share some thoughts on goal-setting at the end of this book in the "A personal challenge" section.)

The key to achieving your goals is consistent action. Persistence. To help you focus your energy and efforts, I recommend you take a moment at the beginning of each week to create a Weekly Action Plan and make a specific time commitment.

At the beginning of each week, plan your activities for that week, and then commit whatever resources in time, money, and effort you'll need to accomplish those tasks. It may be 20 total hours, or four hours a day, or Tuesday and Thursday nights from 8:00 to 10:00 p.m. Whatever it is, make a goal each week in terms of time and specific actions. Some weeks, the only action will be to write. Other weeks, there may be several objectives.

What if you fail to achieve any of these goals? Don't kick yourself or quit. What's past is past. Make a new goal for this week. Learn from mistakes. Your goals are motivators to freedom, not prison wardens. Onward!

Contact Logs

Keep track of all your efforts for legal purposes, for tax purposes, and especially for marketing purposes. The correspondence log is really a submissions log. You keep track of your submissions of query letters and one-sheets (Q), treatments and synopses (T), and scripts (S).

With each contact you make, you will plan a *follow-up*. Schedule it. Maintain some kind of tickler to remind you of follow-ups, or just to touch base.

As you contact people, don't forget to apply the Purpose-Audience-Strategy Principle and other marketing principles we discussed earlier.

5. Implement your plan

Okay, you have protected your work, prepared your screenplay (product) for market, assembled 10 selling tools, and created your strategic marketing plan. But your work is not done. Throughout the remainder of this book, we will explore specific techniques, strategies, and methods for implementing your plan.

How to find an agent

As you might guess, there are many advantages to acquiring an agent. Agents save you time. They know the territory and they know how to negotiate a deal. Because agents are expected by the industry to screen out crummy writers, the fact that you have one greatly multiplies your chances of finding work. Best of all, agents don't cost anything until they sell your script. Some large agencies, such as ICM and CAA, package scripts; that is, they add talent or a director to generate a studio deal. They are generally more difficult to break into than small agencies, but a small agency may be a better choice for the novice.

You may have heard how difficult it is to get read. First of all, it is true that agents will seldom read your script, but their assistants and readers may *if* agents are properly approached.

First, secure a list of approved agencies from the Writers Guild. Keep in mind that the Guild lists agencies but not individual agents. For the names of specific agents, you may need to go to a directory. I recommend IMDb Pro or the *Hollywood Screenwriting Directory*.

Study the various agency lists and directories you have acquired. Some directories list agents in order of seniority. When using those that do, select the agent farthest down the list in a given agency. If you admire an established writer, you may contact the WGA for the name of his or her agent, or look it up at IMDb Pro. As a last resort, call specific agencies and ask, "Who is taking on new clients?" Do not tell an agent or agency that you are a new writer. You are a writer with a new script. And don't ever say that you are "seeking representation." Just ask, "Who's accepting new clients?" Or, "Who would I send a short query to?"

The point is to get the names of *individual* agents. You will *not* send them your script. Instead, you will design a strategy. The following are the best ways to gain the attention of an agent. They are listed in order of effectiveness.

1. Get referred by someone the agent knows. Recall what we have already said about making contacts.

2. Get a producer interested in your script, and ask her to refer you to one or two agents to consummate the deal.

3. Get noticed by an agent or agent's assistant by winning or placing in a contest, or by pitching your work at a pitch-fest or through an Internet broker or some other indirect method. Ask yourself how agents find clients, and position yourself or your script. See the section in this book entitled "Jump-start your career now" for a cornucopia of ideas on how to get discovered and get in the game.

4. Write a query letter, which you will mail, email, or fax to about five or so agents at a time. Simultaneous submissions of queries and scripts are the norm in Hollywood. Do not include a synopsis or treatment with your query. Mailing to five to 10 agents at a time enables you to evaluate their responses and improve your query before you contact more agents. You will only contact one agent per agency. In recent years, query letters have become less effective in reaching agents.

5. Brainstorm other ideas. Approach agent assistants directly by phone or by some other means. If you know a reader who reads for agents, engage that reader for a coverage and, if positive, ask for a referral or call the agent directly: "X wrote a coverage of my script and gave it a 'recommend.' May I send it to you?" This may be a long shot at the buzzer, but it is better than no shot.

I'm sure that other potentially effective methods have not been thought of yet.

WORKING WITH AN AGENT

Let's assume you have interested several agents and one has requested your script. You mail your script to the agent with a cover letter that says, "As you requested, here is your copy of *Hell Bent for Leather*." You will also write "Script requested" on the outside of the envelope. (Only do this if a script was actually requested.) Let's say the agent loves the script and calls.

When an agent calls, she will probably ask the golden question: "What else have you done?" Hopefully, you have written a second or third dynamite script, and have other ideas to pitch. Most likely this agent will want to meet you personally. There are a few issues that you and your agent will want to settle at this meeting.

One is the contract. The agent gets 10%. No reputable agent charges a reading fee. Be wary of requests for cash or for referrals to specific script consultants. However, an agent may legitimately ask you to cover the cost of photocopying your script.

In Writers Guild–signatory contracts, there is a 90-day clause: If the agent has not found you work in 90 days, you can terminate the contract. Before you do, however, remember that selling a script takes time. Many agents will not tender a contract until an offer is made by a producer for your script or services. If your agent is a WGA signatory, this is not a problem—the eventual contract will be WGA-approved.

Your agent will want to discuss your career. What do you want to write? Are any genres of particular interest to you? Do you want to write for television? Are you willing to travel to L.A. for necessary meetings? Are there certain things you are unwilling to write (such as stories that demean women)? Be careful not to sound too picky about what you'll write, but, at the same time, freely express your writing passion. While in Hollywood, choose your battles carefully. Many are not worth fighting; some are.

If you have several scripts, and an agent doesn't like one of them, tell the agent you'd like to try to sell it yourself and either get a release from that script or refer script requests that you get back to the agent. Some agents may ask you to do the legwork anyway as their method of operating. If you feel uneasy about a particular agent, ask him to tell you about his current clients and recent sales. You'll get an idea of his ability. Much of this can be researched on your own.

Always remember, the agent's primary motivation is money, not helping writers with passion (although that can be a secondary motivation). The agent has 20 to 30 other clients, and most of them can bring in a higher commission than you. The agent represents you because he sees bigger sales down the road and believes you can write the material his contacts want, so don't say you want to write a screenplay every so often for extra money.

Instead, communicate to the agent your desire for a writing career, your willingness to work hard and to accept writing assignments and development deals. Keep in mind, though, that screenwriters rarely get assignments for adaptations and rewrites unless they've had a sale, but these are not the only types of development deals available.

In addition to your unwavering commitment, your agent wants to see in you an ability to perform as a writer and as a *pitcher*—how well you present yourself and your ideas.

Most agents work on a weekly cycle. Each Monday, they set out to sell one or two scripts by Friday. They're also hoping to secure writing assignments for their clients. In fact, they'll often meet with their producer contacts to match their writers to the producers' project ideas. If an agent loves your script and sees that it is similar to some producer's goal, they'll have it delivered to that producer. Often, that results in a meeting that you attend with the producer, which (the agent hopes) results in a sale or development deal.

Although agents are not usually writing coaches, they will prepare you for meetings and advise you on the ebb and flow of market tides.

There are four kinds of situations that an agent can arrange:

1. *The outright sale of your spec script.* Your agent will suggest a strategy for selling your script. She will want to generate "heat," and solicit the interest of more than one buyer in your script. In rare instances, this can result in an auction. This is the stuff dreams are made of. You will be paid six figures or higher, plus receive a bonus of a like amount or even greater amount *if* the screenplay is actually produced. There are also residuals on DVDs. It will all be spelled out in your lengthy contract.

2. *A literary purchase and option agreement, commonly called an option.* This is more likely to happen than an outright purchase. Here the buyer is not quite so enthusiastic or simply doesn't want to put a lot of money into the script immediately.

In either of these two cases, the producer buys an option to the rights for a short period of time (six months to a year) for a small "down payment" of anywhere from $1 (referred to as a *free option*) to $20,000 or more. During that *option period*, the producer uses the script to attract talent and/or money. At the end of the option period, the producer will pay the purchase price, renew the option for another period of time by making another payment, or pass. In the case of a pass, you keep any option money originally given to you, plus the rights to the script revert to you.

3. *A development deal.* Here, the agent uses your script as a lure to arrange a meeting or pitching session with a producer where you pitch *your* ideas. This can result in a development deal or sale (if the story you pitch is already scripted).

4. *An audition.* The fourth and most likely scenario is that your showcase script secures you an audition meeting for an open writing assignment, such as a development deal to execute the producer's idea into a script. (We'll cover this in depth when we discuss "How to pitch without striking out.") In the case of episodic television, the deal may be to write a couple of episodes plus get residuals if the show goes into syndication. (We'll discuss TV later.)

You can see why your script needs to be well written. Since there are more development deals than spec sales, you are mainly selling your ability to write. A producer recently sent me a writer's script for evaluation with this note attached: "Please also evaluate the strength of the writer; we want to know whether the writer is competent and capable of staying with this project if we opt to move forward. This writer has additional story ideas which intrigue us, but if the writing isn't competent, then we don't want to proceed."

Once the agent negotiates a deal and conditions are met, the check is sent to the agent, from which he pays you your 90%.

Some agents get you to work for them. You go out and make the contacts. When someone expresses interest in your script, you say, "I'll have my agent get you a copy." And then you will inform your agent. Even if you do all of the work, don't even think of attempting to cheat your agent out of the 10%; you will not succeed.

Stay in touch with your agent. Get together on the phone periodically, or in person. During an active campaign, there should be contact at least once a month.

ENTERTAINMENT ATTORNEYS

An alternative to using an agent is an entertainment attorney. These lawyers are recognized by the industry as acting as agents, but they will charge you $150 to $600 an hour for their services, without any guarantee of a sale. This can get very expensive.

Perhaps a more appropriate situation in which to utilize the services of an entertainment attorney is when you have a legal question or need a contract negotiated or analyzed.

If an attorney misrepresents you, notify the state Bar. If you stop using an attorney, she must turn over her files to you.

MANAGERS

A few writers first find a manager, who then helps them find an agent or sells their script for them. A manager may charge 15% to 25% of your writing income for their services, but they basically run your career for you. When meeting with a manager, ask her precisely what she does and what her commission is.

Whereas agents focus on sales, managers focus on developing you and your work. Managers are generally easier to query than agents, and managers usually have fewer clients so that they can spend more time with each. Sometimes, working with a manager in developing your talents is a good way to find an agent.

Some managers may want to attach themselves as producers of your project. This may or may not work for your project. Personally, I would hesitate unless my "gut" told me to go ahead. If you decide to go ahead with such a manager, make sure the "producer" label is appropriate for what he or she actually does.

Managers are not WGA-affiliated, so they are not obligated to use WGA-approved contracts. So look at any contract they offer carefully. By law, they can't negotiate contracts or find you employment, but that law (the California version is called the California Talent Agencies Act) is seldom enforced.

One of the best ways to find an agent is through a producer, and although agents advise against this procedure, it is worth considering. I'll explain in the upcoming section, "How to sell your work without an agent."

Crafting the query

One of the rules of the game is that you never, ever send a script to anyone unless they specifically request it. You get them to do that by sending a captivating query letter or through some other means. If you respond to ads requesting scripts, do so with a query.

In this business, you often begin the marketing process with a query letter (or pitch letter). It's often how you make your first contact with anyone. A query is a written pitch. In cases where you call, the call will resemble the query letter in structure, tone, and content. I suppose you could call it a "query phone call." Many writers call or email before they query, to verify submission policy or whether they are currently considering new material, or verify the spelling of a name (translated: to see if that person is still there).

One screenwriter/client wrote me with his tip of the day. He said that if you know already that a company does not accept unsolicited queries or screenplays, then tell them directly, "I have an unsolicited rom-com (or a four-quadrant actioner, or whatever it is). Who would I send a short query to?" It's worth a try. What I like about it is the honesty. I've seen too many examples of lying becoming counterproductive and even fatal to people's careers.

If you want to approach a producer directly, with no agent or referral, and you have a great concept, you might try phoning the producer. As you might guess, you may have to pitch to an assistant first. But you may be able to get a meeting or at least the opportunity to pitch your idea over the phone. I hasten to add that pitching over the phone is less desirable than pitching in person. Please recall our previous discussion about "Telephone scripts."

The query letter is a written pitch. Its specific purpose is *not* to sell the script, but to get the recipient to request a copy of the script.

Query letters should be typed on 24-pound (or 20-pound) neutral-color paper (white, ivory, gray, etc.) using a conservative, easy-to-read 12-point font (Times Roman, Helvetica, Sabon, Arial, Palatino, Calibri, etc.), and should look professional. You don't need a fancy printed letterhead, but be sure to include your name, address, phone number, and email address. Don't forget to put these on the letterhead itself.

Don't give yourself the title *screenwriter* or *writer*—it's generally seen as a sign of an amateur. Graphics are not impressive; you are selling yourself as a writer, not as a graphic artist. Every written communication by you is a writing sample and will be seen as such. That's especially true with the query, so focus on the writing.

In terms of format, I recommend *standard block*, which means everything is brought to the left margin. Double-space between paragraphs and don't indent paragraphs. Other business formats are fine. You may adjust your format if it calls attention to your pitch in a clever way.

The letter should always be addressed to a specific individual and should never be longer than a page. The content of the letter should be concise, hard-hitting, and intriguing. As a general rule, shoot for three "brief" paragraphs. However, the letter needs to be long enough to convince the reader to call you, but short enough to lure someone into reading it. Big blocks of black ink look boring.

Don't get chummy, and don't say, "I'm going to make you a billion bucks," or, "Today is your lucky day," or, "Anne Hathaway will want to play the lead." There's a big difference between confidence and unsupported conceit.

Your query letter should communicate five things, and these are not in any particular order:

1. The concept in a sentence or two

This is done with a premise statement (usually in the form of a "what if" question), a logline (a one-sentence story summary), or story hook (e.g., "hard-boiled cop becomes kindergarten teacher"). On rare occasions, your strongest point may be your title (such as *Psycho,* for example). This might be a good time to review the information on high concept in Book I.

2. The title and genre

The hook or story summary should imply the genre. If it doesn't, you may need to state the genre directly. The title is often mentioned in the close (#5 below); for example, May I send you a copy of *The Constipated Cockatoo?*

3. A brief pitch of the story

The pitch should be written in present tense, focusing on character, conflict, and action—the Big Event and enough of the story to intrigue the reader. The story is not about the Mafia, it is about a person in the Mafia with a problem. Your story presentation will be one or two paragraphs, with one being preferred to two.

Show is better than tell. Don't say that your story is jam-packed with action and plenty of romance. Instead, write the query in such a way that the reader perceives as much. Give the reader a reason to believe.

Don't tease the agent or producer with a statement like, "If you want to know how it ends, you'll have to read the script." Of course, it's unlikely you'll include the ending in your query, but don't tease the agent or producer about that. If your story is quite strong, but you have a weak concept, open with your story and forget the concept. The reverse is also true. But provide enough information that the agent or producer will ask for your script. At the most, you have three sentences to grab his attention.

It's unnecessary but okay to use Hollywood buzzwords and phrases such as "hip with an edge"—just make sure they are in current usage, yet not overused. Reading industry publications will help you find that edge that makes you hip.

4. Your qualifications

There are many ways to qualify yourself.

- Referred by someone in the biz. In this case, open your letter with that person's name: "Robert Redford asked me to contact you."

- Any film-related experience.

- Any professional writing experience. "Professional" means you were paid. Be brief. Don't make a list of published magazine articles; just say you've been published in a number of national publications.

- Winner of a screenwriting contest (or placed).

- Endorsed by a professional. The best endorsements are from non-buyers such as working writers and actors. Include their testimonial. Don't quote a producer, because that raises the question, *If she liked your script so much, why didn't she buy it?*

- Expertise in the subject matter. If your central character is a trial lawyer and that's your livelihood, consider mentioning it. I had a student who was a rock singer for 10 years, whose script was about a rock singer. I told her to mention her experience.

- A graduate degree from a recognized film school, such as UCLA, USC, NYU, Columbia, or AFI. It may help a little to mention other education or well-known writing courses you have taken, but it will not be as impressive as actual experience.

If you have no qualifications, omit this section. Never mention a negative. If you live out of state, don't worry about it. If you've written other scripts, mention or imply that fact so the agent or producer won't think that the script you're pitching is your one and only. Don't mention that you've written 10 or more screenplays *if* they have not had any action.

5. Request permission to forward your script

Many writers include an SASE (self-addressed, stamped envelope) or postcard to make it easy for the prospect to respond. On the back of the postcard, give the prospect a couple of options to check. (One will be, "Yes, send me a copy of your script *Love Freight*" [or whatever the title of your script is].) Type his or her name at the bottom, so you'll know where it came from.

Personally, I don't recommend an SASE or postcard. Just ask the prospect to contact you for the script. It's as simple as that. They have a phone right there on their desk. In truth, good news comes via the phone, bad news through the mail (if at all). They can also email you if they wish. Some writers add a line to the query that they'll follow up in a few days; in that case, you will need to call after they've had time to receive the query.

Common blunders

Do not open a query letter with long statements about seeking representation; they know you seek representation. And do not close a query with long expressions of thanks for their consideration and time, or tell them how much you're looking forward to hearing from them. They know you are grateful and how much you want to hear from them. These expressions just take up space on the letter and don't help you get a positive response.

Do not send your script with a query. Do not send a treatment or one-sheet or coverage to an agent unless requested.

If you know in advance how a particular producer or actor or agent likes to be queried, then those instructions supersede my own.

How to send the query

Should you fax, mail, or email the query? Although many writers have had success by faxing, my general recommendation is to mail a query letter the first time you're contacting someone unless your research says otherwise. A few agents and producers may prefer emailed queries. Find out in advance what is preferred, even if that means placing a phone call. If you get a chance to pitch when you make that call, then do so.

Generally, if you can find someone's email address, it means you can email that person your query. Do not attach a file to an email; place the hook in the subject line and the remainder of your pitch in the body of the email.

SAMPLE QUERY LETTERS

As mentioned, queries can be used to approach any industry professional. Always query before sending a script. Keep in mind that the purpose of the query is to obtain permission to forward the script. You accomplish that by getting the reader excited about your story. Here are a few sample queries.

Notice that the first letter does not open with any pleasantries, prologues, or small talk.

The Wizard of Oz

Dear Ms. Big:

A tornado throws a young farm girl into Oz, a magical land where she must defeat vengeful witches and sinister flying monkeys to find her way home. On her way, Dorothy befriends a cowardly lion, an airhead scarecrow, and a sentimental, if rusty, tin woodsman. Each, like Dorothy, feels outcast and misplaced.

They join forces to seek help from the Wizard of Oz, fighting off the Wicked Witch of the West along the way; but when they finally destroy the witch and meet the alleged wizard, they discover that the blessing each traveler seeks has been with them all along.

My latest screenplay, *The Wizard of Oz*, is available on request. Please call me for a copy at 555/555-5555.

Sincerely,

The above letter was created by screenwriter Joni Sensel for her newsletter. She points out in her commentary that she would address the letter to an individual. In the first paragraph, she identifies the central character, her obstacles, and goal. I especially like the last sentence about feeling outcast and misplaced, because it identifies an emotion.

The second paragraph tells the agent how Dorothy overcomes her obstacles. It identifies opponents and suggests the resolution. Note that the author told the story, but did not include the concept. The story itself, in this case, is sufficient. It includes character, conflict, action, emotion, and theme. The genre is implied. She also tells us how the story ends; that's usually unwise, but it works in this instance.

The third and final paragraph succinctly tells the agent what to do without groveling or multiplying words of gratitude. Including her phone number is a plus, even though it's already printed on the letterhead. This well-written letter flows smoothly and logically from point to point. If you use the phone to query, be just as succinct and self-assured.

Bed of Lies

This letter is provided by Kerry Cox, former editor of *Hollywood Scriptwriter*.

Dear Ms. Agent:

Thirteen years ago, J. T. Wheeler woke up at 5:30 a.m., showered, had a light breakfast, and savagely murdered his family of four. He then hopped into his Lexus and vanished from the face of the Earth.

Or did he?

It's a question Susan Morgan, wife of prominent attorney Lawrence Morgan, has to answer fast. The chilling fact is, the more she learns, the more she realizes that Wheeler's killing spree not only wasn't his first . . . it may very well not be his last.

And she might be married to him.

BED OF LIES is a psychological thriller and dark mystery with a strong female protagonist that builds to an ultimate shocker of an ending. It is also a story of trust, of betrayal, and the fine line that divides the two when secrets are buried between husband and wife.

I've written professionally for television, radio, and print, including network TV credits and two published books. I've also worked extensively as a crisis-intervention counselor for Interact, a nonprofit group specializing in teen and marital crisis management.

The first paragraph—with the punch line *Or did he?*—is the hook. The next section is the story setup, including the title, genre, and underlying theme about trust and secrets. He mentions "a strong female protagonist." That would only be necessary if he felt the specific production company he is writing to is looking for just that. Otherwise, omit it. The letter might be clear enough without it anyway.

Kerry's qualifications follow. Kerry's work as a crisis-intervention counselor qualifies him as an expert in the story's subject matter.

His writing style matches the mood of the story and uses detail effectively. If this query were for a comedy, he would probably have written the letter from a humorous slant. Kerry doesn't tell the entire story, which is usually a good idea, but he provides enough story information to hook the reader. The letter may be a little long by most standards, but the extra length, I believe, is warranted in this case.

A Cuban Cigar

How would you whittle down this query letter? It is aimed at an agent, but it could have been addressed to a producer as well.

Dear Ms. Agent:

Not unlike most people, baseball fan Jimmy Lansburger's life didn't turn out the way he always dreamed it would. So when he stumbles across a headline about the greatest Cuban baseball player alive, Renaldo Rapido, he's more than willing to try to become this man's agent and save his hide from bankruptcy. However, Jimmy has two small problems: He doesn't have any money and he doesn't speak Spanish. But he has plenty of gall. He talks his sometimes-girlfriend, Selma, a straitlaced travel agent, into helping him go to Cuba to smuggle Renaldo and any teammates who will come out of Cuba to the land of opportunity.

The two are like fish out of water. Jimmy is a good guy who has never been able to hold down a job for more than a couple of months at a time. And Selma knows just enough Spanish to get her into trouble. This results in a fanciful journey through Cuba, where one crazy incident leads to another. And Renaldo the ballplayer, who is known to love America, starts getting homesick for Cuba before he even leaves. This story will touch your heart with romance and excite you with action and keep you laughing all the way to the happy end, as Jimmy finds out what's important in life.

I'd like to submit ROMANCE IN CUBA for your consideration and possible representation. I wrote ROMANCE IN CUBA with Meg Ryan and Tom Hanks in mind. Who wouldn't love seeing these two together again?

I've enclosed an SASE for your reply. Thanks very much for your time and consideration. I'll be eternally grateful to you.

Sincerely,

Big blocks of black ink act like agent repellent. I doubt if the letter would even be read. Here's my revision, which includes a title change.

Dear Ms. Agent:

Have you found that *one special person* who will turn your life around?

Well, Jimmy Lansburger, certified baseball nut, thinks he has—it's Renaldo Rapido, ace pitcher for the Cuban Nationals. Jimmy's dream is to agent Renaldo and his teammates into the American big leagues, and make a grotesque sum of money.

But this lovable flake can't afford a plane ticket or even a Spanish/English dictionary. So he hornswoggles his no-nonsense travel-agent girlfriend, Selma, into helping him smuggle the sentimental southpaw out of Cuba.

A CUBAN CIGAR is a misadventurous comedy romp where Jimmy finally realizes that Selma, not Renaldo, is that *one special person*. May I send you a copy of the script?

The original query letter is authentic. As you can see, the revision is leaner and more focused. It uses stronger, more concrete words, and it avoids unnecessary repetition and cliché expressions. It "shows" rather than "tells," focuses on concept and relationships, and omits any references to current actors. It also opts for a humorous writing style since the screenplay (hopefully) is written in that style.

The phrase "one special person" is an attempt to bolster and unify the concept, characterize Jimmy, and create humor (since this is a comedy). The word "sentimental" is dropped in to raise the specter of conflict—it's not going to be easy to convince Renaldo to leave Cuba. (Besides, I like the alliteration.)

This letter might benefit from a stronger idea of what happens once they're in Cuba (but not having read the script, I don't know). Whether this letter grabs you or not, please note what changes were made and why they were made.

The writer had no experience or qualifications to mention in the letter—*A Cuban Cigar* was his first script. Thus, nothing was mentioned of qualifications. The writer's name, address, and phone number would appear in plain sight on the letterhead.

The Silk Maze

This example by Jeff Warshaw capitalizes on Hollywood's penchant for sex. Although a one-paragraph story summary would be preferred to three, notice how Jeff's style creates suspense and intrigue. Jeff presented this in class to a standing ovation.

> Dear Mr. Shmoe:
>
> Jonathan Stark thought he knew all the angles. He thought he knew what Lily, his beloved partner-in-crime, wanted from life. He thought he knew how to please and manipulate Celia, the young socialite who seemed to know too much about his sordid past. He thought he could control the heart of Mazie, the one "client" who cared for him. He was wrong.
>
> Jonathan Stark knows next to nothing about the three equally beautiful and treacherous women who rule his life. Trapped between two women who love him for very different reasons, and one who wants to destroy him no matter what it takes, Jonathan must walk the tightrope between the true love he seeks and the easy, smarmy sex life he's come to know.
>
> Will he make the right decision, or is he riding for the biggest fall of his life? Caught in a smooth, alluring web of intrigue, deception, and white-hot sexual subterfuge, Jonathan Stark must stay one step ahead of the game if he hopes to escape THE SILK MAZE.
>
> Call me at (714) 555-5555 for a copy of my fast-paced erotic thriller THE SILK MAZE.
>
> Very truly yours,

Jeff indicates his genre as a fast-paced, erotic thriller. He is wise to give his genre some pizzazz. Erotic thriller is better than thriller. Romantic action/adventure is better than action/adventure. My script *Kumquat* is not a romantic comedy; it is a *romantic comedy against a background of high adventure.* Don't overdo it, however, with something like sci-fi/action/drama/reality-based/environmental Western.

Jeff concludes his letter with his phone number. Make sure that your address and phone number are somewhere on the letter. The envelope is in the round file before the query is ever read.

The brief query

Query letters do not need to be long. In evaluating one client's script, I saw a clever angle to her story and wrote a query letter for her. The letter consisted of just one paragraph, and that paragraph was only five lines long. Even though she had no qualifications, she received 40 requests for her script.

Unfortunately, she had not followed my advice to polish her script before sending the query and to not mass-submit the query. This story, unfortunately, ended in heartbreak. Thus, she felt disinclined to share the letter with others.

The Secret Cave

Here's a letter of my own that pitches a project referred to frequently in these pages as *The Secret of Question Mark Cave.* My script was very nearly purchased for production by Disney [translation: rejected], but I asked Barry Wise (name has been changed) who he thought the story was right for. He liked my script and gave me a referral. Since he used the word "perfect," I quoted him. The query was successful; that is, Ms. Miller (name changed) requested the script. Notice the last sentence in the query identifies the primary demographic she is interested in.

Dear Ms. Miller:

Barry Wise at Disney said my screenplay was "perfect" for you. The story is about...

~ A long-forgotten cave, a "magic" sword...and a family stranded without a TV set ~

It is the adventure of a boy who discovers that the only "magic" he needs is already inside him (his good heart). It is a laugh-out-loud family comedy with a final surprise twist that will touch you deeply.

My experience includes several script sales, including a successful DTV feature (HERCULES RECYCLED), a network MOW (A WINDOW IN TIME), and an award-winning family comedy (THE PENNY PROMISE). In addition, I'm the author of *The Screenwriter's Bible*.

Request THE SECRET CAVE by calling (801-492-7898) or faxing (801-756-5555) your release. Incidentally, I wrote this "hero's journey" for kids aged 7–12 and their parents.

Are you shocked that I revealed so little about the action of the story? My thought was the referral and qualifications were enough to get a request for the script. I was right. The reference to a "release" is a plus to the reader. I was willing to sign one at that time.

Kumquat

Kumquat is an unproduced screenplay that I sold for a nice chunk of change. Here's the entire pitch that got the script read. Notice that this successful query focuses on two characters while communicating important story elements.

Dear Mr. Producer:

Philbert the philosopher—melancholy, pensive, and playing it safe—is on the trail of the ancient Golden Kumquat of Tibet, said to hold the meaning of life.

Cami the costume shop owner—bubbly, resourceful, and chameleon-like—is on the lam and wanted for murder. She tricks Philbert into helping her find the real killer.

Their riotous adventure teaches her to drop the façades and love, and it teaches him how to take the risk to live. Together, they partake of the KUMQUAT.

Wanna bite? Call me for KUMQUAT, a delicious romantic comedy against a background of high adventure.

When I was in the marketing phase for the above project, I also identified some actresses/comediennes who might be right for the lead role and was going to query their respective production companies (but I got a "bite" on the above query before I could do that). Naturally, I employed a different approach in the query to the companies of those actresses. In it, I emphasized the importance of the role (actually three roles in one): ". . .my script features three roles for her to play—the romantic lead (naturally), a predatory New Age guru, and a sultry saloon singer." If you approach talent, make sure the project sounds like it's just right for them.

An old query format with a new twist

I'll let this client tell his own story:

> Dave, here's what I did. I queried three agents; three responded positively. I queried four production companies; two responded positively, and two are pending. Here's what I did differently. I centered my excellent title followed by the genre. I then double-spaced and centered the exact phrase I think their marketers would use on the movie poster. That was followed by a normal paragraph consisting of a two-sentence story summary. In my final paragraph, I listed my writing experience.

Another client had success using bullet points. Still another wrote the letter from the point of view of his central character—"Please help me! The cops are after me and my wife thinks I'm nuts." And so on.

Let the characters speak

C. Daniel Yost quoted characters from his screenplay:

You spend 18 years in prison for killing two boys in a fire. Your wife dies of cancer. Your job goes to another man. Your daughter forgets you ever existed. Only exoneration can set you free...

...But is your innocence worth killing for? Luke Foster must answer this question.

"You didn't kill my sons. They died the day they were born Hamiltons."

—Sharon Hamilton, mother of the boys

"Innocence belongs to our children. Today I die. Today you get justice."

—Gen. James Hamilton, father of the boys

"We're all guilty. It's just a matter of time till our crime fits our punishment."

—Johnny Firstlight, parole officer

Drawing on 10 years' experience as a commercial writer/director, I craft stories with unorthodox characters, provocative themes, and extraordinary endings. Please contact me for a copy of *Foster's Fire*.

Yost also created a website to pitch his screenplay and would direct interested parties there. Another client, Mirko Betz, created a YouTube query for his feature *Jim and Abdul*. Normally, I wouldn't recommend going to the expense of either of these efforts, but they demonstrate there are always alternative ways to get your work out there. I am convinced there are many great ideas out there that have not been thought of yet.

Don't be afraid to be creative with your prose and the formatting of your query. Differentiate your query from the typical query; it's okay to stand out. On the other hand, don't outsmart yourself with something so "creative" that it's incomprehensible. The main thing is to loosen up when you write. If you are like other writers, you will feel some tension and pressure when you write the query. Find a way to get beyond that and relax.

Write two queries

After you have crafted your wonderful query, craft another one taking a different angle. It's a great exercise because once the second query is completed, you start seeing how to improve the first one. Also, you may see that the first approach may not work with a particular prospect. It's nice to have an alternate query on hand.

WHAT NOT TO INCLUDE IN A QUERY LETTER

It can be tough finding the razor's edge between professionalism and creativity. And where does confidence and enthusiasm end and conceit and insolence begin? One rule of thumb is to ask yourself, *What does this agent or producer want to hear?* In other words, get the focus off you and what you want to say, and get into the head of the agent or producer you're writing to.

Here are excerpts from five would-be screenwriters who didn't figure that out. These are from actual query letters collected by writer Joni Sensel.

> A warmhearted, romantic venture into the deepest of human emotions, revolving around the love of one person for another despite overwhelming odds, with a touch of comedy, proving yet again that love conquers all.... And, of course, like all my work, the story concludes with a stunning, unexpected ending.

This could describe a dozen stories. The problem here is that the character is telling instead of showing, and is focusing more on theme than story. Write the story, including the ending, and we'll decide if it's heartwarming and stunning.

I'm 22. I hope this will be my way over the "wall" and give me access to a struggling industry that could use the talents I possess to help it reach its potential. Cinema is my life and I hate to see it in the hands of incapable people.

Don't get cocky, kid.

Your agency has been highly recommended to me by the Writers Guild. I have enclosed a short story that explains why I have chosen to be a screenwriter.

And we're all dying to read it. And please, no false flattery. Be aware of Linda Buzzell's two no-nos: "Don't be dull or desperate" (from *How to Make It in Hollywood*).

Jesus Christ the man and I are both empaths. I'm this way because of Y. The symbol of God is a clock. I would like to meet the Pope someday.

Is this the story or your qualifications?

... the constant epistemological question regarding the perplexing attempt to explain the nature of being and reality and the origins and structure of the world ... the metaphysical conflict between natural law (St. Augustine) and pragmatism (Kant-Dewey-James) and the question of the benefits of merging from ...

Excuse me, please, but I just wanna make a movie.

ONCE THE QUERY IS SENT

The next step is to evaluate the responses to your query. Half or more may not respond at all. Most who do respond do so within four weeks, although responses have come as late as six months later. Usually a phone response is positive. Rejection generally comes through the mail. No response usually means no, although it is possible that the query was lost. If the rejections pile up, then reevaluate your query and your story. Make any necessary changes. Then go ahead and contact more prospects.

If there is no response, when should you follow-up? If you faxed or emailed your query letter, call a few days after. If you mailed your query, wait about two to four weeks before following up. Mention that you are touching base or following up on a query. You might ask if they received it. If they can't find your original letter, offer to fax or email a duplicate right at that moment. If they have your query but haven't read it, ask when you can expect to hear back.

If someone tells you that they do not accept manuscripts from people not known to them, ask them for a referral to an agent or producer who does. You could also ask, "May I call back in a few months to see if anything has changed?" or otherwise use your persuasive powers or simply pitch the one-line hook or concept. At the very least, you may make a contact that will pay off later.

Once an agent or producer responds positively to your query, send your script with a cover letter that opens with a variation of, "As you requested, here is. . . . " Remind the agent or producer of the contents of the original query, or attach the original query to your cover letter. The cover letter will be attached to the screenplay with a paper clip.

The script should be an excellent photocopy. Send it Priority Mail with the cover letter. Do not include return postage or an SASE. Scripts are seldom returned. It's okay to make a personal delivery, but you probably will not get a chance to meet the agent or producer. Write "Script requested" on the package with a Magic Marker.

If your contact asks you to email the script, attach your script as a PDF file (or format requested by the agent or producer).

It can take up to four months or more to hear back on a script submission. Wait at least four weeks before your first follow-up. Try once every couple of weeks or so after that. Be *pleasantly persistent*, not obnoxiously persistent. Generally, the best time to call is in the afternoon. A Thursday or Friday call will remind the agent to get the script read over the weekend.

When someone says, "We'll call you," or "We'll get back to you," your response could be, "Great! May I call in a week or so?" That makes it more difficult for them to summarily dismiss you.

If your script has not been read by your third or fourth call, then it's time to turn to another prospect. But before you do, try to get a referral to another agent or producer. Keep in mind that projects move slowly in this business, so be patient.

If your script is rejected, don't be afraid to ask for honest feedback. (The rejection letter may not be honest.) Ask for a copy of the coverage. Remember, you are always building contacts, learning more about the business, and improving your work; and some of your best future contacts may be today's contacts who rejected you.

Always treat the producer's or agent's assistant like a human being. Learn his name. Treat him with the same respect you'd accord the agent, and don't use the word "secretary." You may very well need to sell this person first. In fact, it's quite possible that the assistant will read the script before his boss does.

No one in Hollywood is an assistant to be an assistant. Everyone is on their way up. So think of the assistant as your friend and accomplice. He can tell you how a particular agency or production company operates. You can ask, for example, "When should I expect to hear from so-and-so?" Or, "When can I call back?"

If a prospect is too busy to read your work now, you can ask, "May I try back in a few months to see if anything has changed?"

Let me remind you that during this long period of searching for an agent and selling your script, you should not stop writing. Once you finish a script, take a week off and then start another one. Chances are you will finish it before the previous one has been sold.

How to pitch without striking out

Most producers have their own ideas to develop if they can just find the right writer. Of course, they'll buy a spec script if they think it is an excellent marketing risk, but they're looking for writers. In fact, the vast majority of deals out there are development deals and other assignments—producers hiring writers to execute their ideas, develop sequels to previous movies, rewrite scripts in preproduction or development, adapt novels, and so on. The spec market tends to go in cycles. Some years can be excellent for spec scripts, other years not so good.

What happens when your agent decides to market your script?

Your agent will contact the highest-level executives and producers he knows. These will be producers with deals or executives at studios. Producers with deals are producers with contacts or other connections with studios or financial sources. The studios are usually the last to be contacted, because their rejection closes the doors to outside producers wanting to bring the project to them.

Your agent will use the same or similar pitch or premise that you used in your query letter. If the development executive or producer asks for your script, she will normally give it to a *story editor* who will assign it to a *story analyst* or *reader*. As you know, the reader will write a *coverage* and make a recommendation. If the recommendation is positive, the development executive will read at least a portion of your screenplay. (The process is the same whether your agent submits the script or you submit it directly to the producer yourself.)

A development executive must love your script to champion it. Assuming she does love it, she will pitch it to other execs using the same or similar pitch or premise that your agent used with her. These other producers will then read your script, probably during the weekend. It will then be discussed at the Monday morning conference or some other meeting. The decision will be made to 1) buy it or 2) not buy it.

1. If they decide to buy it, you could be rolling in six figures. Or, they'll pay for an option (as explained earlier) and use your script to interest other parties (talent, director, other producers) and/or bring it to a studio. The script will likely be further developed by you and/or by other writers.

Eventually, the project is either *greenlit* or not. A *green light* means it will go into production. Money and fame will soon be yours! If it is not greenlit (and most scripts that get this far aren't), then either the rights will revert back to you (in the case of an option) or the project will go into *turnaround*, that is, be offered for sale to another studio or entity that is willing to cover the costs to date. There are many variations on this theme and many other pathways deals can take.

Even if your script is not greenlit, it may make *The Black List*. That's a list of the ten best unproduced specs floating around Hollywood. The list is released every December by Franklin Leonard.

2. If they decide to pass on the script, *but* they like your writing, the executive will call you or (if represented) your agent and ask to meet you. This means you're a semifinalist in your bid to secure a development deal or other writing assignment. Your agent will arrange a meeting with the producer. This meeting is an opportunity for you to *position* yourself and your work in the minds of executives and get some kind of deal.

PREPARING TO PITCH

The purpose of any pitching opportunity

From your viewpoint, the goal of almost any pitching session is to get your script in the hands of decision makers. In the scenario described above, where you or your agent has set up a meeting with someone who already loves your script, the goal is a deal.

From the viewpoint of the executive, producer, agent, or assistant listening to you, the goal is to answer two questions:

Is this the writer (or project) we're looking for? This is why you are there.

Is this a writer we can work with? This is why you will not arrive drunk.

Before any pitch

Prior to a meeting with a producer, pitch mart, pitch-fest, writing conference, or other pitching venue, find out as much as you can about the company(ies) and the people you are meeting or may meet. If you have an agent, he should be a big help. Research these questions:

- Who are these guys and what are their titles?

- What are their most recent credits?

- How much total time will you be allotted to pitch?

- How many pitches will they expect you to pitch?

- What genres are they most interested in? Who is *their* audience?

- What major talent has appeared in their most recent productions?

- Do they work with high or low budgets?

- What are they looking for now?

The single best way to prepare for a pitch is to sit down with some writer friends or invite some neighbors over and pitch to them. If the pitch appears clear and interesting to them, then feel encouraged. Practicing your pitch in front of real people (not the mirror) will help you immensely in preparing for the real thing. You might even role-play the entire meeting from beginning to end in a writer's group session if you belong to a writer's group.

What should you bring to the pitch? Bring anything you think they might want. If they haven't seen a sample script, bring one. If coverage has already been written on your script by a professional reader, and it's positive, bring it with you. Bring written one-sheets (one-page story summaries) of any projects you may pitch.

Be prepared to answer questions. In the case of a brief pitch, be ready to continue your pitch after the initial two minutes have passed. Have about two to five additional pitches ready to go—just in case. Have a brief bio or résumé in mind (not written) in case they ask you what you've done.

Also, after or during the pitch, they may ask you who you see in certain roles. Be ready with ideas about casting. The main reason they may ask this is that it helps them get a clearer picture of how you see your characters. It's seldom for casting purposes.

What do you wear? Dress comfortably, but don't come in rags. Generally, you do not wear a suit, but you may if you wish. For men, I suggest nice jeans, a T-shirt or collared shirt, and a sports jacket. Wear loafers or attractive sneakers that don't stink. Slacks are okay. For women, I recommend something similar or slacks, casual dress, or skirt and top. Don't wear a short skirt or show cleavage. Keep them focused on the pitch.

Finally, in driving to the meeting or event, allow adequate time to arrive and park. Take into account possible traffic jams. Be on time. It's okay to bring a pen and notepad to take notes. Bring a firm handshake as well.

During the meeting

If the pitching opportunity is a meeting set up by you or your agent because the producer has read or loves your script, then expect about 30 minutes to about an hour, but it could be less. You'll know that when the meeting is set up. Some of the time is spent with getting-to-know-you conversation. At the beginning of the meeting, they will tell you how much they love your sample script. They're trying to make you feel relaxed. They will offer you a soda or water. This is not an adversarial confrontation; they hope you will do well. Let that be of some small comfort to you.

Be as conversational and natural as you can. At the same time, retain a level of professionalism. Don't try to get too chummy or be too charming. Be your best self. Be willing to engage your "new friends" with small talk. First names are okay. Having a good sense of humor is a plus. Project positive energy—not Pollyanna, not God's gift to Hollywood—be upbeat and confident. Ask about something in the room—a trophy or painting. Listen more than you talk. (Incidentally, if you are participating in a pitchfest or similar venue, there may be no small talk or very little.)

If they are interested in hearing your ideas with an ear toward developing one of them, they will ask you to pitch them. These will be short pitches, or at least start out as short pitches. They just want to get a feel for your work, your creativity, and your personality. After all, pitching is as much about making contacts and developing relationships as it is about swapping "stories."

If they are interested in the possibility of giving you a writing assignment, they will audition you by asking you what you've been working on, as already discussed above. Afterwards, they may then pitch some ideas to you. For example, a producer may say, "We're looking for a Faustian comedy for Tobey Maguire. What do you think?"

If you respond positively and intelligently, the executive may say, "Well, if you come up with a story for us, then let us know. We'd love to hear the pitch." Interpreted, this means: *Congratulations, you are now a finalist in your bid to secure a development deal. Have your agent call us (or you call us) when you have something for us.*

Here's what's really happening: You and a half-dozen other finalists will create and pitch a Faustian comedy for Tobey Maguire. This way, the producer can develop her ideas without investing a dime of her own money. The producer will pick the pitch she likes best—which, naturally, will be yours— and you will get the development deal to write the script.

THE LONG PITCH

In the scenario above, you have been asked to come up with a story for a Faustian comedy. You were given this opportunity based on your "sample script" or previous body of work and the previous meeting. Now you have one of those rare occasions where you will deliver a 10–20 minute pitch.

You will prepare for this opportunity in much the same way as for any pitch. You will need to outline a complete story—beginning, middle, and end. Have one or two alternate angles to the story just in case the story doesn't grab your listeners.

In the body of the pitch, focus on character, the goal, what's at stake, the emotional high points, theme, how the character will grow, the major dramatic twists, and, of course, how it ends. In some long pitches of complex stories, consider opening with the title, genre, and a brief introduction to your main characters.

In the next section we will discuss the content of short pitches, and then we will consider how to deliver any pitch.

THE SHORT PITCH

By far the most common pitch is the short pitch. A short pitch can range from 30 seconds to two to three minutes. Some writers call this the *elevator pitch*—the elevator of opportunity opens and closes, and that's how much time you have.

The short pitch is used in chance encounters, on the phone, pitch marts, pitch-fests, writing conferences, and other meetings. On occasion, you may be given five minutes or more per pitch.

Brief pitches come in two stages—the story hook in 25 words or less and a brief rendition of the storyline. In other words, the structure of this short pitch is quite similar to a query letter. And much of what we discussed about written pitches applies to oral pitches.

The opener
When the time comes, just dive into your pitch. If you wish, you can transition into your pitch by mentioning what inspired you to write this story. Don't be afraid to let your passion flow.

The hook must grab the decision maker's attention and set a tone. The hook could come in the form of a premise, a logline, or a concept statement. Often the Big Event is the hook. Here are some examples of openers:

- *"Honey, I Shrunk the Kids"* (said in a distressed, confessional tone). In this case, the descriptive title may be enough to grab the attention of the executive. This particular title implies the Big Event— the shrinking of the kids.

- *"An alien child, accidentally left behind on Earth, is befriended by some children who help him find his way home."* You just cast your logline and you're hoping the hook sets.

- "The Queen of Rock falls for a tabloid reporter on the way to marry the King of Fashion. *Celebrity Wedding.* Who doesn't want to go to one of those?" That's from Yours Truly.

- *"What if the President of the United States were kidnapped?"*

- *"Rom-com adventure. Okay, here it is: When her sister is kidnapped, a lonely romance writer tries to save her, only to find true romance in the process."* This is a variation of the old pitching formula: When X happens (the Big Event), so-and-so tries to get Y, but ends up with Z.

- *"Imagine you are driving down a dark road. Late at night. And someone is behind you. You turn; he turns. He is following you. You decide to get on a lighted street and suddenly find yourself at a stop light. Nowhere to go, and the car behind you gets closer and closer. Finally, he pulls up next to you and stops. You look over and he resembles you exactly. He is you!"* This is a little long, but it's suspenseful. Use your voice.

When you prepare for a pitch, it may take a little time to find your hook or logline. The key is to focus on the golden nugget at the center of your story or determine the strongest point of the story. For example, here is the original, poorly crafted logline written by a client:

A cantankerous old man courts Sunshine (60), a platinum blond gold digger, and ignites a family feud when he threatens to change his will, to give his estate to her if she will marry him. But to everyone's surprise, Sunshine refuses to marry and becomes a catalyst for change when she attempts to set things right in his dysfunctional family.

Here is the final revision:

An aging platinum blonde gold-digger falls in love with a hunk who marries rich old women on their deathbeds.

When Gene Roddenberry pitched *Star Trek*, he had problems. No one was interested in sci-fi. A popular TV show at the time was *Wagon Train*. So Gene pitched *Star Trek* like this: "*Wagon Train in space.*" He hitched his "star" to a "wagon," and the rest is history. He combined the familiar with the unique—a new twist on a recently successful idea.

These days, you want to avoid the "cheap pitch." *Driving Miss Daisy meets the Men in Black.* Or: *Napoleon Dynamite in the Hurt Locker.* Or: *Good Will Hunting falls in love with Avatar.* It's okay to refer to recent successful movies, but it should not be the core of your concept or pitch. Yes, *Alien* was pitched as *Jaws* in space, and *Titanic* was *Romeo and Juliet on the Titanic.* Use your common sense and don't abuse this cliché tactic. There is some resistance to it now anyway. If you have a *bona fide* comparison that helps you present "the successful with a twist," then use it as a hook.

In light of the above, it's both fun and instructive to watch the opening sequence of *The Player* and see all the established writers stumble through pitches.

Most often, development executives must sell your idea to higher-ups, and higher-ups will sometimes pitch your idea to other producers or a studio. It's the script's story concept, logline, or hook that helps them sell these contacts. Likewise, distributors and exhibitors need a simple, easily understood idea to attract moviegoers to their movies.

However, if a producer's past work consists of literary films (such as *Emma* or *Howards End*), a blood-and-guts, special-effects, high-action pitch may not be appropriate; in fact, you may even be perceived as a hack. Be wise.

The body and conclusion of the pitch

Once you have awed them with your hook, you will be favored with a nod or otherwise be encouraged to continue. Build on what you have already told them as you set up the story. In a short pitch, you only have time to pitch the story up to the Big Event. As you know, the Big Event is when the character loses control of her life or something changes her life. You may have room for an additional turning point beyond that.

Avoid thematic and abstract pitches: "This is about love's greatest attribute." Focus on a character with a problem. In fact, you can include two or three characters. Emphasize conflict, emotion, and action. Don't forget the emotional beats. Avoid hyperbole ("This will make you hundreds of millions") and negatives ("Are you afraid of political movies?"). Only in rare circumstances should you tell them how your movie ends. Just give them enough to make them want your script.

How do you end the pitch? You could end it by shutting your mouth and sitting back with a confident grin. You could ask a dramatic question; for example, *How will Johnny ever find his way home?* The best way to end is to ask, *May I give you a copy of the script?* And, of course, you'll have a copy right there with you. You'll also have a one-sheet handy in case they don't want the script. Try to leave them with something.

If you're pitching several ideas, open with your best shot. Don't go into a pitching session with more than three to five pitches, unless the venue requires it. Too many pitches make you look like a watch salesman in front of a hotel. The listener is evaluating two things: *Do you have good ideas? Can I work with you?*

In some venues, you may be allowed to further develop the pitch. "Tell me more." Be prepared to reveal more of the story if that situation occurs. If asked how it ends, provide more about what leads to your shocking end and then give them what they want.

DELIVERING YOUR PITCH

In most pitching situations, you'll be seated on a couch or chair facing one or more people. Sometimes this is across a table. When you sit down, place your hindquarters hard against the back of the chair or couch—this helps you project your voice and maintain good posture.

You will feel nervous. As a public speaker, I can tell you that you will not appear as nervous to others as you feel inside; knowing that may help you relax a little. Be as conversational and natural as possible. The pitch should not sound canned.

Decision makers love passion and adore enthusiasm. Put some energy into your voice. That doesn't mean you have to bring pom-poms and lead a rah-rah session; just be *naturally* enthusiastic. Allow me to explain what I mean. Imagine watching a movie that you love. You're excited about it. You go home to loved ones to tell them about this wonderful movie. Your tone in that telling will be "naturally enthusiastic" for you. That's the voice of conviction that will help you more than any single thing other than the quality of the story content.

Use words that appeal to the senses. Use specific language. Pitch in the style of your story. If the story is funny, the pitch should be funny. Speak clearly. There's a tendency when we are nervous to race to the finish like Seabiscuit. Slow down a little; you can still win!

Do not ever read your pitch. But it is okay, in longer pitches, to have 3"×5" cards or notes to prompt you.

Be as clear and animated as your personality allows. Let your passion flow.

Two common traps to avoid in any pitch:

> First, don't try to cram your entire story, all the subplots, and all the characters into your pitch. It shouldn't sound too complicated. In a short pitch, focus on two to three characters in the majority of cases. Don't include details that are important in the script but irrelevant in a pitch. In a short pitch, don't tell them how it ends.
>
> Second, don't present a rundown of scenes: *This happens and then this happens and then this happens. . . .* Your story will sink into the mud and you'll be dead in the water. Get to the heart. Talk them through the story. People can't follow all the details anyway, so hit the high points, and don't forget the emotional moments.

Here's the opening of a successful short pitch I delivered for *The Secret of Question Mark Cave.*

My story is about a secret cave, a magic sword, and a family stranded without a TV set.

[I'm smiling, hoping for a chuckle, and then I grow suddenly solemn.]

Seebee, age 11, feels that his dad hates him. He does everything he can to please his dad, but Frankie berates him, criticizes him, hurts him. It's not that Frankie hates his son—he doesn't. He just wishes he knew how to show his affection.

[The energy level rises in my voice with the next line. I get real excited when I arrive at the word "Wow."]

Well, one night, Seebee sneaks into the attic against Frankie's orders and finds the old journal of his great-great-grandfather. The journal tells the boy about a secret cave and a magic sword. Wow—with a sword like that, Seebee could solve all his problems! He vows to run away to the mountains, but then he hears a noise! Frankie is downstairs, and boy is he mad.

Please note that I emphasized the first turning point (the Catalyst) and the *emotions* of the characters. The pitch needs to touch the executive's cold heart. I learned this lesson when a producer asked me the following question after one of my pitches: "But when do I cry?"

The above pitch excerpt is 49 seconds long. I still have enough time to bring you to the Big Event (the next important turning point), assuming I have two minutes to pitch. I may need to adjust my pitch depending on how much time I have.

Don't refer to actors in the pitch itself, except maybe in a long pitch, and even then, any such references would be rare and handled in a casual manner.

Don't tell them what *they* are looking for. Don't say, "I know you'll like it because it has plenty of sex and violence." Remember, show is better than tell.

Don't lie. Don't say that Ron Howard is looking at the project if he is not. The producer will simply call Ron Howard to find out. They follow up. Don't think they don't. Don't say that no one has seen the script if, in truth, dozens of executives already have a copy. On the other hand, if DreamWorks is interested in it, don't be afraid to say so.

In some pitches, you may be interrupted with questions, requests for clarifications, and suggestions. Go with the flow and be flexible, but do not allow the pitch to lose momentum. Be open to suggestions and be prepared to present a different angle on the story. Don't be afraid to express yourself. They want you to. If appropriate, let them contribute to the story, so they can own it too. Respond respectfully and quickly, and get back on track; you may need to recap to do so.

Don't oversell. Once they say no, STOP. Once they say yes, STOP. Don't keep blabbing on. In truth, you may want to end before your allotted time. That's to allow for questions and discussion. You will also want to ask the listening party if she'd like a copy of the script. It's also okay to take notes when you're listening to them, although I would ask permission: "Is it okay if I jot this down?"

When they are done with you, they will excuse you without telling you their decision. The truth is that they may not be the decision makers. When a decision is made, it will be conveyed to you. Regardless of the outcome, send a note of thanks.

Creativity

In preparing for a long pitch, you might consider a creative touch. A minor innovation may make your pitch stand out from the dozens of humdrum presentations that have dulled the producer's senses that week. One client used action figures to represent his characters in a 20-minute pitch. He introduced them one by one and spread them out on the table. The development executive was enthralled.

However, usually props are not a good idea, particularly in a short pitch. Don't try to act out your pitch, and don't hire actors to perform your pitch for you. On the other hand, don't be afraid to use your voice for emphasis. Use your common sense and put your creativity into the content of your pitch.

AFTER THE PITCH

If your pitch does the trick, the producer may read your script, and may even buy it. Or, if you pitched to an agent, you may find representation. This is called *Screenwriter's Heaven.*

Another scenario is, the producer ends up offering you a development deal. This is called *Development Hell,* but at least you're being paid good money to suffer, plus your career is moving forward. I'll explain further in a moment.

Your first development deal will probably also be a step deal, which means that you can be cut out at any step in the writing process. You'll be paid a portion of the total purchase price at each step. Although there are many possibilities, it could work like this: 25% advance, 25% on treatment (first step), 25% on first draft (second step), 25% on polish (third step). If the film is eventually produced, expect a production bonus.

Personality

One thing's for sure: If any agent or producer decides to take you on, he or she will be spending a lot of time with you developing the story. So almost as important as your ideas is your personality. Some meetings are arranged purely for interpersonal relations, and for developing contacts and relationships. In any case, they want to know what you are like to work with. On one worksheet of your Strategic Marketing Plan, you are asked to do a personal inventory.

There are four personality traits that are key to any situation when you're meeting Hollywood types: enthusiasm, objectivity, ambition, and grace.

Enthusiasm. Do you have the voice of conviction? Do you have a passion for your work? Do you communicate confidence? Do you believe in your ideas? I cannot over-emphasize the power of enthusiasm. By the same token, don't get so excited that you hyperventilate and pass out. They dock points for that.

Objectivity. Can you separate your ego from your work? Can you be objective about the pluses and minuses of your script? This does not diminish your passion. It means that you can adjust to what lies ahead: story development hell.

Story development hell refers to the process of working with the notes and other feedback you'll receive while developing the project. You may be amazed at how these professionals view your script. One producer read a sci-fi script and commented, "A Martian wouldn't say that" (incident taken from *A Martian Wouldn't Say That* by Stern and Robison). Well, that raises the question, "Well then, what *would* a Martian say?" The producer is likely to respond, "I'll know it when I see it."

It may be difficult, but be open to criticism. Be diplomatic and firm where it matters. If you are defensive and rigid, then you're difficult to work with (from their point of view). Often, you will find that the suggestions you receive are helpful.

Ambition. Do you love the business? Do you want to be a full-time writer or do you want to just write an occasional script from your cabin in the woods? The correct answer is "full-time writer." Convey a feeling of confidence in your script and in your writing ability. Communicate that you are a writer; that's what you want to do all the time, with occasionals break to eat and sleep.

Grace. Are you gracious? Do people enjoy meeting you and talking to you? Do you have any natural charm? Are you the opposite of dull and desperate?

Now don't present a façade personality or disparage your weaknesses; just project your best self, focusing on your strengths, whatever they are.

Golly, do I have to pitch?

You may be wondering, *Why can't I just give producers a synopsis of the story in writing? Why do I have to pitch it?* One reason is because they cannot "legally" ask for anything in writing without paying you for it. That's because they are signatories to the Writers Guild of America contracts. However, many writers leave a one-sheet or synopsis on the table after their pitch.

If you're dealing with a producer who is not a signatory to the Guild, then you can give him a synopsis or treatment directly and avoid pitching altogether. This is discussed in depth in the next chapter.

Summary

Do you see a pattern in this chapter? The dance proceeds as follows: You write two or three spec scripts. The spec script that best shows your talent becomes a sample script that finds you work. Sometimes you sell that spec script outright. Usually, you don't. Instead it becomes a divining rod that finds you an agent and/or gains you admittance to a meeting with a producer where you can sing for your supper. Having established that, now let's move onward!

Synopses, one-sheets, treatments, and outlines

A *synopsis* is a one- or two-page story summary, usually single-spaced, using a conservative 12-point font such as Times Roman. Keep in mind that many people use the term *synopsis* to refer to any summary that is not used for marketing purposes and the term *treatment* to refer to any story summary used as a selling tool.

A *one-sheet* (occasionally called a *pitch on paper* or *POP* and sometimes called a *one-pager*) is a one-page synopsis headed by the title, the hook or logline, genre (if not otherwise obvious), followed by the story summary, and concluding with your contact information. Unlike a synopsis, it can include information about you and your work at the end, and since it is a "selling document," you can inject your personal style into it just as you would with a query. You may include your ending or not, depending on what you think works best.

In preparing your one-sheet, use a conservative typeface (Times New Roman, Arial, Helvetica, etc.). Otherwise, the format is up to you. Since the story is king, this is mainly a written document, although you may wish to include a small graphic, but only if it really pops out and helps your pitch. Some writers will put something visual on the reverse side; don't do that unless it is superb and professional looking.

You can leave your carefully prepared one-sheet behind at pitch meetings or hand it off at gatherings or pitch-fests. Thus, it is essentially a synopsis used as a marketing tool, so make sure your name and contact information are on it.

Besides its most prominent use as a "leave behind" after oral pitches, it can be mailed directly to producers, actors, agents, or directors (if requested or in lieu of a query).

A **treatment** (actually *spec treatment*) used to market your script is not the long, 50-page document that you're sometimes paid to write in a development deal. A *spec treatment* is usually three to five pages long, but can be as long as 12 pages. Keep in mind that many people use the term *treatment* to refer to any story summary that is used for marketing purposes. Thus, it is possible that someone could request a two-page treatment.

When a producer or agent asks for an **outline**, he or she is usually referring to a *spec treatment*. Although it is possible that she is asking for a simple *list of scenes* or a **beat sheet** (a list of the key events or turning points in the script), it is unlikely that she is. Since the words *synopsis*, *treatment*, and *outline* are often used synonymously, ask the person making the request about how many pages they're expecting. Then you will have a better idea of the type of document to prepare.

Given what we have established above, I will use the term *treatment* throughout this chapter. In your discussions with professionals, you should use the term *treatment*, unless the other person uses one of the other terms.

A one- to two-page treatment will not usually need a title page, so be sure that your name and phone number are on it. You can do that with a header or simply by typing the contact information in the top left corner of the first page.

The title page of a longer treatment (3–12 pages) should look like the script's title page. The treatment should be written in a conservative font such as Times New Roman. Do not bind with brads. Instead, send it loose or stapled.

A short treatment is usually double-spaced or one-and-a-half-spaced, but it can be single-spaced. There is not a specific standard for spacing. If you single-space your treatment, you should double-space between paragraphs, and don't indent the paragraphs. That's the style I am using in this book.

Treatments, one-sheets, and synopses can be registered with the Writers Guild. Follow the same process as registering a screenplay.

Think of the treatment as a written pitch—analogous to the long pitch discussed earlier. In fact, it may be voluntarily left behind after a pitch. It should be written in present-tense narrative (short story) form with no or little dialogue. It's not a scene-by-scene rundown, and you will only focus on about three to five characters. You cannot include all of the subplots. It emphasizes the crucial moments, the key events of the story, and the emotional highs and lows of your characters. In a script, you cannot describe what a character is feeling or thinking, but you can in a treatment.

A treatment not only tells the story, it sells the story. It is a marketing piece. You write it for producers, talent, and directors. You want them to love the story. You want them to say, "What a great story! Let me read the script!"

Some treatments begin with a description of the setting or "world" of the story. Others open with a story hook. A very few open with a brief description of the characters. Grab the reader's attention from the beginning in a manner that works best for your story.

I think it will be instructive to actually see the difference between a professional story synopsis written for informational purposes and a treatment written for marketing purposes. Some time ago, I asked longtime Hollywood story analyst Leslie Paonessa to read my old script, *The Secret of Question Mark Cave*, and write a coverage.

Her coverage consisted of her recommendations, an analysis, and a story synopsis. When she wrote her synopsis, her objective as a professional story analyst was not to pitch the story but to create a clear and complete summary of the story. As you will see, she did a superb job . . . but it is not a selling document.

I suggest you read Leslie's "synopsis" now (found in the upcoming chapter "How to sell your script without an agent"), and then return to this page to read my selling treatment (below) of about the same length. Please note the differences in tone and emphasis.

● ● ● ● ●

The brief treatment that follows *treats* the same story as the story analyst's synopsis. Why is the writing style different? Because it is written for a different purpose. Incidentally, this treatment and the associated screenplay convinced four Disney executives to recommend the script for production, while the fifth nixed the deal. However, I was given an opportunity for a development deal.

My strategy for this treatment was to apply the principles already stated in this chapter. The short length of the treatment forced me to focus on the essential story in terms of plot, character, and emotion.

Because a treatment is a written pitch, consult the section about pitching. Most of those tips apply to writing a treatment as well. Although not necessary, I open this treatment with the story hook.

THE SECRET OF QUESTION MARK CAVE

by Dave Trottier

This is the story of a long-ago promised sword, a secret cave, and a family stranded without a TV set.

SEEBEE (nickname for Percival), age 11, fancies himself a knight, although he is kicked out of the Explorers Club for failing to perform a brave deed. Worse, his own dad (FRANKIE) calls him a "nothing kid." Actually, Frankie loves his son; he just doesn't know how to connect with him, and he's too busy watching TV to find out. Meanwhile, Seebee practices with his little wooden sword.

One night, Seebee sneaks into the attic against his father's wishes and discovers several beautifully carved wooden knights. He also finds the journal of his great-great-grandfather, Captain Cole. The journal tells the story of a "magic" sword (at least Seebee thinks it's magic) hidden in a secret cave deep in the mountains. Seebee vows to find the sword; he's sure it will solve his problems.

That day, Seebee and his friend GLODINA witness a bank robbery through the window. When the RED HAT BANDIT races toward them, Seebee tells Glodina to hide in a car for safety, but the car she chooses is the robber's car. Seebee unsheathes his little wooden sword to defend the car, but his fear paralyzes him— he's no brave knight. The bandit drives away with Glodina still hidden in the back seat. Seebee hightails it home only to do something even worse—he accidentally breaks his dad's TV set. So Frankie breaks Seebee's cherished sword in half, breaking his heart as well.

Seebee feels dejected and powerless; but that night, he dreams that his great-great-grandfather, CAPTAIN COLE, gallops up on his horse and offers Seebee the sword mentioned in his journal. Cole says, "You have a power all your own," and Seebee awakens.

Emboldened, the boy tapes the pieces of his *wooden* sword together. He runs away with his Explorers Club buddies to find the "magic" sword so he can use it to rescue Glodina. They overcome conflicts and natural obstacles until they discover Question Mark Cave. Inside, they find Glodina (she is safe)—the cave must be the bandit's hideout! A deeper search produces evidence of Captain Cole, but *not* the wondrous sword in his dream. Seebee is discouraged.

Just then, the Red Hat Bandit arrives. He's about to "rub out" the little band of four, but Seebee tricks the robber, and the four children escape from the cave and race down the trail. But the robber is right behind, and boy is he mad!

Meanwhile, Frankie gets fired. Like his son, he feels dejected and powerless. Upstairs in his own secret cave (the attic), his precious wooden carvings gather dust. He might carve more if his tools hadn't been stolen years ago. Enough of his troubles; he needs to find his runaway son.

Back on the trail, the bandit pursues Seebee and his friends until he catches them at a cliff that hangs over a canyon stream. There, Seebee unsheathes his taped wooden sword and courageously holds the robber at bay while his friends get over the cliff to safety. When Seebee attempts to cross, the bandit catches him. In the struggle, Seebee defeats the bandit with his wooden sword, and the famous Red Hat Bandit tumbles into the stream below, breaking his leg.

Seebee now realizes that he doesn't need a magic sword, because he has *"a power all his own."* His dream has come true! Plus, he has performed a brave deed to get back into the Explorers Club. In fact, he's president now! When Frankie arrives, Seebee offers his portion of the "Red Hat Bandit reward" to buy a new TV to replace the one he broke. But no, Frankie can use that money to buy new carving tools. Maybe now he's brave enough to do the work he loves. His "little knight" has healed his wound.

So Frankie takes Seebee into the attic (the secret cave) and removes Captain Cole's sword from a secret hiding place! Father, like son, had once wanted to be a knight, and had journeyed to Question Mark Cave years ago and had found the ancient sword. The sword becomes Frankie's connection with his son, the connection he has longed to find.

On the front lawn for all to see, he then knights his son "Sir Percival" and gives him the sword he deserves. Seebee then "knights" Glodina his "brave princess."

• • • • •

Don't expect to find work based on a treatment alone until you are established. You must have a finished script. If a producer loves your treatment—your story—but you have no script, he may buy the treatment for much less than he would for a script, and then hire a proven writer to write the script. Hollywood has plenty of ideas, but not as many great writers. Great ideas are not worth much without a script.

On the other hand, a great spec treatment can earn you a deal if you have contacts and some kind of track record that demonstrates your writing ability. Such treatments can be as long as 20 pages, but are usually much shorter.

The following is a treatment by David S. Freeman; the story is by David and a colleague. This story treatment was purchased by Paramount Pictures for $45,000. Not bad for five pages!

Readers might note some similarity between this story and the film *S1m0ne*. It's worth noting that Paramount bought this story several years before that film came out.

Regarding treatment writing, David says, "Keep it short. Keep it colorful. You don't have time to get lost in the details or the subplots. The treatment should focus on giving us (1) the main beats of the story, (2) the principal characters—who they are, why they're unique, why we care about them, and how they change (if they do)—and (3) the flavor of the story.

For those who don't know David, he has sold scripts to many studios. He also teaches "Beyond Structure" (www.beyondstructure.com), which has grown to be one of the most popular screenwriting workshops in Los Angeles, New York, London, and elsewhere in the United States and around the world.

THE "IT" GIRL

LOS ANGELES... ROD TRENTON has been a Junior Editor at a half-dozen trendy magazines. He's got wit, he's got sharp, offbeat insights into contemporary life...and he's got a little too much cynicism and attitude. That's why he's never been promoted to Managing Editor. (It's also why he's single.) His latest haunts: *Centre* magazine, peeling back the onion skin of pop culture.

Media mogul DALTON QUINCE-TAYLOR, whom rebel Rod hates for his renowned anti-humanism, just bought *Centre*. Dalton gives his Managing Editor a mandate: Increase profits by downsizing staff. Rod learns he's next to go. He's desperate to save his job, for he's burned bridges everywhere else.

Rod decides to do a story on "The Most Irresistible Face in the World." Together with a computer-literate friend, he merges the faces of five beautiful women. Rod gives this captivating, phantom woman a name: "CHRISTIANA SARINS."

Rod writes his story on "Christiana" (aka "The 'It' Girl"). Using some nefarious antics, Rod gets "Christiana" on the cover. The face captures the imagination of the public and the magazine sells like crazy. The editor, who thinks that Christiana is a real woman, demands a follow-up "interview" of the young woman, and soon *Entertainment Tonight*, *Oprah*, *David Letterman*, and other shows demand Christiana.

But, since she's not to be found, people begin to suspect a hoax. The Managing Editor gives Rod an ultimatum: Produce Christiana or he's fired. Rod's desperate, for he's burned too many bridges to land an equally good job elsewhere.

Rod spends a frantic week crisscrossing the South and Midwest, locating any small-town beauty queen who might look like Christiana. No luck. Gloom overcomes Rod. Then he discovers TAMARA MILLS, a sincere wannabe actress from a white-trash neighborhood outside of Cincinnati. She looks close enough to the mythical Christiana that she could pass. While some might dismiss Tamara as unsophisticated, she more than compensates with her love of life, her quirky charm, and her corny but endearing sense of humor.

Rod spills his predicament to her. Will she pretend to be Christiana? She'll be thrust into fame. Tamara's reluctant—this violates her ethics and her beliefs. But the idea of a short road to Hollywood is too tempting. She takes the deal.

In a *My Fair Lady* type of development, Rod becomes her mentor, giving her a crash course in civilization, Los Angeles style. Making his job more difficult is the contempt he feels for her small-town ways. However, Tamara's great qualities soon win him over—especially her guilelessness and her emotional responsiveness. She's very present and very genuine.

Rod's defenses can't hold out forever, and soon it's unclear who's re-creating who. If he's turning her into an urban sophisticate, she's softening his rough edges and thinning out his protective coating. In truth, he's falling in love. They both are.

The one thing that Rod can't teach Tamara is how to be a Hollywood starlet. He calls on his actor friend JASON KAROW, who takes over Tamara's "education." Jason teaches her survival skills for the upwardly mobile actress in Tinseltown, like how to walk into a room and capture every man's eye while pretending to be totally ingenuous, how to laugh so that everyone else wishes they could be as happy as they think she is, or how to use a Little Black Dress as a weapon.

The big evening arrives, although Rod is merely a spectator. Jason takes Tamara to a fancy movie premiere. "Christiana's" appearance causes a sensation. As the paparazzi's cameras snap away, Tamara handles the "audition" with splashy aplomb. She's a hit!

Rod's life is a dream. Things are going well at *Centre* and he's got a woman he loves. But the bloom is soon to fade from the rose....

Tamara adjusts to the high life very quickly, and she adjusts to Jason Karow just as rapidly. Rod's bright, sure, but Jason can take her right into the middle of a world she's always dreamed of. Nothing compares to the fun and glamour of Hollywood.

What's happened is that, in a way, Rod and Tamara have changed places. He's learned to open up and become genuine; she's learned how to bask in the superficial.

Or at least that's how Rod sees things when she breaks off their budding relationship. She tries to let him down easily.

Rod is devastated. That short burst of warmth that Rod had bathed in disappears and is replaced by bitterness. As for Tamara, the world's her oyster as she becomes a hot item and signs on the dotted line with CAA. Next comes Leno and Letterman and magazine covers. She fails to notice the irony in how she occasionally acts superior to those around her, just the way others used to act superior to her before she was "remade."

Tamara is in such demand that her agent lands her a movie role in a film with a big male star. The rehearsals are very rough. Although Tamara studied acting in Cincinnati, although she has talent, and although she gets help from an acting coach and others on the set, she knows she's over her head. She needs time to bring her acting skills up to the level demanded of her.

Back at the magazine, Rod's writing has become more cynical than ever.

Tamara becomes increasingly ambivalent about being surrounded by people who just want her stardom to rub off on them. She tries in vain to find someone real she can talk to. Of course, there's Jason...until she catches him having sex with another woman. And so ends another Hollywood romance.

Tamara has a crisis of the soul. Tired of living a lie, the next day on the set she spills the entire truth about her past and announces that she's leaving the picture. She wants the roles, the stardom, the whole works—but when she's earned it, as herself, not pretending to be someone else. She's going to concentrate on her acting craft for a year. And then she'll return—as Tamara Mills, not as Christiana Sarins.

The tabloids make humiliating fodder out of her story, although some admire her courage and honesty.

Tamara, having regained her integrity, wants to give it another go with Rod. She tracks him down in Aspen, where he's having discussions with Dalton Quince-Taylor, the hard-edged publisher of *Centre*. Dalton is about to fulfill Rod's dream by giving

Rod his own magazine to helm. The magazine will bear the stamp of Rod's incisive, increasingly sarcastic wit.

When Tamara approaches Rod, he brushes her off. He tells her that he did love a woman once, a small-town girl with a radiant smile. But she turned into Christiana Sarins, who liked glamour over substance. He dismisses her and turns away.

Later, Dalton commends Rod for putting women in second place. Hearing this, Rod realizes that he's *turned into* Dalton, whom he has always despised. Rod's out of there in a flash. He abandons *Centre*; he even abandons this new magazine, which was going to be his own creation.

Rod flies to Cincinnati to pursue Tamara. When they connect, Rod is awkward. This time it's his turn to bare his soul. Tamara listens, torn. Tamara is hurt and reluctant... but love will not be denied.

We see Rod pitching an idea for a new magazine. Cynicism is out, he argues; it's an occasional fun indulgence but no one wants it for a steady diet.

His new vision for a magazine is one that examines the scope of our lives, and all the seeming impossibilities of living. How do you find passion for life if you hate your work? How do you love your body if all the commercials and movies say that only young is beautiful? How do you stay honest when your political leaders tell lies? How do you stay genuine and still climb the ladder of success?

This is the focus that Rod pitches...to a group of IMPRESSED INVESTORS. And so Rod's new magazine, *Scope*, is born. And love is rekindled for Tamara, whose acting career has been revitalized, and who is at Rod's side when it happens.

How to sell your script without an agent

Much has changed during the last few years. Hollywood is inbreeding more. In other words, the system has become more closed to outsiders, and it's more difficult to break in. It's hard to find a place at the table.

Creating a marketing plan will help you penetrate the market at the same time you are searching for an agent.

Would you be surprised if I told you that most first scripts that are sold are sold without the services of an agent? It's true. And although it's a distinct advantage to have an agent, it's possible for you to sell your script without one. In fact, one of the best ways to find an agent is through a producer who loves your script and then refers you to one or more agents. After all, as a general rule, producers are a little easier to connect with than agents.

If you are going to try to sell your script without an agent, make sure that you assemble your 10 marketing tools (including your pitch elements, a pithy query, and one-sheet) and create a strategic marketing plan.

PENETRATING YOUR MARKET

Once you have your 10 selling tools in your toolbox (you don't necessarily need all 10 at one time) and a completed marketing plan, you can mastermind and implement your campaign.

Make sure that your screenplay is original, and don't market a script that will cost $100 million to produce if you are approaching independent production companies who make low-budget features in the $500,000 to $2 million range.

Don't be overly concerned with Hollywood trends. Keep in mind that your first script usually becomes a sample script that you use as a calling card. That's one reason my advice is to write what you have a passion for. You need that energy to get you through that first script. Even so, consider the advice of William Goldman, who said, "Don't write *American Beauty* because Alan Ball did" (*Hollywood Scriptwriter*, June 2000). Don't write this year's hit. Don't imitate what others have written. Write your best original screenplay.

There are five markets you can approach to sell your script without an agent:

1. Writers Guild–signatory producers
2. Independent producers (the indies)
3. Actors and directors (talent)
4. Television markets
5. Everything else (see the chapter "Jump-start your career now")

Before discussing each of these, let's look at the crucial role of the story analyst.

READERS

Story analysts, commonly called *readers*, read scripts for everyone in the industry. In fact, some people joke that readers are the only people in town who still read scripts. When an agent or producer receives your script, they send it to a reader; you live and die with the result. If a reader does not recommend a script, that's the end. The person paying them is not going to read it.

Readers read five scripts or so over the weekend, *plus* what they read on weekdays. When a reader reads your script, she wants a correctly formatted narrative that flows like a river through her mind. She wants a "good read" [translation: readable and riveting], and if it isn't a good read, she gets even on the coverage. Frankly, a reader takes a risk in recommending a script; if the recommended script turns out to be unworkable, the reader suffers. The easy path is to *not* recommend a script.

The *coverage* is what she writes when she finishes reading your script. A coverage is a brief synopsis and analysis that *covers* the story. And it contains her recommendation to the agent or producer who hired her. A sample coverage follows:

SAMPLE COVERAGE

Here is an actual sample coverage by story analyst and script consultant Leslie Paonessa.

STORY REPORT

TITLE:	THE SECRET OF QUESTION MARK CAVE	FORM:	Screenplay
AUTHOR:	DAVID TROTTIER	PAGES:	100
CIRCA:	Present day	SUB. BY:	Author
LOCALE:	The Rocky Mountains	SUB. TO:	Leslie Paonessa DATE: 7/25/96
GENRE:	Family drama	ANALYST:	Leslie Paonessa DATE: 7/30/96

LOGLINE: A boy and his friends go searching for a "magic" sword that belonged to his great-great-grandfather, and in the process, they catch a bankrobber who has kidnapped another friend.

	EXCLNT	GOOD	FAIR	POOR
CHARACTERIZATION		X.....X		
DIALOGUE	X.........X			
STRUCTURE	X			
UNIQUE STORY		X		
SETTING/PROD VALUE		X		

BUDGET: _____ HIGH   _____ MED.   _X_ LOW

RECOMMENDATION: _X_ YES   _____ NO   _____ MAYBE

THE SECRET OF QUESTION MARK CAVE
COMMENT

This is an unusual story that will attract a family audience, especially the youngsters. It has elements of fantasy, humor, and family values set against an entertaining and exciting adventure. It has a bit of dramatic tension, if somewhat simplistic, but it will certainly capture the imagination of kids as they get caught up in the story and identify with the characters.

SEEBEE, STINKY, RALPH, and GLODINA are the youngsters who live out the adventure. Seebee is our "hero" who comes from a very dysfunctional family. Father FRANKIE has been laid off from his job and does little but watch television. He is, in fact, a TV junkie, and it's not at all a positive image. We don't find out until near the end that he once was a creative artist, and it would strengthen his characterization if we could see his internal struggle a little more. We sense that he has some love inside when he nearly comes into Seebee's room to apologize but can't. Perhaps his relationship with Seebee's mother, FREDA, could help. She is caught up in all kinds of occult interests so that she rarely relates in a warm, motherly manner. Everyone in the story -- neighbors, Frankie, the cops -- thinks she's a nut. Though she provides good comic relief, there could be more poignant moments through her. It's only at the very end that we have any hope that Seebee can get love in this family.

Because the characters are broad, we assume that this story is for children, and to make it more of a crossover film, it would help if it weren't aimed at quite so young an audience. Teenagers will find this too juvenile. The RED HAT BANDIT never seems truly evil, and surely the writer was aware of not making him too frightening for young children.

Seebee as the lead character starts off as a victim, but then finds his own power. It's a very good transformation, and it's through the action that we see him gain strength. He has a mission and goes for it, gaining the admiration of his friends as he does so. Even his father has to admit that he's a hero, and their bonding together at the end is very satisfying. We also see Frankie regain his pride.

The pacing of the story is strong, especially when we go out on the trail with Seebee and friends in the quest for the sword and Glodina. It's an exciting adventure, and it's written in a very visual manner. There could be more worry at the homefront with more intercutting to build the tension further.

This is a story that could be produced on a modest budget, possibly for an alternative to the huge summer releases. It's an ensemble piece for young actors and could have wide family audience appeal.

THE SECRET OF QUESTION MARK CAVE
SYNOPSIS

SEEBEE LANCE, 11, and his two friends, STINKY MARANTZ and RALPH HARDY, play their favorite game as adventurers. Seebee's trademark is his wooden sword, and he's even proficient in swordsmanship. Stinky uses a bow and rubber-tipped arrows. Ralph is a large boy dressed in camouflage. The game is interrupted when Seebee's mother, FREDA, calls him and his younger sister, VICKY, to come home.

Freda is a bit of a kook, often preoccupied by astrology, card-reading, and the occult. FRANKIE, husband and father, has just been laid off from his job and spends most of his time as a television junkie. At a family picnic in the park, Freda tells Seebee about his great-great-grandpa, CAPTAIN PERCIVAL COLE, for whom Seebee is named. She also says that he had a sword with magical powers that may still be in the attic. Though Seebee is intrigued, Frankie forbids him from going into the attic.

GLODINA SANCHEZ, 11, tries to come up into the tree house used by the boys. All but Seebee object. They tell brave-deed stories, but Seebee is ostracized because he's afraid to jump off the high dive at the pool. Seebee and Glodina begin to grow closer.

Seebee makes a ladder and uses it to go up into the attic at night. He finds relics from Captain Cole, including a fascinating journal. Under the bedcovers later, Seebee continues reading the journal and fantasizes about Captain Cole and the sword. In the morning, Seebee tells Glodina the lore about his namesake, and that the sword is in a secret place called Question Mark Cave. He also sees how a loving family acts when Glodina's mother invites him for a morning hug. Later, in an effort to bond with his father about a TV show, Seebee accidentally thrusts his sword through the television screen. Frankie is furious, and Seebee leaves, hurt.

Seebee can't get the club to go with him to find the sword, because Stinky's the boss who makes the decisions. Seebee is left with Glodina, and he's depressed. They find Frankie's car on Main Street. He's in the bank, trying to get a loan, when the RED HAT BANDIT enters with a red ski mask, cap, and a gun! Seebee and Glodina are making believe they're truckers in Frankie's car. The Red Hat Bandit takes Frankie's car for his getaway. The Bandit tosses the bags of money into the car and tosses Seebee out, but he doesn't see Glodina in the back seat until he's on the road.

Seebee tells Ralph and Stinky what has happened, while Frankie returns home and tells Freda that his car was stolen. He takes out his anger on Seebee, saying that he stole Captain Cole's journal. He breaks Seebee's wooden sword and banishes him to his room. Though Frankie later feels a bit sorry about this, he is unable to do anything. Freda comes in to try to comfort Seebee, but she can only seem to resort to her kookie brand of spiritualism.

Alone in his room later, Seebee prays for Glodina and asks for a blessing on his sword so he can help her. That night, each member of the family has dreams. Seebee's makes him accept his own power and the need for him to save Glodina by going to Question Mark Cave -- guided by Captain Cole.

In the morning, Ralph comes in through Seebee's bedroom window, and hears the story of Seebee's dream and the journal. They go up into the attic to look for the sword, and they're almost caught when Frankie comes home. They meet later on the hill with Stinky, and the boys are dressed for the occasion as Explorers. Ralph even has a BB gun.

Glodina sits in a dark room inside a cave. The Red Hat Bandit has gone out to get snacks and brings back licorice for Glodina. He warns Glodina not to try to escape.

When the boys reach the canyon, Seebee consults the journal and finds the map to the cave. Stinky grabs it away, but Seebee sticks up for himself and retrieves it after a fight. Now he's the leader and takes the boys across the river cliff by hanging onto exposed tree roots, though Ralph is terrified. Back at home, the mothers find that their boys are gone. The POLICE arrive to talk to them.

Seebee spots the hidden opening of Question Mark Cave and is the first one to enter, feet-first. Then Stinky and Ralph go, using flashlights. They explore further and find the Red Hat Bandit's clothes in a second room! Then they find the money bags and hear Glodina's voice calling them. They find her with blankets, food and water, though she's a little dirty. Seebee is her hero.

Seebee asks her about Captain Cole's "magic" sword, but Glodina hasn't seen it. He sees a crevice and enters another room, where he finds Captain Cole's skeleton but no sword. He falls back into Glodina's room and is dizzy but manages to bash the Red Hat Bandit in the face when he shows up. Seebee wishes he had the sword now as he and the other boys run toward the cave opening. Seebee realizes that they've left Glodina behind. When the Bandit's head pops out, the boys throw rocks at him. Now he's really mad. He pulls a gun on Stinky and Ralph, but Seebee is above on a ledge. He finally jumps -- like he was afraid to do at the pool -- and knocks the Bandit over! They overpower the Bandit and knock him out. Glodina is rescued, but the Bandit comes to and chases the kids down the trail.

Back at the house, Frankie goes into the attic and finds his precious wood carvings he was unable to sell when his old partner made him sign a paper forbidding it. OFFICER JONES is certain that he can now sell them, and Frankie seems to regain his pride. He also says he knows where Seebee is. The Police already have men at the canyon looking for the Red Hat Bandit. Frankie runs out. The kids stop to make a plan to ambush the Bandit. Ralph's BB gun and the others' primitive weapons slow the bandit down.

Then Seebee uses his swordsmanship and wooden sword to force the Bandit into the raging river, where he breaks his leg. The kids meet up with Frankie, who is being pursued by a GOOFY COP who thinks he is the bandit. Seebee gives his father some of the stolen money to replace the television set he broke, but Frankie returns it as a matter of principle. The Bank President rewards all the kids.

When they get home, Frankie goes into the attic with Seebee and shows him where the sword is hidden. He gives it to him, and the family is reunited. The neighborhood watches as Frankie knights his son "Sir Percival."

WRITERS GUILD–SIGNATORY PRODUCERS

The studios and other large production companies are signatories to the Writers Guild. That means that they have agreed to use Writers Guild–approved contracts. Their names can be easily found in a variety of directories.

What are large producers looking for? Their perceived needs can change monthly, or even weekly. They're constantly assessing the markets. In general, they want something that can be easily pitched to other producers, studios, distributors, and moviegoers. So the concept or central idea must grab them immediately. They also want something written for an actor. They want a script that makes the difference between Johnny Depp doing the movie and George Hamilton doing it, or Julia Roberts as opposed to Gertrude Kowalski. The executive's contacts will want to know whom she can attach, who will direct, who will act.

Realize that Hallmark Entertainment is looking for a different script than Castle Rock, but all producers have their markets foremost in their minds. What do their moviegoers want to see, and who do they want to see? They probably don't want a film-noir sci-fi Western that they cannot sell to the moviegoing public. And who's the mainstream moviegoing public? Mostly high school boys, college men, and other male and female thrill-seekers between the ages of 15 and 32, although don't discount the baby boomers.

I should note that when a producer produces the script of a new writer, he's putting his job on the line. If the resulting movie fails, he could be canned for trying someone new. Whereas if a picture using a proven writer fails, it can be seen as a fluke. All producers have their lists of A, B, and C writers, actors, directors . . . and also their up-and-coming. When a producer hires you, she's hoping you're up-and-coming.

These large production companies have *deals* with studios, meaning that they have contractual arrangements to produce a certain number of pictures with a studio or another production company. Or a studio may have right of first refusal, which means the studio has the right to be the first to see the project and either accept it or refuse it if they don't like it.

Midsized production companies have deals with large companies, and small production companies have deals with the midsized and large companies. Independent production companies don't have deals with anyone. If you do not have representation, don't approach the studios unless you have a good referral. If a studio passes on your script, then it means those companies who have deals with the studio also necessarily pass. Do you see the logic? I'll illustrate with an example.

A few years ago, I wrote what I thought was an arty script that I felt was just right for Hallmark or a similar company, but I didn't approach Hallmark or those other companies. Instead, I searched in directories, on the Web, and elsewhere and found out what producers produced for Hallmark. That way, I could approach those one at a time, and if one became interested, it could take the project to Hallmark. However, if I approached Hallmark first and they passed, then it wouldn't make sense to approach these other production companies with deals with Hallmark. When Hallmark passes, it effactually passes for any company that has a deal with them. By the way, I optioned the project.

Sometimes it makes sense to think small and approach small and midsized production companies that may not require you to have an agent to make a submission. After all, most large producers and studios accept submissions only from agents.

Where do you find the names of producers? You can use IMDb Pro (www.imdb.com), the *Hollywood Screenwriting Directory*, or the trades (*Variety* and *The Hollywood*

Reporter), where current productions are listed weekly. If you are in L.A., see what is available at the WGA library. Use Done Deal (www.donedealpro.com) to view the details of recent deals. There are also a few online tracking services that might be helpful. And of course, the credits for any film can be easily researched.

If you don't have an agent, how do you reach companies of any size?

1. The best way is to get referred by people known to them. This is why it's important to make contacts and build relationships.

2. Place yourself in a position to be discovered. You can do that by winning contests, taking advantage of pitching opportunities, using Internet brokers, and/or writing for an independent film. Additional methods are discussed in the chapter entitled "Jump-start your career now" (page 409).

3. Devise other creative means. Brainstorm ideas. See "Creative strategies" a little later in this chapter, and recall our discussion of "How to find an agent."

4. Craft a query letter and one-sheet. If your pitch is strong enough, there are some WGA-signatory producers who may accept a script without an agent. In such rare cases, they will require a *submission agreement* or *release*.

A submission agreement is a legal document that basically absolves the producer or executive of responsibility if your work is accidentally stolen. It sounds horrible, but you should consider signing the release to get your work sold and produced. Many smaller production companies with deals will accept a script without an agent if you are willing to sign a release.

You will find a sample release form on the next page. It is provided for informational purposes only.

SAMPLE RELEASE

TO _____

I, _____, acknowledge that the material

___ (title and description)

_____

_____

_____ that I am submitting to you was created
and written by me without any suggestion or request from
you. I represent that I am the author of the material and
that the material is original with me; that I have the
exclusive rights to submit the material to you on the terms
and conditions set forth in this agreement; and that I have
the power and authority to grant to you all rights in this
material.

I realize that many ideas, programs, slogans, scripts,
plans, suggestions, and other literary and/or dramatic
and/or musical material (herein collectively referred to
as "material") which are submitted to you are similar to
material previously used, previously submitted by others, or
already under consideration by you. I further realize that
you must protect yourself against any unwarranted claims by
refusing to examine any material submitted to you unless you
are assured that you shall have the unqualified right to
finally determine whether such material or any part thereof
is in fact used by you or your successors, assignees, or
licensees, and what compensation or other consideration, if
any, should be paid for such use.

I am submitting certain material to you herewith. In
order to induce you to consider this material, I hereby
irrevocably waive, release, and relinquish any and all
claims which I, or any person, firm, or corporation
claiming under or through me, may now or hereafter have
against you, your successors, assignees, and licensees,
and your and their respective officers, employees, and
representatives, for any alleged use that you or your
successors, assignees, or licensees may make of any such
material.

I agree that, should I bring any action against you for wrongful appropriation of the material, such action shall be limited to an action at law for damages, and in no event shall I be entitled to an injunction or any other equitable relief. If I am unsuccessful in such action, I agree to pay you all the costs and expenses involved in defending such action.

I further understand and agree that you are not responsible for the return of any material submitted, and I acknowledge that I have retained a duplicate copy of such material in my possession.

I hereby acknowledge that I have read and understood this agreement and that no oral representations of any kind have been made.

Very truly yours,

[Signature]

[Typed or printed name]

[Address]

[Telephone number]

Why the release? Because these companies are afraid of lawsuits. Sometimes an executive hears a pitch or reads a script that resembles something already in development. When the writer sees the resulting movie, he sues the production company on the basis of that pitch or script.

Generally, these folks aren't interested in stealing your story. Theft occurs occasionally, but large producers are more interested in avoiding lawsuits than they are in theft. *Writer's paranoia* is the hallmark of an amateur. You've got to get your ideas out there. Perhaps your best protection is your writing ability, industry savvy, and completed scripts.

When querying these companies, consider asking them for their release form. That shows you understand the business and their needs, and it might make them a little more open-minded about your pitch.

Another angle is to pitch to producers on the phone rather than via a written query. Ask to speak to a specific development executive or producer, but realize you'll end up speaking to that person's assistant. Pitch to the assistant. You might conclude your oral pitch by giving the assistant a choice: "If you fax me your release, I can send you a synopsis or a script. Which would you prefer?" It just may be that the assistant will want to discover you and make points with the executive he works for.

When a producer receives a script from an agent or from you, it is handed to a story editor who checks to see if they already have a coverage written on it. If a coverage is already written, that means one of their readers has already read your script sometime in the past. That old coverage will then be attached to your script (even if this is a new, revised version) and returned to the development executive. That's why once any company *passes* on your script (that is, rejects it), you can't resubmit it for consideration.

Actually, there is a possible way around that. Revise the script and make sure the page count has changed. If the page count of your revised script differs from the page count listed on the coverage, the producer may assume that this truly is a revision and have another coverage written on it. Changing the title alone usually does not work.

If the development executive likes the coverage, then she will read a few pages and sometimes the entire script. Development executives "read" 10 to 15 scripts a week. So yours had better capture their imagination. If it does, they'll have others in the company include it in their weekend read. If everyone feels comfortable with it, they will finance it themselves or, more likely, take it to another producer or to a studio.

If the production company you contacted is interested in your script, they will refer you to an agent or list of agents. This is perhaps the best way to find an agent. Ideally, agents want you to approach them first so that the marketplace is untouched, but they will not turn down an easy commission. If a producer refers you to more than one agent, interview each and try to determine which is most genuinely interested in your career as opposed to getting a quick sale. I've had a few clients who found agents in just this way.

The company will either buy your script outright or option it. The option is a smaller investment for them, and it gives them time to shop your script around before having to commit more money.

The producer may actually be more interested in your writing ability than in your script. She might hire you to "develop" one of her ideas or a sequel or some other project. In other words, she will offer you a development deal. Please recall our earlier discussion in the "Working with an agent" section of the chapter "How to find an agent," and also in the chapter "How to pitch without striking out."

THE INDIES

Declare your independence!

There are about 40,000–50,000 independent feature productions every year. Many a writer, director, and actor has gotten his/her start with an independent film. Don't you love Jack Nicholson as the masochistic dental patient in Roger Corman's *Little Shop of Horrors*? The best part of working in the indie realm is you don't need an agent, and it can be a lot of fun and certainly an education.

Keep in mind that most of the Indies are not signatories to the Guild, so there are fewer restraints keeping them off the paths of temptation. Also, they are relatively poor. If you are taken to the cleaners in this biz, it will more likely be by an independent producer than a studio. I urge you to negotiate a written and signed deal with an independent producer before you start writing.

It's not uncommon to be offered a deal where you are paid a few thousand dollars or (more likely) your pay is deferred until the film is distributed. Seldom are you paid anything up front. In fact, they normally offer an option. With an option, a producer can tie up the rights with just a few dollars. In fact, it is not unusual for an indie to ask for a "free" option—no money down. During the option period (usually six months), the producer uses your script to attract talent, a director, or another producer. Once he has a *package*, he goes to the money people and shops for a deal. If a deal is secured, he pays you for the script. If he doesn't secure a deal, you will have difficulty approaching people who have already seen your script.

Don't be tempted to sign a deal that's bad for you. Don't write until you have a completed deal. And if you're not being paid as stipulated, stop writing. And before you sign a deal with anyone, ask yourself these questions: Can this guy get the movie made? Can I work with this person? Such questions may not be easy to answer, but they are worth thinking through. Also, it's better to work with a jerk that loves your script and can get a deal than with a sweetheart that's going nowhere. If you have questions about a certain producer, contact the Producers Guild to see what information they might have.

If a producer asks you to rewrite your script for free before making any kind of deal, only do so if the script will be genuinely improved and you retain 100% ownership of the material, even if you use some of their ideas. Get an agreement to that effect.

If a contract is slow in coming, request a *deal memo*. A deal memo is a quickie contract that presages the larger edition later on. It can be used to clinch a deal, any kind of deal. The deal memo is simply a letter delineating the basic points of the deal. Sign the letter and return it. Sometime later, the actual contract will arrive.

When you negotiate your deal, try to get paid as much up front as possible. When it comes to an independent production, I'd rather take $40,000 now than $100,000 on the "back end" or "on deferment."

I was paid a small sum to develop a screenplay for indie producer Tanya York. I was given a long list of parameters. For example, I was allowed one outside location, one burn (where a guy is lit on fire), one car crash of two late-model cars, and so on. I took it on as a creative challenge. Remember, one experience can lead to another. The idea is to get some momentum to your career.

Be professional in contacting independent producers, beginning with a query letter, one-sheet, or phone call. They seldom require submissions through agents, but may ask you to sign a release. Many independent producers (large and small) use Internet brokers (such as InkTip, for example) to find writers.

Even if you're paid very little for your first assignment, a sale is a sale. You can begin building your career on such a sale. And credits, at this point, are worth more to your career than money. On the other hand, I had one student who sold his first script to an independent producer in New York for $110,000. So there is a wide variety of opportunities in these markets.

A great number of independent producers are continually searching for scripts for very low-budget productions ($100,000 to $500,000 and up) with as few as one or two locations and just a handful of characters. This market should not be overlooked. These indie projects can range from *Sex, Lies, and Videotape* to *The Blair Witch Project*.

Don't overlook these smaller, independent market opportunities. They can be stepping-stones to more lucrative assignments down the road. The independent market is broadening every day through the growth of film festivals devoted to independent films, the availability of lower-cost technology, and the growth of a variety of indie-friendly venues.

Every year, independent producers, foreign sales agents, and others gather for the American Film Market (AFM) in Santa Monica. A directory is printed by both the AFM and *The Hollywood Reporter*. This directory contains the identities of many independent companies that are players.

APPROACHING TALENT

Don't approach actors (often referred to as *talent*) and directors through their agents, because their agents will not see you as potential money and will not likely pass the script along. Most agents of big stars are more interested in offers than in scripts. I had one client who emailed me to say she had succeeded in getting a script to an actor through his agent. So there's your exception that proves the rule.

One way to approach these people is to make a personal delivery. This is easier said than done. One writer found an actress in a public place and fell to his knees. With his script in hand, he gushed obsequiously, "I adore you. You have such range. Here, I wrote this for you and for you alone. Please, would you read it?" She did.

Many actors and directors have their own production companies, which are set up specifically to find projects equal to their talents. Most require script submissions through agents. Many will accept a script with a release. My personal experience and that of my clients has shown that these production companies have a greater openness to queries than the large producers.

CREATIVE STRATEGIES

Sometimes you need a creative way to bring attention to your script. For example, one writer dressed up as a custodian after hours and dropped the script on someone's desk. That sounds too dangerous to me.

A friend of mine dressed up as a UPS man and delivered his script to Harrison Ford. Harrison Ford actually signed for it. Too bad the script was a dog. Another writer sent his script in a pizza box. This tactic did not work.

The Ticking Man was sold by an agent who sent ticking clocks to about 20 producers. A note said, "The ticking man is coming." This resulted in a bidding war, and the script sold for $1 million. (Note: The agent did *not* wrap these up like bombs.)

Gimmicks like this work rarely, and usually they backfire. Some time ago, I received a call from a writer who was at the Beverly Hills Police Department—he had become too clever for his own good. I told him that he should call his attorney, not me.

On the other hand, if you can find small, clever ways to differentiate yourself from the pack, then that's usually a plus, even if it's as simple as a clever format for a query. After graduating from my course, Robert Olague imprinted the logline for his screenplay *The Coming* on the back of a jacket, and attended a writers conference. The logline read, "In an attempt to take over the world, an alien imitates the coming of a messiah." Robert made many key contacts that night.

Discrimination?
Don't let the rumors of ageism, sexism, and racism slow you down. You will not likely encounter such bias until you have broken in, and maybe not even then. When an agent or producer reads a great script, they don't care who wrote it. A client contacted me recently to refer me to an article in *Fade In* about her. She's a 49-year-old woman who lives outside the Los Angeles area who sold her script to a producer without the services of an agent.

There are almost as many ways to break into the business as there are writers. Look for your opportunities and find a way. Just remember, before you parachute into Tom Cruise's backyard, be sure you are carrying a great script. Don't leave home without it.

For additional strategies and markets, see my upcoming chapter entitled "Jump-start your career now," but first let's explore the television markets.

Television markets

There are many opportunities in television. And television is where the money and power is for writers. Television is generally character-driven (although an occasional exec may respond to a high concept pitch), and most of it is staff-written. That's because producers want to use proven talent.

If you're interested in breaking into TV writing, I highly recommend Ellen Sandler's book *The TV Writer's Workbook*. I like the book so much that I have asked Ellen to contribute the following section on television. Ellen was nominated for an Emmy for the CBS hit series *Everybody Loves Raymond*. She has written for many other primetime network TV comedies and has created original pilots for ABC, CBS, NBC, Fox Family, Oxygen Network, and the Disney Channel. For more about Ellen and her services, visit www.sandlerink.com.

THE TV BUSINESS AND EPISODIC TV

The consensus is that the most exciting writing in Hollywood right now is in series television, and, in the current market, TV is where the action is for writers. The Writers Guild annual report shows that more than two-thirds of the paying work for writers in Hollywood comes from TV contracts. If you want to be a working writer in show business, give television writing serious consideration.

The TV business runs differently than the film business. You can write a terrific feature script and a studio may option it. Whatever they do with it—make the movie, don't make the movie, hire another writer to rewrite it—doesn't matter, you sold a script and got the money. That's *not* how it works in TV.

Television producers, also known as *show runners*, don't buy scripts, they hire staffs. What they want is you and the craft and talent you can bring to their writing tables. Therefore, your script is more of an audition piece, an introduction to you as a writer, than a product for sale, and you will need to have more than one script for consideration.

If you are as yet an unproduced or relatively unknown writer, when a show runner or an agent likes your script, he or she will most likely want to see another. They want to see that your great script is more than a lucky fluke. They want to know you can do it more than once. Writing for a television series is like running a marathon. You have to be able to write fast, and write a lot. Every day, for many weeks. No writer's block. No missed deadlines. To be a working TV writer you have to be able to turn out *quantity* as well as quality.

WHAT TO DO

What should you write to demonstrate your abilities? It used to be that a new writer would write specs [spec scripts] of currently airing shows. Not so much anymore. Original pilots have become the writing sample of choice. However, writing a pilot is a huge challenge, even for experienced writers. Trying to create a whole new show without ever writing an episode of an existing show is not likely to turn out the polished script that your spec pilot needs to be.

If you are new to the form of TV writing, I recommend writing a spec script of an existing on-air show as a warm-up. The exercise of writing a spec will give you a working knowledge of television formatting as well as practical experience with story structure and the requirements of your genre. I think it's the best preparation you can have for writing an original pilot.

TIPS:

- Choose a show that is the same genre as the pilot you want to write, maybe one with a similar character or arena that you plan to use in your pilot.

- Get some scripts of that show, and study them carefully. [Ellen's book *The TV Writer's Workbook* has an entire chapter devoted to breaking down scripts for study.] Then write a story outline and at least one draft of a script for that show.

- I also suggest you get some professional support, but don't wait until you've finished your script to get help. Using a script consultant or a class while you are developing the story and writing the script will teach you how to build a solid foundation for your story and help you stay on track throughout the writing process.

If your spec comes out not so good, so what? Consider it like the first pancake: You make it to test the griddle and then usually throw it out. Isn't it a lot better to work out the uphill learning curve on a script that didn't cost you as much time and energy as your original pilot will?

BONUS: If this on-air spec does turn out to be something you feel good about, you can use it as a sample to open a small crack in some heavy doors. Ask friends—other writers or anyone who knows anything about the business--to give you feedback. The advice can be invaluable in learning what to do, and what not to do with your pilot. You can submit it to agents and managers too. You may get responses like, "I can't do anything with a spec script, but if you write something original I'd like to see it." They may be saying that to shine you on, but it qualifies as an invitation. Now you won't be cold-calling when you're ready to show your pilot. That's working the room.

Next step is to write that pilot, and while you're writing, you also need to be building relationships with other writers. You'll need them for feedback on your work, industry information like where to get copies of scripts to study, when a writer's assistant job may be opening up, what contests are worth submitting to, and all the other things a community of like-minded people can do for each other.

Don't minimize the importance of this aspect of the marketplace. Other writers are the main source of how you get a writing job in this industry. It only *seems* like they are your competition; in actuality, they can be your best allies. If someone you know gets a job, that's great for them, *and* it's also good for you. You now know someone who could be in a position to recommend your excellent pilot to her show runner. This assumes that you are pretty good friends and she likes you and respects your work. So take classes, belong to writers groups, participate in writing chatrooms and blogs. Go to writers conferences and pitch-fests. But don't just go; while you're there, make the effort to meet lots of people, and after the event continue to build relationships with the ones you like. Be kind and generous, supportive and cheerful; your relationships will grow exponentially and they will pay off in ways you can't predict.

When you have the opportunity to show your material to someone, it has to be "good." What anyone—a show runner, a development exec, an agent or manager—who reads your scripts wants to see is how you tell a story and if you can write characters that we believe in and care about. If it's a comedy, is it funny? Are the jokes fresh? If it's a drama, is there enough suspense? Most important: Does your story work? Is there a clear setup and a strong follow-through? Does the story make sense? Is the resolve satisfying? How's your plot? If it's contrived and manipulative, you'll get a pass. If it's the result of motivated character action and consequence, you're likely to get a call.

TAKING A MEETING
You can't affect or second-guess what your potential employer's needs are; but what you can do is make your script conform to industry standards and at the same time sing with originality. That's an outstanding pilot script and it can generate interest from many quarters. [If you need guidance writing a pilot, visit Sandlerink.com and put yourself on the mailing list.]

For example, maybe a development exec likes your writing, but not this particular concept. She'll call you in to meet you and she'll want to hear what you're working on next. Be sure you've got something to say. A professional writer is always working on something (or at least can say she is). A good thing to be working on is another pilot. Be prepared to tell what that next project is about in a couple of conversational lines. Please don't have a memorized poster catchphrase. They don't want to hear a promo line. You're a writer not a marketer; they want to know what it's about for you.

Another possibility: Your great pilot script may be in the same vein as a current show and you could be asked to come in and pitch story ideas for an episode. Are you wondering how your script came to the attention of the show runner in the first place? Those other writer friends mentioned earlier are the most likely way—especially if you don't have representation yet.

You may pitch to the show runner or to the whole writing staff. Use the pitching guidelines presented in this book. Keep in mind that producers often make up their minds in the first 30 seconds of the pitch, so don't start at the beginning; lead with the key conflict and the essence of your story, not with the opening dialogue or setup scene. Take a look at the pilot for *Breaking Bad* for a terrific example of a hitting the story on the high point of the action and then presenting the exposition and setup after the audience is hooked.

If the show runner hears a story idea he likes, he and the staff will probably work on that idea with you, often changing what you came in with—that's a good thing, by the way. Never object to their suggestions. It's their show and you want to work on it with them. If the story shows promise and you've been agreeable and fun to work with in the meeting, you'll be asked to go home and write an outline based on what's been discussed. Congratulations, you have just sold a story!

In a week or so they will expect you to turn in your outline, and if comes in looking a lot like the story they discussed, you may then be asked to write the script. That's the jackpot—not only are you getting paid, but even more important, you're getting a "written" by credit. With credit comes viability. Other show runners will want to meet you and agents will want to represent you. You are now in the game!

CHILDREN AND TEEN PROGRAMMING

Children's programming (The Disney Channel, Nickelodeon, and others) is an active market that can often be more open to new writers. While it pays less than prime time, it can be a good opportunity to get experience. A lot of these shows are animated, and you might want to consider writing a spec animation show. If you do, be sure to study the conventions and formatting thoroughly, as they are different than live action.

Some of the production companies that supply programming to these networks use new writers and may be willing to look at your specs without submission by an agent. Of course, just like anything else, it's always much better if someone can refer you, like, for example, another writer who has worked for them (see above, about making friends). You can try submitting your specs for consideration directly to the networks that do kids' shows. Write query letters to the Development Executives in the Children's Programming Departments. Executives move up and around frequently, but you can find out who is currently sitting in the chairs through the company's corporate website or the *Hollywood Creative Directory*.

TV MOVIES AND TRUE STORIES

The Movie-of-the-Week (MOW) is a rare, if not extinct, format for the major networks, but some cable networks do produce made-for-TV movies. Most are based on existing material, either true life stories or published books. If a company or cable network has optioned rights to a life story or book, they will then be looking for a writer to adapt the material for filming. A client of mine wrote a spec pilot which remains unsold, but the development execs at Hallmark Network read it, loved her work and she got three (3!) made-for-TV movie assignments for them.

If you know of a true life story or published material that has not been picked up by a network, and it's a story you love and think could be adapted for a TV movie, or made into a series, you could write the script as a spec. But before you write a word, you MUST get the rights. Writing a script without the rights is A) illegal and B) a huge waste of your time and creativity.

Acquiring the rights to a story does not necessarily mean you will have to pay big bucks; you may be able to acquire the rights for as little as $1, or what is essentially a free option. However, if you are adapting any preexisting material, you must consult an entertainment attorney to arrange such a deal and that will cost you, but it is smart money. You need an option that protects you and covers all contingencies, An entertainment attorney will know what those are. Your college pal who is now an assistant DA will not—neither will your dad's tax lawyer. Even though they might be willing to do it for you as a favor, you won't get the protection you need, and you could wind up losing the whole project.

CAUTION: Having the preexisting material can be a bonus and might add interest to your package, but do not write the story thinking that if you interest a company in the project, they will spend the money for the rights. They may very well be willing to buy the rights, once you have kindly brought it to their attention, but there is no incentive to keep you on a project if you do not hold rights to it. You can't copyright your script, because it is based on material you don't have rights to. They can bypass you entirely, and you will have no recourse.

Get the rights and, during the option period, write the script and approach producers who have deals with the networks and studios. If they think it's salable they will know the appropriate places to take it.

Where do you find these producers? In the weekly list of "Television Productions" found in *Variety* and *The Hollywood Reporter*. You can go to the Internet Movie Database (www. imdb.com) and look up projects that have been done recently that are similar to your material. You'll be able to find out which network aired it and who the producers were; now do some more research and find out how to contact development people at those companies. You can find this information in the *Hollywood Creative Directory* or often online.

[For more on "true stories," see "Find a True Story" in the next chapter.]

MINISERIES

If you think your TV movie or series idea is a miniseries, like *Game of Thrones* or *House of Cards*, do not write the whole miniseries. Write only the pilot episode and a short synopsis of subsequent episodes to indicate how the series story arc plays out. There is no advantage to writing all those episodes on spec. For one thing, no one will read an entire series of episodes. They are thinking ahead to marketing and know they will have to hook an audience on the first episode; therefore, if the concept doesn't generate enough interest from the pilot story, they simply won't be interested in the project.

REALITY TV

You can make money "writing" for reality shows, but you should consider it a day job, not a building block for your writing career. The workload is demanding and you will not have time to make dental appointments, shop for food, or ever get enough sleep, much less pursue your own writing. You might be better off at Starbucks. At least as a barista you get to go home and write your spec script.

While much of the work you would be doing on a reality show would involve structuring plot points and even suggesting dialogue, which is indeed writing, it is not recognized as such. You will not receive any kind of writing credit—and without credits you will still be at pre-entry level with regard to scripted television series.

Your job description on a reality TV show will be something like "Segment Producer," and that will lead to moving up the ranks of producing more reality shows. Nothing wrong with that. It can be creative and fun and it pays. But it will not be considered experience by scripted television show runners and will not in all likelihood lead you to any credited writing assignments. You will still need to write those spec scripts.

As an aspiring writer you would probably do better working as a dog walker to the stars, an on-set gofer, or a desk receptionist in an agent's office. You won't be getting paid for writing, but you will be playing in the right ballpark. You will meet other ambitious people on the way up—these are your new best friends. You may even meet some higher-ups who will be interested in reading what you write because now they know you. And most important, you will have some downtime for writing your own scripts and pursuing your dreams.

Jump-start your career now!

After you write your first screenplay, the path to glory seems clear: find an agent who will get you a six-figure deal. A hundred and fifty query letters later, you're languishing at your laptop. You've received a lot of encouragement, but, as Pauline Kael put it, "Hollywood's the only town where you can die of encouragement." Maybe it's time to try another approach.

BUILD A PLATFORM

In the film marketing business, if you lack resources but have a winner, you *platform* that winner by showing it to one or two markets at a time and letting it accumulate positive reviews. In other words, you build momentum. *Chariots of Fire* and *American Beauty* were both distributed in this manner.

If you've written a winner, maybe it's time to build a platform so that Hollywood players can see you and "discover" you. Your first sale may not be a blockbuster, but it could lead to one later in your career—maybe sooner than later. The idea is to gather strength with each positive step you take and get in the game rather than pace on the sidelines.

What follows are numerous platforming strategies that you can use to give your career momentum and direction. Success in any of these can lead to more successes, until you are recognized as the next great screenwriter and a *bona fide* player. These include many small markets that are often overlooked.

WRITE THE BOOK

For the last several years, there has been a greater movement towards writing the novel version of your script, and selling rights to both the novel and screenplay at the same time. The large agencies (CAA, ICM, William Morris) and some small agencies (Paul S. Levine, Charlotte Gusay, David Higham in the UK, among others) handle book-to-screenplay deals.

Another angle is to write the graphic novel version of your script. Screenwriter Joseph Calabrese did that with *The Eyes of Mara* and Frank Miller with *Sin City.*

BECOME A READER OR ASSISTANT

Almost any writer can find a job as a story analyst, that is, as a *reader.* It pays almost nothing, but the experience teaches you what works and especially what doesn't work in a screenplay. You will also make connections. Michael Arndt, screenwriter of *Little Miss Sunshine,* started out as a story analyst, as did Sherry Lansing, former Paramount CEO.

Apply for this position with agents and producers. A college education is a plus, especially if you majored in literature or something similar. Submit a résumé plus a coverage of a script for a produced movie, one that they will be familiar with. Offer to write a free coverage for a script that they are currently considering. It's not particularly important where you live, but don't ignore local opportunities. One of my Texan students reads for local production companies and festivals. That experience and the contacts made led to a deal to write a screenplay. The script is being produced and she is getting a writing credit.

Get a job as an assistant. If you become an assistant to a TV staff writer or TV producer, for example, you may get a chance to write for a TV show. Duppy Demetrius from Pittsburgh started this way. He became an executive story editor for *The Closer.* It is not unusual.

The same is true for agent assistants, production assistants (gofers for the production crew), script coordinators, desk receptionists, transcribers, and so on. Michael Nachoff began his career as a set decorator and grip at the Canadian Film Center. He later became a postproduction staffer for Brightlight Pictures. That led to writing a spec, and the spec led to two writing assignments: *Bloodrayne: The Third Reich* and *In the Name of the King: Two Worlds.* Both were produced.

Some writers take advantage of internships offered by some production companies and studios. You will meet people and learn about the business. Many writers and other film professionals begin this way. If you live in L.A., you might try a temp agency, such as Apple One. Studio temp pools keep résumés on hand.

Apply for these jobs like you would for any other job. Send résumés to studio or production company HR departments, TV show runners, networks, and so on. Get your hands on the UTA Job Board, a job list circulated among agency assistants.

MAKE A SHORT FILM

Learn more about the business by making a short, inexpensive film that you can enter in a festival of some kind or even show on Youtube. The experience of producing and directing will improve your skills as a writer, plus the film might get recognized and find you valuable contacts. If you act in it, you will—at last—fully understand *subtext*.

Hollywood types often view short films and peruse YouTube and similar sites. Filmaka (www.filmaka.com) is an organization that you might find helpful in terms of networking and getting your short film noticed.

Dozens of my clients and students have made short films and won awards. One of those is Tom Basham (www.sapfilms.com), who recently produced his first feature film, *Bright Lights & Promises*. He is in the game.

One example of a successful short film is *The Pizza King*, which has won four festival awards. Jared Hess wrote and directed the 10-minute film *Peluca* while at BYU; it was shown at the Slamdance Film Festival. The cost of the shoot was $500 and the film attracted an executive producer to finance the feature film, entitled *Napoleon Dynamite*. The feature film was produced for $400,000 and was sold at the Sundance Film Festival for over $3 million.

EXPOSE YOURSELF

Virtually all of the platforming strategies I name are aimed, at least in part, at meeting people, getting discovered, and making contacts—networking. Never underestimate the value of a contact. A former student and now working writer (Max Adams) tells the story of when she was just trying to break in. She met "an assistant to an assistant of an industry pariah." This assistant went on to become a studio executive. Together, the ex-wannabe writer and ex-assistant put together a feature deal that the studio bought.

There are three things writers do: They continue to learn their craft, they burn the midnight oil writing, and they yearn so much for a writing career that they get out and connect with people. There are plenty of seminars, workshops, publications, conferences, expos, pitch-fests, writers groups, professional organizations (including online organizations) to help you meet people and continue your education. Wherever you go, schmooze. Part of the schmoozing art is to remember that you have two ears and one mouth, and to use them in that proportion. Don't try to be cool; be you. If you are already cool, that's hot, which is supercool.

Literary manager Mason Novick saw Diablo Cody's blog and contacted her about her work. Get yourself and your writing out there. Some established and beginning writers have used Facebook or developed a website as a pitching tool and/or to post credits. Here is one example: www.joelenders.com.

If you create a website, you will need to drive traffic there. Perhaps, when you meet someone or deliver a short pitch, you could give that person your URL and perhaps a password to your secret projects. That person could read or view your pitch, read your synopsis or treatment, and use the password to read your script.

WIN CONTESTS

I recommend you look into two or three contests that seem right for your script and that have some kind of reputation behind them. Some contests provide notes, and some writers have made valuable connections with people associated with the contest they entered. See the section on "Contests" in the chapter entitled "Create your strategic marketing plan."

USE INTERNET SERVICES

Some writers have sold their scripts through Internet marketing services such as InkTip, Triggerstreet, Script P.I.M.P., and others. I tend to favor a focused approach rather than a shotgun approach. Nevertheless, you may find these services to be worthwhile.

There are many Internet writing-services companies that promise to get your story concept or synopsis seen by executives. Many advertise promising results. In evaluating these, I recommend caution but also an open mind. Try to substantiate their claims. Scrutinize success stories. Ask yourself questions as you study the specifics of the deal. Is the site connected with industry professionals? (That might be a good sign.) Are they contacting potential buyers directly, or are they just hoping buyers will find their site? How are they contacting potential buyers? And so on.

BECOME A HYPHENATE

Billy Wilder was once asked why he became a director. His answer: "To protect the script." If you decide to produce and/or direct the movie yourself, that makes you a writer-producer-director (a hyphenate). However, before attempting a feature production, make a short film and get a feel for the head-banging experience putting together a film is.

You've heard of Murphy's Law—*If anything can go wrong, it will?* Well, Murphy was a filmmaker, so you want to be prepared. There are books and short courses available, some only a weekend long. Oh, and don't use your own money to cover production costs. What follows are some tips on becoming a hyphenate.

Package your project
You already have the script; now add talent (an actor or director) or other creative element, and—*shazam!*—you have a package. A client of mine added a known singer to his package, and now has access to her music. With a package, you can act as a producer and approach other producers about your project, or you can simply mention your package elements in a query letter or pitch.

My co-writer for *Hemingway's Twin* worked as a kid for the Hemingways at their house at Walloon Lake. Based on that relationship, we secured family cooperation on the script. I also secured a letter of interest from Mariel Hemingway to play the main role and, with the help of others, Alfonso Arau (*Like Water for Chocolate*) to direct. On that basis, I made a deal with a producer who had a deal with 20th Century Fox, but some legal issues got in the way of a production and everything fell apart. The bottom line: I was paid, I met people, and I still own the script in case someone is interested.

Why not take the initiative yourself to put together the players to make a movie? When you interest talent in your script, you are "packaging an element"—a function of a producer. When you secure the rights to a true story and take the story to a producer, you are, in effect, co-producing.

Adapt a book
About half the movies made are from material adapted from another medium. Novels, children's books, plays, graphic novels, and even short stories are converted into movies, usually because an audience already exists for the story. You cannot compete with the majors for the rights to "event" books, but there is material out there you can acquire. Search for that golden nugget that is not getting noticed. Screenwriter Michael Seitzman optioned the rights to a book and wrote the screenplay for the produced film *North Country*.

Suppose you want to secure the rights to a novel or other work. You will contact the subsidiary-rights department of the book publisher, or hire an entertainment attorney to do this for you. Find out who controls the rights; it may be the author or the publisher. You will need to convince that person or persons that you can write a salable screenplay. Having some kind of writing credits will be helpful.

You will make an offer to buy an option to the rights of the book. You do that by making a "down payment" of a small amount of money (even as low as $1) for the exclusive rights to the book for a period of time. That way, you only tie up a little money, but you must write the script and sell it before the deadline of the option agreement. The longer the option period, the better for you; you need plenty of time to write the script and sell it to producers. If you buy the rights outright, obviously you are under no deadline because there is no option period. Make sure you avail yourself of the services of an entertainment (intellectual property) attorney for the legal stuff.

Keep in mind *Trottier Rule #9*: Don't adapt it until you own it. You will only get hurt and waste time if you write a script on something you don't own. Don't write the sequel to anything unless you control the rights. Don't use a song as the basis of your screenplay unless you own the rights to the music. Naturally, there are exceptions to *Rule #9*, but you are in a much better bargaining position if you control the rights.

When you buy rights or buy an option to the rights of anything, be sure an entertainment attorney (intellectual property lawyer) reviews the contract and verifies copyright. She should also make sure there are no liens or encumbrances attached to the work.

Don Moriarty and Greg Alt played it smart. They got their start by buying the rights to the book *The Mark of Zorro*. Then they, with the assistance of Yours Truly, wrote a screenplay entitled *Zorro, the Comedy Adventure*, which evolved into *Zorro, the Gay Blade*. They were able to attract a producer because they owned the rights to the book.

Exploit a life

What about writing about famous people? First, consult an entertainment attorney. Second, don't assume anything. Third, don't write anything until you control the rights. As a general rule, if the person has exploited his life by granting interviews or running for office, etc., then he is "fair game"—probably. You don't want to run the risk of lawsuits or a libel charge. Truth is a defense of libel so long as there is an absence of malice. (Sounds like a movie I saw.)

History, of course, is in the public domain, but history books are not. For example, although the life of Charles Lindbergh is in the public domain, Steven Spielberg still paid a large sum of money for the rights to A. Scott Berg's biography of Charles Lindbergh.

414

If you *base* your story on real people or a real incident, just make sure that your script is totally fictitious. If your script is based on a real person, and if that person's peers can deduce from the movie who the movie is about, then that could be *invasion of privacy*.

My advice is to avoid anything that could possibly get you into a legal entanglement. You should think twice even about buying an option to the rights to a book or someone's story. Make sure you want to make the financial investment. If you decide to forge ahead, you will want to avail yourself of the services of an intellectual property (entertainment) attorney. It's expensive, but worth it.

If you decide that you want to be the producer from start to finish, then you need to do your homework. This is an area where you can lose your shirt if you are not careful. Read books and talk to other producers. Consider the Hollywood Film Institute's two-day course or the New York Film Academy's courses.

Find a true story

What if you are aware of a little-known but compelling incident or interesting person and don't want to fictionalize the event or the person's story, but want to tell it straight? Follow the same procedure as with an adaptation of a book. Buy an option to those rights first.

After you have secured the necessary rights—and that might involve contracts with more than one person—write the script, and take one of the following approaches: 1) produce the screenplay yourself from start to finish, 2) package the project and take it to a producer, or 3) approach producers that specialize in true stories.

National true stories are already locked up before you've even thought of them as a possibility. However, sometimes you can find unknown stories about major events. *Oklahoma City—A Survivor's Story* is a TV movie about a woman saved by a fireman after the Oklahoma City bombing of 1995. A few movies have been made of unknown stories stemming from 9/11.

[For more information, read the section "TV movies and true stories" in the preceding chapter, "Television Markets."]

GET CORPORATE BACKING OR A GRANT

Ask Procter & Gamble to help you. Approach corporations for funding. The makers of the independent film *Film Camp* received help from PepsiCo and Ty Inc. One client wrote a screenplay that indirectly highlights the sights of a particular city. She contacted that state's tourism office and film commissioner for financing and production assistance leads, which she received.

I worked as a script doctor with the producer of a $40 million animated film. They have raised $20 million already from businesses and organizations interested in the content of the film (including Procter & Gamble). To get you started, the blog financingfilms. blogspot.com chronicles corporate and other sources for indie film financing. There are also funding organizations like Kickstarter (kickstarter.com), which focuses on funding within the United States, and RocketHub (rockethub.com) which is global. IndieGoGo (indiegogo.com) operates a little differently from the other two and is riskier.

There are many grants available for making documentaries and other films. You'll need to do your research to find these. Also, beware of scams. Perhaps one place to start your search is to Google Michigan State University's compiled list of film grants.

EXPLORE OVERLOOKED TV MARKETS

There are many small TV markets besides those mentioned in the previous chapter on "Television markets." See the section in that chapter on "Children and teen programming."

There are hundreds of cable channels and TV stations looking for content (movies, sitcoms, reality shows, and so on), including HBO, Showtime, Turner Broadcasting, and other cable networks, stations, and channels.

Have you considered a documentary? Erik Stahl wrote two documentaries, which led to his producing and hosting a TV show in Colorado. Another client, S. A. James, wrote a feature screenplay for the big screen, and that sample eventually led to an adaptation of a Danielle Steele novel for a TV movie.

One evening after presenting a seminar on the East Coast, I received a call from a very young 18-year-old who had never written so much as a page. He told me that he had called a PBS station and presented a series idea over the phone. The producer loved it, but since the kid did not have a sample script, the producer suggested that he connect with a professional writer or write a script himself. Imagine! If this kid had had a decent sample script (or had been willing to write one), he may have been hired.

The PBS network includes such stalwart affiliates as KCET in Los Angeles, WNET in New York, WGBH in Boston, and ETV in South Carolina. Approach these stations individually or PBS directly. Investigate local stations.

Don't ignore the many magazine shows, educational shows, soap operas, children's shows, game shows, and infomercials (direct response television).

ANIMATION

Thanks to the information age and the development of computer software, animated productions continue to increase, but historically animation has gone through many ups and downs. Feature animation projects (such as *Shrek*, *The Incredibles*, and *Finding Nemo*) are developed much like feature films are, since they feature top talent voicing the characters. There is little chance that you can sell a spec animation script for a blockbuster animation film. You have a better shot at smaller films or TV.

Although most animated TV shows do not have staff writers, they use a pool of writers to write scripts. There are two kinds of animated series: weekly and daily. Because of the greater number of episodes produced by daily shows, they might be better targets for new writers.

For your information, animated scripts for television can *include* camera directions and angles. (That's because they're being written for a storyboard artist rather than a director.)

You will probably need only one imaginative and fanciful sample script to break in, and animated shows generally are open to queries from writers without agents. If your sample script gets you noticed, you can pitch with treatments, synopses, and even premises. Research the show you are interested in before contacting them.

The pay for animated TV scripts and feature direct-to-DVD projects is about half of the basic rate for projects featuring human characters (rather than toons). Generally, you earn no residuals, no ancillary rights, and no royalties on toys based on your characters.

REGIONAL AND FOREIGN MARKETS

Dig in your own backyard. *Acres of Diamonds* is the story of a man who searched the world for diamonds without success and finally returned home to realize that there were acres of them on his own farm. So what's available in your own backyard? Look at regional markets and specialty markets (such as the Christian market, for example). Contact your state film commissioner (and nearby state film commissioners) about local production companies. My screenplay *The Penny Promise* was produced by a Utah company. The film won "Best Feature Comedy" at two film festivals, plus I got paid.

The BBC set up the Writer's Room (http://www.bbc.co.uk/writersroom/) to assist writers interested in writing for the BBC.

Since there is no major studio in Canada, the Canadian film business operates much like the independent film market operates in the United States, in terms of selling your work as a writer. Many American films are produced in Canada with Canadian talent and writers. That's because the government provides financial incentives for those who produce in Canada. If you are Canadian, your research question is this: Who produces or is about to produce in Canada? There may be an opportunity there for you. There are also many Canadian productions for the Canadian market. One Canadian writing resource is the Writers Guild of Canada (www.wgc.ca).

If you live south of the border or overseas, realize that the film business is increasingly global. There is a growing market for films written and produced in Spanish, if that is your first language.

And some online companies like amazon.com are now producing movies and other media.

GO INDEPENDENT

Consider the huge independent motion picture market. See the section entitled "The Indies" in an earlier chapter of this book (Book V).

DIRECT-TO-DVD

The direct-to-DVD market (formally referred to as the direct-to-video market) provides opportunities for many writers. These are low-budget features ($1 to $1.5 million, but often in the $50,000 to $250,000 range) made specifically for DVD sales. The most common genres are horror, action/adventure, and thrillers, and they are not released theatrically. To find the names of these producers, simply look for the credits on recent direct-to-DVD releases and otherwise conduct your research.

I received a thank-you letter from a prior student, Daniel Springen, who wrote, "I... have six feature films available for rent." Daniel is in the game.

Related to this area is the information/instructive DVD market. Films such as *Buns of Steel* and *How to Remodel Your Home* are examples. Keep in mind that regardless of the market, the basic approach is similar in each.

In years to come, direct-to-DVD productions may give way to Internet feature productions. In view of that, let's look at the current Internet market next.

THE NEW MEDIA

Become a writer or hyphenate for a New Media production. Atom Films was one of the first short-film Web producers in this arena. They were bought by MTV and eventually became part of Comedy Central. Initially, Atom Films productions were often paid for, at least in part, by ads.

The *Web series* phenomenon is well established. Some of the original Web series, such as *Quarterlife* and *Afterworld*, can still be seen on YouTube although they were once featured at their own Web sites. In the early days (which was not long ago), *webisodes* were about three minutes in length. With *Afterworld*, there was little dialogue but a lot of narration, and no big action scenes. These days, webisodes of Web series such as *Broad City, Burning Love, Neil's Puppet Dreams*, and *Misadventures of Awkward Black Girl* (which premiered on YouTube) are about 3–12 minutes in length.

Internet productions such as these may be a place to start and get noticed. Some productions have had tens of millions of views per webisode, and that will increase in years to come. And Web series can also be viewed on smartphones. You can create your own pilot or write webisode scripts for other shows. It's a wonderful challenge and opportunity for writers.

If you create your own series, you can promote it on YouTube, Facebook, MySpace, and similar sites and/or secure funding through some other means, including via corporations and organizations. *The Guild* in its early days solicited donations from fans and produced episodes from those donations.

Do you carry an iPod, iPhone, or iPad? Consider writing for that arena. A *mobisode* is an episode of a show written specifically for mobile phones, iPods, and similar devices. Most Web series can now be viewed on smartphones; in fact, most new media can be viewed on most devices. The production company Fun Little Movies (funlittlemovies. com) produces "fun little movies" for your cell phone. Check them out.

You can learn a great deal about writing for, or producing for, Internet movie companies by searching the Web. The WGA now has a section for New Media writers. Sign up for their updates. New Media companies are monitored by feature producers. You may get noticed with a New Media production. Many companies have Internet connections or are Web-driven. One example is the Oxygen channel.

The New Media market is growing rapidly, and the parameters may change rapidly as well. There are many interactive companies now. Most studios and many special-effects companies have formed interactive divisions. Contact them directly or have your agent call.

Certainly, additional opportunities for writers will materialize as new distribution channels are created and innovative technology continues to expand. I foresee more entertainment distributed directly to home computers, tablets, smartphones, and future devices.

GAMES

Videogames, videos based on video games, virtual reality, 3DO, interactive programming, and multimedia represent markets on the rise. This broad area has become a huge growth industry with increasing opportunities for writers. In fact, production has increased markedly in recent years, and agents have materialized to handle multimedia material.

Producers in these areas are generally open to ideas. Surprisingly, it is better to approach these people with a treatment than with a completed script—at least for now. Also include game concepts and flowcharts if applicable. Your final script may earn you tens of thousands of dollars. For information on writing or designing video games, I recommend *Creating Emotion in Games* by David Freeman (www.freemangames.com).

SUCCEED IN OTHER WRITING AREAS

Diablo Cody, before she wrote *Juno*, wrote a critically acclaimed book entitled *Candy Girl: A Year in the Life of an Unlikely Stripper*. Prior to that, she wrote for a Minneapolis newspaper. Why not sell a short story to a magazine or write in some other area to get your career moving in a positive direction? Some screenwriters keep body and soul together with business writing, magazine writing, copywriting, column writing, and so on.

I started out as a copywriter of marketing collateral, advertising, and scripts for business videos before moving on to more "creative" areas. I learned that more money is spent in non-broadcast audiovisual than in the U.S. motion picture industry. Writing video and DVD scripts for business and education can be both profitable and fun.

You will contact media producers for possible assignments, or call video production managers at corporations. Present yourself as a freelance writer and have a sample

10- or 12-page script handy. In some instances, your other writing experience may be sufficient.

Pay is about $150 per finished minute of the eventual DVD, or 10% of the budget. That comes to about $1,500 a week for your time.

You can earn up to $10,000 writing an infomercial show. Infomercials are written by writers, so why not you? Find producers by searching the Internet or reading direct-response magazines such as *Response Magazine*. Visit www.retailing.org.

GET YOUR "DEGREE"

The position of screenwriter or TV writer is a profession, like a doctor or a lawyer. Usually, it takes years of education to prepare for a profession; consider these platforming strategies as part of your professional education.

There is one step you should take before you try any of the above platforming strategies, and that is to write one or more original, feature-length screenplays. You will need them as proof you can write, and by applying some of the above strategies, you might even sell them and become a player in the game.

How to break into Hollywood when you live in Peoria

Living outside of the Los Angeles area is not a problem when you are selling your first script. You can sell it from anywhere. It is seldom a problem even after you've sold your first script. In fact, one's domicile is becoming less and less of an issue in our technology-laden society.

Most Hollywood producers are more concerned about your writing ability than your current address. If you write well and know what you're talking about, their fears will be allayed. However, an L.A.-based agent will want to know if you are willing to visit Los Angeles on occasion to attend meetings with producers and executives.

That raises the following question: Don't L.A. writers have an advantage over others? Yes, of course they do. It's simply easier to meet more people. But it is not a requirement for success. People break in from all over the world.

The idea of relocating after your first big sale may occur to you or be suggested. Obviously, if the deal is sweet enough and the situation warrants it, you will relocate. But you likely will not have to. And even if you do, it won't be forever. Once you have established your name, you can buy an island in the Caribbean and write there. On the other hand, you may want to move to the Los Angeles area, just to have more opportunities to meet people. Living in L.A. does have its advantages.

If you want to write for episodic television, you must live near production headquarters, but don't move until you get the assignment.

You'll be pleased to know that more regional opportunities are opening up all the time. There are three reasons for this: Union shoots in Southern California have become very expensive, California is generally unfriendly to business, and the Information Age has created a huge demand for programming.

Many new opportunities exist in areas outside of Hollywood. Production companies are sprouting up all over the map. Some of these can be found in industry periodicals, directories, or literary reference guides. Call around. Your state film commissioner should have up-to-date information concerning the film industry in your state. Revisit the previous chapter.

In summary, don't let your current residence deter you from pursuing a screenwriting career. Concentrate on your writing first and your geographical issues second.

A personal challenge

Now just a few words concerning your writing career. Take it seriously. You are a screenwriter.

Create a vision for your career. Pretend that 20 years have passed and that the PBS program *American Masters* is going to present a tribute to you and your career. Or, if you prefer, *Entertainment Tonight* is spotlighting your work. How do you want to be remembered? What kind of work will you do during the next 20 years? Where is your career going to be in 20 years? (Or 10 years, if you prefer.) Write this down.

What would you like to accomplish this year (or within the next 18 months)? What excites you the most? Is it to sell your spec script to a company like Imagine? Is it to be a story editor for a TV show? Set this milestone goal. Spend some time with this; you need this motivating energy.

Think of the script you're working on now. When do you plan on finishing the first draft? How about the final draft? Or, if you're beginning the selling process, by what date do you want to sell your script? Or how many requests for your script do you want by a certain date?

Remember, goals should be specific and measurable. They help you work faster and with more focus. Use them as motivators, not guilt inducers. If you fail to achieve a goal, learn from the experience and set new goals.

Have a writing schedule. Four hours a day is ideal, but if that is unfeasible, try to set aside whatever time you can. That's your time to write. Your loved ones need to understand that. I recommend weekly goals, which is why I have included a "Weekly Action Plan" worksheet in this book. How many hours will you spend writing next week?

Keep logs of contacts, power lunches, phone calls, script submissions, queries, and anything that would affect the "business" of your career. You need this information for follow-ups. This business is built on contacts and relationships. Even when your script is rejected, if anything positive takes place between you and the contact, nurture that contact with occasional notes (once or twice a year), emails, or calls. In doing this, do not impose on their time. And hold on to your screenplay—it may be the perfect vehicle 10 years hence.

Keep track of your expenses. I'm afraid the IRS will insist on it. You will use the Schedule C to report income and business expenses. As a sleeping aid, consider reading IRS Booklet 334 for small businesses before going to bed.

If you have a writing partner, make a written agreement before you write.

Keep a writer's notebook of thoughts, ideas, clippings, bits of dialogue, etc. Many writers use their smartphones for this. Treat your writing career with respect.

Continue your education, but don't stop writing while you learn.

Learn how to take criticism. Be able to stand apart from your work and look at it objectively. Don't rush into rewrites; let advice sink in. Consider what others suggest, but remember that you are the screenwriter and the script is yours until it is sold.

Most of all, enjoy writing for the sake of writing, whether you sell anything or not. Creating something new and original is its own reward. Writing is a fundamentally worthwhile way to spend your time. It is the best therapy I never paid for. If you write because you want to, then the financial rewards are more likely to follow.

Writers write.

Now, finally, I'd like to take a moment to salute you. You have not chosen an easy road. You will need to draw upon your inner resources and believe in yourself. When you get up in the morning, face the person in the mirror and say, "I am the next great screenwriter." Then perhaps one morning, you may awaken to find that you are the next great screenwriter. Don't be surprised. Just keep writing.

Resources

Numerous links to resources can be found at the Community page of my Web site **keepwriting.com**. These include Internet sites, industry organizations, writer organizations and groups, schools, software, directories, periodicals, bookstores, and contests. You will also find helpful information on contests in Book V; use the handy-dandy index to find the exact pages.

When you visit my Web site, make sure you subscribe to my **free viewsletter** for more screenwriting tips and tricks at **keepwriting.com**.

If you would like copies of all of the worksheets in this book, visit the store at my Web site where you can purchase them for a nominal fee. Otherwise, please feel free to photocopy anything from *The Bible*, as long as it is for your individual use only.

For more information on formatting, consider my book *Dr. Format Tells All*, which can be purchased at my Web site store.

For updates and changes to this work, visit **keepwriting.com** and click "Community" and "Book Updates."

My "Keep Writing with Dave Trottier" Facebook page is at **www.facebook.com/keepdave**. Also, you can follow me on Twitter at **www.twitter.com/DRTrottier**.

My clients and students include two Nicholl winners, a National Play Award winner, and dozens of working writers. For more information, visit **keepwritng.com** or email me at **dave@keepwriting.com**

Visit the Consulting page at keepwriting.com for information about my script consulting services. I also evaluate query letters and one-sheets.

Index

You'll find four types of entries in this index.

Titles of screenplays and movies appear in italics

Formatting terms appear in all-CAPS

Names appear last name first

All other topics appear in regular upper- and lower-case type